By "TODAY'S KING OF GOURMETS"
(Time Magazine)

JAMES BEARD'S
FISH COOKERY

". . . a fascinating book replete with recipes both usual and unusual—more than 400 pages of delectable possibilities and a world of information about edible creatures of the sea." (The Hartford Courant Magazine)

"This excellent cookbook not only contains a multitude of wonderful recipes for cooking fish, but the directions are so clear that even a neophyte can follow them easily." (King Features Syndicate)

"A COMPLETE GUIDE FOR FISH FANCIERS AND A TREAT TO READ . . . . SIMPLE DIRECTIONS FOR BRINGING OUT THE BEST IN EVERYTHING . . . ." (Pasadena Independent)

Books by James Beard

James Beard's Fish Cookery
The Best of Beard

Published by
WARNER BOOKS

JAMES BEARD'S
FISH COOKERY

WARNER BOOKS

A Warner Communications Company

CONTENTS

5

Fresh-Water Fish

Shellfish

Terrestrial Animals Prepared Like Fish

Introduction

THIS RICH LAND of ours is richer still because of the living things that swim or crawl in its waters. In the seas and gulfs along our shores, in our innumerable lakes and ponds, and in our rivers and lesser streams are hundreds of different sorts of edible fish and shellfish. Yet I suppose that of this great variety the average American has cooked no more than three or four kinds. Few people have tasted all the species that are sold in our markets. Many Americans eat fish regularly without really knowing what fish they are eating.

For centuries the French, Italians, Russians and Chinese have been great fish cooks. It is regrettable that skill in cookery is not an inherited trait among human beings, and that the art of preparing fish could not have been transmitted effortlessly from Old World generations to those of the New. But then, of course, there would have been no need for this book, the purposes of which are to encourage Americans to eat more fish, and to help them enjoy it more through the expedient of cooking it well.

All my life I have been fond of fish, and I have been fortunate in having lived where fish were plentiful. I was brought up in the Pacific Northwest, a region that is remarkable in its range of both salt- and fresh-water fish. Later, in California, New York and Europe, I managed to eat every form of seafood I could catch or buy.

Nearly all the recipes I offer were tested at one time or another in my own kitchen. Through the years I have had much expected pleasure and many exciting surprises in cooking varieties of fish that were new to me, in trying new recipes and in refining traditional ones. I urge you be adventurous, as I have tried to be, in your approach to fish cookery. And I suggest only one general rule: Don't overcook fish.

A number of people have been exceptionally kind to me in the development of this book. Rose G. Kerr of the Department of Fish and Wildlife in Washington, D.C., has been

8

patient and informing. Helen Ridley and Frances Smith of the National Fisheries Institute and the Shrimp Association of the Americas have been of great help. Isabel Callvert of New York has been an invaluable aid in assembling material. Stuart Clayson of Los Angeles, owner of the Neptune Seafood Company, has been generous with his time and advice. Helen Evans Brown of Pasadena has been most obliging in giving me tips on West Coast fish. My thanks also go to John van Glahn of the Fishery Council in New York, and to many others—friends, acquaintances and fish enthusiasts—for information and suggestions.

JAMES A. BEARD

GENERAL INFORMATION
ABOUT FISH

Buying and Preparing Fish

FRESH FISH

Like other kinds of food, most varieties of fish have their seasons—the particular times when they are in most abundant supply, at their best and cheapest. These seasons vary greatly from coast to coast and from fish to fish. Everything considered, the best authority on when to buy fresh fish is your own local fish dealer. In a number of respects, however, you must supplement his advice with your own judgment.

When you buy whole fish, make sure you are getting the freshest by checking these points:

1. The eyes must be bright, clear and bulging.

2. The gills should be reddish or pink, clean and fresh-smelling.

3. The scales should be bright, shiny and tight to the skin.

4. The flesh should be firm and should spring back when pressed.

5. There should be no strong or unpleasant odor.

You will need about ⅓ to ½ pound of fish for each person, but this means edible fish. Do not count the bones, head, tail, and so on. As a general rule, figure on buying about 1 pound of whole fish per person.

Fish spoils easily. As soon as it comes from the market, wrap it in moistureproof paper or place it in a covered dish, and store it in the refrigerator.

FROZEN FISH

The frozen food companies now produce a wide variety of frozen fish, and their selections are often excellent buys. If you live far from the fresh supply, or if you have your heart set on a fish that is not at the height of its season, the frozen product can solve your problem with little or no sacrifice in flavor or texture. The amount per person is the same as for fresh fish: ⅓ to ½ pound of edible fish per person. Keep frozen fish, packaged in the original container, in the

11

freezing unit or the frozen-food compartment of your refrigerator until you intend to use it. Thawed fish must be used at once.

To thaw: Fillets, steaks and dressed fish may be cooked without thawing, but you must allow additional time in the cooking process. If you wish to bread or stuff the fish, take it out of the package and place it in the refrigerator (not the freezing compartment), allowing it to thaw slowly at 37° to 40°. Thaw it just enough to make it easy to handle. Thawing is always necessary for whole fish in order to clean it. Whole fish may be thawed more quickly by placing it under cold running water. Thawing at room temperature is unwise, as the fish is apt to become shapeless and soggy.

Cleaning and Dressing Fish

MUCH of the fish sold today in the markets is already cleaned and dressed, filleted or steaked. If you are a fisherman and catch your own, or if you are fortunate enough to have sportsman friends who give you some of their catches, then you need to know just how to clean and prepare fish for cooking. Here is the process (for further directions for blowfish, see index).

1. *Scaling:* Place the fish on a table, holding it firmly by the head with one hand. In the other hand hold a sharp knife, and starting at the tail, scrape toward the head, taking off the scales. Be sure to remove all scales around the fins and the base of the head. Wet fish can be scaled more easily than dry, so you can simplify this job by soaking the fish in cold water for a few minutes before you begin work.

2. *Cleaning:* With a sharp knife slit the belly of the fish the full length from the vent (anal opening) to the head. Remove the intestines. Next, cut around the pelvic fins (those on the underside toward the head) and pull them off, being careful not to tear the fish.

Take off the head by cutting above the collarbone, and also remove the pectoral fins (on either side just back of the gills). If the backbone is large, just cut through to it on each side of the fish; then place the fish on the edge of the table so the head hangs over, and snap the backbone by bending the head down. Then cut any remaining flesh that holds the head to the body.

Cut off the tail. Next remove the dorsal fin (the large one on the back of the fish). Cut along each side of it and give a quick pull forward toward the head to remove the fin and its root bones. Take out the ventral fins (at the back on the underside) in the same way. Do not take fins off with shears, for simply trimming them will not remove the little bones at the base.

Now wash the fish in cold running water, being sure it is free of any membranes and viscera. It is now dressed and ready for cooking. Large fish may, of course, be cut crosswise into steaks.

3. *Filleting:* With a sharp knife cut along the back of the fish from the tail to the head. Next, cut down to the backbone just back of the head on one side of the fish. Then, laying the knife flat, cut the flesh down one whole side, slicing it away from the ribs and backbone. Lift the whole side off in one piece. Turn the fish over and repeat on the other side.

4. *Skinning:* Many people like their fillets skinned. Place the fillets skin side down on the table. Hold the tail tightly and with the knife cut down through the flesh to the skin about ½ inch from your fingers. Flatten the knife against the skin and cut the flesh away by sliding it forward while you hold the tail end of the skin firmly.

Cooking Methods

MUCH too much fish is overcooked until it becomes flavorless and uninteresting. The Fishery Council of New York has one basic rule that I feel all of us who love fish should follow: "Fish is cooked to develop flavor, not to make it tender." No amount of cooking will ever make fish tenderer than it is when it comes from the water. Overcooking only robs fish of its delicious juices and makes its texture dry and flabby.

Any fish may be cooked by any of the methods given in this section. Sometimes you may hear people say that such and such a fish is "too fat" to broil or, that another fish is "too dry" to eat with mayonnaise. These are silly notions. Don't believe them.

Fish is most responsive to flavoring during the actual cooking process. Some varieties of fish require special flavors to complement natural flavors that are somewhat neutral. Others need only salt and pepper to make them outstanding. And don't forget that good butter, olive oil, sweet cream, sour cream and wine enhance fish and give it added goodness.

BAKING

The fish should have its fins run (see directions for cleaning fish) and should be scaled and rubbed well. The head and tail should stay on for decorative purposes. Are you the squeamish, tenderhearted type that cannot bear the sight of a head on the platter? Well, perhaps you'll get used to the idea after a while. You might begin by considering the fact that a fish cooked with head intact is usually a more juicy fish. Naturally, if you are baking just a piece of fish, you cannot follow this rule.

Oil the bottom of the pan well, or place a bed of vegetables —carrots, onions, celery, all cut very fine—on the bottom of the pan. Dot these with fat. Place the fish on top, and lay strips of salt port or bacon over it, or oil it well. Add white wine or broth to the pan to use in basting.

I recommend an oven of 400° to 425° for baking fish, rather than a slower oven. You should know the approximate weight of the fish before baking. If you stuff the fish, count the dressed weight, not the stuffed weight. Figure about 8 to 10 minutes cooking time per pound, but the actual time will depend somewhat on the thickness and texture of the fish. Test for doneness with a fork; the fish is done when the flesh flakes easily.

BROILING—CHARCOAL GRILLING

There is no doubt about it. Fish grilled over charcoal has an entirely "different" flavor. Use a hinged grill so the fish will stay in place, and be sure the grill is hot when you put the fish into it—it should be hot enough to mark the fish.

Whether whole, half, fillets or steaks, the fish should be well floured and oiled before going into the grill and should be brushed well with oil several times during the cooking process. Steaks or fillets without skin will need more lubrication than whole fish.

It is mostly your sense of doneness that will finally produce the perfectly grilled fish. Better to have it slightly undercooked than to overcook it. It is done when it flakes easily with a fork or toothpick. For a good-sized whole fish, this might take about 6 minutes per side, whereas a thin fillet will take perhaps 5 minutes altogether.

OVEN BROILING

If you broil in your range, the rules are somewhat different. Heat your broiler to top heat for about 10 minutes before you cook your fish. Oil the broiler well. Filleted fish or steaks may be broiled in a separate pan placed on top of the broiler rack. This pan should be well oiled or lined with foil so that the fish does not stick.

Baste the fish once or twice during the broiling process. You may use butter, oil, wine, or a mixture of wine and melted butter. Steaks and whole fish should be turned once, but fillets do not need to be turned.

Fillets: Flour the fillets and oil them well with butter, oil or other fat. Place them about 2 inches from the flame and baste them once or twice during the cooking process. Be certain not to turn them. Fillets will take from 5 to 8 minutes to broil, depending upon their thickness. Season after cooking.

Steaks: Dust the steaks with flour and dot them well with butter, or brush them with oil. Place them on the oiled rack or flat pan about 2 inches from the flame. Steaks should be turned once during the broiling, and it is wise to allow more of the cooking time after the turning than before; then the serving side will have a nice brown color. Baste once or twice, and be sure to give the steaks an extra basting after you turn them to help them brown well. Allow 6 to 10 minutes cooking time, depending on their thickness and on the variety of fish. Season steaks after removing from the broiler.

Split fish: You may split fish at home or have the fish dealer do it for you. I like a fish broiled with its backbone intact—it seems to make a difference in the juiciness and the flavor. Place the fish skin side down on the oiled broiling rack or in a separate pan. Dust it with flour and dot it heavily with butter or brush it with oil. Broil it 2 to 3 inches from the flame. Very delicately meated fish, such as carp, pike and whitefish, should be placed a bit farther away. Baste it several times during the cooking and be sure you do not turn it. Broiling time for split fish varies with the thickness of the fish. The doneness is something you will have to judge for yourself. In any event, the time should not be less than 6 to 10 minutes. Season the split fish after cooking.

Whole fish: A whole fish with the head on will be much juicier than one without the head. Dust the fish with flour, and butter or oil it well on one side. Oil the second side after turning. Place smaller fish about 3 inches from the flame, and larger ones about 6 inches away. Allow 3 to 5 minutes broiling time for the first side, depending on the thickness of the fish. Turn and allow 5 to 8 minutes for the second side. Fluke, flounder and sole are usually not turned during broiling. Baste often and season after cooking.

PANNED

This is a good method for cooking fillets or fish steaks that are to be served with a simple sauce or merely with butter and lemon.

For every 2 pounds of fish, beat up an egg with a tablespoon of milk or water. Melt butter and oil in a skillet—about 6 tablespoons or more. Dip the fish in flour, then in the egg and milk (or water) mixture, and finally into dry bread crumbs. Sauté in the fat until nicely browned on one side. Turn, and brown on the other side. Salt and pepper to taste.

SAUTEED (SAUTE MEUNIERE)

This is the preferred method of cookery for small whole fish, rather than for fillets or steaks. If you wish to cook fillets or steaks this way, there is no "rule" against it. And they will taste very good. Trout, sole, butterfish, porgies, dabs, fresh sardines, smelt—all these take to this treatment in a fine way.

Dip the cleaned fish in milk and roll in flour. Melt plenty of butter in your skillet. When it is hot but not burned, add the fish and sauté until nicely browned on one side. Turn and brown the other side. Remove to a hot plate, salt and pepper to taste, and sprinkle with chopped parsley. Melt a little additional butter in the pan and pour it over the fish. No wine, no other seasoning—nothing but the butter and parsley.

DEEP FRYING

Heat the fat in your deep fryer to 375°. Dip the fish in beaten egg, and roll in flour, corn meal or bread crumbs. Place in the frying basket and lower into the fat. Cook 3 to 5 minutes. Drain on absorbent paper and season to taste.

Be sure the temperature of the fat goes back to 375° before frying other pieces of fish. Be careful not to overcook. Fish done this way can be deliciously juicy and tender, or it can resemble sawdust. Deep frying is perhaps the riskiest method of cooking fish. It is difficult to do perfectly.

BRAISING

This method is little known in this country, but very popular in France. If you've never tried it, I urge you to make the experiment. The results are excellent.

Cut 3 carrots, 2 stalks of celery, 3 onions, and a clove of garlic in thin strips. Sauté them in 3 tablespoons of butter for 5 minutes. Arrange them on the bottom of a baking dish, fish boiler or saucepan. Place your fish on the bed of vegetables, salt and pepper it, and place a few strips of bacon or salt pork across the top. Add enough liquid—red or white wine or a mixture of wine and fish bouillon—to half cover the fish. Let it come to a boil, and either cook it very slowly on top of the stove, or put it in a 350° oven. In either case baste carefully during the cooking process.

Fish cooked in this manner is usually served with a sauce made of the cooking liquid, put through a sieve and mixed with other ingredients. Sometimes part of the skin is removed after cooking and the fish is decorated with garnishes —mushrooms, truffles, pickles, lemon slices, anchovy fillets.

COOKING IN COURT BOUILLON

In the next section are recipes for various court bouillons (see index). In general, here are important points about the process:

For small fish and for fillets that are to be cooked in bouillon, prepare the mixture in advance and cook the fish very quickly without letting it boil. It should barely simmer without any bubbling of the liquid.

Large whole fish must cook long enough in the liquid to take on its flavor. Therefore, put the fish in the cold bouillon and bring it to the boil. Then simmer, without any visible movement of the liquid, until the fish is done. This will take about 6 to 8 minutes per pound, depending upon the size of the fish. Most whole fish are prepared with the head and tail on the fish, but scaled and with the fins run. For ease in handling, wrap the fish in cheesecloth. Leave long ends on the cloth to serve as tabs at each end of the fish, and grasp these when you lift it.

17

Shellfish should not be left in bouillon after they are cooked. They will be overdone and tough.

When you cook fish in court bouillon, the critically important point to remember is that the liquid never boils—never bubbles. The bouillon may boil before the fish goes in, but never afterward. Do not discard the broth. It may be used for sauces, aspics, and in any way you use fish stock.

SOUPS AND CHOWDERS

For these methods of cooking, see the section on fish stews, chowders and soups.

Serving Wine with Fish

MOST fish dishes are enhanced by dry white wine, well chilled. This is neither rule nor ritual but simply a time-tested expression of popular taste and preference. Fish generally has a delicate texture, and its flavor is often elusive. Dry white wines, lacking the roundness and robust taste of the reds, improve the flavor of the fish but do not overwhelm it.

Not everyone agrees. If you are among those people who genuinely like red Burgundy with broiled halibut or sauternes with bouillabaisse, then these preferences are your own special pleasures. No one can say for certain that you are "incorrect." If, however, you are serving fish to guests whose tastes are unfamiliar to you, probably the wise procedure would be to accompany the dish with the traditional dry white wine.

What if the fish has been cooked in red wine, or if the sauce contains red wine? Should the householder set aside a jug of red "cooking wine," distinct and separate from the wine that is to be served with the fish?

The existence of "cooking wine" is a culinary myth. Wine is used in cooking as a flavoring agent; the better the wine, the better the flavor. And so some authorities say that it makes good sense to serve the same wine that was used in cooking the fish. I think it might be more accurate to say that the predominating flavors of a dish, and the intensities of these flavors, should determine what sort of wine is served. If the sauce for a fish is pungently accented with herbs, spices

18

and garlic, then red wine or *rosé* may be preferable to white. For example, the famous California dish cioppino is customarily served with red or *rosé* wine. A number of highly seasoned baked fish dishes—red snapper, redfish, sea trout— seem to call for *rosé*.

There are also some other exceptions to the traditional affinity between fish and dry white wine. Some salmon dishes, for example, are perfect with *rosé* and also go well with a light red wine. The same is true of some of the heavier fish stews. Many people enjoy *rosé* or light red wine with swordfish, since its texture is heavier than that of most fish, and its flavor rather "meaty."

The incomparable and universal beverage, champagne, is happily married to all fish dishes—hors d'oeuvre, stews, entrees. Besides champagne, pleasant accompaniments for hors d'oeuvres based on fish and shellfish are dry sherry, *rosé* and dry white wine. All should be chilled, although I think that sherry has more character when it is not icy cold.

FRENCH WINES

There are no greater wines than the great French wines, and there is no greater complement to a fine fish dish than one of the superb white wines of the Côte de Beaune. The great French wines are readily available in good wine shops in New York, Boston, San Francisco and other large American cities, but they are often hard to find in smaller cities.

In those localities where French wines are available, fish lovers have this advantage: generally speaking, the finest of France's dry white wines and *rosés* are less costly than the very great reds. Superb white wines, the greatest in the world, may be had for less than $4.00, and many excellent white wines of less distinction may be obtained for around $2.00.

Champagne. Complementary to all fish, but never cheap. Among the famous names are Pommery and Greno, Dom Perignon, Louis Roederer, Bollinger, Veuve Clicquot, Pol Roger, Taittinger. The dryest champagne is labeled *brut* and *English Market*. Despite the implication, *extra dry* is not the dryest.

White Bordeaux. The white wines of Graves, once popular in England and the United States, are no longer so eagerly sought by wine lovers. A notable exception, almost a curiosity, is the very dry Château Haut-Brion Blanc, regrettably scarce and expensive. A good dryish Graves is Château Olivier. In general, sauternes and Barsac are too sweet for fish dishes.

White Burgundy. Perfect with fish. The communes that are world-famous for dry whites include Vougeot, Aloxe-Corton, Meursault, Chassagne-Montrachet, Puligny-Montrachet. In a special class of its own is Chablis, greenish golden and dry as flint. It is superb with oysters. Not sufficiently appreciated by Americans is Pouilly-Fuissé, excellent with all fish and quite reasonable.

Rhone. The Hermitage white wines are excellent with fish. One of the most charming white wines in the world is Clos de Chante-Alouette. Try it with a delicate sole dish.

Loire. For a pleasant experience with fish, try Pouilly-Fumé, which is fresh and fruity, with a taste of the soil. Also pleasant, and very reasonable, is Muscadet.

Alsace. For wonderful summer drinking, especially with cold fish try Gewurztraminer, Traminer, Riesling.

Rosé wines. The Tavel *rosé* wines are delicious when chilled. To a somewhat lesser extent than champagne, they are congenial with nearly all fish dishes.

GERMAN WINES

The Rhine and Moselle districts of Germany produce some of the world's most famous white wines. Rhine wines tend to be full-bodied and long-lived, while the Moselles are lighter and often delightfully fragrant and delicate. Personally I have never considered German wines to be the equal of the fine French white wines, yet I must acknowledge that they are highly prized and that the renowned bottlings, such as Schloss Johannisberg and Bernkasteler Doktor, command exceptional prices. Many of the dry German wines are excellent with fish, and the Moselles, especially, are delicious with cold fish dishes served on warm summer days.

Some of the most expensive Rhine wines are exceedingly rich and sweet, and these, of course, are not congenial with fish. German wines labeled *Auslese* (selected picking of the grapes) and *Spätlese* (late picked) tend to be dryish, while those labeled *Beerenauslese* (selected overripe grapes) and *Trockenbeeren Auslese* (selected semidried grapes) are very sweet.

AMERICAN WINES

Wines produced in the United States must be judged and enjoyed in proper perspective. From none of our vineyards do we obtain dry white wines comparable to those of France and Germany, where growers benefit from the accumulated wisdom of centuries of viticulture. Still, American wine is good and is steadily becoming better. It is now possible to buy many types of domestic wine that go well with the best fish dishes. Prices are generally less than for imported wines. In many communities the only wine available is domestic wine.

Wine production in this country is centered in three regions: California, where most of the grape varieties are those that flourish in Europe; the Finger Lakes area in New York State, and the Lake Erie Islands area in Ohio, where "native" American grape varieties are cultivated.

Most fine California wines are now known by their grape varieties rather than by names copied from French and German wine districts. The wise purchaser seeking a dry white California wine to serve with fish therefore looks for such varietal names as Johannisberg Riesling, "Riesling," Pinot Blanc, Chardonnay, Sauvignon Blanc, Folle Blanche, Sylvaner, Traminer. Most of the best dry whites come from the counties near San Francisco Bay, from the Livermore, Napa, Sonoma and Santa Clara valleys, and these geographic names are also general clues to quality. Pleasant *rosé* wines are produced in the Napa and Santa Clara valleys.

The "native" wines of New York and Ohio are distinctly different from those of California. Some people describe their flavor as "foxy" or "grapy." To my taste the whites are much more interesting than the reds, and several of them are ideal with fish. In buying Eastern wines, check grape varieties on the labels. Among the best are Delaware, Elvira, Moore's Diamond, Diana, Catawba and Dutchess, in about that order.

Those who have had no experience in buying or tasting domestic wines may sometimes find it difficult to buy merely through label information. Despite a growing tendency to label by varietal names, quite a number of American producers still identify their products as "Chablis," "Burgundy," or "Rhine wine," although the wine inside the bottles may bear no resemblance to such European wine types. When in doubt, consult your wine merchant.

ITALIAN WINES

The people of Italy like their own wine so much that no great amount of it is exported to this country, and a wide choice of Italian wine is available only in cities like New York, where the Italian population is large. White Chianti, though not abundant, can be purchased in large cities. It is quite good with highly seasoned fish dishes. Not so well known but worth trying are Orvieto (buy the *sec* or dry) and a pleasant wine with the curious name Est! Est! Est! Prices are reasonable.

Court Bouillons and Essences of Fish

FISH differs greatly in flavor, texture, gelatinous content and delicacy of meat. Some fish and shellfish need strong bouillon to bring out and complement their flavors. Others have such distinctive flavors in themselves that they need practically nothing to enhance them.

SIMPLE COURT BOUILLON I

Sea bass, striped bass, red snapper, and other similar fish should be poached in a simple salt and water bouillon. They have distinction and flavor in themselves and should not be assaulted with artificial seasonings.

SIMPLE COURT BOUILLON II

This bouillon can be used for whiting, halibut, cod, and many of the small white fish. Combine equal quantities of milk and water with just a little salt. Bring to a boil before adding the fish. Reduce the bouillon over a fairly brisk flame after the fish is cooked and you can use it for sauces.

COURT BOUILLON FOR COLD FISH DISHES

If you are doing a large piece of salmon, or a whole one, or a large piece of any fish to be served cold, you then want a bouillon that has a pleasant blending of flavors and is well punctuated with herbs and seasonings. Such a court bouillon may be used as the basis for a remarkably good aspic. Reduce the court bouillon after removing the fish. Clarify by adding white of egg and egg shell to the broth for 3 to 5 minutes. Then strain it through a linen napkin.

For a large fish:

3 quarts water	4 carrots, finely cut
1 quart white wine	2 stalks celery
1 cup wine vinegar	1 bay leaf
3 onions	1 teaspoon thyme
9 cloves	4 to 5 sprigs parsley
1 tablespoon salt	

Put 3 cloves in each onion. Combine all ingredients and bring to a boil. Simmer for an hour before adding the fish.

RED WINE COURT BOUILLON

This is really an essence of fish for it uses the bones and heads to make a richer bouillon. It is an excellent base for aspics or sauces, or it may be cooked down to about ⅓ of its volume and used as a flavoring agent or glaze for fish dishes.

2 pounds fish bones and heads	2 stalks celery
3 quarts water	1 onion stuck with
1 quart red wine	cloves
Bouquet garni (thyme, parsley, leek)	3 carrots cut in quarters
	1 tablespoon salt

Cook the bones and heads of fish in 2 quarts of water for 30 minutes. Add the remaining water and all the other ingredients and continue cooking for 20 minutes. Add the fish and cook according to the recipe.

RICH WHITE WINE COURT BOUILLON FOR ASPICS

1 pound fish bones and heads	2 onions stuck with
1 quart water	cloves
1 quart dry white wine	2 carrots, diced
1 teaspoon dried thyme	2 cloves garlic
	1 bay leaf
	Salt, pepper

Cook the fish bones and heads in the water for 30 minutes. Strain through fine cloth. You should have about a quart of bouillon. Add all the other ingredients, bring to a boil and simmer for 20 minutes before adding the fish. For aspic, reduce the bouillon over a brisk flame after the fish is removed. Clarify it with egg white and shells and strain through a linen napkin.

COURT BOUILLON FOR SHELLFISH

Use either the red or the white wine court bouillon for any of the shellfish. If, however, the shrimp, lobster, langouste or crayfish are to be served with a highly flavored sauce, it is often more desirable to poach the fish in a plain salt and water bouillon—or in sea water, if available.

FISH ESSENCE

This can be used for flavorings, aspics, soup, and—if reduced to a heavy jelly—glazes.

1 cup mirepoix (carrots, onions, celery)	2 quarts white wine
3 tablespoons butter	2 pounds fish bones and heads
Salt, pepper	4 sprigs parsley
	1 teaspoon thyme

Make the mirepoix by cutting the vegetables in very fine julienne and cooking them in the butter until they just begin to color. Salt and pepper to taste. Add the wine and the fish bones and heads. Bring to a boil, remove any surface scum, and add the parsley and thyme. Simmer for 2 hours.

Clarify and strain through a very fine sieve or linen napkin.

Sauces for Fish

SAUCE VELOUTE

2 tablespoons flour	1 cup fish stock
2 tablespoons butter	Salt, pepper

Combine the flour and butter and cook together until they are slightly browned or yellowish in color. Gradually stir in the fish stock; continue stirring until it thickens. Cook 10 minutes and season to taste. This makes 1 cup of velouté.

It is customary when you serve a plain velouté to add cream and egg yolks to the sauce. To 1 cup of velouté add 1 cup of cream and 3 egg yolks. Beat the cream and egg yolks together well and gradually stir into the basic sauce; continue stirring until the sauce is properly thickened and heated through. Be careful not to let the mixture boil after the egg yolks have been added. This will make 2 cups of sauce velouté.

Shrimp Sauce. To 1 cup of sauce velouté add ½ cup of finely chopped cooked shrimp.

Lobster Sauce. To 1 cup of sauce velouté add ½ cup of finely chopped cooked lobster meat.

Oyster Sauce. Use ½ cup of the oyster liquor in making the basic sauce velouté, and add ½ cup of chopped oysters.

Clam Sauce. Use ½ cup of the clam liquor in making the basic sauce velouté and add ½ cup of minced clams.

Crabmeat Sauce. To 1 cup of sauce velouté add ½ cup of flaked, cooked crabmeat.

SAUCE AURORE

1 cup sauce velouté
½ cup tomato puree
½ cup cream
2 egg yolks

Combine the sauce velouté with the tomato puree. Gradually add the cream and egg yolks, which have been well mixed. Stir until thickened and smooth, but take care the mixture does not boil. Taste for seasoning.

SAUCE MORNAY

1½ cups sauce velouté
½ cup grated Gruyère cheese
½ cup (more or less) cream
Few grains cayenne

When the sauce velouté has thickened, stir in the grated cheese and continue stirring lightly until the cheese is melted. Dilute with cream, if needed. Season with cayenne and taste for salt.

FRENCH CURRY SAUCE

This is a good choice if you like a mild flavor of curry. It is also easier to make than the regular curry sauce.

2 cups sauce velouté
½ cup cream
Curry to taste

Combine the sauce velouté with the cream and as much curry as you like, and heat well. Use on any type of fish.

SAUCE SOUBISE

1 large onion, finely chopped
Butter
1 cup sauce velouté

Steam onion in butter until soft and transparent. Add to sauce.

BASIC BROWN SAUCE FOR FISH
(SAUCE ESPAGNOLE)

1 quart fish essence	4 to 5 mushrooms or stems
⅓ cup Madeira or sherry	4 tablespoons butter
¼ cup tomato puree	4 tablespoons flour

Combine the fish essence, the wine, the tomato puree and the mushrooms, and cook down for 1½ hours or until it is reduced one half. Strain. Melt the butter in a skillet. Add the flour and let it cook until fairly well colored. Add the reduced stock and stir until the sauce is thickened. Season to taste and cook for 15 minutes.

This brown sauce is the basis for many more elaborate sauces served with fish, but if you wish to serve it plain, you may add more wine or more tomato paste.

SAUCE BORDELAISE

3 shallots or 2 small white onions	3 tablespoons butter
3 to 4 mushrooms	1 cup white wine
	1 cup basic brown sauce

Peel and chop the shallots and slice the mushrooms very thin. Melt the butter in a saucepan, add the shallots (or onions) and brown lightly. Add the mushrooms and the wine and let it reduce to half its volume. Stir in the brown sauce and continue stirring until mixture has thickened and is thoroughly blended. Correct the seasoning and serve with any grilled or fried fish.

SAUCE FINES HERBES

1 cup white wine	1 cup basic brown sauce
Herbs (1 teaspoon each of chopped parsley, tarragon, chives, chervil)	2 tablespoons chopped herbs (same mixture)
	Juice of a lemon
Salt, pepper	

Combine the white wine with a teaspoon of each of the herbs and bring to a boil. Let it steep for a half hour. Strain through a cloth. Combine with the brown sauce and bring it to the boiling point. Add the additional herbs and continue cooking for 2 minutes. Just as you remove it to a sauce boat add the lemon juice and correct the seasoning.

BASIC SAUCE BECHAMEL

4 tablespoons butter	1 cup milk
3 tablespoons flour	Salt, pepper
½ cup fish broth	Nutmeg

Melt the butter, add the flour, and cook until slightly colored. Add the fish broth and stir until smooth. Gradually add milk and continue stirring until nicely thickened. Cook 5 minutes and season to taste with salt, pepper and nutmeg.

VARIATIONS

Tomato Sauce. Add 3 tablespoons of tomato puree.

Tomato-Curry Sauce. To the tomato sauce add 1 to 1½ tablespoons of curry powder.

Anchovy Sauce. Add 2 or more tablespoons of anchovy paste, 1 tablespoon of butter and the juice of half a lemon.

Cheese Sauce. Add 1 cup of grated Cheddar or Gruyère cheese, a few grains of cayenne and ½ teaspoon of dry mustard.

Egg Sauce. Add 3 hard-cooked eggs, thinly sliced.

Parsley Sauce. Add ⅓ cup of finely chopped parsley. Flavor, if you wish, with 1 tablespoon of onion juice.

Piquant Sauce. Add 1 tablespoon of finely chopped onion, 1 finely chopped, hard-cooked egg, 1 finely chopped dill pickle, and 1 tablespoon of finely chopped parsley.

Mustard Sauce. Add 1 tablespoon of French mustard and 1 teaspoon or more of dry mustard.

White Wine Sauce. Stir in ½ cup of white wine and 2 egg yolks. Heat through, stirring constantly, but do not let the sauce boil.

Dill Sauce. Add 1 teaspoon of chopped fresh dill.

Cream Sauce. Follow the basic sauce béchamel recipe, but substitute cream, or half cream and half milk, for the fish broth and milk.

SAUCE CARDINAL

1 cup fish stock	½ cup heavy cream
1 truffle (optional)	1½ cups sauce béchamel
4 tablespoons lobster butter	

Using a brisk flame, reduce the fish stock to ½ cup. While it is reducing, you may add a truffle to the stock, if you wish. Combine the stock with the cream and the béchamel. When

27

it is smooth and thickened, remove it from the fire and stir in the lobster butter (see index).

HORSERADISH SAUCE

½ cup grated fresh horseradish   1 cup béchamel
Juice of ½ lemon

Add the horseradish to the sauce, blend well, and add the lemon juice. If you use bottled horseradish, be sure you drain it well before you mix it with the sauce, and omit the lemon juice.

SAUCE VILLEROI

This is a sauce that steals its way into many recipes. It is merely a highly reduced sauce béchamel, or a heavy cream sauce, flavored with mushrooms or tomato or truffles. It is often used for masking fish or shellfish before rolling in crumbs and deep frying or baking.

SAUCE POULETTE

1 cup white sauce   Juice of ½ lemon
2 egg yolks   Chopped parsley

Make a basic white sauce, add the egg yolks and blend well with a wooden spoon or whisk. Season with lemon juice and parsley. Be careful not to let the sauce boil after the egg yolks are added.

SAUCE BOURGUIGNONNE

This is a simple version of the famous sauce.

1 small onion   1 cup red wine
6 mushrooms   Salt, pepper
4 tablespoons butter   Beurre manié
2 cups fish stock   Chopped parsley

Chop the onion very fine and slice the mushrooms very thin. Sauté them in butter until they are cooked through. Add the fish stock and the wine and let it simmer until reduced one half. Correct the seasoning and thicken with beurre manié (balls of butter and flour kneaded together). Add chopped parsley just before serving. Serve with poached fish such as salmon, salmon trout or sturgeon.

VARIATION

Add anchovy paste to taste along with a dash of lemon juice.

SAUCE HOLLANDAISE

This is sometimes called sauce Isigny. The secret of a good Hollandaise is to use the finest of sweet butter, to be sure the pan in which you make it does not touch the water below, and to be sure that the water never boils. Use either a wooden spoon or a wire whisk (I think the latter is better).

3 egg yolks	Few grains cayenne
1 or 2 teaspoons water	Few grains salt
¼ pound (½ cup) butter, cut into small pieces	Lemon juice or tarragon vinegar

Combine the egg yolks and water in the upper part of a double boiler and whisk over hot water until the eggs are well mixed and slightly thickened. Gradually add the butter. Whisk all the time, and be certain that the water below does not boil. If your sauce becomes too thick, dilute it with a little water. If it curdles, you can bring it back with a little boiling water. When it is properly emulsified, add the cayenne and a few grains of salt and the lemon juice (or vinegar) to taste.

SAUCE MOUSSELINE

This is a combination of equal parts of Hollandaise and whipped cream. It is one of the most delicate sauces in cookery.

SAUCE BEARNAISE

This is prepared exactly like a Hollandaise except that it has some added flavorings. Take 2 teaspoons of chopped fresh tarragon or 1 teaspoon of dried, 2 teaspoons of finely chopped shallots or green onions, a small pinch of salt and a pinch of black pepper. Add these to 3 tablespoons of wine vinegar and cook it down until it is practically a glaze. Add this glaze to the egg yolks and then proceed as for Hollandaise. Flavor with finely chopped tarragon, parsley and chervil, and a speck of cayenne. Add more lemon juice or tarragon vinegar, if you like.

BEARNAISE TOMATE

This is a blend of Béarnaise and tomato paste, flavored with a little salt and pepper and a bit of tarragon.

29

DUXELLES

1 medium onion	6 tablespoons butter
½ pound mushrooms	1 teaspoon chopped parsley
	Salt, pepper

Chop the onion very fine. Chop the mushrooms—caps and stems—very fine and press them in a cloth or sieve to release any natural moisture.

Melt the butter in a skillet. Add the onion and let it become just transparent. Add the mushrooms and let them cook down to almost a paste. Add the parsley, salt and pepper to taste, and cook until there is practically no moisture left. This may be stored in the refrigerator and used for various sauces.

SAUCE DUXELLES

This is a very practical sauce as it can be served with a great number of fish dishes.

¾ cup white wine	3 tablespoons flour
¾ cup fish stock or bouillon	½ cup strong stock (fish or
2 tablespoons chopped shallots	meat)
or onions	½ cup tomato puree
3 tablespoons butter	3 tablespoons duxelles

Combine the wine, the fish stock and the chopped shallots or onion. Bring to a boil and let it reduce one half. Melt the butter in a large saucepan or skillet, combine with the flour and let it cook until lightly colored. Gradually stir in the additional stock, the tomato puree and the reduced wine and broth mixture. Stir until thickened and well blended. Add the duxelles and blend again. Taste for seasoning.

SAUCE A L'AMERICAINE

3 tablespoons butter	3 tablespoons chopped
1 small chopped onion	parsley
6 chopped shallots (or green	1 tablespoon chopped fresh
onions)	tarragon (or 1 tea-
5 ripe tomatoes, peeled, seeded	spoon dried tarragon)
and chopped	1½ teaspoons thyme
1 chopped clove of garlic	Salt, pepper
	3 tablespoons tomato puree

Melt the butter and sauté the onion for a few minutes. Add shallots, tomatoes, garlic and herbs and simmer for 1 hour. Season to taste and let cook down and blend thoroughly. Add the tomato puree at the last.

NOTE: Actually, sauce à l'Américaine is usually added to fish (generally shellfish) as it cooks in white wine. During the cooking process the sauce and the wine blend. The fish is then dished out on a platter and the liquid poured over and around it. The amount of sauce given above will blend with 1½ cups of wine or fish stock.

SAUCE ITALIENNE

Brown roux
12 mushrooms
3 tablespoons butter
1 cup tomato puree (or 1 can condensed tomato soup)
¾ cup fish stock
2 tablespoons of chopped herbs (parsley, tarragon, chervil or dill)

Make a brown roux by browning 4 tablespoons of flour and combining with an equal amount of butter.

Chop the mushrooms very fine and cook them down in the butter until they are a paste.

Heat the tomato puree and the fish stock, which should be reduced a bit; when this has almost reached the boiling point, stir in the mushrooms and the roux and continue stirring until properly thickened. Add the chopped herbs and taste for seasoning.

CURRY SAUCE

⅔ cup grated coconut or ground almonds
1 cup milk
2 onions
1 apple, cored but unpeeled
2 tomatoes, peeled and seeded
4 tablespoons butter
2 tablespoons curry powder
Salt
1 cup white wine
Cream, if needed

Put the coconut or almonds to soak in the milk.

Chop the onions, apple, and tomatoes. Melt the butter in a skillet and cook the onion until just soft. Add the apple, the tomatoes, the curry powder, and salt to taste. Cook slowly until the vegetables are tender. Add the wine and simmer for ¼ hour; then add the coconut or almond milk and simmer for 15 minutes more. Force the sauce through a fine sieve, return it to the stove and let it cook down for a few minutes until well blended and thickened. Add a little cream if necessary. Taste for seasoning.

31

SAUCE DIABLE

6 shallots or 1 small onion with 1 clove garlic finely chopped
3 tablespoons butter
1½ teaspoons dry mustard
½ cup consommé (or fish broth)
½ cup white wine
2 tablespoons Escoffier Sauce Diable
½ teaspoon salt
Cayenne pepper
Juice of ½ lemon

Sauté the shallots or onion and garlic in butter. Add mustard. Gradually add the consommé and wine, blending well. Add Escoffier Sauce Diable, and salt and pepper to taste. Just before serving add lemon juice.

BARBECUE SAUCE

2 medium-sized onions, finely chopped
¼ cup olive oil
1 cup Italian tomato paste
1 teaspoon salt
1 teaspoon basil
½ cup steak sauce
¼ cup Worcestershire sauce
1 teaspoon dry mustard
½ cup strained honey
½ cup red wine

Sauté the onions in olive oil until lightly browned. Add the tomato paste, salt, basil, steak sauce, Worcestershire sauce, mustard and honey. Allow to simmer 5 minutes, stirring constantly. Add the wine and allow the sauce to come just to the boiling point. Taste for seasoning. Strain through a fine sieve.

ANCHOVY ONION SAUCE

2 large or 4 medium-sized Spanish onions
4 tablespoons olive oil
10 anchovy fillets
¼ cup chopped parsley
Thyme
Fresh or dried basil
1 cup tomato puree (Italian type)
¼ cup white wine

Peel the onions and chop them fine. Sauté them until delicately golden, but not brown, in olive oil. Add the anchovy fillets, each cut in 2 pieces. Mix very carefully with the onions and add chopped parsley, a few leaves of thyme and basil. Stir in the tomato puree mixed with the wine and let the entire sauce cook down very slightly. Taste for seasoning. Whether you need additional salt depends on the saltiness of the anchovies.

SAUCE PROVENCALE

12 ripe tomatoes	1 teaspoon black pepper
⅔ cup olive oil	1 teaspoon sugar
1 teaspoon salt	2 cloves garlic, crushed
1 tablespoon chopped parsley	

Peel, seed and chop the tomatoes and combine them with the olive oil, which you have heated to the smoking point. Add the seasonings, the garlic, and the parsley.

Cover and simmer for 30 to 40 minutes, or until the sauce is smooth and well blended.

BEURRE NOISETTE

This is really browned butter. Heat the butter in a small skillet or pipkin until it is a delicate brown but not burned.

MAÎTRE D'HOTEL BUTTER

Beurre noisette (browned butter) with lemon juice to taste.

BLACK BUTTER (BEURRE NOIR)

Heat 6 tablespoons of butter until well browned. Add lemon juice or wine vinegar to taste and blend well.

LEMON BUTTER

Heat the amount of butter needed and add lemon juice to taste.

VARIATION

Lime Butter. Substitute lime juice for lemon juice.

LOBSTER BUTTER

Grind or pound cooked lobster shells until very fine. Combine with the quantity of butter needed for the recipe and force through a fine strainer. To each ¼ pound of butter add the shells from a 1-pound lobster.

ANCHOVY BUTTER

Cream ½ cup butter until it is light. Fold in 6 anchovy fillets, finely chopped, or use anchovy paste to taste. Add a few drops of lemon juice and 1 teaspoon chopped parsley.

You may melt the butter and stir in the anchovy paste. Season with a few drops of lemon juice.

CAVIAR BUTTER

Cream 6 tablespoons of butter until light and add 1 tablespoon of caviar (more or less, according to your taste). Season with a few drops of lemon juice.

HERB BUTTER

Cream ¼ pound of butter and blend in 1 tablespoon each of finely chopped parsley, chives, chervil and tarragon. If you use the dried tarragon and chervil, use 1 teaspoon each.

VARIATIONS

Tarragon-Chive Butter. Cream butter and add chopped chives and tarragon to taste.

Parsley Butter. Cream butter and add chopped parsley to taste.

AIOLI

This sauce is a regular Friday dish for many people living in the South of France. It was formerly made by pounding the garlic in a mortar, but you can make it much more easily with an electric mixer or blender.

4 cloves garlic	Olive oil or peanut oil
2 egg yolks	Lemon juice
Salt	

Chop the garlic very fine or put it through a garlic press. Add the egg yolks and beat in the electric mixer or blender.

Gradually add the oil—between 1 and 2 cups—and when thickened and the consistency of a mayonnaise, add lemon juice to taste and salt. The garlic flavor should be dominant.

SAUCE MAYONNAISE

2 egg yolks	½ teaspoon dry mustard
1 teaspoon salt	1 pint peanut or olive oil
Lemon juice or vinegar	

Beat the egg yolks, the salt and mustard together and gradually add the oil, beating constantly until well thickened and stiff. Thin with lemon juice or vinegar to taste.

If your mayonnaise starts to curdle, begin over with another egg yolk and a little oil, and gradually add the curdled mixture. I find that it is important to have your eggs and oil at the same temperature.

You may make mayonnaise with a fork, a rotary beater, a whisk, or an electric blender or mixer.

VARIATIONS

Sauce Andalouse. To 1 cup of mayonnaise add ½ cup of tomato puree and 2 pimientos, finely chopped. Season with ½ teaspoon of paprika.

Mayonnaise with Jelly. Combine equal quantities of mayonnaise and aspic—either lemon or fish. Beat it well with a wire whisk and chill. Use it for masking fish, or a decoration piped through a pastry tube. (This is also called **Chaudfroid.**)

Green Mayonnaise (Sauce Verte). To 2 cups of mayonnaise add 1 cup of mixed herbs (spinach, water cress, parsley, chives, tarragon) which have been chopped very fine—almost to a powder. Blend well.

SAUCE REMOULADE

2 cups mayonnaise
2 cloves garlic, finely chopped
1 tablespoon finely chopped tarragon
1 teaspoon dry mustard
2 hard-cooked eggs, finely chopped
1 tablespoon capers
1 tablespoon finely chopped parsley
1 teaspoon anchovy paste

Mix all the ingredients thoroughly and let stand for 2 hours before serving.

RUSSIAN DRESSING

2 cups mayonnaise
1 teaspoon dry mustard
2 tablespoons finely chopped onion
2 ounces caviar
1 tablespoon Worcestershire sauce

Blend well and let stand for 2 hours before serving.

THOUSAND ISLAND DRESSING

2 cups mayonnaise
2 tablespoons finely chopped onion
1 finely chopped hard-cooked egg
1 teaspoon dry mustard
⅓ cup chili sauce
1 tablespoon capers
2 tablespoons finely chopped parsley

Blend well and let stand for 2 hours before serving.

35

TARTAR SAUCE

2 cups mayonnaise
3 tablespoons finely chopped onion
2 teaspoons lemon juice
2 tablespoons finely chopped parsley

2 tablespoons finely chopped dill or
3 tablespoons finely chopped dill pickle

Blend well and let stand for 2 hours before serving.

LOUIS DRESSING

1 cup mayonnaise
2 tablespoons grated onion
¼ cup chili sauce

2 tablespoons chopped parsley
Few grains of cayenne
⅓ cup heavy cream, whipped

Mix the mayonnaise, onion, chili sauce, parsley and cayenne thoroughly. Let them stand to blend while whipping the cream. Fold in the cream until it is well mixed with the mayonnaise mixture. This is excellent on cold shellfish.

VINAIGRETTE

Vinaigrette is nothing more than oil, vinegar, salt and pepper,—the oil and vinegar being apportioned according to your taste. I prefer 3 to 4 parts of oil to 1 of vinegar.

This is often erroneously called "French dressing" in this country.

SAUCE GRIBICHE

This sauce is often mistakenly called "vinaigrette."

3 yolks of hard-cooked eggs
1 teaspoon dry mustard
1 teaspoon salt
½ teaspoon freshly ground pepper
1 cup olive oil
1 tablespoon wine vinegar
3 egg whites, hard-cooked and finely chopped

1 tablespoon finely chopped pickle
1 teaspoon finely chopped capers
2 tablespoons finely chopped mixed herbs (chives, parsley, tarragon, chervil)

Crush the egg yolks with a fork and blend well with the mustard, salt and pepper. Gradually stir in the oil. When it is all absorbed, add the vinegar, egg whites, and other seasonings. Let the sauce stand for at least an hour to bring out the flavors.

BOILED SALAD DRESSING

2 tablespoons sifted flour	½ cup lemon juice or
3 tablespoons sugar	vinegar
1 teaspoon dried mustard	2 eggs, separated
1 cup white wine	½ cup olive oil
	Salt, pepper
½ cup sour cream	

Combine the flour, sugar, mustard, white wine, and vinegar or lemon juice together in the top of a double boiler. Add the egg yolks, the oil, and salt and pepper to taste. Heat over hot water until the mixture thickens. Beat the egg whites until stiff. Add the sour cream and the stiffly beaten egg whites to the mixture and beat with a whisk or wooden spoon until the dressing is thoroughly blended. This can be used hot or cold.

CUCUMBER SAUCE

1 cup sour cream	1 teaspoon finely chopped
½ cup seeded, grated	fresh dill
cucumber	2 teaspoons chopped chives
½ teaspoon salt	
½ teaspoon black pepper	

Blend all the ingredients well. Allow the sauce to stand for 1 or 2 hours in the refrigerator before serving.

SOUR CREAM SAUCE

Season 1 cup of sour cream to taste with salt and freshly ground black pepper. You may add grated onion or chopped chives if you wish.

COCKTAIL SAUCE I

½ cup chili sauce	½ teaspoon dry mustard
1 tablespoon Worcestershire	½ teaspoon salt
sauce	1 tablespoon horseradish
½ cup tomato catsup	1 teaspoon ground black
	pepper

Blend all ingredients well.

COCKTAIL SAUCE II

6 tomatoes, peeled, seeded,
  chopped
1 green pepper, seeded and
  chopped
1 medium onion or 4 shallots,
  peeled and chopped

1 teaspoon dry mustard
1 tablespoon horseradish
1 teaspoon freshly ground
  pepper
2 teaspoons lemon juice
  Salt to taste

½ cup olive oil

Chop the vegetables very fine, add the seasonings and olive oil and mix thoroughly. Chill before using.

Stuffings and Fish Forcemeat

STUFFINGS for baked fish vary from the simple to the elaborate —from a bit of chopped onion and parsley to the complicated fish forcemeat. There are plain bread stuffings, vegetable stuffings, and stuffings that include meats or other fish or shellfish.

The recipes listed here are a few general favorites, the ingredients of which may be varied to suit your own taste. You may also select any of the number of stuffings given in various recipes throughout the book. In making your selection, keep in mind the other foods you plan to serve at the meal, and the sauce, if any, that you will serve with the baked fish.

SIMPLE BREAD STUFFING

2 large onions, sliced
4 tablespoons butter
1 cup bread crumbs
¼ cup finely chopped parsley

½ teaspoon thyme
2 tablespoons chopped
  celery leaves
1 teaspoon salt

1 egg, well beaten

Sauté the onions in the butter until soft. Add all the other ingredients and mix thoroughly.

VARIATIONS

1. Add sautéed chopped mushrooms.
2. Omit the thyme and celery and add chopped toasted almonds.

VEGETABLE STUFFING

2 onions
1 clove garlic
Butter
1 green pepper, seeded and
chopped

4 ripe tomatoes, peeled,
seeded and chopped
Chopped parsley
Salt, pepper

Sauté the onions and garlic in butter just until soft. Add green pepper, tomato, parsley, and salt and pepper to taste. Fish baked with this stuffing is especially good served with a tomato sauce made with red wine.

PUNGENT STUFFING

½ cup finely chopped onion
4 tablespoons butter
2 tablespoons olive oil
2 cups dry bread crumbs or
zwieback crumbs

1 cup ground cooked ham
¼ cup chopped parsley
1 teaspoon dried or 1
tablespoon fresh tar-
ragon
Salt, pepper

Sauté the onion in butter and oil until soft; add the other ingredients and blend thoroughly. If the stuffing is too dry, add a little dry vermouth or sherry.

OYSTER STUFFING

6 green onions, chopped
¼ cup celery, minced
¼ cup green pepper, minced
5 tablespoons butter

1½ cups bread crumbs
½ pint oysters and liquor
½ cup chopped parsley
Salt, pepper

Thyme

Sauté the onions, celery and green pepper in butter until just soft. Add the crumbs, the oysters and their liquor, and cook for 3 or 4 minutes. Add the parsley and season to taste with salt, pepper and thyme.

CRABMEAT STUFFING

2 cups cracker crumbs
½ cup chopped celery
½ cup chopped onion
¼ cup chopped green pepper
½ cup crabmeat

3 eggs
1 teaspoon salt
Dash of cayenne
1 teaspoon dry mustard
½ cup melted butter

Mix all the ingredients together.

VARIATIONS

You may substitute shrimp, chopped, for the crabmeat.

SCANDINAVIAN STUFFING

Stuff the fish with anchovy fillets and pieces of uncooked bacon. This is especially good if you baste the fish with white wine during the cooking.

FISH FORCEMEAT

This is one of the most complicated stuffings. It is very flavorful and used in several ways: as a stuffing for baked fish, as a spread on rolled fillets, or as small fish balls poached in court bouillon.

1 cup soft bread crumbs	4 egg yolks
Milk, about ½ cup	Salt, pepper
1 pound pike or other white	Thyme
fish	Tarragon
1 egg	Heavy cream

Soak the bread crumbs in milk until all the milk is thoroughly absorbed. Grind the fish several times or pound it in a mortar. It must be exceedingly pasty. Add the bread crumbs to the fish; add the egg, the egg yolks, the seasonings and enough cream to smooth the mixture. Work it in a mortar or with a heavy wooden spoon until smooth and thoroughly blended.

Fish Stews, Chowders and Soups

IT seems to be human nature to like stews, chowders and heavy soups made of many ingredients. Almost every country has produced its specialty, and perhaps the most famous of all is the bouillabaisse. This splendid concoction is usually associated with the port of Marseilles, but it has been known for centuries, in one form or another, to the residents of the whole of Southern France.

BOUILLABAISSE

This is the recipe of Jean Suprenat, who owns the restaurant La Méditerranée in Paris.

Certain Mediterranean fish, not available in this country, are traditional in the bouillabaisse, but excellent substitutes can be found. A good selection for an American bouillabaisse is haddock or bass for the hearty fish; then lemon sole, whiting, red snapper, flounder—practically any other fish you want. And always eel. For shellfish, use lobster, mussels, sea urchins. For a large bouillabaisse:

3 pounds fish:	3 cloves garlic
1 pound eel	3 tomatoes
1 pound haddock or sea bass	⅓ cup olive oil
1 pound red snapper (Or you may use a larger variety of fish—½ pound each of 6 different kinds.)	Bouquet garni (thyme, bay leaf, parsley, celery, rosemary)
	Pinch of saffron
	Water or fish broth
3 pounds lobster	Salt, pepper
3 dozen mussels	Cayenne
3 leeks	Croutons fried in garlic-flavored olive oil
2 large onions, chopped	

Cut the fish into small serving-size pieces. Keep the richer, heavier fish—eel, haddock, cod, bass—separate from the more delicate types. Cut the live lobsters into pieces (see directions for Broiled Live Lobster). Wash and clean the mussels.

Cut the white part of the leeks into small pieces. Chop the onion and the garlic. Peel and seed the tomatoes.

Heat the olive oil in a large kettle. Add the vegetables and let them cook well together. Add the bouquet garni and the heavier fish. Let this cook about 7 or 8 minutes. Add the lighter fish, the lobster, and a good pinch of saffron. Cover with water or fish broth, season to taste with salt, pepper and cayenne, and bring to a boil. Cook for 15 minutes. Add the mussels and cook until they open. Place the fish in a deep serving dish and pour the hot liquid over it. Serve garlic flavored croutons separately.

VARIATIONS

1. Boil heads and bones of fish with water and white wine—3 quarts of liquid to 3 pounds of heads and bones—for ½ hour. Then simmer until the liquid is reduced to 1½ quarts. Strain, clarify and use as liquid for the bouillabaisse.

2. Substitute ½ cup of butter for the olive oil. The result is a more delicate dish.

AIGO-SAU

This is similar to bouillabaisse and is also native to the South of France. It is simple to prepare and has interesting variations.

1½ pounds fresh fish	Salt, pepper
5 or 6 potatoes, peeled and sliced	Seasonings (bay leaf, fennel, parsley, celery, grated orange rind)
2 tomatoes	
1 onion	⅓ cup olive oil
2 cloves garlic	Boiling water

Dry bread

Arrange the fish, cut into serving-size pieces, in a large saucepan and cover with the potatoes. Add the tomatoes, onion, and garlic—all peeled and finely chopped. Add the seasonings—salt, pepper and herbs. Pour the olive oil on this, and add enough boiling water to cover. Boil quickly for 20 minutes or until the potatoes are tender. Pour the broth into dishes over slices of dry bread—toasted or not, as you wish—that have been well rubbed with garlic. Serve the fish and the potatoes on a separate plate. This recipe serves 4 to 6 people.

This dish is sometimes served with what is called "rouille," which is not a sauce, but more of a condiment.

ROUILLE

Pound in a mortar, or chop exceedingly fine, 2 cloves of garlic and 2 hot red peppers. Add 3 tablespoons of fine bread crumbs and mix well. Work in 3 tablespoons of olive oil and blend the whole with 1 cup of the bouillon from your fish dish. Serve in a sauceboat. This may also be served with bouillabaisse.

VARIATION

You may prepare aigo-sau with only one fish or with as many as you please. It is also made without fish, and eggs are poached in the broth just before serving. In this case it is sometimes called bouillabaisse borgne.

COTRIADE—A BRETON BOUILLABAISSE

4 large potatoes, peeled and quartered	Bouquet garni (thyme, bay leaf, rosemary, parsley)
4 large onions, peeled and quartered	Salt
Fish heads	Water, about 1 pint per person

3 pounds fish (mackerel, eel, fresh sardines, mullet, cod)

Put the potatoes, onions, fish heads, bouquet garni, and salt in a pot and cover with water—a pint per person. Bring to a boil and simmer for 20 minutes. Remove the fish heads. Add the fish, which has been cut in serving-size pieces. Cook until the potatoes are tender and the fish cooked through—about 15 minutes.

Serve in two bowls, one for the broth and the other for the fish and vegetables.

BOURRIDE

There are about as many types of bourride as there are of bouillabaisse. It is difficult to offer one recipe that is representative, so I suggest two that are very different.

BOURRIDE I (CHIBERTA)

2 onions
2 cloves garlic
2 tomatoes
Bouquet garni (thyme, bay leaf, fennel, parsley)
2 quarts water
Salt
2 tablespoons olive oil

1½ pounds small fish (sole, smelt, sea bass)
Pinch of saffron
6 fillets sole or flounder
6 large slices day-old bread, fried in garlic-flavored olive oil
2 egg yolks

Peel and chop the onions and garlic. Peel, seed and chop the tomatoes. Add these with the bouquet garni to the water. Add salt to taste and 2 tablespoons of olive oil. Bring to a boil and add all the fish except the fillets. Simmer for 15 minutes and add a pinch of saffron.

Remove the fish to a hot dish and allow the bouillon to cook down for a few minutes. Strain it and rub the vegetables and seasonings through a fine sieve. Reheat the bouillon and poach the fillets until they are just cooked through. Remove them to a hot plate and keep the bouillon hot.

Fry the bread in garlic-flavored olive oil until nicely browned.

Beat 2 egg yolks well and stir them into the bouillon. Do not let it boil. Place each piece of fried toast in a soup plate, top each one with a fillet and cover with sauce aioli (see index). Surround with the rest of the fish and the broth.

BOURRIDE II

2 pounds fish (bass, haddock, flounder)
1 medium onion, finely chopped
Bouquet garni (thyme, bay leaf, fennel, peel of half an orange)

Salt, pepper
Boiling water
12 slices bread
Garlic
2 cups sauce aioli

Prepare the fish—fillets will do. Cut it into small serving-size pieces. Place it in the bottom of a saucepan and cover with the onion, bouquet garni, and salt and pepper to taste. Add boiling water to cover and a little above and let it boil for 10 minutes.

While the fish is cooking, toast the bread and rub well with garlic. Place them in a large tureen or deep platter. Then prepare enough sauce aioli (see index) to use 1 cup in the sauce and have enough left (at least another cupful) to serve separately. You may estimate 1 egg and ¼ cup of oil per person.

When the fish is cooked, remove it and keep warm. Strain the bouillon and combine it, little by little, with 1 cup of the aioli. Mix well without letting it curdle. When it is all mixed, put it in a saucepan over very low heat, or over hot water, and stir with a wooden spoon until the sauce just coats the spoon. *It must not boil.* Pour this sauce over the pieces of toast and serve the fish separately with additional aioli.

BOUILLINADE DES PECHEURS

This is a fisherman's dish that is a combination of French and Spanish cuisine, and while it shows some relationship to the Provençale dishes, it has a personality quite its own. It is properly made in an earthenware pot, but since few people have much success in top of the stove cookery in earthenware, I think it is better to use a copper or stainless steel container.

⅓ cup olive oil	2 pounds fish
⅓ cup butter	6 to 8 soft-shelled crabs or
1 onion, finely minced	2 hard-shelled crabs
3 cloves garlic, finely minced	broken in pieces

2 large minced sweet red pep-
   pers or pimientos, cut in
   fine julienne
	2 to 3 dozen mussels
	⅓ cup flour
	Sauce aioli

1 pound potatoes, peeled and sliced or quartered	

Place the olive oil and butter in the bottom of the pan (the Rousillon natives like rancid lard, but the flavor is not pleasant to our palates); add to this the onion and garlic, the peppers or pimientos, potatoes, and fish—a mixture of haddock, sea perch, sea bass, and red snapper, or whatever fish you find available—cut in small serving-size pieces. Top this with the crabs and mussels, and sprinkle with flour. Cover the fish

44

completely with water. Bring it to a boil and boil for about 15 minutes or until the potatoes are soft.

Thicken the sauce with aioli as in the preceding recipe. (The traditional way to make the sauce and thickening for this dish is to pound the liver of the fish with garlic, oil and egg yolks; however, we seldom get fish livers in this country and the method I give you is far simpler.)

This recipe will serve 6 to 8 people.

ZUPPA DI PESCE

This is an Italian version of the dishes above.

½ cup olive oil
1 large onion, finely chopped
  Herbs (bay leaf, fennel, parsley)
½ cup white wine
1 teaspoon salt, pepper
2 pounds fish (eel, sea bass, skate, red snapper, or cod, with lobster, clams or mussels)
2 quarts boiling water
6 to 12 slices of stale bread fried in olive oil
Chopped parsley, a little garlic, finely minced
Black pepper

Heat the olive oil in a deep kettle, add the onion and herbs and let them cook for a few minutes. Add the wine, salt and pepper and let it all blend thoroughly.

Cut all the fish in pieces for serving, and cut the live lobster in sections. Wash the clams, and wash and clean the mussels. Add the heavier fish to the hot olive oil mixture and cook for just a minute. Add boiling water and cook for 4 minutes. Add the lighter fish and the shellfish, and cook for 5 or 6 minutes more. Taste for seasoning.

Meanwhile, brown 6 to 12 pieces of stale bread in olive oil until crisp. Remove the cooked fish to a tureen. Let the broth cook down for a few minutes and pour it over the fish. Sprinkle with chopped parsley, a little garlic and a dusting of black pepper. Serve on top of the fried bread in soup bowls.

CIOPPINO

This is a California dish with a noble history that is now tarnished by commercialism. It was originally made by the Portuguese fishermen along the coastal counties of California; much care went into the preparation. In recent years, a bastardized version has become standard fare in many seafood restaurants—one of those "specialties of the house" resting for hours on a steam table.

1 sea bass or striped bass	1 green pepper
1 pound shrimp	½ cup olive oil
1 quart clams or mussels	1 large onion, chopped
¼ pound dried mushrooms	2 cloves garlic, chopped
(Italian variety)	3 tablespoons chopped
1 West Coast crab or lobster	parsley
3 or 4 tomatoes	⅓ cup tomato puree
	1 pint red wine

Salt, pepper

Cut the raw fish into serving-size pieces. Shell the shrimp, leaving the tails intact. Clean and steam the mussels or clams and save the liquid. Soak the mushrooms in cold water. Break the crab apart, or if you use lobster, cut it in pieces. Peel and chop the tomatoes and chop the green pepper.

Place the olive oil in a deep pot, and when it is hot add the onion, garlic, parsley, mushrooms, and green pepper and cook for 3 minutes. Next add the tomatoes and the puree, the wine and the liquid from the mussels or clams. Salt and pepper to taste, cover and let it simmer for 30 minutes. Add the cut-up fish, the shrimp and the crab or lobster, and cook until done. Serve with plenty of red wine and garlic bread.

VARIATION

Helen Evans Brown of the *West Coast Cook Book* adds oregano and basil to her recipe, which give it an Italian touch. She also says that there are recipes calling for white wine, sherry, and other wines.

It is my opinion that cioppino is a result of the various Mediterranean cuisines that met on the shores of California.

MATELOTE

The matelote is another French version of a soup stew. These days we consider it the main course of a meal, but in heartier times it was served as the first course and followed by several others.

3 pounds fish (eel, carp, pike,	⅓ cup cognac
perch, whitefish)	12 small white onions
Bouquet garni (thyme, bay	Powdered sugar
leaf, parsley, onion)	12 mushroom caps
2 cloves garlic	4 to 6 tablespoons butter
1 clove	Lemon juice
Salt, pepper	Beurre manié
Red wine to cover (about 1	Fried bread
bottle)	

Cut the fish into small serving pieces. Place them in a large pot with the bouquet garni, the garlic, the clove, and salt and pepper to taste. Add enough wine to cover, and place over a low flame. When it comes to a boil, add the cognac and let it simmer for 12 to 15 minutes. Remove the fish to a hot dish. Let the broth cook down for 2 or 3 minutes and strain. Return it to the pot.

While the fish is cooking, peel and sauté the onions in butter, and add a sprinkling of powdered sugar to give them a glaze. When they are nicely browned, cover and steam them until they are cooked through. Cook the mushrooms in butter and a little lemon juice.

Thicken the broth with beurre manié and stir until smooth. Pour this over the fish and surround with the onions and mushrooms. Serve with fried toast.

PAUCHOUSE BOURGIGNONNE

The pauchouse is what some people call a fresh-water bouillabaisse. It's a hearty dish and may be reheated the following day, when it will often taste even more delicious.

There is one "must" in any pauchouse. That is eel. As for the other fish, use any of the following or choose your own combination: pike (almost a "must"), perch, carp, lake trout, whitefish.

5 pounds fish	12 to 18 small white onions
2 quarts court bouillon (see index)	1 tablespoon butter
	Powdered sugar
4 slices salt pork, cut in small dice	Beurre manié (see index)
	1 cup heavy cream
3 tablespoons butter	⅓ cup armagnac or cognac
Fried toast rubbed with garlic	

Cut the fish into serving-size pieces and prepare the court bouillon. After the bouillon has simmered for about 20 minutes, add the fish and poach for about 15 minutes. Remove fish to a deep hot serving dish. Strain the bouillon and return it to the pan. Reduce it for 10 minutes.

During the time the bouillon is cooking, try out the salt pork in 3 tablespoons of butter. Cook the onions in a very little water until just tender. Brown them in butter with a little sprinkling of powdered sugar.

Now thicken the bouillon with beurre manié, add the crisp bits of salt pork, the onions, and the cream. Stir until well blended. Pour the armagnac or cognac over the fish and ignite.

Pour the sauce over the fish and serve with fried toast heavily flavored with garlic.

WATERZOOI

Popular throughout Europe, this is one of the great national dishes of Belgium.

Fish heads and bones
Salt, pepper
1 onion
Celery
Seasonings (bay leaf, 2 cloves, parsley, fennel)

3 quarts water
3 pounds fish
Fried bread rubbed with garlic
Chopped parsley

Prepare a rich stock with the heads and bones of fish, salt, pepper, onion, celery and seasonings. Start with 3 quarts of water and cook it down until half of the water is reduced. Strain.

Cut the fish—preferably fresh-water fish—into finger-sized pieces and place them in a saucepan. Cover with the reduced broth and poach the fish until it is just tender. Serve with garlic-flavored bread, toasted or fried, and sprinkle heavily with chopped parsley.

SOLIANKA—A RUSSIAN FISH STEW

2 pounds fish bones and heads
1½ quarts water
Salt, pepper
2 onions
4 dill pickles
3 large tomatoes
Oil

1 pound salmon
1 teaspoon capers
1 teaspoon chopped green olives
1 teaspoon chopped black olives
1 bay leaf
Parsley
4 tablespoons butter
Lemon slices

Prepare a fish bouillon with the heads and bones and water, well seasoned with salt and pepper. Peel the onions and chop them with the dill pickles. Peel, seed and chop the tomatoes and cook them in a little oil until they form a paste. Cut the salmon into strips and place them in a pan with the onion, pickles, tomato paste, capers, and chopped olives. Cover with the fish broth, which you have strained. Add the bay leaf and a sprig of parsley, and cook gently for 15 minutes. Add the butter.

Serve in bowls garnished with chopped parsley, olives, and thin slices of lemon.

RUSSIAN FISH STEW

1 pound flounder or sole
1 pound pike
½ lemon
6 potatoes in ½-inch slices
3 large onions, sliced

2 carrots cut in fine julienne
2 quarts water
1 bay leaf
1 teaspoon salt
Pepper

Paprika

Slice the fish in serving-size pieces. Cover them with lemon juice and place in the refrigerator for several hours.

Prepare a bouillon with the vegetables, water and seasonings. Cook for nearly an hour. Add the fish and simmer for about 15 minutes. Serve very hot.

UKHA

2 quarts water
Bouquet garni (leek, celery, carrot, onions, bay leaf, thyme)
Salt, pepper
1 pint white wine

2 pounds carp
1 pound pike
1 pound eel
Lemon juice
Croutons
Garlic-flavored oil or butter

Combine water, bouquet garni and seasonings and simmer for 30 minutes. Add the wine and the carp and simmer until the fish begins to fall apart—about 35 to 40 minutes. Strain and force the fish and the seasonings through a fine sieve. Return the broth to the pan and bring it to a boil. Add the pike and eel cut in small serving-size pieces. Simmer for 15 minutes. Taste for seasoning and add lemon juice (about 4 tablespoons) just before serving. Serve with croutons fried in garlic-flavored oil or butter.

MATELOTE OF EELS NORMANDIE

Mirepoix (see index)
2 pounds eel
1½ cups cider
Parsley
Tarragon
1 teaspoon salt
3 tablespoons butter

3 tablespoons flour
2 egg yolks
½ cup cream
fresh sorrel (if available) or lemon juice
12 small onions
Butter

Fried croutons

Prepare a mirepoix and put it at the bottom of a large saucepan. Cut the eel in serving-size pieces and place it on top. Add the cider, parsley, tarragon, and salt. Bring to a boil

49

and simmer for about 20 minutes. Remove the eel to a hot platter and keep hot.

Reduce the bouillon to 1 cupful. Strain. Melt the butter in a saucepan or double boiler and blend in the flour. Add the bouillon gradually, stirring constantly, until the sauce is thick and smooth. Remove from the flame and add the egg yolks and cream; stir until well blended and taste for seasoning. If available, add a few leaves of chopped sorrel—or a good squeeze of lemon juice. Pour the sauce over the eels and surround with small white onions that have been browned in butter and steamed until tender. Serve fried croutons, or slices of bread fried in butter and flavored, if you wish, with garlic.

CRAB GUMBO

There seems to be great difference of opinion about this famous dish, and I cannot tell who is right. So I give a New Orleans version and a Western version, and will let you fight it out on your own stove.

CRAB GUMBO, NEW ORLEANS VERSION

12 crabs (either hard- or soft-shelled)	6 ripe tomatoes, peeled and chopped
3 tablespoons butter	Seasonings (thyme, bay leaf, parsley, salt, cayenne)
1 large onion, chopped	Water
1 pound okra	

Boiled rice

Clean the crabs. If you use the hard-shelled variety, break off the claws and cut the body in quarters. If you use soft-shelled, leave them whole.

Melt the butter in a large pot and cook the onion until lightly browned. Add the okra and tomatoes, cover and cook for 15 minutes. Uncover and add the seasonings, the crabs, and enough water to cover and a little over. Simmer for 40 minutes.

Serve very hot in bowls with boiled rice.

CRAB GUMBO, WESTERN VERSION

2 Dungeness crabs	¼ pound diced smoked ham
4 tablespoons butter	Salt, pepper
2 large onions	3 quarts boiling water
5 large tomatoes	1 pound okra
1 green pepper	Boiled rice

50

Clean the crabs and remove all the meat from the shells. Melt the butter in a large kettle and sauté the coarsely chopped onions until they are golden; add the peeled and chopped tomatoes, the green pepper cut into strips, the ham, salt, pepper, and the boiling water. Cover and simmer for 20 minutes. Uncover and add the okra cut into 1-inch lengths. Cook for 10 minutes. Add the crab meat and cook until gelatinous. If you like it thicker, add a little beurre manié.

Serve with boiled rice and a good white wine, well-chilled.

NOTE: It is my opinion that these dishes, authentic as they are, overcook the crab. I believe that you will enjoy the dish more if you do not add the crab until about 5 minutes before serving. Or add only part of it to flavor the gumbo and the rest just at the last. The fish will then retain the texture and flavor of crabmeat and will not end up merely as part of a mush.

NEW ORLEANS COURT BOUILLON

This is not to be confused with the court bouillons that are used generally in cooking fish and shellfish. This is a particularly interesting development in regional cookery. It is definitely related to the court bouillon of French cookery and more distantly to the bouillabaisse; it has also the heaviness of Indian and Negro adaptations of foreign dishes that have sprung up in the South.

3 pounds filleted red snapper	1½ quarts boiling water
1 cup flour	1 pint red wine
½ cup olive oil	1 tablespoon Worcestershire
¼ pound butter	sauce
2 pounds onions	1 lemon, sliced
4 stalks celery	1 bunch parsley
3 cloves garlic	2 bay leaves
2 sweet peppers	Salt, pepper
12 ounces tomato paste	Fried croutons

Prepare a roux with the flour and oil. When it is well thickened, add the butter, and the onions, celery, garlic and peppers, all of which have been chopped very fine. Stir constantly so as not to scorch the roux; add the tomato paste, and gradually add the boiling water. Add the wine and other seasonings. Simmer gently for 30 minutes. Add the fillets of snapper, and cook just until they flake easily with a fork. Correct the seasoning and serve with fried croutons and a chilled white wine.

SOUPE DE POISSON MARSEILLAISE

2 leeks	2 quarts water
2 onions	2 pounds fish (small lobster, crab, snapper, haddock)
4 tablespoons olive oil	
2 tomatoes, chopped	Salt, pepper
2 cloves garlic, crushed	1 pound fine spaghetti or vermicelli
Bouquet garni (fennel, bay leaf, orange rind)	Pinch of saffron

Cut the leeks and onions very fine and cook them for a few minutes in the olive oil. Add the tomatoes, garlic and bouquet garni. Cook for a few minutes, stirring with a wooden spoon, and then add the water and fish. Bring it to a boil, and let it boil rapidly for 15 minutes. Strain into a large saucepan. Press the fish and seasonings in a sieve or colander so that all the juice and bits of flesh are forced through into the bouillon. Salt and pepper to taste. Bring this bouillon to a boil again and add the spaghetti or vermicelli (or any finely cut paste). Add a pinch of saffron and cook very slowly until the paste is soft. Serve this hearty soup to 6 or 8 people with a bottle of *rosé* wine and some well-toasted French bread.

VARIATIONS

1. If you wish to be dressy, serve as a garnish on each plate of soup a few small shrimp cooked in butter and sprinkled with parsley.

2. Prepare this soup with only one fish or shellfish—red snapper, lobster, mussels, clams, or any fish you like. Then set aside a bit of the fish that does not get overcooked and use it as a garnish.

3. Add a dash of Madeira to the soup just before serving.

SOUPE DE POISSON A LA MARSEILLAISE

This recipe is from Monsieur Pascal, who operates the charming restaurant L'Auberge de France in New York City. Flounders, fish bones, crabs and mussels can be added, but no oily fish like mackerel.

4 quarts of rockfish (sea bass, blackfish, etc.)	20 peeled and chopped tomatoes
1 cup olive oil	½ pound vermicelli
Salt and pepper	1 pinch of saffron
4 large onions	½ pound grated Swiss cheese

Clean and wash the fish (no scaling is necessary)and cook it in ¾ cup of olive oil, stirring often to prevent burning and to flake the fish. When the fish is reduced to pieces, fill the pot with water, add salt and pepper to taste and cook as long as you deem it necessary in order to extract all the flavor.

In another pot, put ¼ cup of olive oil and cook the grated or finely chopped onions until they are soft (not brown). Add the chopped tomatoes and cook for 15 minutes.

Strain the fish through a fine mesh strainer or squeeze it through a piece of cloth. Add the resulting broth to the vegetables and bring to a boil. Add ½ pound of medium-sized vermicelli, cut small, and when almost cooked, add a pinch of saffron. Let it simmer for a few minutes. This should give 8 quarts of soup. When served, sprinkle each bowl with grated Swiss cheese.

CLAM CHOWDER

This, among fish soups, is my oldest love. It was the first fish soup I ever had and it has remained my favorite through the years. It can be made with either the minced razor clams of the Pacific Coast or the littlenecks of the East Coast.

With the littlenecks: Place 1 quart of clams in a saucepan with a little white wine or water. Cover and steam until they open. Pour off the liquid and strain it. Remove the clams from their shells and set aside. If you use the minced razor clams (fresh or Pioneer canned), you will need about 1½ cups of clams, drained. Save the broth, of course.

Clams (about 1½ cups, drained) and clam liquor	2 medium potatoes
	Salt and pepper
3 or 4 slices salt pork or bacon, cut in fine pieces	2 cups light cream
	Thyme
1 medium onion, finely chopped	Paprika
Chopped parsley	

Fry out salt pork or bacon. Remove it when it is crisp, and lightly brown the onion.

Peel and dice the potatoes, and cook them in boiling water until just tender. Take them out and let the water cook down a bit. Combine the bacon, onion, potato and potato water in a saucepan, and add the clam juice. Bring this to a boil and let it simmer for 5 minutes. Season to taste. Add, gradually, the cream, and when it has just come to the boiling point, add the clams. Just let them heat through. Sprinkle with the merest pinch of finely rubbed thyme.

53

Serve in heated cups with a dash of paprika and a little chopped parsley.

You may add more clam broth and use milk instead of cream. The result is a lighter, less hearty soup.

MANHATTAN CLAM CHOWDER

Proceed as for clam chowder but substitute tomato juice for the cream and add more clam broth.

WIN'S CLAM CHOWDER

This rich and unusual version of New England clam chowder is the recipe of Irwin Chase, an excellent Yankee cook.

¼ pound salt pork	¼ teaspoon garlic powder
2 medium onions	¼ teaspoon celery salt
1 green pepper	1 pint quahogs or other
6 medium potatoes	clams, with liquid
2 tablespoons salt	1 pint water
¼ teaspoon white pepper	Sour cream

Dice the salt pork and fry it until brown. Chop the onions and green peppers very fine, and add them to the salt pork and drippings. Let them sauté to a light brown. Chop the quahogs or clams in small pieces. Dice 3 of the potatoes. Add the chopped quahogs with their liquid and the diced potatoes to the salt pork, onion and pepper. Add the seasonings and let it all simmer until the potatoes are done.

Cut the remaining 3 potatoes into small pieces, put them in a Waring Blendor with 1 pint of water, and blend until creamy. Add this to the clam mixture and simmer for 5 more minutes. Serve with a dab of sour cream.

FISH CHOWDER

This is a hearty dish for a number of people. It can be cut in half, if you wish, but I like it best for a big party.

10 pounds fish, plus heads and bones	2 to 3 pounds potatoes, sliced about ⅜ inch thick
½ pound salt pork	2 to 3 quarts milk
½ cup butter	Salt, pepper
1 cup chopped onion	Thyme

Use several kinds of fish and order the heads and bones as

well; cover these with water and simmer them for 1 hour. Strain the broth.

Cut the salt pork into small dice and try it out until crisp in 2 tablespoons of butter. Add the chopped onion, and brown lightly. Boil potatoes in salted water till just tender.

Cut the fish into small fingers and simmer these in the fish broth for about 15 to 20 minutes. Add the potatoes, onions and salt pork and let it come to the boiling point. Add the milk and season to taste. Let the mixture come just to the boil and simmer for 5 minutes. Add the butter and a sprinkling of thyme.

Fish chowder is usually served with pilot crackers, but I prefer fried bread with mine.

CARIBBEAN CHOWDER

¼ pound salt pork or bacon	3 large potatoes
Butter	Milk or light cream
2 cloves garlic, chopped	Salt, pepper
1 large onion, chopped	Oregano
1½ pounds fish (grouper, snapper)	Thyme
	1½ pounds lobster
½ pound shrimp	

Cut the salt pork into small dice and try it out in a little butter. Add the garlic and onion and brown lightly.

Chop the fish or put it through a fine grinder. Cook the potatoes in boiling salted water until just tender. Put the potatoes and the chopped fish through a puree machine or force them through a fine sieve. Add them to the salt pork and onion mixture, and add enough milk or light cream to make a soup. Season to taste with salt, pepper, oregano, and thyme.

Cook the lobster and shrimp in boiling salted water for 5 minutes. Shell the shrimp and cut them in small pieces. Remove the lobster meat from the shell. Add the lobster meat and chopped shrimp to the soup and heat it to the boiling point. Correct the seasoning.

VARIATIONS

1. Add ½ cup of sherry or Madeira to the soup before serving.

2. Blaze the lobster and shrimp meat with brandy before adding it to the soup.

MARGARET JENNINGS'S CRAB SOUP

This is one of those soups that, seasoned by mistake, became a notable gastronomic discovery.

1 pound crabmeat	2 cups sauce béchamel
½ cup milk	1 cup cream, or more
2 tablespoons butter	⅓ cup Scotch whisky

Heat the crabmeat in the milk and butter. Prepare a light béchamel and add the cream to it after it has come to the boiling point. Add the crabmeat and heat again until it reaches the boiling point. Season to taste, and add more cream if it needs thinning. Just before serving, stir in the Scotch. Serve in heated cups with a sprinkling of finely chopped parsley.

CREAM OF SEAFOOD SOUP

12 shrimp	Bouquet garni (onion,
4 cups fish bouillon	parsley, thyme)
12 crayfish or 1 small lobster	12 oysters
¼ pound butter	3 tablespoons flour
12 mussels	Salt, pepper
½ cup white wine	Cayenne
	2 cups cream
3 egg yolks	

Shell the shrimp, and poach just the shells in court bouillon (see index) for 3 minutes. Leave the shells in the broth. Poach the lobster, or crayfish, for 8 minutes. If you are using lobster, remove the meat from the shell and cut it in small pieces. (With crayfish, remove the meat from the tails.)

Grind the lobster (or crayfish) shells or pound them in a mortar and mix with 4 tablespoons of butter. Force this through a fine strainer.

Put the mussels in a large pan with the wine and the bouquet garni. Cover and steam until they open. Remove the meat from the shells and strain the broth.

Remove the oysters from the shells.

Reduce the court bouillon and add the broth from the mussels and any oyster liquor there may be. Strain the bouillon—you should have about 4 cups.

Prepare a velouté with the flour and 4 tablespoons of butter, gradually stirring in 2 cups of the bouillon until the sauce is thickened. Add the remaining bouillon, bit by bit, and taste for seasoning. Mix the cream and egg yolks and stir into the soup. Add the various seafoods. Heat until the oysters are heated through, but do not let it boil. Finally stir in the lobster butter. Serve with croutons.

VARIATIONS

1. Add a healthy slug of either sherry or Madeira just before serving.

2. Make substitutions or additions to the list of seafood: clams, scallops, crabmeat, or others.

3. Make the soup with only one fish, if you prefer. Be sure, however, that you adjust the amounts of the other ingredients.

BISQUE

No matter what your seafood happens to be, the procedure for making bisques is the same. The recipe I suggest here is based on lobster.

Mirepoix (onion, carrot, celery, leek)	½ cup rice
3 tablespoons olive oil	1 quart stock or fish bouillon
1 lobster, 1½ to 2 pounds	Salt, pepper
1 cup white wine	1 cup heavy cream
¼ cup cognac	3 or 4 tablespoons butter
	Cayenne

Prepare a mirepoix by cutting the vegetables into very fine julienne strips and sautéing them for 2 or 3 minutes in 3 tablespoons of olive oil. Add the live lobster which has been cut in half. Toss it around with wooden spoons until its shell turns red. Add the wine and cognac and simmer for about 6 minutes. Remove the meat from the lobster shell and keep it warm. Pound the shells in a mortar, or break them up and put them through the grinder. Return to the pot.

Meanwhile, cook the rice gently in broth or stock for about 45 minutes. Combine the cooked rice, the mirepoix, and the ground lobster shells and put all through a puree machine or fine sieve. Dilute the mixture with stock of bouillon until it is the consistency of a very thick soup. Season to taste. Reheat, adding the cream and 3 or 4 tablespoons of butter. Add a few grains of cayenne and serve with the finely cut pieces of lobster meat and a little chopped parsley. This will serve 6 people.

Tiny quenelles (see index) are sometimes used for garnish with various bisques. This is a lot of work, but may be worth while for an extra-special occasion.

Crayfish, Shrimp, or Clam Bisque. This same procedure may be followed for crayfish (use about 18), for shrimp (use about 15 to 18), for clams (use about 24). In using clams, save the juice for the broth. Do not try to crush the shells. Instead, combine them whole with the rice, and then strain it. Add the clam broth to the stock in which the rice is cooked.

Oyster Bisque. Heat 1 pint of oysters with the mirepoix and when they are plumped, chop them very fine. Add the rice, which has been cooked in stock with the oyster liquor added. Force all through the puree machine or sieve and proceed as above. Serve several oysters in each dish as a garnish. (As with clams, do not try to crush the oyster shells.)

SALT-WATER FISH

Barracuda

SOMETIMES called a sea pike or "brochet de mer," which it resembles, barracuda is eaten principally on the Pacific Coast and is seldom marketed elsewhere. Anglers respect it as a game fish. It has treacherous teeth, and there are occasional reports of its striking at bathers close to shore.

Those who have eaten barracuda—their number is not impressively large—regard it as a good dish. It is a fat fish, and I think it is exceptionally fine when smoked. The food barracuda averages 12 to 15 pounds, but some of the species may weigh as much as 100 to 150 pounds.

In some parts of the country, barracuda is considered poisonous. This is an old wives' tale.

BROILED BARRACUDA

Use either steaks or fillets. Follow the directions for broiling under "Cooking Methods." Serve with mustard sauce, black butter, or parsley butter.

CHARCOAL-BROILED BARRACUDA

Barracuda is really best baked, for my taste, but I do think it is wonderful broiled over charcoal. In that case, follow this California method.

Use a small whole fish, clean it, and place it in an oiled hinged grill. Broil it slowly, close to the charcoal, so that the skin comes close to burning. Baste it with soy, sesame, or peanut oil, and whiskey (bourbon is best) or sherry—using equal parts of the oil and liquor. Add any seasonings you wish to the basting sauce. Sometimes you may like a few slivers of ginger, or perhaps you would enjoy adding crushed garlic. Serve the sauce separately.

SAUTEED BARRACUDA

Follow the basic rules for sautéing. Serve with sour cream

sauce, mustard sauce with tarragon added, or a tomato-curry sauce.

BAKED BARRACUDA

The directions for baking salmon (see index) or halibut (see index) apply equally well to barracuda.

BAKED BARRACUDA CALIFORNIA

Select a small whole barracuda and clean it. Make a basting sauce as for charcoal-broiled barracuda (see recipe above). Place the fish in an oiled baking dish, pour the sauce over it, and bake at 400° until the flesh flakes easily when tested with a fork. Baste frequently with the sauce during the cooking process. When the fish is about half done, sprinkle it liberally with sesame seeds. If you have a baking thermometer, cook the fish to 140° internal temperature. You will find it deliciously juicy.

BAKED BARRACUDA NICOISE

4 barracuda steaks	Fillets of anchovy
Olive oil	Slices of peeled tomatoes
2 cloves garlic	Black olives
1 medium onion	1 cup red wine
Flour	Chopped parsley
Salt, pepper	Fresh tarragon

Oil a baking dish well. Chop the garlic and onion and sprinkle in the bottom of the dish. Dip the steaks in flour and place them on top of the garlic and onion. Season with salt and pepper. Arrange anchovy fillets and sliced tomatoes over the top and sprinkle with black olives. Add red wine and bake at 400° for 20 minutes, basting about 3 times during the process.

Sprinkle with chopped parsley and a little fresh tarragon, if available. Serve with a mound of buttered rice.

BRAISED BARRACUDA SANTA BARBARA

6 tablespoons of butter	3 cloves
4 barracuda steaks	2 slices onion
Flour	Milk
Salt, pepper	Grated Switzerland Swiss
1 bay leaf	cheese

Paprika

Melt the butter in a baking dish or casserole. Dust the steaks with flour and brown them in the butter. Salt and pepper them to taste, add a bay leaf, 3 cloves, 2 slices of onion, and enough milk to cover ¾ of the thickness of the fish. Sprinkle with grated cheese and paprika. Bake at 350° for 20 minutes, or until the fish is done and the cheese nicely browned on top.

BARRACUDA ROE

1½ pounds barracuda roe	½ cup white wine
Court bouillon (see index)	1 cup cream
¼ cup butter	Salt, pepper
1 clove garlic	Rosemary
4 tablespoons flour	Buttered crumbs

Poach the roe for 10 minutes in court bouillon. Melt the butter, add the garlic and cook it for 2 minutes. Remove the garlic clove and add the flour to the butter, blending well. Cook for 3 minutes. Gradually stir in the white wine, ½ cup of the court bouillon, and the cream. Season to taste with salt, pepper, and a trace of rosemary.

Cut the poached roe in fairly small pieces. Arrange them in baking shells, and cover with the sauce. Top with buttered crumbs and bake until brown.

VARIATION

Poach the roe as above and serve in a Newburg sauce (see index) made with 1 cup heavy cream, ¼ cup sherry, 3 egg yolks for thickening, and salt and cayenne.

Black Drum

THESE are probably the most musical of all fish. They are loud and harmonious, and on a quiet evening a school of them can put on an impressive symphonic program.

Black drums are also gluttons. They often stand on their heads, sometimes with their tails showing above the water, while they suck up great quantities of clams, the shells of which they crush as they gorge.

Drums grow to large size, but those marketed average only 8 to 20 inches long. They are more popular in the South, especially in Texas and Louisiana, than in other parts of the country.

BROILED DRUM

The drum is a rather dry fish, so oil it well before broiling, and baste it frequently with oil or butter. Follow directions for broiling under "Cooking Methods." Serve with tartar sauce, lemon butter, parsley butter, or brown butter.

BAKED DRUM

Follow any of the recipes for baked redfish.

Blowfish (Sea Squab)

ALSO called the puffer or globefish, this creature can suck in water and air and enlarge itself until it is nearly round. Only the meat around the spine is eaten. In Eastern markets you will see the prepared fish looking something like large chicken drumsticks from which the skin had been pulled. In this form it is known commercially as sea squab. Good eating but expensive.

If you catch your own blowfish, there is a special procedure for extracting the edible portion. Hold the tail of the fish in your left hand, and with a sharp knife cut right through about 1 inch back of the eyes, removing the head. Then peel the skin back, stripping it off the fish. Cut away the entrails. This will leave you one solid round piece of meat with the spine bone running through it—a sea squab.

SAUTEED SEA SQUAB

Follow directions for sauté meunière under "Cooking Methods."

BROILED SEA SQUAB

Follow directions for broiling under "Cooking Methods."

FRIED SEA SQUAB

Follow directions for deep frying under "Cooking Methods.

Bluefish

THIS fine-looking, fine-tasting fish is fairly common all along the Atlantic Coast and in the Gulf. It is a spirited fish that often puts up a good fight before landing.

Bluefish may run up to 10 pounds, but about 3 to 6 pounds is the usual weight. It is nicely meated and may be prepared a number of ways, although I think it is best broiled or baked. Bluefish is so delicate in flavor that it does not need heavy seasonings to enhance it. Simple herbs, white wine, salt and pepper are the only additions necessary.

BROILED BLUEFISH

You may either split the fish or broil it whole, whichever you prefer. Follow the general rules for broiling.

VARIATIONS

1. Serve the broiled fish on a bed of dried herbs: thyme, fennel, bay leaf, parsley. Pour ¼ cup of cognac or rum over the fish and herbs and ignite it. Let it burn, smoking the herb flavors into the fish. Serve with lemon butter and plain boiled potatoes.

2. Split the fish, dot it with butter, and add bacon strips. Broil it about 4 inches from the flame until the bacon is crisp and the fish cooked through.

SAUTED BLUEFISH

Small whole bluefish or pieces of bluefish may be sautéed à la meunière or à l'Anglaise (see index).

Avoid the highly spiced sauces for this delicate fish. Serve with something simple, such as lemon butter, parsley butter, or anchovy butter.

BAKED BLUEFISH

Clean and split a bluefish and place it on an oiled baking dish or pan. Dot it heavily with butter, sprinkle with salt and pepper, and bake at 425° for about 20 minutes. This should be ample time for a 3 to 4 pound fish. Test with a fork to see if the fish flakes easily. Serve with lemon or parsley butter.

1. Stuff the bluefish with crabmeat, and sprinkle the stuffing with salt, pepper and butter. Tie the fish up, place it on an oiled baking dish, dot with butter, and season with salt and pepper. Bake at 425° for 20 to 25 minutes. Serve with lemon butter.

2. Arrange a split bluefish on an oiled baking dish. Lay strips of bacon or salt pork across the top of the fish. Bake at 425° for 20 to 25 minutes, or until the fish flakes easily when tested with a fork. Serve with lemon wedges, boiled potatoes, and a cucumber salad made with a sour cream and dill dressing.

3. Stuff a bluefish with a few sprigs of parsley, fresh dill, and 2 or 3 slices of lemon. Dot the interior with butter and sprinkle with salt and pepper.

Oil a baking dish and cover the bottom with 3 shallots and 4 green onions, finely chopped. Lay the stuffed fish on top, dot it with butter and sprinkle with salt and pepper. Add 1 cup of white wine. Bake at 425° for 20 to 25 minutes, basting often. Remove the fish to a hot platter.

Take out the herbs and add them to the pan juices. Put the juices through a sieve or a food mill. Return to the stove and add ½ cup of heavy cream and 2 egg yolks. Stir until thickened, but do not let it boil. Taste for seasoning and pour the sauce over the fish. Sprinkle with chopped parsley and dill.

BABY BLUES

The small bluefish, called "baby blues," which are caught late in the summer, are bluefish that have not yet grown to full size. They should be cleaned and cooked whole. Follow the recipes for broiled or sautéed bluefish.

Butterfish

THESE small silvery fish are among the most delicately meated and thoroughly pleasing fish in the sea. They are caught in great quantities and are available in Eastern markets throughout most of the year.

BROILED BUTTERFISH

Since butterfish are very small—some weighing as little as

¼ pound—they should be broiled very quickly. My preference, as usual, is to sauté them. However, if you do broil them, use plenty of butter and oil and place them near the flame. Serve with a sauce Béarnaise.

SAUTEED BUTTERFISH

Follow the directions for sauté meunière (see index). Serve with lemon wedges or lemon butter. A strong sauce is not good with this delicate fish.

VARIATION

Add canned buttered almonds to the pan at the last minute.

BUTTERFISH NICOISE

Sauté butterfish as for sauté meunière, but substitute olive oil for the butter. Grill or sauté tomatoes in olive oil and season them with a little tarragon and garlic. Arrange the fish on a bed of the tomatoes, top them with strips of anchovies and garnish with ripe olives. Serve this with sautéed potatoes and a bountiful salad and you will have a satisfying meal.

BUTTERFISH WITH CURRY AND TOMATOES

Sauté 1 medium onion, finely chopped, in butter. Dip 4 small butterfish in flour that has been heavily seasoned with curry powder, and salted to taste. Sauté the fish in the pan with the onion. Remove the fish to a hot platter and rinse the pan with a little white wine. Serve with a tomato sauce laced with more curry, and rice.

BUTTERFISH IN CASES

This is definitely a party dish.

Prepare a bread case, large enough and deep enough to hold a whole fish, for each serving. Butter the cases well and dry them out in a 300° oven.

Make a sauce duxelles (see index). For each fish, sauté 3 large mushroom caps in butter.

Flour the fish and sauté them according to the directions for sauté meunière (see index). Spread a little sauce duxelles in each bread case, place a fish in each case, add more sauce, top with the mushroom caps, and garnish with chopped parsley. Serve with additional sauce.

PAN-FRIED BUTTERFISH

Dip in seasoned flour, then in beaten egg, and roll in any of the following: buttered crumbs, cracker crumbs, corn meal, chopped nuts mixed with crumbs, or sesame seeds. Sauté quickly in butter or olive oil and serve with lemon wedges.

VARIATIONS

1. Sauté whole slices of orange, peel and all, with the fish and serve as a garnish.

2. Add 1 teaspoon of tarragon to the pan and rinse it with ¼ cup of white wine. Pour over the fish.

BUTTERFISH EN PAPILLOTE

Butterfish (1 per serving)	Grated onion
Cooking parchment	Butter
Ham slices (1 per serving)	Salt, pepper
Anchovy butter	Thick tomato puree
Chopped parsley	

Cut heart-shaped pieces of cooking parchment big enough to accommodate the fish. On each piece of parchment, place a slice of ham near one edge. Spread it with anchovy butter and a little grated onion. Top with a butterfish, dot with butter, season with salt and pepper, add a teaspoon of tomato puree, and sprinkle with chopped parsley. Fold the other side of the parchment over this, crimp the edges together so that they are tightly sealed. Bake at 425° until the paper is brown and puffy.

SMOKED BUTTERFISH

Smoked butterfish is found in many delicatessens and fish shops. It is delicate and very pleasant. Try it as a first course for dinner or as a light luncheon dish. Serve it with lemon, a sprinkling of capers if you like, or chopped onion.

California Black Sea Bass

THIS Pacific Coast fish is sometimes called the jewfish, but it is not the same as the Florida jewfish or giant sea bass. It is a good game fish and is sold to a certain extent for food. The flesh is flaky, white, and well-flavored. The fish is large, weighing as much as 700 to 800 pounds, and is usually sold in steaks or fillets.

Two smaller fish, the cabrilla and the grouper, are sold in fillets in California markets as "golden bass." The rock bass, averaging about 18 inches in length, is popular in the West both as a game and a commercial fish.

BROILED CALIFORNIA SEA BASS

Follow directions for broiling under "Cooking Methods."

SEA BASS FILLETS PACIFIC

See index.

BAKED CALIFORNIA SEA BASS

Follow directions for baking under "Cooking Methods."

BARBECUED SEA BASS STEAKS CALIFORNIA

¼ cup melted butter	1 clove garlic, crushed
2 tablespoons soy sauce	2 pounds sea bass steak
Juice of 1 lemon	½ cup sesame seeds
2 ounces whiskey or brandy	Lemon or lime wedges

Prepare a basting sauce with the butter, soy sauce, lemon juice, liquor and garlic. Brush the steaks with this, place them in an oiled hinged grill and cook over a charcoal fire, basting often and turning. When nearly done, sprinkle heavily with sesame seeds and continue cooking until the seeds are toasted. Serve with lemon or lime wedges.

JEWFISH STEAKS TROPICAL

3 cups toasted crumbs	3 eggs
2 tablespoons chili powder	4 tablespoons heavy cream
2 teaspoons paprika	6 to 8 rashers bacon
1 teaspoon salt	1 clove garlic
1 teaspoon oregano	3 pounds jewfish steaks
Flour	

Roll the crumbs fine and combine with the chili powder, paprika, salt and oregano. Beat the eggs lightly and add the cream. Try out the bacon and add the garlic to the bacon fat. When the bacon is crisp, remove it to absorbent paper. Brush the fish steaks with flour, dip them in the eggs and cream, and then cover them thoroughly with the crumb mixture. Sauté them gently in the bacon fat until crisp and brown and cooked through. Serve with tomato sauce and a bacon garnish.

California Kingfish

IN order to avoid confusion, I must resort here to Latin: the California kingfish is a *Genyonemus lineatus*, which means that it is a different fish from the East Coast fish, which is a *Scomberomorus Cavalla* and closely resembles the Spanish mackerel (see index). The West Coast fish is sometimes mistaken for tomcod, a similar fish.

California kingfish comes in sizes of about ¾ to 1¼ pounds and are usually eaten whole. The meat is excellent.

BROILED CALIFORNIA KINGFISH

Broil the fish whole or split, according to the directions under "Cooking Methods."

FRENCH-FRIED CALIFORNIA KINGFISH

Clean, wash and dry the fish. Dip it in flour, then in milk, and roll it in corn meal. Heat fat in the deep-fat fryer to 360°. Fry the fish until it is browned and crisp. This will take about 4 minutes. Drain on absorbent paper, season with salt and paprika, and serve with tartar sauce or mustard sauce.

BAKED CALIFORNIA KINGFISH WITH ANCHOVIES

Split 2 kingfish and stuff them with anchovy fillets, sliced onions, and chopped parsley. Fold them over, place on an oiled baking dish, dot with butter, and sprinkle with pepper. Bake at 400° for about 15 minutes, or until the fish flakes easily. Serve with lemon quarters.

BAKED CALIFORNIA KINGFISH ITALIAN

Split the fish and stuff them with finely chopped onion, parsley and thyme. Place them on a well-oiled baking dish and brush with olive oil. Add ½ cup of white wine and bake at 400° for 15 minutes, basting once or twice during the cooking. Season with salt and pepper and serve with tomato sauce or lemon quarters.

California Pompano

THIS fish is not the true Florida pompano, but is a relative of the butterfish. It is found only on the California Coast. It is always served whole and is a delicious and delicate morsel.

Prepare it according to the recipes for Florida pompano (see index).

California Whitefish

THIS is an entirely different fish from the fresh-water white-fish of the Great Lakes. It is a good game fish and is sought by anglers as well as commercial fishermen. Fairly large, it comes to the market whole, filleted, and in steaks.

BROILED CALIFORNIA WHITEFISH

Broil steaks or fillets according to the directions under "Cooking Methods." Serve with butter flavored with tarragon or sauce Béarnaise (see index).

BAKED CALIFORNIA WHITEFISH AU GRATIN

3 pounds whitefish fillets
Court bouillon (see index)
2 cups sauce béchamel
Tarragon

¼ cup of chopped parsley
Grated Swiss or Cheddar cheese

Cut the fillets into strips 1 inch wide. Poach them in court bouillon for 3 minutes, then remove them to an oval baking dish or casserole. Using the fish broth and some cream, make 2 cups of sauce béchamel. Season it with tarragon and parsley and pour over the fish. Sprinkle with grated cheese and bake at 350° for 15 minutes. Serve with buttered noodles and chopped spinach seasoned with a little garlic.

POACHED WHITEFISH HOLLANDAISE

Poach 3 pounds of whitefish fillets or steaks in salted water for 5 or 6 minutes, or until the fish flakes easily. Serve with Hollandaise sauce, boiled parsley potatoes, and green beans.

You may substitute shrimp, lobster or poulette sauce for the Hollandaise.

Cod

ONE of the most important food fishes in the world, cod comes mainly from the banks of Newfoundland, from New England waters, and from the coast of Norway. Close cousins of the Atlantic cod are caught in North Pacific waters, and other relatives are taken in the colder regions of the southern hemisphere.

An average cod weighs about 10 pounds, but specimens weighing 50 pounds and more are sometimes caught. It is an active hunter with an excellent appetite, preying relentlessly on shellfish and on practically any fish that live on the bottom or close to it. Sharks and dogfish are among the few species that can cope successfully with a husky cod.

The annual haul of cod is over a billion pounds, and it is sold as flakes, shredded, pickled, green or smoked, in salted slabs, whole, in steaks, and in frozen and fresh fillets. Cod is also the source of cod-liver oil, a fact of slight gastronomic interest.

I am so fond of salt cod that I sometimes forget that fresh cod can be prepared in many interesting ways, and that the so-called "scrod," which is a young cod weighing 1½ to 2½ pounds, is fine eating. Young haddock, pollock, and other similar fish are also often called scrod.

FRESH COD

If you live near the source of supply, you can buy the whole fish, steaks, or center cuts. Most unsalted cod, however, comes to market as fresh or frozen fillets, and these can be prepared in any of the ways given for ocean perch or haddock (see index). Here are other recipes for fresh cod:

BROILED CODFISH

Broil either steaks or fillets according to the directions under "Cooking Methods."

BROCHETTES OF COD ITALIAN

Cut 2 to 3 pounds of cod into small cubes about 1½ to 2 inches square. Alternate them on skewers with fresh or "broiled in butter" mushrooms. Sprinkle them with salt and pepper, dip in flour, brush with butter or egg yolks, and roll in crumbs. Then sauté them quickly in oil or butter until they are nicely browned on all sides. Serve with a rich tomato sauce and risotto.

SAUTEED COD

Either steaks or fillets may be used. Follow the directions under "Cooking Methods." Serve with your favorite sauce.

COD SAUTE, INDIAN STYLE

1 large eggplant	1½ cups rice
6 to 8 tomatoes	2 pounds cod fillets
1 large onion	Flour
⅓ cup olive oil	Curry powder
1 clove garlic	Butter or oil
Salt, pepper	Tomato sauce or parsley
Sweet basil	butter

Peel and dice the eggplant. Peel, seed, and chop the tomatoes. Peel and chop the onion. Heat the olive oil and sauté the onion. Add the garlic and tomatoes. Season to taste with salt, pepper and basil. Cook for 10 minutes and add the eggplant. Cover and cook for 20 minutes, or until the eggplant is tender and the tomatoes cooked down.

Cook the rice according to your usual method.

Cut the cod fillets into strips 2 inches wide and roll them in flour and curry powder. Sauté them quickly in butter or oil until they are nicely browned on all sides.

Make a ring of the rice on a large platter, heap the fish in the center, and make a border of the tomatoes and eggplant. Serve with a tomato sauce flavored with more curry powder, or parsley butter with curry added.

CODFISH STEAKS IN WINE

4 cod steaks	6 tablespoons butter
Salt, pepper	Chopped parsley
1½ cups white wine	Lemon slices

Arrange the steaks in a baking dish, season to taste, and

cover with white wine. Let them soak in the refrigerator for several hours.

When ready to cook, dot the steaks heavily with butter, and bake at 400° to 425° until the fish flakes easily when tested with a fork. Baste often during the cooking process. Sprinkle with chopped parsley and garnish with lemon slices. Serve with small artichoke hearts and fresh peas.

BAKED COD

Cod may be baked in any of the ways given for striped bass or halibut. (See index.)

BAKED STUFFED COD

1 whole cod (2 to 4 pounds)	1½ cups bread crumbs
Lemon	½ pint oysters and liquor
6 green onions, chopped	½ cup chopped parsley
¼ cup minced celery	¼ teaspoon black pepper
¼ cup minced green pepper	1 teaspoon salt
5 tablespoons butter	½ teaspoon thyme
Butter or bacon fat	

Clean and split the fish. Rub the interior with lemon.

Sauté the onions, celery and green pepper in butter until just tender. Add the crumbs, the oysters and their liquor, and cook for 3 or 4 minutes. Add the parsley and season to taste with salt, pepper, and thyme. Stuff the fish with this mixture, secure it with toothpicks and string, and place it in an oiled baking dish. Season with salt and pepper, dot with butter or bacon fat, and bake at 400°, allowing 10 minutes per pound of fish.

Serve with lemon butter or with sauce béchamel to which you have added onion and parsley.

NEW ENGLAND TURKEY

This is one of the truly authentic American dishes.

Clean and split a whole cod and stuff it with your favorite bread stuffing. Sew it up or secure it with toothpicks and string. Arrange it in an oiled baking dish in an S-shaped design. Cover with strips of salt pork from head to tail and bake at 400° for 25 to 35 minutes, depending upon the size of the fish. (Allow about 10 minutes per pound.) Baste with the pan juices during the cooking.

Remove to a hot platter, garnish with plain boiled potatoes and green peas, and serve with an egg sauce or parsley sauce.

COD IN THE FASHION OF THE BAKER

For this recipe you may use either a medium-sized whole fish, or a large center cut of cod.

Steam 12 to 18 small potatoes in butter until almost tender. Brown 12 small white onions in butter, and cook until nearly done. Clean the fish, arrange it in a greased baking pan, sprinkle it with salt, pepper, thyme, and powdered bay leaf. Surround it with the potatoes and onions and pour over it the melted butter in which the vegetables were cooked. Bake at 400° for about 20 minutes, basting every 5 minutes with the pan juices. Garnish with chopped parsley and lemon slices.

BAKED COD WITH CREAM

Use either a whole fish or a large center cut.

Clean the fish, place it on an oiled baking pan and dot heavily with butter. Add 1 cup of fish broth or chicken broth, or 1 cup of hot water in which you have dissolved a bouillon cube. Season to taste and bake at 400° for 20 to 25 minutes, or until the fish flakes easily when tested with a fork. Baste often with the pan juices. Arrange the fish on a hot platter and surround it with a ring of sautéed potatoes.

Thicken the pan juices with beurre manié and add ½ cup of heavy cream. Pour the sauce over the fish.

POACHED COD

You may poach a whole fish, a center cut, steaks or fillets. Wrap the fish in cheesecloth and poach in boiling salted water or in a court bouillon (see index) until the flesh flakes easily. Serve with lemon butter, Hollandaise sauce, or an egg sauce made by adding chopped hard-cooked egg and a bit of sherry to sauce béchamel.

CODFISH CUSTARD

1½ teaspoons cornstarch	Salt, pepper,
1½ cups milk	1½ pounds cod, poached
2 eggs, well beaten	and flaked
¼ cup melted butter	

Dissolve the cornstarch in the milk, add the eggs, butter, seasoning to taste, and the fish. Pour into a buttered casserole and bake at 350° for about 40 minutes, or until the custard

75

is not quite set in the middle. This is a Rhode Island dish and is often served with their native johnnycake.

COD LOAF

2 cups cooked, flaked cod	1 cup sifted toasted crumbs
¼ cup each chopped onion, celery, green pepper	Salt, pepper
	1 teaspoon tarragon
½ cup chopped walnuts	2 eggs, separated
¼ cup chopped parsley	½ cup milk
½ cup melted butter	

Combine the fish, vegetables, nuts, parsley, crumbs, salt, pepper, and tarragon. Beat the egg yolks and add them to the mixture with the milk and melted butter. Fold in the stiffly beaten egg whites and pour into a buttered mold or pan. Set in a pan of hot water and bake at 375° for about 40 minutes, or until set. Unmold on a hot plate and serve with egg sauce or Hollandaise sauce.

COD FLORENTINE

Poach 1 fillet of cod for each serving in boiling salted water. Arrange the poached fillets on a bed of chopped cooked spinach lightly flavored with nutmeg. Top with sauce Mornay (see index), sprinkle with grated Parmesan cheese, and run under the broiler flame for a few minutes to brown.

COLD POACHED COD

Cold poached cod is delicious if it is firm and not over-cooked. Serve it with mayonnaise, sauce gribiche, sauce rémoulade, tartar sauce, or Russian dressing (see index).

If you wish to serve the fish in aspic, follow the directions for Rich White Wine Court Bouillon for Aspics.

COD CHEEKS AND TONGUES
(SOUNDS AND TONGUES)

These delicacies come either fresh or salted. If salted, they must be soaked overnight. (See salt cod in index.)

Drain them the next morning. Cover with cold water and simmer for 5 minutes. Drain again. After this preparation they are ready for use in recipes. Plan 1 pound for 4 people.

BOILED COD CHEEKS AND TONGUES

Cover with boiling water and simmer for 5 or 6 minutes. Serve with sauce Mornay, sauce béchamel, or sauce poulette (see index). The sauce poulette, to my taste, is the best for this dish.

SAUTEED SOUNDS AND TONGUES

Prepare the sounds and tongues as above, if salted. Drain them and sauté in butter until nicely browned. Serve with lemon butter or parsley butter.

SOUNDS AND TONGUES PROVENCALE

Prepare sounds and tongues and sauté in ⅓ cup of olive oil. Just as they have browned lightly, add 3 cloves of garlic, finely chopped, and ⅓ cup of chopped parsley. Mix these thoroughly with the fish and continue cooking until well heated and blended.

ESCALLOPED SOUNDS AND TONGUES

Prepare sounds and tongues as above. Arrange them in a baking dish. Sauté 3 tablespoons of onion lightly in butter and sprinkle over the fish. Top with sauce béchamel, sprinkle with buttered crumbs, and bake at 375° until brown and bubbling.

SALT COD

My favorite codfish dishes are based on the salt cod. In preparing salt cod, it is always necessary, of course, to remove the salt. There are two ways to do this. You may soak the fish for several hours; or you may cover it with cold water, bring the water to a boil very slowly, and then rinse the fish in cold water. Here are recipes that demonstrate the versatility of the salt cod.

POACHED CODFISH WITH VARIOUS SAUCES

Soak 1 pound of salt codfish in cold water for 4 hours. Rinse the fish thoroughly. Place it in a skillet or shallow saucepan and cover it with cold water. Bring slowly to a boil and let it boil feebly for about 15 minutes. Remove the fish to a hot platter and surround with plain boiled potatoes sprinkled with parsley. Serve with:

1. Melted butter
2. Parsley sauce (see index)
3. Hollandaise sauce (see index)
4. Egg sauce (see index)

CODFISH BÉCHAMEL

1 pound salt codfish
2 cups sauce béchamel

Chopped parsley
Fried toast

Soak the codfish in cold water for 4 hours. Remove, rinse, place in cold water and bring to a boil very slowly. Remove the fish from the water and cut into small pieces or flake with a fork. Combine with sauce béchamel and serve hot over fried toast. Sprinkle with parsley. Plain boiled potatoes are a natural accompaniment.

VARIATIONS

1. Prepare the codfish béchamel as above and pour into a flat baking dish or gratin dish. Sprinkle with buttered crumbs and grated Gruyère cheese and place under the broiler for a few minutes. If you don't have Gruyère, try Cheddar or a good store cheese.

2. Sauté 1 medium onion in 4 tablespoons of butter; when it is just light-colored, add 1 tablespoon of curry powder and ½ teaspoon of black pepper. Combine with the cooked codfish and season to taste—possibly you may want additional curry. Serve with rice. French-fried onion rings, very crisp, are good with this.

3. Combine 1 cup of grated Cheddar or Gruyère or Swiss cheese with sauce béchamel (see index) and mix well with the codfish. Pour into a flat baking dish or gratin dish and sprinkle with grated Parmesan cheese. Run under the broiler for a few minutes. Serve accompanied by plain boiled potatoes with butter and parsley.

4. Sauté ½ pound of sliced mushrooms, 2 tablespoons of finely chopped onion and 4 tablespoons of chopped parsley and combine with the fish. Mix with the sauce béchamel and serve in patty shells or in a large vol-au-vent. (This is an overgrown patty shell. You may order one from a good French baker if you wish to serve something spectacular.)

5. Sauté ½ cup of blanched shredded almonds in 4 tablespoons of butter until crisp and brown. Combine with the

fish and sauce béchamel. Serve with large baked potatoes topped with paprika.

6. Add 4 sliced hard-cooked eggs and ¼ cup of finely chopped parsley to the sauce béchamel after combining with the fish. Add to this 1 tablespoon of paprika and blend well. Serve with buttered noodles.

ARMENIAN CODFISH

1 pound codfish	Vinegar
8 tomatoes	6 green peppers
6 tablespoons oil	5 tablespoons butter
Salt, pepper	4 tablespoons oil

Put the fish to soak in cold water for 4 hours. Peel and chop the tomatoes very fine, combine with the oil, and let them cook down to a paste. Add salt and pepper to taste, and a touch of vinegar to cut the oil. Seed and cut the peppers into julienne strips. Sauté them in butter until tender.

When the fish has soaked, rinse it and put it in a skillet with cold water and bring to a boil. Drain off the water, add 4 tablespoons of oil, and sauté the fish until just lightly browned and cooked through. Serve on the tomato paste topped with the sautéed peppers. Pass rice and additional tomato sauce, if you wish.

CODFISH, SPANISH STYLE

1 pound codfish	½ cup olive oil
2 medium onions	6 to 8 tomatoes
2 cloves garlic	Beurre manié (see index)
2 green peppers	Pimientos
Parsley	

Soak the codfish, rinse and poach for about 15 minutes. Chop the onions and garlic, seed the peppers and cut them in fine strips, and brown in the olive oil. When tender, add the tomatoes, peeled and chopped, and a little of the fish broth. Thicken with beurre manié. Let it cook down for ½ to 1 hour, add the pieces of codfish and the pimientos, chopped, and heat again. Serve in a flat dish topped with chopped parsley and garnished with fried toast points.

CODFISH SOUFFLE

1½ cups flaked codfish	Black pepper
4 tablespoons butter	4 egg yolks
4 tablespoons flour	6 egg whites
1 cup milk	Sauce béchamel (see index)
Nutmeg	or Hollandaise (see index)

Soak the codfish and poach for about 15 minutes. Flake into shreds.

Combine the butter and flour in a saucepan; when they are well blended, gradually add the milk, stirring until it is thickened. Season with a little nutmeg and black pepper. Add the egg yolks, beaten, blend well and add the codfish. Beat the egg whites until stiff and fold into the mixture. Pour into a buttered soufflé dish and bake at 375° for 35 to 45 minutes or until puffy and brown. Serve with a béchamel or Hollandaise sauce—and forget you ever ate a fish cake.

FRIED CODFISH STRIPS

1 pound filleted codfish	Pepper
Flour	Fat for frying
Tartar sauce (see index)	

Soak the codfish for several hours. Cut in diagonal strips about 1 to 1½ inches wide. Roll in flour, sprinkle with pepper and fry in deep fat at 365°. Drain on absorbent paper and serve hot with a tartar sauce.

CODFISH LYONNAISE

Naturally the combination of onion and codfish is elegant. So it is not surprising that there should be a Lyonnaise version, for the traditional dishes of that city use onions a great deal.

1 pound codfish	2 medium onions
6 medium potatoes	Butter or oil
Chopped parsley	

Soak the codfish for several hours. Sauté the potatoes and onions as you would for Lyonnaise potatoes. Flake the codfish and brown it nicely in butter or oil; combine with the potato-onion mixture and let it cook down for a few minutes. Sprinkle generously with chopped parsley. This is a wonderful Sunday breakfast dish.

CODFISH CARCASSONNE

1½ pounds codfish	2 cloves garlic
1½ pounds small new potatoes	3 to 4 tablespoons flour
Butter or fat	Pepper

Chopped parsley

Soak the codfish for several hours and poach for about 15 minutes. Cut into small pieces.

Scrape or peel the potatoes and brown them in butter or fat until they are just golden. Add garlic, finely chopped, and sprinkle with flour. Season with freshly ground pepper and a bit of parsley. Add broth from the fish and water mixed in equal parts—enough to cover the potatoes. Let them simmer until tender. About 4 or 5 minutes before you remove them from the heat, add the codfish and let it all blend well together.

CODFISH MARSEILLAISE

Here is another tasty way of combining salt cod and potatoes:

1½ pounds codfish	Pepper
Flour	Sage
½ cup olive oil	Thyme
1 large onion, chopped	Salt
1 clove garlic, chopped	6 potatoes cut in quarters
5 large or 6 medium tomatoes	White wine

Chopped parsley

Soak the codfish. When it is freshened, cut it into even-sized squares. Roll these in flour and sauté them in hot oil until nicely browned. Remove them from the pan and in the same oil sauté the onion and garlic until they are light-colored and soft. Add the peeled, seeded and chopped tomatoes, black pepper, a pinch of sage, a bit of thyme, and let this simmer about 15 minutes. Season to taste with salt.

Oil a casserole, put the quartered potatoes in the bottom, pour the sauce over them and add just enough white wine and water mixed to cover. Add the pieces of cod, cover the casserole, and bake at 350° for 30 minutes, or until the potatoes are tender. Remove the cover and sprinkle with chopped parsley.

CODFISH CROQUETTES

1 cup codfish soaked, poached and flaked	1 tablespoon chopped parsley
¾ cup sliced sautéed mushrooms	Dash of nutmeg
	1¼ cups heavy white sauce
1 teaspoon freshly ground pepper	Sifted bread or cracker crumbs
	1 egg, beaten
Oil or fat for frying	

Mix the codfish, mushrooms and seasonings and combine with the heavy white sauce. Let it cool thoroughly and form into balls, cylinders or pyramids. Let these chill for an hour or so. Heat the fat in your fryer to 375°. Dip the croquettes into crumbs, then into beaten egg, and finally cover thoroughly with crumbs again. Fry 3 or 4 minutes or until nicely browned. Drain on absorbent paper.

VARIATIONS

1. Add another cup of codfish and omit the mushrooms.
2. Use sautéed onions in place of the mushrooms. The onions should be finely chopped and sautéed until just soft. Use ½ cup of onions to 1¼ cups of codfish flakes.

CODFISH CAKES I

There are as many recipes for this delicacy as there are counties in all the New England states. One of the newest has come to me from Charles Triggs, who is an authority on fish and a man who knows codfish. His recipe is:

1 pound codfish	1 egg
7 or 8 medium-sized potatoes	Fat for frying

Cut the codfish across the grain into about ½-inch pieces. Pick the pieces apart, place in a skillet, cover with hot water, stir and drain. Repeat two or three times, then cover with cold water and let it come to a boil. Change the water, let it come to a boil again and simmer for a few minutes.

Boil and mash the potatoes. Drain the codfish and mix with the mashed potatoes, using wire masher. When thoroughly mixed, add one egg and beat with a fork. Take a tablespoon at a time and drop into deep fat, or into a frying pan with a fair amount of fat. Drain on absorbent paper.

NOTE: This recipe can be changed according to taste—some may prefer a larger percentage of codfish, some less.

CODFISH CAKES II

This is a recipe from Martinique that is served in a pleasant restaurant in Paris specializing in food from the Antilles.

2½ cups flour
1 teaspoon baking powder
1 clove garlic, finely chopped
4 shallots, finely chopped
2 tablespoons chopped parsley
Fat for deep frying

Black pepper
Beer, enough to make a batter (about 1 cup)
½ pound shredded codfish, soaked and poached

Sift flour and baking powder together. Add the garlic, shallots, parsley, and a good grind of black pepper. Stir in enough beer to make a batter and add the shredded codfish.

Heat fat in your fryer to 380°. Drop the batter by spoonfuls into the hot fat and fry until nicely browned. Drain on absorbent paper.

CODFISH CAKES III

The mixture of equal quantities of mashed potatoes and cooked shredded codfish is the traditional codfish cake. Some like less potato, and others like more. Vary it to suit yourself.

1 cup shredded cooked codfish
1 cup mashed potatoes
1 or 2 eggs

Freshly ground pepper
Butter or hot fat
Flour or crumbs (if desired)

Mix the codfish, potatoes, eggs and pepper, and form into cakes. Sauté in plenty of butter or bacon fat, or roll in flour or crumbs and fry in deep hot fat.

VARIATIONS

1. A teaspoon of ground ginger or a little finely chopped green ginger does wonderful things for codfish balls. This is a recipe that my mother's old chef used, and the codfish balls he made were always in demand. He added plenty of butter to the mashed potatoes and then sautéed the codfish balls, spiked with ginger, in additional butter. They were crisp and rich with the mixed flavors of butter, ginger and salt cod.

2. Southerners are apt to add finely chopped green onion to the traditional codfish cake mixture, which gives it a different flavor. Sometimes a bit of finely chopped green pepper is also added.

3. For cocktails, make the cakes very small, roll them in flour and crumbs, and deep fry them for about 3 minutes at 390°. A demitasse spoon is perfect for dropping this size ball into the basket for frying.

You will find some rather good codfish cakes in tins—all prepared ready to roll into balls or pat into cakes and fry. They are a good addition to your emergency shelf and come in quite handy for guests who drop by unexpectedly at late Sunday breakfast or luncheon time.

A barbarian combination is codfish cakes served with tomato sauce. I can't imagine why it is served, for the two flavors do not blend well. I feel codfish cakes need no sauce so long as they are well seasoned and well cooked. If you must have a sauce, perhaps it should be a sauce béchamel or a sauce soubise (see index).

Another rather barbarian combination, which you may observe occasionally in the New York area, is codfish cakes served with tired spaghetti. It is hard to think of anything so uninteresting or so poorly balanced.

BRANDADE DE MORUE

1 pound salt codfish	½ teaspoon freshly ground
⅔ cup olive oil	pepper
⅓ cup heavy cream	Toast triangles fried in
2 cloves garlic	olive oil

Soak the codfish for several hours. Wash it and bring it to a boil in cold water. Reduce the heat and simmer for about 10 minutes. Drain the fish and shred it very fine, removing any bits of bone.

Heat the olive oil and the cream separately. Crush the garlic—in a mortar if you have one—and add the fish; if you don't have a mortar, put both garlic and fish through the food grinder twice, using the fine blade. The fish must be very fine, so if two grindings do not seem enough, work it with a heavy wooden spoon in a bowl. When the mixture is practically a paste, put it in a heavy saucepan over very low heat and stir well with a fork. Now add the olive oil and the cream alternately and work them both in well. Continue until all the oil and cream are absorbed and the mixture has the consistency of mashed potatoes. Season with freshly ground black pepper, heap it up in the center of a serving dish and surround it with fried toast triangles.

Beat mashed potatoes into the mixture. This gives a completely different texture to the dish and a more delicate flavor. It is called Benedictine, and the true eggs Benedictine are served on a bed of this. Eggs Benedict is another dish entirely.

Croaker

THIS fish gets its name from the air bladder it uses to give off tuneful sounds. There are a number of varieties on both coasts, and in some localities they are marketed. The croaker is a good game fish.

BROILED CROAKER

Broil whole croakers according to directions for broiling under "Cooking Methods." Serve with any of the fish butters—anchovy, lemon, or parsley.

CROAKERS SAUTE MEUNIERE

To my taste, this method of preparation is usually preferable to pan frying. Dust the fish with flour and sauté lightly in plenty of butter. Season to taste and serve the fish with chopped parsley, lemon, and more butter.

PAN-FRIED CROAKERS

Roll the fish in seasoned crumbs or corn meal and sauté in butter or oil. Serve with a sauce rémoulade or tartar sauce (see index).

Cusk

EVEN more streamlined than the hake, this fish is distinguished by a long black fin extending from just behind the head to the tail. It is found in northern waters and is nearly always caught on line. It puts up a good fight when hooked.

You will not often see the whole fish in the markets, but quite a bit of it is sold as fillets that are labeled something else besides cusk. It has good flavor and texture and ought to be more popular in its own right.

Cusk may be prepared in any of the ways you prepare haddock or fresh cod.

Eels

EELS are erroneously called fresh-water fish by most French authorities. They are both fresh-water and marine. All the European and American eels are born in the same place, a deep spot in the ocean south of Bermuda. From there they migrate to localities previously frequented by their parents— European eels go to Europe, and American eels to America. They ascend the fresh-water streams, stay for a while, and then return to the spawning grounds in the Atlantic.

Eels are a traditional dish during the Italian celebration of Christmas Eve, and they are in greatest demand at the holiday season. Smoked eels are available all year, and fresh eels can now be bought the year round in markets that maintain tanks in which to keep them.

PAN-FRIED EELS

First, the eels must be skinned. The traditional method is to nail the head of the eel to a wall, and then skin it with one full sweep of the hand. You may also cut the eel skin around the head, and peel it back very slowly. You may need the aid of pliers to get it started. Once the eels are skinned, remove the intestines, wash the fish and cut them into 3-inch pieces. Dip these in flour and sauté them in butter or oil until delicately browned. Season to taste and serve plain or with a tartar sauce.

EELS SAUTE PROVENCALE

2 large eels or several small ones	6 tablespoons olive oil
	Salt, pepper
Flour	3 cloves garlic, chopped
¼ cup chopped parsley	

Skin and clean the eels, cut in 3-inch pieces and dredge with flour. Heat the olive oil in a skillet and sauté the pieces of eel quickly. When they are done—in 7 or 8 minutes—season to taste and add the garlic and parsley. Toss these about in the pan for a minute or two. Serve the eel with the garlic and parsley poured over the top.

EELS NAPOLITANA

2 or 3 large eels
2 cups browned crumbs
1 teaspoon salt
1 teaspoon cinnamon
1½ teaspoons sugar
Flour
Beaten egg
Butter
Lemon wedges

Skin and wash the eels, and cut in pieces. Mix the crumbs, salt, cinnamon and sugar. Dip the eels in flour, then the beaten egg, and finally in the crumb mixture. Sauté quickly in butter until tender and nicely browned. Serve with lemon wedges.

NOTE: The traditional way of preparing this dish is to tie the eel on a spit and roast it in front of the fire, basting it with its own juices. However, this is a little involved for most people.

EELS COMMACHIO

The Italians, like many Europeans, are very fond of eels. In fact, true international gourmets find it difficult to understand why Americans neglect this delicious fish. Here is a famous Italian recipe that does justice to it.

6 eels
½ cup olive oil
1 large onion, sliced fine
Salt, pepper
1 teaspoon sage
1 cup tomato puree
1 cup white wine

Skin and clean the eels, and cut them in 3-inch lengths. Heat the olive oil in a skillet. Add the onion, sage, and the pieces of eel. Sauté until nicely browned. Season to taste, and add the tomato puree and white wine. Cover and simmer until the eel is tender. Serve with rice baked in broth.

MATELOTE OF EELS, NORMAN FASHION

3 onions
2 carrots
3 stalks celery
24 small white onions
12 small croutons
Butter
2 to 3 pounds of eels
Salt, pepper
Thyme
Tarragon
1½ cups cider
3 tablespoons flour
3 tablespoons butter
2 egg yolks
½ cup heavy cream
Chopped fresh sorrel

Prepare a mirepoix by cutting the onions, carrots, and celery into very fine julienne strips. Peel the onions and put them to cook in salted water. Fry the croutons in butter. Skin and clean the eels and cut them into 3-inch pieces.

Put the mirepoix on the bottom of a saucepan and top with the pieces of eel. Season with salt, pepper, thyme and tarragon. Pour the cider over this and simmer until the eel is tender. Remove it to a hot dish or tureen.

Prepare a sauce béchamel with the broth; reduce the broth to 1 cupful and strain. Blend the flour with the butter and stir the broth into it. Continue stirring until thickened. Mix the egg yolks and the cream and stir this into the sauce. Continue cooking and stirring until smooth and well blended, but do not let it boil. Add a few leaves of chopped fresh sorrel, if it is available.

Pour the sauce over the pieces of eel and surround with the small white onions and the fried croutons.

MATELOTE PROVENCALE

This is prepared in the same way as the preceding recipe, except that white wine and water (half and half) are used in place of cider, and 3 cloves of garlic are added. Sautéed mushroom caps are used as garnish along with the onions and croutons.

OLD-FASHIONED NEW ENGLAND EEL STIFLE

6 eels	Pepper
6 fairly large potatoes	Flour
4 large onions	Salt pork
Butter	

Skin and clean the eels and cut them into 4-inch lengths. Peel and slice the potatoes and onions. In a buttered baking dish or casserole, place a layer of the potatoes, a layer of the onions, and a layer of eels. Sprinkle each layer lightly with pepper and flour. Cover the top with small bits of salt pork, dot with butter, and add almost enough water to cover. Cover and bake at 375° until tender, or cook slowly on top of the stove until done.

EELS BORDELAISE

This dish is usually made with the lampreys caught near Bordeaux. It is a specialty of the house in one of the famous restaurants in St. Emilion, where some of the finest wines of that district are used to prepare the food, and, of course, are drunk with it. Strangely enough, St. Emilion is famous for another gastronomic delight—macaroons.

3 pounds of eels	1 teaspoon salt
Carrot, thinly sliced	1 teaspoon freshly ground
Onion, thinly sliced	black pepper
1 clove garlic	Red wine to cover
Pinch thyme	6 to 8 pieces of the white
1 leaf and stalk of celery	of leek
Several sprigs parsley	⅓ cup diced raw ham
1 bay leaf	3 tablespoons butter
4 tablespoons flour	

Skin and clean the eels and cut them in 4-inch pieces. Line a skillet or saucepan with sliced carrot and onion. Put the pieces of eel on top. Add garlic, thyme, celery, parsley, bay leaf, salt, pepper, and red wine to cover. Cover the skillet, bring it to a boil, and simmer for 10 minutes.

Meanwhile, brown the pieces of leek in butter. Add the ham and the eel, after it has cooked 10 minutes. Make a roux of the butter and flour and add it to the broth in which the eel was cooked. Simmer for 20 minutes. Force this sauce through a sieve onto the eel, leeks, and ham. Simmer this all together for 15 or 20 minutes, stirring occasionally. Taste for seasoning.

Arrange the fish and leeks on a serving dish. Thicken the sauce with beurre manié (see index) if necessary, and pour it over the eel.

BAKED EELS, NEW ENGLAND FASHION

Skin and clean 6 eels but do not split them. Cut them in lengths of 3 to 4 inches. Remove the intestines with a fine-pointed knife, or a fork or skewer. Arrange the pieces on an oiled baking pan, season, and top with slices of onion and salt pork. Bake in a 350° oven for 30 minutes or until the eel is tender.

POACHED EELS

Skin and clean eels and cut them into 3-inch lengths. Poach them in a court bouillon (see index). They should be tender in about 8 or 9 minutes. Remove them to a hot dish, reduce the broth and use it to prepare a sauce velouté (see index). Pour this over the eels and garnish with chopped parsley.

1. Prepare a curry sauce (see index). Pour the sauce over the poached eels and serve with rice and chutney.

2. Poach the eels. Prepare the sauce velouté and lace it heavily with paprika. Serve with buttered noodles.

3. Poach the eels in white wine. Sauté 24 mushroom caps in butter. Brown ½ cup of artichoke hearts in butter. Arrange these in a baking dish or casserole with the eels. Add 3 pimientos cut in fine strips. Prepare a white wine sauce with the broth (see index), season it with paprika, and pour it over the eels and vegetables. Heat in 350° oven for 12 minutes.

4. Cut the eels into lengths of 5 or 6 inches and poach in a court bouillon for about 6 minutes. Let them cool in the broth. When cool enough to handle, wipe them well, dip in flour, then in beaten egg yolk, and roll in crumbs. Grill or broil until nicely browned. Serve with tartar sauce (see index).

MARINATED EELS

3 eels	1 stalk celery
Red wine	3 or 4 sprigs parsley
Garlic	Pinch thyme
1 carrot	1 leek
1 onion stuck with cloves	Salt, pepper

Prepare a marinade of all the ingredients except the eels. Skin, clean, and cut the eels in pieces. Soak them in the marinade. Poach them in the marinade for 15 or 20 minutes. When tender, remove them to a hot dish. Reduce the broth and put it through a fine sieve or food mill. Reheat and pour over the pieces of eel.

COLD EEL (EELS IN JELLY)

6 large eels	Chopped parsley
White wine court bouillon	1 envelope gelatin (if desired)
3 cloves garlic	Sauce rémoulade or sauce gribiche
Olive oil	

Skin and clean the eels, and cut them in 3-inch pieces. Prepare the court bouillon (see index). Poach the eels until tender, remove them, and arrange in a mold.

Chop the garlic and sauté in olive oil until brown. Add these to the mold. Sprinkle chopped parsley over the pieces of eel.

Reduce the bouillon and strain. It should make a good jelly without the addition of gelatin. However, if you will feel safer, use 1 envelope dissolved in ¼ cup of water. Stir it into 2 cups of the hot broth. Chill slightly and pour over the pieces of eel. Stand in the refrigerator until firm. Unmold on a platter with your favorite garnishes and serve with sauce rémoulade or sauce gribiche (see index).

FLEMISH GREEN EELS

This is certainly one of the finest of cold dishes. I like it as an hors d'oeuvre or as a full course for a summer buffet.

3 pounds of eels	Savory
6 tablespoons butter	Rosemary
¼ pound chopped sorrel or spinach	Sage
½ cup chopped parsley	Thyme
¼ cup chervil	Salt, pepper
1 tablespoon fresh or 1 teaspoon dried tarragon	White wine
	4 egg yolks
	1½ tablespoons of lemon juice

Skin and clean the eels and cut them into 3-inch pieces. Brown them in the butter, and when they are just colored add the herbs. Mix the herbs well with the pieces of eel, add salt and pepper to taste, and cover with white wine. Cover the pan and poach just until the eel is tender. Remove the fish to a large earthenware or glass dish.

Stir the slightly beaten egg yolks into the broth, and continue stirring and cooking until lightly thickened. Be careful not to let the sauce boil. Taste for seasoning, add lemon juice, and pour over the pieces of eel. Chill and serve cold.

SMOKED EEL

Smoked eel is excellent as a cocktail snack, as a first course, or as part of a smoked-fish platter at a buffet or supper party. You may buy it by the pound.

It is not necessary to skin it and cut it up for serving, but it does make a nicer appearance that way. Its oily flesh takes well to a sprinkling of freshly ground black pepper and a little squeeze of lemon juice.

CANNED EEL

There are several different varieties of canned eel in jelly, and they are all good for cold snacks and summer luncheons.

Serve on a bed of greens with a garnish of thinly sliced onions. Use a sauce rémoulade or green mayonnaise (see index).

Fluke

THIS is a fish that has become popular with summer fishing enthusiasts along the central Atlantic coast. It is also known as the summer flounder, and is in fact a member of the flounder family. It has much more spirit, however, than its close relatives, and this accounts for its appeal as a game fish.

In some local areas in southern New England, especially on the island of Nantucket, fluke is called plaice, although it bears no relationship to the European fish of that name. It is found in the markets only during the summer months, when it comes close to shore to feed.

Although fluke can grow to 25 pounds, the average size caught is 1 to 5 pounds. It is a delicious food fish with white meat of an unusually delicate texture. Prepare it in any of the ways suggested for sole or flounder.

Groupers

THE many varieties of groupers are all members of that large family of fish known as sea bass, which is so common all through the Atlantic coastal area, and in fact, common all over the world. The red grouper is probably the best known, and it is important commercially from Virginia on south. The Nassau grouper is found around Florida, while the yellowfish and black grouper and the gag are mainly Gulf fish.

An interesting characteristic of the grouper family is the ability of its members to conceal themselves by taking on the color of their surroundings. In coral or seaweed they camouflage themselves with stripes. When they rise to the surface of the sea, they turn pale, almost colorless, blending with the water. Apparently this ability is something they can flash on and off at will, for they can turn on their colored bands when they see a fish of a different species approaching.

Another interesting fact about groupers is that they seem to be very friendly. One scientist who made underwater investigations some years ago found that red groupers he had been feeding would let him handle them and would even poke around in his pockets in search of tidbits.

Groupers can weigh as much as 40 pounds, but the market fish generally weigh from 5 to 15 pounds. They are sold whole, in steaks or fillets.

Groupers can be cooked in any of the ways suggested for sea bass or red snapper, see index.

Grunion

THESE amusing fish are *gathered* on shore instead of being hooked or netted in the sea. During their spawning season, grunions come up on the beach and dig holes in the wet sand, where they deposit their eggs. Their floundering antics have always reminded me of a disorderly, unrehearsed ballet.

The grunion "run" can be forecast from year to year, and the seasonal sport of gathering them has many followers on the West Coast. I have never encountered grunions on the Atlantic seaboard. The fish is small, delicate and flavorful, and somewhat resembles the smelt.

BROILED GRUNIONS

Clean the dish, dip them in flour, dot well with butter, and broil under a hot flame. Brush with oil or butter during the cooking process. Season to taste and serve with a tartar sauce.

FRIED GRUNIONS

Here are grunions at their best.

Heat the fat in your French fryer to 370°. Clean the fish, dip them in flour, then in beaten egg, and roll them in corn meal. Fry until brown and crisp—about 4 minutes. Drain on absorbent paper and season to taste with salt and pepper.

Serve with lemon butter or parsley butter and lemon quarters.

Haddock

THE haddock and the cod are close relatives, but you can easily tell them apart once you have seen them side by side in the market. The haddock is usually smaller, the average market fish weighing about 2½ to 3 pounds; its mouth is smaller than that of the cod; and it has a black, rather than a whitish, lateral line.

A great deal of haddock is sold in fillets, either fresh or frozen, and like ocean perch and cod, it is shipped frozen all over the country. Americans now consume over 100,000,-000 pounds of haddock a year.

Finnan haddie—or smoked haddock—is an extremely popular dish of Scottish origin. Years ago it was known as Findon haddock, after the Scottish fishing port of Findon.

Fresh Haddock

BROILED HADDOCK

See directions for broiling fish under "Cooking Methods."

SAUTEED HADDOCK

See directions for sauté meunière under "Cooking Methods." For fillets, see recipes for ocean perch.

FRIED HADDOCK

See directions for frying fish and fillets under "Cooking Methods."

HADDOCK TURBANS WITH LEMON SAUCE

6 haddock fillets	Parsley
½ pound shrimp	Court bouillon
Fresh dill	Sauce velouté (see index)

1 tablespoon lemon juice

Place one or two shelled, uncooked shrimp on each fillet and a little fresh dill and parsley. Roll the fillets and secure with toothpicks. Poach them in court bouillon until they are just cooked through and will flake easily when tested with a fork. Remove to a hot serving dish. Reduce the stock, prepare the sauce velouté, and add the lemon juice at the last minute. Pour the sauce over the fillets.

HADDOCK FILLETS VERONIQUE

6 haddock fillets	Sauce velouté (see index)
Court bouillon	½ cup white seedless grapes
White wine	Half-whipped cream

Poach the fillets in court bouillon and white wine until just cooked through to the point of flakiness. Arrange them in a shallow baking dish. Make a sauce velouté with the bouillon and some heavy cream and add the white seedless grapes. Pour this over the fillets. Dribble a little half-whipped cream on top, and run under the broiler for a minute or two to give it a glaze.

FILLETS OF HADDOCK IN CREAM SAUCE

Sauce béchamel (see index)
2 tablespoons sherry or Madeira
Chopped parsley
Fresh fennel or fennel seeds
6 haddock fillets

Prepare the sauce béchamel and flavor it with sherry or Madeira and the fennel or fennel seeds. Place the fillets in a flat baking dish and pour the sauce over them. Bake for 25 to 30 minutes in a moderate oven, about 325°. Remove and sprinkle liberally with chopped parsley. Serve with crisp fried potatoes and a cucumber salad.

BAKED HADDOCK FILLETS IN WHITE WINE AND TARRAGON

6 haddock fillets
Fresh or dried tarragon
Salt, pepper
3 egg yolks
1½ cups white wine
Butter
½ cup heavy cream

Arrange the fillets in a shallow baking dish and sprinkle liberally with tarragon. Salt and pepper to taste. Add the white wine and dot with butter. Bake at 400° for 25 minutes or until the fish flakes easily when tested with a fork. Remove fish to a hot platter. Reduce the wine to ¾ cup and combine with the heavy cream mixed with the egg yolks. Stir until the sauce is thickened, but do not let it boil. Season to taste, pour over the fillets and sprinkle with additional tarragon.

STUFFED FILLETS IN WHITE WINE

Fish forcemeat (see index)
6 haddock fillets
Chopped shallots or green onions
1 cup white wine
Butter
18 cooked shelled shrimp

Prepare a fish forcemeat or your favorite stuffing for fish. Spread this on the fillets and fold them over. Arrange the

95

stuffed fillets on a bed of chopped shallots or green onions in a baking dish and add the wine. Dot with butter and bake at 400° for 25 minutes or until the fillets are flaky. Baste often with the pan juices. Remove the fish to a hot platter, and prepare a wine sauce with the pan juices. Pour this over the fillets and garnish with the shrimp.

HADDOCK FILLETS IN PAPER CASES

½ pound mushrooms	Dash of lemon juice for
5 tablespoons butter	each fillet
Salt, pepper	Finely chopped green
6 haddock fillets	onion
	Butter

Mustard sauce (see index)

Chop the mushrooms and sauté slowly in 5 tablespoons of butter until they are black and rich. Salt and pepper to taste. Spread each fillet with this mixture, add a dash of lemon juice and a little chopped onion and fold over.

Cut large heart-shaped pieces of cooking parchment or heavy wax paper or foil, and place one fillet on each piece, putting it toward the edge so that you can fold a layer of paper over the top. Dot the fillets with butter, spread with a little mustard sauce, and fold the paper over the top. Crimp the edges so that you have a tightly closed bag. Arrange on a baking sheet and bake at 400° for about 15 to 20 minutes, or until the paper is puffed and brown.

BAKED STUFFED HADDOCK

Clean a 3-pound haddock and split it for stuffing. Leave the head and tail on the fish.

Prepare the following clam stuffing:

½ cup chopped onion	1 tin minced clams (7
¼ cup butter	ounces) with liquid
2 cups buttered crumbs	Salt, pepper
¼ cup finely chopped parsley	Nutmeg

2 eggs, well beaten

Sauté the onion in butter and mix with all the other ingredients. Stuff the fish with this, sew up the sides, and put strips of bacon or salt pork on top. Place on an oiled baking dish and bake at 400° for 25 to 35 minutes. Serve with a sauce tartare or with lemon butter.

HADDOCK PROVENCALE

1 good-sized haddock	Salt and pepper to taste
1 large onion in paper-thin slices	½ cup olive oil
12 to 16 anchovy fillets	Fennel seeds
2 cloves garlic, finely chopped	Sliced tomatoes
18 to 20 ripe olives	1½ cups tomato puree
1 green pepper, finely shredded	1½ cups red wine
Chopped tarragon	Chopped parsley

Clean and split the haddock. Mix together the onion, anchovies, garlic, ripe olives and green pepper. Salt and pepper to taste.

Pour over this the olive oil and a sprinkling of fennel seeds. Stuff the fish with the mixture, sew it up, and place it in a well-oiled pan or baking dish. Top with sliced tomatoes and pour over it the tomato puree and red wine mixed together. Bake for 25 to 35 minutes at 375°, basting the fish often with the tomato-wine mixture. Just before serving, sprinkle well with chopped parsley and tarragon, mixed.

STUFFED WHOLE HADDOCK

1 haddock	1 teaspoon salt, or more
1 cup fine bread crumbs	½ cup melted butter
¼ cup chopped parsley	1 teaspoon fennel or tarragon
¼ cup finely chopped green onions or chives	2 eggs

Choose a 3-pound haddock, or larger. Have your fish dealer make a gash in the fish and remove all the meat and bones, leaving the skin intact and the head and tail on. Grind the meat well and combine it with all the other ingredients.

Blend well, stuff the fish skin with this mixture, and sew it up after pressing it into shape.

Poach in a white wine court bouillon (see index) for about 40 to 45 minutes. Remove the fish to a hot platter and prepare a white wine sauce (see index) with the court bouillon after reducing it.

BOILED HADDOCK, NEW ENGLAND STYLE

Split a 3 to 4 pound haddock, clean it and rub the inside well with salt. Let it stand for 3 hours. Rinse it and wrap it in cheesecloth, leaving long ends of the cloth for handles. Simmer in boiling salted water for 25 to 35 minutes or until the fish flakes easily when tested with a fork. Remove it to a hot platter, garnish with crisp bits of salt pork, and surround with boiled potatoes and boiled buttered beets. Serve with parsley sauce or egg sauce (see index).

HADDOCK CUSTARD

5 eggs, well beaten	Salt, pepper
2 cups light cream	Nutmeg
2 teaspoons finely grated onion	2 cups flaked cooked
2 tablespoons finely chopped parsley	haddock

Beat the eggs thoroughly, add the cream, beat another minute, and then add all the seasonings. Arrange the flaked fish in a well-buttered baking dish and pour the custard sauce over it. Bake at 350° for about 40 minutes or until it is not quite set in the middle. Serve with crisp fried potatoes and a distinctive relish.

VARIATIONS

1. Line a deep pie tin with pastry and pour the mixture in this. Bake at 400° for 10 minutes. Then reduce to 350° for 25 minutes or until the custard is not quite set. Serve with a shrimp sauce (see index)

2. Line a 12-inch pie tin with pastry. Arrange the flaked fish, chopped parsley and onion, and bits of crisp bacon in the bottom. Add a good sprinkling of grated Swiss or Parmesan cheese, or a mixture of the two. Pour the custard over this and bake at 375° for 35 minutes or until the custard is not quite set.

HADDOCK LOAF

2 cups flaked cooked haddock	1 cup chopped toasted almonds (they come in tins)
1 cup fine bread crumbs	
¼ cup finely chopped parsley	Salt, pepper
¼ cup finely chopped green onions or scallions	3 egg yolks, well beaten
	3 egg whites, beaten stiff

Combine all the ingredients except the eggs. Then blend in the well-beaten egg yolks, and finally fold in the stiffly beaten egg whites. Turn into a well-buttered mold and bake at 375° for 35 to 40 minutes or until set. Serve from the mold, or unmold on a hot platter and serve with a shrimp or oyster sauce (see index).

COLD HADDOCK

Follow the recipes for cold ocean perch (see index).

Finnan Haddie

Finnan haddie—or smoked haddock—comes in fillets and whole fish, and there is a great argument over the merits of each type. Sometimes I think that the whole fish has a better flavor, and other times I think that the fillets I happen to be eating are as good as anything could possibly be.

BROILED FINNAN HADDIE

Arrange fillets or a whole fish on a broiling rack over a little hot water. Dot the fish with butter and run it under the flame. Broil it slowly so that the fish does not burn or dry out.

FINNAN HADDIE BROILED IN MILK

Place a whole fish or fillet in a broiling pan and dot with butter. Pour warm milk over the fish to cover the bottom of the pan. Broil until the haddock is well heated through and lightly browned. Baste it often with the milk. Serve with boiled potato.

POACHED FINNAN HADDIE

Poach the finnan haddie in milk, or in half milk and half water, or in a mild court bouillon. Serve with parsley butter.

VARIATIONS

1. Poach the finnan haddie, flake it and combine with ¼ cup of butter in a saucepan. Add 1 cup of heavy cream, 4 sliced hard-cooked eggs, and flavor with cayenne, nutmeg, and black pepper. Blend thoroughly.

2. Combine flaked, poached finnan haddie with sauce béchamel (see index), sprinkle with buttered crumbs and run under the broiler for a few minutes.

3. Combine flaked, poached finnan haddie with sauce Mornay (see index), sprinkle with grated Swiss cheese, and brown under the broiler.

4. Combine 2 cups of flaked, poached finnan haddie with 1½ cups of sauce béchamel, ¼ cup of chopped pimiento, ½ cup of chopped olives, 3 sliced hard-cooked eggs, and 2 teaspoons of onion juice. Arrange in a baking dish, sprinkle with grated cheese, and brown under the broiler for a few minutes.

FINNAN HADDIE SOUFFLE

1½ cups flaked poached finnan haddie
¾ cup heavy sauce béchamel
4 egg yolks

Salt, pepper
Nutmeg
6 egg whites
Butter

Combine the finnan haddie with the sauce béchamel (see index). Beat in the egg yolks. Season to taste with salt and pepper and add a few grains of nutmeg. Beat the egg whites until stiff and fold them into the mixture. Pour into a buttered soufflé dish and bake at 375° for 35 to 40 minutes or until well puffed and brown. Serve with a sauce Mornay (see index) or a sauce béchamel.

FINNAN HADDIE CAKES

1½ cups flaked cooked finnan haddie
1½ cups seasoned mashed potatoes

½ teaspoon ginger
1 egg, well beaten

Combine the finnan haddie with the mashed potatoes—potatoes which have been mashed with plenty of butter and well seasoned with salt and pepper. Add the ginger and egg. Form into small flat cakes and sauté in butter until nicely browned on both sides. Serve with crisp bacon.

Hake

A TREMENDOUS amount of hake is marketed all over the country, but I suspect that the number of people who actually recognize the fish when they see it on the stands is amazingly small. Filleted and salted, it is sold, along with haddock, cod, and other white fish, as "deep sea fillets."

The whole fish is readily identified. It is long and streamlined, with large eyes and only two dorsal fins, the second being very long. It is also equipped with a feeler.

The flesh of the hake is delicate, soft and white. Prepare it in any of the ways you would cod or haddock.

COLD HAKE

To me, a cold hake is one of the most delicate and delightful dishes.

Poach the fish in a court bouillon (see index) and serve it, chilled, with your favorite sauce. My choice with hake is mayonnaise, but many people may prefer something more highly seasoned.

SALT HAKE

A great deal of the salted codfish sold throughout the world is actually salted hake. Salt hake can be prepared in the same manner as salt cod (see index).

Halibut

THE halibut is popular, but not nearly so popular as it ought to be. It resembles the famed turbot of Europe,* and many of the fine turbot recipes may be used in its preparation.

The Latin name for halibut is most appropriate—*Hippoglossus hippoglossus*. An ordinary halibut may weigh 50 to 100 pounds. Some weigh as much as 600 pounds. Small members of the species, known as chicken halibut, are caught occasionally on the West Coast, and still less frequently on the East Coast.

Halibut is usually bought in steaks, sometimes in fillets. For an unusual occasion, such as a very large gathering, you might possibly buy a whole fish. Halibut cheeks are available from time to time on the West Coast, where they are cooked in the same way as salmon cheeks.

BROILED HALIBUT

A steak about 1½ to 2 inches thick seems to me to be the ideal piece for broiling. Follow the general directions for broiling fish steaks under "Cooking Methods," brushing well with butter and lemon juice several times during the cooking process. Sprinkle with salt and paprika before serving.

* Some people claim there is no turbot in American waters, but it is sometimes caught off the coast of Oregon.

Serve with maître d'hôtel butter (see index), lemon butter (see index), Hollandaise sauce (see index) or parsley butter (see index).

HALIBUT SAUTE

SELECT a halibut steak about 1 to 1½ inches thick. Dip it in flour and sauté it gently in butter or oil, turning once during the process. A steak weighing 1½ to 2 pounds should take 6 to 8 minutes, depending upon its thickness. Salt and pepper well and serve with lemon butter or parsley butter.

VARIATIONS

1. Dip the halibut steak into flour mixed with 1 teaspoon of salt, 1 tablespoon of paprika, and 1 teaspoon of freshly ground pepper. Sauté as above, sprinkling with additional paprika if needed. Remove to a hot platter. Add 1 cup of sour cream to the pan and blend well. Heat through but do not let it boil. Pour the sauce over the fish and serve with steamed rice.

2. Dip the halibut steak in lemon or lime juice, then in flour, again in lemon or lime juice, and then in fine bread crumbs. Or dip in beaten egg and crumbs. Sauté very quickly in butter or, preferably, olive oil until the fish is nicely brown on both sides and flaky when tested with a fork. Salt and pepper to taste and remove to a hot platter. Serve with plenty of chopped parsley, boiled potatoes and peas.

3. Follow the preceding recipe. When you have removed the fish to a hot platter, add to the pan ¼ cup of Worcestershire sauce, ¼ cup of white wine or sherry, 1 tablespoon of prepared mustard and 1 teaspoon of dry mustard. Blend well with the pan juices. Pour the sauce over the fish.

4. Sauté the halibut steak in butter and add 1 teaspoon of dried tarragon or 1 tablespoon of fresh tarragon, salt and pepper. When the fish is cooked and nicely browned, remove it to a hot platter and add ½ cup of white wine to the pan. Let it cook down very quickly and pour over the fish.

BAKED HALIBUT

You may bake either a large piece of the fish or steaks, depending on the size of your family or the number of your guests. Follow directions for baking under "Cooking Methods."

BAKED STUFFED HALIBUT STEAKS

Choose 2 good-sized halibut steaks, about 4 pounds or more. Prepare the following stuffing:

¼ cup finely, chopped onion	¼ cup finely chopped parsley
4 tablespoons butter	1 teaspoon salt
½ cup sliced mushrooms	½ teaspoon black pepper
½ cup dry bread crumbs	¼ teaspoon thyme

Heavy cream

Sauté the onion in the butter. Add the mushrooms, bread crumbs, parsley, salt, pepper and thyme. Mix thoroughly and moisten with a little heavy cream.

Oil a baking dish or pan and put one of the fish steaks on the bottom. Spread it with the stuffing and top with the second steak. Secure the two steaks together with toothpicks or tie lightly with string. Brush with butter or oil and sprinkle with salt and pepper. Bake for 30 to 40 minutes at 400°. Baste often during the process. Serve with a sour cream cucumber sauce (see index) or with parsley sauce (see index).

Tiny buttered new potatoes and green peas bonne femme are excellent with this.

VARIATIONS

1. Begin the preparation of a stuffing with 6 rashers of bacon cut in bits and tried out until crisp; remove to absorbent paper. Add 1 large onion, finely chopped, to the fat and sauté gently until soft. Add ½ cup of bread crumbs, 1 7-ounce can of minced clams with the liquor, 1 teaspoon of salt, 1 teaspoon of coarsely ground black pepper, and ½ teaspoon of thyme or more. Mix well, adding a few more bread crumbs if the stuffing seems too soft. Finally, add the crisp bacon pieces. Spread this on one steak, cover with the other, and place in a baking dish or pan. Top with strips of bacon and bake at 400° for 30 to 40 minutes or until the fish is flaky. Serve with parsley butter.

2. Stuff the fish with your favorite stuffing and place in an oiled baking dish or pan. Cover with sour cream, and bake at 350° for 35 to 40 minutes or until the fish is flaky. Sprinkle well with paprika and chopped parsley just before serving.

3. Stuff the fish with your favorite stuffing, place in an oiled baking dish and brush with butter. Add ½ cup of white wine to the pan and bake at 425° for 30 to 35 minutes. Baste with additional butter and white wine. Remove the fish to a hot platter, add balls of beurre manié (see index) to the liquid in the pan, and stir until thickened. Add ½ cup of heavy cream and heat thoroughly. Serve with the fish.

4. Prepare a stuffing with 1 small onion, finely chopped and sautéed in butter with ½ green pepper, finely chopped. Add ¾ cup of crumbs, 1 teaspoon of salt, 1 teaspoon of freshly ground black pepper, and 1 cup of chopped oysters. Blend well, stuff the steaks and place them in a well-oiled baking dish or pan. Brush with butter and bake at 425° for 30 to 35 minutes, basting every 10 minutes. Serve with a sauce béchamel (see index) prepared with some of the oyster liquor. At the last moment add ½ pint of oysters to the sauce and taste for seasoning. The oysters should be small, or else they should be cut in several pieces.

5. Place a halibut steak on an oiled baking dish or pan. Top with a layer of paper-thin onion slices, a layer of peeled tomatoes sliced very thin, a layer of thinly sliced green pepper, a layer of chopped parsley, and another layer of sliced onions. Dot each layer with a little butter and sprinkle lightly with salt. Top the whole with the second steak and brush well with butter or oil. Add 1 cup of red wine to the pan and bake at 400° for 30 or 40 minutes, basting occasionally. Remove the halibut to a hot platter. Add an additional ⅔ cup of wine to the pan juices and bring it to a boil. Add to this ¼ cup each of finely chopped parsley and green onion or scallion. Season to taste and, if you wish, thicken the sauce with small balls of beurre manié.

6. Stuff the halibut with a layer of thick tomato puree, a layer of finely chopped garlic, a layer of anchovy fillets, a layer of ripe olives, a layer of pimientos, and another layer of the tomato puree. Add some fennel or basil, salt and pepper. Place in an oiled baking dish or pan and add 1 cup of tomato puree mixed with 1 cup of red wine. Bake at 400° for 30 to 40 minutes, basting occasionally. Serve with the juices in the pan and sprinkle lavishly with chopped parsley and sliced black olives.

7. Chop very fine ½ cup of fresh dill sprigs, 1 cup of parsley sprigs, and 6 to 8 green onions or scallions. Blend with ¼ cup of butter and spread on a halibut steak. Season to taste and top with another steak. Brush with butter and bake at 425° for 25 to 35 minutes or until the meat will flake easily

when tested with a fork. Serve with boiled potatoes and a sauce tartare heavily flavored with dill.

FRIED HALIBUT

Buy halibut steaks cut about ¾ inch thick. Cut them into fingers about the same width, roll them in flour, dip in beaten egg and crumbs and deep fry according to the directions on page 16. Serve with a rémoulade sauce (see index).

POACHED HALIBUT

Halibut is firmly meated but has a certain delicacy that lends itself well to poaching. Have a piece about 1½ to 2 inches thick cut for you, and poach it in a well-seasoned court bouillon. Serve it in any of the following ways:

VARIATIONS

1. Serve with Hollandaise sauce (see index). Pass boiled potatoes with parsley.

2. Serve with aioli (see index). Serve with parsley potatoes, string beans, and tomatoes Provençale.

3. Prepare a sauce velouté (see index) with the court bouillon and a little cream added. Spike it with lemon or lime juice.

4. Add ½ pound of shelled shrimp to the court bouillon for the last five minutes of cooking. Remove the shrimp and halibut. Reduce the bouillon and make a sauce béchamel (see index). Add the shrimp to the sauce and season it well with chopped fresh dill and black pepper.

5. Prepare a sauce béchamel, using oyster liquor and some of the court bouillon. Add ½ pint or more of small or chopped oysters to the sauce and let them just heat through.

6. Poach the halibut in salted water instead of the bouillon. Prepare a sauce béchamel using clam juice, and add 1 7-ounce tin of minced clams and some chopped parsley to the sauce.

7. Poach the halibut in salted water. Prepare a curry sauce (see index) and serve with a ring of saffron rice; garnish with chutney, bits of crisp bacon and chopped hard-cooked eggs.

8. Poach the halibut in salted water. Serve with a highly seasoned tomato sauce, baked rice and a cucumber salad.

105

HALIBUT MOUSSE

1 pound halibut	Nutmeg
3 egg whites	Cayenne (if desired)
1 cup heavy cream	Finely chopped fresh dill
Salt, pepper	(if desired)

Chop the halibut or put it through a fine grinder. The preferred method is to grind it and then pound it in a mortar or work it with a heavy wooden spoon. Place the bowl with the fish over cracked ice and gradually beat in the egg whites, using a whisk or wooden spoon to smooth the fish and make it absorb all the liquid. Then gradually stir in the cream, making sure every bit of it is absorbed as you work it in. Add salt, pepper and a little nutmeg—you may add cayenne or finely chopped fresh dill if you wish. Let it stand over the ice for an hour.

Butter a fish mold and stir the mixture thoroughly before pouring it into the mold. Cover it with waxed paper or buttered brown paper and place it in a pan with about 1 inch of hot water. Bake at 350° for 25 minutes or until the mousse is firm.

Serve with a sauce mousseline (see index), a sauce béchamel with shrimp or lobster added (see index), or with a cucumber sour cream sauce (see index). Tiny new potatoes and sliced cucumber salad are good accompaniments.

HALIBUT AU GRATIN

Poach a 3 to 4 pound halibut steak. Prepare a sauce Mornay (see index). Place the fish in a flat baking dish and cover it with the sauce. Sprinkle with buttered crumbs and finely grated Swiss or Cheddar cheese and run under the broiler for a minute to brown.

HALIBUT SOUFFLE

Prepare as you would salmon soufflé (see index). Serve with a Hollandaise, shrimp, or oyster sauce (see index).

HALIBUT WITH LOBSTER

1 large lobster (2 to 2½ pounds)	Salt, pepper
Court bouillon	Chopped parsley
2 halibut steaks (4 pounds)	Artichoke hearts filled with peas
2 tablespoons flour	Potato balls browned in butter
2 tablespoons butter	
Heavy cream	

Poach the lobster in court bouillon (see index). When it is cool, remove the meat from the shell, setting aside the tomalley and coral, if any. Return the shells to the bouillon. Cut the lobster meat into pieces and keep it warm.

Poach the halibut steaks in the bouillon until they flake easily when tested with a fork. Remove them to a hot platter. Strain the court bouillon and reduce it to 1 cup. Prepare a sauce velouté (see index) using the bouillon, flour, butter, heavy cream and seasonings; add the lobster tomalley and the coral. Arrange the lobster meat on one of the steaks, top with the other, and sprinkle with chopped parsley. Garnish the platter with artichoke hearts filled with tiny green peas and small potato balls browned in butter. Serve the sauce separately.

COLD HALIBUT

Court bouillon	Sliced cucumbers, hard-cooked eggs, or other garnish
Large piece of halibut or 2 halibut steaks	
1 egg white	Vegetable salad (mixed vegetables, finely cut, small whole tomatoes and green peppers)
2 envelopes gelatin	
2 cups well-seasoned mayonnaise	

Prepare a rich court bouillon with fish bones and heads (see index). Poach a large piece of halibut or 2 halibut steaks. For cold dishes, some people prefer one or two large pieces without bones. Others like the appearance of one large piece cut right through the center of the fish with the bone left in.

When the fish is done, remove it to a plate to cool. Reduce the bouillon to 4 cups. (This amount is for a large piece of fish.) When the liquid is reduced, strain, and clarify it with the white of an egg. Strain it again, this time through a linen napkin. Return it to the stove, bring it to a boil and add the gelatin, which has been softened in ½ cup of cold water. Stir well and cool.

Skin the fish and arrange it on a serving dish. When the

gelatin mixture is almost set, combine 1 cup of it with the mayonnaise and mask the fish with it. Decorate the top with slices of cucumber, ripe olives, hard-cooked eggs, tarragon leaves, or anything you like.

Prepare a mixed vegetable salad, using finely cut cooked vegetables. Mix it with some of the jellied mayonnaise. Hollow out a few small tomatoes and small green peppers and fill them with the vegetable salad. Surround the fish with these. When the first coating of jelly is almost firm on the fish, add a coating of the plain jelly. Brush the tops of the stuffed tomatoes and peppers with jelly and chill thoroughly. When ready to serve, chop the remaining jelly and surround the fish with it. Serve with a mayonnaise sauce.

VARIATIONS

1. Poach halibut in a simple court bouillon or in plain salted water. Serve cold with mayonnaise and a potato and cucumber salad.

2. Poach the halibut and serve with a sauce rémoulade (see index), cole slaw and sliced tomatoes.

3. Poach the halibut and serve with parsley, hard-cooked eggs, and a mayonnaise heavily spiked with dill.

4. Serve the poached halibut with a Russian dressing, a tossed green salad, sliced cucumbers and hard-cooked eggs.

STEAMED FISH (HALIBUT) PUDDING
OR TIMBALE

Irma Rombauer is surely beloved by thousands, or probably millions, of young Americans, and her cook book is a "must" for brides. Not only are her recipes excellent, but she somehow seems to convey the glow of her own deep enjoyment in her home and kitchen.

This is a fish pudding that was one of her favorites as a child, and she has graciously passed it on to me for this book. It is a perfect way for using up leftover fish. This recipe is for 6 people. If you wish to serve 3, cut the ingredients in half and steam the pudding in a 1-pound baking powder tin or a small mold.

2 cups flaked or ground halibut, or other fish	2 teaspoons lemon juice or 1 teaspoon
¾ cup bread crumbs	Worcestershire sauce
¼ cup melted butter	Salt
3 eggs, separated	Paprika

Combine the fish, crumbs, butter, egg yolks, and seasonings. Beat the egg whites stiff and fold them into the mixture. Pour it into a well-buttered timbale mold or pudding tin, and steam for 1 hour. Unmold onto a hot platter and serve with cream sauce flavored with Worcestershire sauce, or a mustard or tomato sauce (see index).

Herring

HERRING is one of the most plentiful catches in the Atlantic. There is no great demand for it fresh, but it is enormously popular in other forms—smoked, pickled, salted, kippered. Every year millions of herring find themselves in cans labeled "sardines."

For centuries herring have been a mainstay of commercial fishermen, and for many more centuries they have been the prey of practically every voracious fish in the sea. So great is the general chase for herring that the supply fluctuates sharply, and no one can accurately predict the catch.

Fresh herring weighing over a pound are seldom found in the markets. In fact, they are usually much smaller. They can be cooked whole or cut into fillets. Plan one or two fish per serving, depending on the size of the fish.

Fresh Herring

GRILLED HERRING

Split the fish and remove the backbone. Brush well with butter or oil, sprinkle with salt and pepper and a dash of paprika. Grill according to directions under "Cooking Methods."

VARIATIONS

1. The whole fish may be grilled without splitting. Be sure to turn it once during the cooking process.
2. Baste with butter, and sprinkle dried fennel or thyme on top a few minutes before the fish is done.

HERRING SAUTE MEUNIERE

Clean and trim the fish. Roll in flour, and follow the directions for sauté meunière under "Cooking Methods."

HERRING, ENGLISH FASHION

Split and remove the bones from 8 small herring. Dip them in milk, then in finely rolled crumbs, and sauté quickly in 6 tablespoons of butter. Turn once. Salt and pepper to taste and sprinkle with lemon juice. Serve with tartar sauce (see index).

VARIATIONS

1. Dip the herring in milk and then in corn meal seasoned with salt, curry powder, and a little chopped garlic. Sauté as above and serve with mayonnaise blended with chutney.

2. Add finely chopped tomato to the pan while you are sautéing the fish. Or add ½ cup of tomato paste to the pan after the fish are removed. Heat the paste, add 4 tablespoons of sherry or red wine, let it cook up, and pour over the fish. Sprinkle with chopped parsley.

FRIED HERRING

Clean the fish and fillet them. Dip them into beaten egg, and then into crumbs, and deep fry according to directions under "Cooking Methods."

BAKED HERRING BOULANGERE

Oil	2 large onions
4 large herring	Salt, pepper
Butter	Pinch of dried thyme
4 large or 6 medium potatoes	

Oil a flat oval baking dish. Clean the fish and arrange them in the dish. Dot them with butter, cover with a layer of thinly sliced potatoes, and then a layer of thinly sliced onions. Dot with butter again, season with salt, pepper, and a little dried thyme. Bake at 350° until the potatoes are cooked through. Baste from time to time with the pan juices.

VARIATION

Omit the potatoes and cover the herring with 3 large onions, thinly sliced and steamed in butter for 15 minutes. Dot with butter and season with salt and pepper. Bake at 400° for 20 minutes, basting often. A few minutes before the fish is done, sprinkle the top with grated Gruyère or Swiss cheese. Serve with plain boiled potatoes.

SMOTHERED HERRING

6 shallots or green onions	Butter
4 tablespoons butter or oil	Salt, pepper
8 split, boned herring or fillets	White wine

Beurre manié (if desired)

Chop the shallots very fine and sauté them in the butter or oil for 5 minutes. Place the herring, or herring fillets, on top of this. Dot them with butter and season with salt and pepper. Cover them with white wine. Bring to a boil over a medium flame, reduce the heat and simmer for about 6 minutes, or until the fish flakes easily.

Remove the fish to a hot platter. Reduce the liquid one half, and pour over the fish. If you wish a thicker sauce, add beurre manié (see index) to the pan juices and stir over low heat until smooth and well blended.

BAKED SPICED HERRING

Butter	Sprig of thyme
3 carrots, chopped	6 peppercorns
3 onions, chopped	Pinch of allspice
1 clove garlic, chopped	2 cloves
4 sprigs of parsley, chopped	12 small herring
White wine	Rings of sliced onion
1 bay leaf	Thin slices of carrot
Salt, pepper	¼ cup wine vinegar

Butter a large baking dish or casserole and cover the bottom with the chopped carrots, onions, garlic, and parsley. Salt and pepper to taste, add white wine to cover, and a bay leaf, a bit of thyme, the peppercorns, allspice, and cloves. Bring it to a boil and simmer for 20 minutes, or until the vegetables are tender.

Clean the fish and place them on top of the vegetables. Cover with onion rings and carrot slices, add the wine vinegar and more wine—enough to cover. Bake at 350° for 20 minutes. Let the fish cool in the liquid, and serve them chilled as a main course for luncheon, or as a first course for dinner.

VARIATIONS

1. Add ½ cup of olive oil and ½ cup of tomato puree to the mixture.

2. Add 2 tablespoons of curry powder, ½ cup of tomato puree, and 4 pimientos cut in strips.

COLD HERRING HORS D'OEUVRE

4 large tomatoes, peeled and seeded	1 teaspoon fresh basil
3 medium onions	1 teaspoon salt
2 cloves garlic	1 teaspoon freshly ground pepper
6 tablespoons olive oil	¼ cup tomato puree
4 or 5 pimientos	8 small herring

Chop the tomatoes, onion and garlic, and sauté them in the olive oil until soft. Add the pimientos cut in strips, the basil, salt, pepper, and tomato puree. Oil a baking dish, arrange the herring in it, top with the sauce, and cover tightly. Bake at 425° for 20 minutes. Let the fish cool in the sauce.

Serve cold on greens with lemon slices, capers, and chopped parsley.

HERRING ROE

Herring roe, like the roe of salmon, shad, and whitefish, is excellent when poached or sautéed. See index for shad roe.

Herring in Brine

If your family likes cured fish, you will find herring in brine one of the most versatile foods you can buy. The 9 to 10 pound kegs of the Holland or German variety are excellent. But before using this fish, you must freshen it in cold water for 24 hours. Change the water several times. After the fish has soaked, cut off the head, split the fish in half, bone it, and, if you wish, skin it.

ROLLMOPS

To make 12 rollmops:

6 herring in brine	2 bay leaves
12 sweet or 3 dill pickles	1 clove garlic
4 medium onions	1 teaspoon thyme
1 cup vinegar	3 or 4 allspice
1 cup water	3 or 4 cloves
2 tablespoons brown sugar	8 peppercorns

Prepare the herring as above, but do not skin them. Rinse them well, and on each half herring place 1 sweet pickle or ¼ dill pickle. Roll up and fasten with a toothpick. Arrange the rollmops in a large bowl or crock that has a cover. Top with a layer of thinly sliced onions.

Combine the vinegar, water, sugar, bay leaves, garlic, thyme, and spices. Bring to the boiling point. Pour this hot pickle over the rollmops and cover them. Chill in the refrigerator for 48 hours. Serve as a luncheon dish or as hors d'oeuvre.

MARINATED HERRING

6 herring in brine	Dry mustard
Sliced onions	Pepper
Diced raw apple	White wine
Bay leaves	Sour cream

Soak and prepare the herring as above. Arrange a layer of the herring halves in the bottom of a glass or earthenware dish. Add a layer of sliced onions, ½ apple diced, 1 bay leaf, a sprinkling of mustard and pepper, and 3 tablespoons of white wine. Arrange another layer of the fish and repeat. When all the ingredients are used, cover the whole with heavy sour cream.

Cover the dish and chill for 24 hours. Serve as an appetizer or as a main course at luncheon with rye bread and beer.

VARIATION

Chop the herring into small dice and place in a large jar with 2 chopped onions and 1 chopped apple. Add 2 bay leaves, crushed, 3 tablespoons of vinegar, and ½ cup of dill and parsley mixed. Top with sour cream, cover, and chill for 24 to 36 hours. Serve as hors d'oeuvre.

PICKLED HERRING

6 herring in brine	Sliced lemon
Onion slices	1 cup wine vinegar
Bay leaves	½ cup white wine
Cayenne	2 tablespoons prepared mustard
1 teaspoon sugar	

Prepare the herring as above. Place a layer of the fish in a large dish, add a layer of onion, a bay leaf, a dash of cayenne, and a layer of lemon slices. Repeat.

Mix the vinegar, wine, mustard, and sugar and bring to a boil. Pour this over the fish. When cool, cover and chill for several days.

VARIATIONS

1. Omit the vinegar and sugar and double the white wine.

2. Arrange the herring in the dish with onion rings. Blend ⅔ cup of French mustard with ½ cup of olive oil. Season with a dash of cayenne and 2 tablespoons of chopped fresh dill. Add ½ cup of white wine. Pour this sauce over the fish, cover, and chill for 2 days.

HERRING SALAD

There are many versions of this dish, all good and all excellent changes from the usual supper or buffet dish.

3 herring in brine	1½ cups cooked veal, diced
4 diced cooked potatoes	½ cup olive oil
5 diced cooked beets	¼ cup wine vinegar
2 tart apples, sliced	1 tablespoon sugar
1 onion, diced	Coarsely ground black
1 or 2 dill pickles, diced	pepper, to taste

Wash, soak, and prepare the herring as above. Remove both the bones and the skin. Cut the flesh into small dice and combine with all the other ingredients. Mix well, and chill thoroughly.

Serve on a bed of greens and garnish with hard-cooked eggs.

Smoked Herring

Smoked herring comes in fillets. They are rather heavily smoked and should be trimmed and soaked in water, water and milk, or white wine for several hours. The length of time you soak them will depend on how much smoky taste you like. I recommend soaking the fillets in a mixture of half water and half milk.

HERRING IN OIL

This is the customary way to serve smoked herring. After they have soaked for 2 hours or more, remove them from the liquid and dry them. Arrange a layer of the fillets in a dish, top with a layer of sliced onions, and then sliced carrots. If you wish to be elaborate, scallop the edges of the carrot slices. Add several bay leaves. Repeat these layers. Cover the fish and vegetables with olive oil and chill for 48 hours.

Serve the fillets on lettuce with lemon quarters. Have some good German or French potato salad—made by pouring oil and vinegar over the hot sliced potatoes.

HERRING SALAD, RUSSIAN STYLE

Make a potato salad: Mix sliced cooked potatoes with finely cut onion and parsley and dress with oil and vinegar. Arrange this on a large platter. Top with a layer of sliced tart apple dressed with oil and vinegar. Arrange the herring fillets on top in a lattice design. Surround with quartered hard-cooked eggs, quartered tomatoes, and sliced cucumbers marinated in a sweet-sour dressing. Serve with sauce vinaigrette (see index) heavily laced with grated horseradish.

KIPPERED HERRING AND BLOATERS

Both kippers and bloaters are herring. The bloaters are simply older and fatter. I think that the kippers available in the fish markets are far superior to the canned variety.

Both kippers and bloaters are best if heated through. They may be placed in a baking dish, skin side up, dotted with butter, and warmed in the oven. Or you may dot them with butter and heat under the broiler flame. Be careful not to overcook them or they will be decidedly dry and uninteresting.

Serve them with scrambled eggs and crisp toast and you have a very good breakfast. Personally I prefer tea, rather than the usual coffee, with this breakfast menu.

Kingfish

THIS giant, which may weigh as much as 75 pounds, is a relative of the Spanish mackerel. It preys upon lesser fishes off Florida and in the Gulf. It is strong, fast and gamy, with sharp teeth that can easily ruin fishing gear. Sometimes it is seen leaping as high as ten feet out of the water. (See also California Kingfish.)

Gastronomically, the kingfish has a distinguished flavor. It is sold from November to March, whole, filleted, or in steaks.

BROILED KINGFISH STEAKS

Select good-sized steaks and brush them well with olive oil. Broil according to directions under "Cooking Methods."

1. Broil thick steaks, basting them with oil. Add salt and pepper to taste. When they are done, arrange them on a bed of dried thyme, rosemary and fennel, and top with parsley. Pour ⅓ cup of rum over the fish and ignite. Let it blaze until the herbs have burned down and flavored the fish steaks.

2. Broil thick steaks. Season with salt and pepper, sprinkle well with paprika and dot with buttered crumbs. Serve with a devil sauce (sauce diable, see index).

SAUTEED KINGFISH

Use either steaks or fillets, dip them in flour and proceed as for sauté meunière under "Cooking Methods."

SAUTEED KINGFISH A L'ANGLAISE

Dip steaks into flour, beaten egg and crumbs, and sauté in butter or bacon fat until nicely browned and cooked through. Salt and pepper to taste and serve with a tartar sauce or a sauce rémoulade (see index).

BAKED KINGFISH STEAKS AU GRATIN

Choose 1 steak per person. Dip in flour and arrange in an oiled baking dish or pan. Dot with butter and sprinkle with salt and pepper. Bake at 375° for 25 minutes. When they are cooked through, cover with a sauce velouté (see index) and sprinkle with buttered crumbs and grated Parmesan cheese. Brown under the broiler for 3 or 4 minutes.

1. Proceed as above, but add 1 cup of seedless grapes to the sauce velouté before pouring it over the fish. Omit the cheese.

2. Arrange the steaks in the oiled dish or pan. Top with paper-thin slices of onion and a slice of tomato. Salt and pepper and dot with butter. Bake 25 minutes at 400°, basting often. Serve with a tomato sauce (see index).

BAKED WHOLE KINGFISH

If you find a smaller-sized fish, one that you can cook whole, stuff it with your favorite stuffing and bake in an oiled baking pan with red wine. Bake at 375°, allowing about 9

minutes per pound of fish. Baste frequently with the red wine
and serve with a tomato sauce (see index) or a Spanish sauce
(sauce Espagnole, see index).

KINGFISH STEW

4 leeks, well cleaned	1 bay leaf
2 carrots	Sprig of thyme
3 stalks celery	Several sprigs of parsley
4 tomatoes, peeled and seeded	1½ pints fish stock
2 medium onions	6 slices kingfish
1 green pepper	Butter
6 tablespoons olive oil	½ pound shelled shrimp
2 cloves garlic	1 pint oysters

Salt, pepper

Cut the vegetables in julienne strips. Sauté them in the olive
oil. Add the garlic, bay leaf, thyme, parsley, and the fish stock,
made from the heads and tails of fish.

Brown the kingfish slices lightly in butter and add them to
the stock and vegetables. Simmer for 10 minutes. Add the
shrimp and oysters and cook for 3 minutes longer. Season to
taste.

Pour into a large tureen or bowl, garnish with lemon slices
and serve with garlic-toasted French bread.

COLD KINGFISH

Poach a whole kingfish (or a large piece of kingfish) in a
court bouillon (see index). When it has cooled, remove the
skin and serve with mayonnaise and cucumbers, or with a
sauce rémoulade (see index).

Ling Cod or Long Cod

DESPITE the name, this Pacific Coast fish is not a member of
the cod family, nor does it resemble the cod. It is a greenish
fish with brown spots, and its flesh has a greenish cast.

Ling cod averages about 12 pounds. It is sold whole, and in
steaks and fillets. The fresh fish sells well in West Coast
markets and the smoked ling cod is popular, too.

BROILED LING COD

Use steaks or fillets and follow directions for broiling on

page 15. Serve with lemon butter, parsley butter, Hollandaise sauce (see index), or sauce Béarnaise (see index)

BAKED LING COD FINES HERBES

Split and bone a small ling cod. Place it in a well-oiled baking dish, flesh side up, and sprinkle with chopped chives, tarragon, and parsley. Season with salt and pepper, dot with butter, and bake at 425° for 20 minutes, or until the fish flakes easily.

BAKED DEVILED LING COD

Split and bone a small ling cod. Place it in a well-oiled baking dish, flesh side up. Season with salt and pepper, cover with crisp crumbs, and dot with butter. Bake at 425° for 20 minutes, adding melted butter to the crumbs during cooking, if necessary. At the last minute, run it under the broiler flame to brown. Serve with sauce diable (see index).

BAKED LING COD MORNAY

Split and bone a small ling cod. Place in a well-oiled baking dish, dot with butter, and add ½ cup of white wine. Bake at 425° for 20 minutes, or until the fish flakes easily. Baste with the wine in the pan during the cooking process. When it is done, cover the fish with sauce Mornay (see index) and sprinkle with grated Swiss cheese. Run under the broiler flame to melt the cheese and brown the top.

POACHED LING COD

Follow the recipes for poached striped bass (see index).

LING COD TIMBALES

1 pound cooked ling cod	¼ cup heavy cream
3 egg yolks	Salt, pepper
3 egg whites	White wine or sherry

Flake the fish and pound it in a mortar, or mash it well. Blend in the egg yolks. Beat the egg whites until just light and gradually work them in with a wooden spoon. (It is better to do this over a bowl of ice.) Add the heavy cream and work it in thoroughly. Season to taste with salt and pepper and add a dash of sherry or white wine.

118

Pour the mixture into a buttered mold, and place the mold on a rack in a pan of hot water. Bake at 300° until the fish is firm, but be careful not to let the water boil. Keep the top from browning by placing several thicknesses of paper over the mold. Unmold and serve with shrimp or oyster sauce (see index).

Mackerel

EVERY spring the first mackerel boats are eagerly awaited by those who fancy this regal, well-flavored fish. The first taste of it is every bit as good as that of the year's first shad and salmon.

Not so many years ago, salt mackerel was a standard dish for Sunday breakfast, along with boiled potatoes and fresh hot biscuits. Nowadays, since the fresh fish is available the year round thanks to freezing, the salt variety has become rare.

Mackerel comes in sizes up to about 16 inches long. You may buy the whole fish, cuts, fillets and frozen fillets. It is rich eating.

BROILED MACKEREL

Split the fish and broil according to the direction under basic broiling methods.

FRIED MACKEREL

See fried fish under "Cooking Methods."

MACKEREL FILLETS SAUTE MEUNIERE

See directions for sauté meunière under "Cooking Methods."

POACHED MACKEREL I

Mackerel may be poached whole in court bouillon, or you may poach it as slices or fillets. Allow 8 to 9 minutes per pound.

Poach 6 mackerel fillets in court bouillon. Remove to a hot dish and surround with thin slices of fried eggplant covered with a tomato sauce. Reduce the bouillon and add it to a sauce

Mornay (page 25) well seasoned with cayenne and dry mustard. Pour the sauce over the fillets, sprinkle with grated Gruyère cheese or Swiss cheese. Brown the whole platter under the broiler for a few minutes.

VARIATION

Add 2 tablespoons of curry powder to the sauce Mornay.

POACHED MACKEREL II

Poach 6 mackerel fillets in court bouillon and remove to a flameproof serving dish. Reduce the bouillon by half and use it to prepare a rich velouté (see index). Season the sauce heavily with paprika. Cover the fillets with mushrooms sautéed in butter and seasoned with paprika. Add the sauce, sprinkle with more paprika, and run under the broiler flame to glaze.

VARIATIONS

1. Substitute curry powder for the paprika and serve with rice and chutney.
2. Add 1 cup of sour cream to the sauce at the last moment. Pour over the mackerel and glaze under the broiler flame. Serve with fried toast and a cucumber salad.

MACKEREL ITALIAN

6 mackerel fillets	¼ pound sliced mushrooms
Flour	6 or 8 chopped shallots or
Beaten egg	green onions
Crumbs	Tomato sauce
Olive oil	Parmesan cheese

Dip the fillets in flour, then in beaten egg, and roll in crumbs. Cook them in hot olive oil until nicely browned on both sides. Arrange in a flat baking dish. Add to the pan the mushrooms and shallots or green onions. Sauté them lightly and arrange on top of the fish fillets. Cover the fish and vegetables with a rich tomato sauce (see index).

Sprinkle with crumbs and Parmesan cheese and brown under the broiler flame for a few minutes. Spaghetti with oil and garlic is excellent with this dish.

SAUTEED MACKEREL FLORENTINE

2 pounds spinach or 2 packages frozen spinach	Pinch of nutmeg
4 tablespoons butter	6 mackerel fillets
Grated onion	Beaten egg
1 teaspoon salt	Crumbs
Juice of 1 lemon	Butter for sautéeing
	French-fried onions

Wash the spinach and cook, or prepare the frozen spinach. Drain, chop, and mix with the butter, onion, salt, lemon juice, nutmeg. Oil a baking dish and arrange the spinach in a layer on the bottom.

Dip the fillets in beaten egg and then in fine crumbs. Sauté lightly in butter until browned. Place the cooked fillets on the bed of spinach and top with a layer of crisp French fried onions. Serve with a tartar sauce (see index) and plain boiled potatoes dusted with chopped parsley.

VARIATIONS

1. Mix 3 cups of rich mashed potato mixture with 2 egg yolks. Arrange in mounds, or pipe through the large rosette end of a pastry tube on the bottom of a greased baking dish. Brush with butter and brown under the broiler flame. Place the sautéed fillets on top of this potato bed, sprinkle with chopped parsley and dress with lemon butter. Serve with a mustard sauce (see index).

2. Serve the fillets on a bed of sautéed onions. Top with grated Swiss and Parmesan cheese mixed. Run under the broiler flame to glaze. Surround with broiled tomatoes and garnish with anchovy fillets and black olives.

ESCABECHE OF MACKEREL,
HELEN EVANS BROWN

This is an excellent hors d'oeuvre or summer supper dish.

6 mackerel fillets	3 tablespoons lemon or lime juice
Lemon or lime juice	
Flour	⅓ cup orange juice
6 tablespoons butter	¼ cup green onions or scallions, chopped
2 cloves garlic, crushed	
⅓ cup olive oil	Dash of tabasco sauce
Salt	

Dip the mackerel in lemon or lime juice, then in flour, and sauté in butter until golden. Arrange the cooked fillets in a flat serving dish.

Prepare a sauce with the garlic, olive oil, lemon or lime juice, orange juice, green onions or scallions, and a dash of tabasco sauce. Season to taste with salt. Pour over the fish and chill for 24 hours. Serve garnished with quartered limes or lemons and ripe olives.

VARIATIONS

1. Sauté the fillets in ⅓ cup of olive oil. Remove to a serving dish. Add to the oil in the pan 5 cloves of crushed garlic, 1 finely chopped onion, and one shaved carrot. Cook until they are just colored. Add ¼ cup of vinegar, ¼ cup of water, ¼ cup of white wine, 1 teaspoon of salt, 2 tablespoons of finely chopped green pepper, a sprig of thyme, and ¼ cup of chopped parsley. Simmer for 10 minutes. Pour over the fish and chill for 24 hours.

NOTE: This recipe may be used for almost any filleted fish.

2. You may add any of the following seasonings to the sauces in either of the two preceding recipes: ground coriander; finely chopped Chinese parsley, or fresh coriander, or cilantro; toasted coriander seeds.

BAKED MACKEREL

Clean a mackerel weighing 2 to 4 pounds. Oil a large oval baking dish or pan and place the fish on it. Dot with butter, sprinkle with salt and pepper, and bake at 425°, allowing 10 minutes per pound of fish. Baste often. Serve with Hollandaise sauce (see index) or a tomato sauce (see index).

BAKED STUFFED MACKEREL I

Stuff the cleaned fish with thinly sliced onions, tomatoes, green peppers, and parsley. Sprinkle with salt and pepper and dot with butter. Sew the fish or tie it securely with string. Cook as above.

BAKED STUFFED MACKEREL II

1 whole mackerel	Butter
2 medium onions, finely chopped	2 tomatoes, seeded and chopped
8 mushrooms, finely chopped	3 eggs
1 clove garlic, chopped	Salt, pepper

Sauté the onions, mushrooms and garlic in butter. Mix with the tomatoes and lightly beaten eggs. Salt and pepper to taste.

122

Stuff the mackerel with this mixture, sew it up or tie securely. Bake as above and serve with a mustard sauce (see index) or a tomato sauce (see index).

BAKED STUFFED MACKEREL WITH WHITE WINE

1 whole mackerel	White wine
Stuffing for fish	4 tablespoons butter
Thinly sliced onions	4 tablespoons flour
Salt and pepper	Cayenne
½ cup heavy cream	

Clean and stuff the fish with your favorite stuffing. Arrange a bed of thinly sliced onions in the bottom of an oiled baking dish. Season and cover with white wine. Place the fish on top, and bake as above. When the fish is cooked, remove it to a hot platter. Put the onion and wine mixture through a fine sieve. Melt the butter in a saucepan, blend in the flour, and gradually add the strained pan juices. Stir until smooth and thickened. Taste for seasoning, add a little cayenne and the heavy cream. Blend thoroughly. Pour over the fish.

MACKEREL, CHINESE STYLE

1 2-pound mackerel	1 clove garlic
4 stalks celery	¼ cup bland oil
4 green onions	2 tablespoons soy sauce

Clean the mackerel and make diagonal slits on each side, slashing it to the bone. Chop the celery, onions, and garlic. Mix with the bland oil (preferably sesame or peanut oil) and soy sauce. Arrange this mixture on the bottom of a flat pan and place the fish on top. Cover and steam gently for a half hour, or until the meat separates easily from the bone. Serve with rice and something crisp—bean sprouts with almonds, perhaps, or asparagus cooked in the Chinese manner.

NOTE: The Chinese steam such dishes on the platter, plate, or bowl in which it is to be served.

Mullet

THE mullet, of which there are about a hundred varieties, has appealed to the tastes of the most diverse civilizations. The Egyptians cultivated it in the deltas of the Nile. The Romans were fond of it and planted it successfully in fresh-water ponds and lakes. It was also a favorite of the Polynesians and of the early settlers of Hawaii, where it was similarly cultivated. Today the mullet is the principal food fish of the South.

The striped, or jumping, mullet is the species that is so plentiful in the coastal waters of the Carolinas and Florida. A beautiful silvery acrobat, it is so active that fishermen locate schools of the fish at night by listening for splashing sounds.

Mullet is marketed chiefly in the South, but occasionally you find it elsewhere. It is usually sold whole, and averages 2 to 3 pounds in weight.

BROILED MULLET

The small whole fish are the best for broiling. Follow directions under "Cooking Methods." Serve with lemon wedges, lemon butter, or parsley butter.

SAUTEED MULLET

Either the small whole fish or the fillets may be sautéed. Follow directions for sauté meunière, under "Cooking Methods."

BAKED MULLET A L'ANGLAISE

Allow 1 small fish per serving, or 1 medium fish for two. Clean the fish, dip in milk, and roll in crumbs. Place on an oiled baking dish, season with salt and pepper, and dot with butter. Bake at 450° for 12 minutes, or until the fish flakes easily when tested with a fork.

Serve with maître d'hôtel butter (see index), lemon butter (see index), or tartar sauce (see index).

BAKED SPLIT MULLET

1 whole mullet, 4 to 5 pounds	Thyme
1 cup lightly sautéed onion rings	Salt, pepper
	Butter
½ cup chopped parsley	Finely chopped parsley

Clean and split the mullet. Place it on an oiled baking pan and top it with the onion rings. Sprinkle with chopped parsley, a little thyme, salt and pepper. Dot with butter and bake at 425° for 20 minutes or until the fish flakes easily. Serve with the pan juices and a little additional butter kneaded with finely chopped parsley.

NOTE: Recipes for striped bass (see index) may be used in preparing mullet.

Ocean Perch

THE term "ocean perch" appearing on frozen fillets, is the official trade name for rosefish, redfish, red perch, and sea perch. The fillets are apt to be any of these. Together, these fish account for a large proportion of the fish eaten in this country. The flesh is firm and rather coarse, and the flavor is delicate. Ocean perch is ideal for those who do not like a strong fish flavor but who enjoy the texture of fish. Since it is so bland, it adapts well to all sorts of cookery and sauces, and combinations of foods.

The fillets run about 6 to a pound and are practically boneless. They will thaw overnight in the refrigerator or in 3 or 4 hours if left out in the room. They may be cooked in the frozen state if you allow additional cooking time.

Some ocean perch fillets will have the skin on. Refer to instructions for cleaning and dressing fish, if you wish to remove the skin before cooking.

BROILED OCEAN PERCH FILLETS

Butter the fillets well and follow directions for broiling fish under "Cooking Methods." Serve with lemon wedges, lemon butter (see index), parsley butter (see index), or Hollandaise sauce (see index).

OCEAN PERCH SAUTE MEUNIERE

Flour the fillets and follow the directions for sauté meunière under "Cooking Methods." Serve with chopped parsley and lemon wedges.

OCEAN PERCH AMANDINE

8 to 12 ocean perch fillets	⅔ cup slivered blanched
Lemon juice	almonds
Flour	Salt, pepper
6 tablespoons butter or oil	Chopped parsley

Thaw the fillets. Dip them in lemon juice and then in flour. Sauté in butter or oil until delicately browned on both sides.

125

Remove to a hot platter. Add the slivered blanched almonds to the pan and let them brown very quickly. Salt and pepper to taste, add a dash of lemon juice and the chopped parsley. Pour this over the fillets.

Buy the chopped buttered almonds in tins and add these to the pan at the last minute.

FRIED OCEAN PERCH FILLETS

Follow the directions for deep frying fish under "Cooking Methods." Serve with a very highly seasoned tartar sauce (see index).

VARIATION

Marinate the fillets in lemon juice for 2 hours before frying them.

BAKED PERCH ESPAGNOLE

1 large or 2 medium onions	2 cloves
5 tablespoons butter or oil	1 bay leaf
1 clove garlic, chopped	2 grated carrots
½ cup chopped celery	½ cup white wine
¼ cup chopped green pepper	Salt, pepper
1½ cups tomato puree	12 ocean perch fillets
Grated Parmesan cheese	

Chop the onions and sauté them in the butter or oil. Add chopped garlic, celery, and green pepper and cook until tender. Add the tomato puree, cloves, bay leaf, grated carrots, wine, and salt and pepper to taste. Simmer for ¾ hour.

Oil a large baking dish and arrange the fillets on the bottom. Season with salt and pepper, top with the sauce, and bake at 350° for about 25 minutes, or until the fish is flaky. Sprinkle with grated cheese and serve with noodles or rice.

OCEAN PERCH FILLETS POLONAISE

Crumbs	3 medium onions, sliced
Flour	Fresh dill or dill pickles
Salt, pepper	Sour cream
8 ocean perch fillets	Chopped parsley

Line a well-oiled loaf pan with crumbs. Dredge the fillets in flour and season them with salt and pepper. Place a fillet or two in the bottom of the pan, top with slices of onion, then chopped fresh dill (or thinly sliced dill pickle), and cover with sour cream. Repeat these layers until all the fillets are used. Mask the top thoroughly with sour cream and bake at 375° for 25 to 30 minutes, or until the cream is a golden color. Unmold the loaf and sprinkle with chopped parsley and fresh dill, if available.

Serve with boiled potatoes topped with parsley, and cole slaw.

DEVILED FILLETS

12 ocean perch fillets	1 teaspoon dry mustard
½ cup Worcestershire sauce	1 teaspoon freshly ground
Juice of 3 lemons	pepper
¼ cup beefsteak sauce	Salt
½ cup chili sauce	Buttered crumbs
¼ teaspoon cayenne	Butter

Mix the Worcestershire sauce, lemon juice, beefsteak sauce, chili sauce, cayenne, mustard, and black pepper and spread this mixture on the fillets. Let them stand for ½ hour.

Oil a baking dish and place the fillets in it. Bake at 425° for 20 minutes, or until the fish is flaky. A few minutes before the fish is done, season to taste with salt. Remove the pan from the oven, sprinkle with buttered crumbs, dot with butter and run under the broiler to brown.

Serve with a sauce diable (see index) or mustard sauce (see index).

FILLETS MORNAY

Poach 12 fillets in a court bouillon (see index) until they flake easily. Remove them to a hot platter, and reduce the bouillon. Prepare a sauce Mornay (see index), using some of the bouillon. Arrange the fillets in a baking dish and cover with the sauce. Sprinkle the top with grated cheese (Gruyère, Cheddar, or Swiss), and run the dish under the broiler flame to melt the cheese and brown the top.

CURRIED OCEAN PERCH FILLETS

12 ocean perch fillets	5 tablespoons butter
Court bouillon (see index)	1½ tablespoons curry powder
½ cup each of chopped onion,	½ cup white wine
apple, and green pepper	Beurre manié (see index)

Poach the fillets in court bouillon for about 8 minutes or

just until they flake easily. Remove them to a hot platter and reduce the bouillon to 1½ cups.

Sauté the onion, apple, and green pepper in butter until tender. Add the curry powder and white wine and simmer for 10 minutes. Add the reduced bouillon and cook 5 more minutes. If you wish a thickened sauce, add beurre manié, and stir until smooth and well blended. Pour the sauce over the fillets.

Serve with rice, chutney, and chopped toasted almonds.

STUFFED FILLETS FOYOT

8 to 10 ocean perch fillets	Salt, pepper
1 tablespoon chopped onion	Court bouillon (see index)
½ cup chopped mushrooms	3 tablespoons butter
4 tablespoons butter or oil	3 tablespoons flour
1 tablespoon chopped parsley	½ cup cream
1 cup crabmeat	1 egg yolk
Lemon juice	

Thaw the fillets. Sauté the chopped onion and mushrooms in butter or oil until tender. Add the chopped parsley, crabmeat, and salt and pepper to taste. Blend well. Spread this mixture on the fillets, roll them and fasten with toothpicks.

Poach the fillets in court bouillon for 8 to 10 minutes or until they flake easily. Remove them to a hot platter and reduce the bouillon to 1½ cups. Add the butter and flour blended together to the bouillon, and stir until thickened and smooth. Gradually stir in the cream mixed with the egg yolk. Heat thoroughly but do not let boil. Taste for seasoning and add lemon juice. Pour over the fillets.

Serve with tiny boiled new potatoes and sautéed mushroom caps.

COLD OCEAN PERCH FILLETS

This is an excellent dish for a buffet supper. You can make it as simple or as decorative as you wish.

12 ocean perch fillets	1 envelope gelatin
Court bouillon (see index)	Garnish of tarragon leaves,
Egg white and shell	olives, hard-cooked egg

Poach the fillets in court bouillon for 8 to 10 minutes, or until they flake easily. Remove to a platter and let them cool. Reduce the bouillon to 2 cups, clarify with egg white and shell, and strain.

Dissolve the gelatin in ¼ cup of cold water and add to the

boiling court bouillon. Cool, and when it is almost set, cover the bottom of a large platter or serving dish with part of the jelly. Arrange the fillets on top. Decorate the fillets with tarragon leaves, olives, and hard-cooked egg cut into designs. You may make these as elaborate as you wish. (For suggestions on decorating cold fish, see recipe for Cold Halibut.) Brush the top of the decorated fillets gently with some of the jelly and set aside to chill thoroughly.

Serve with garnishes of salade Russe (see index), stuffed eggs and olives, and sauce rémoulade (see index).

Ocean Sunfish

THIS is a peculiar round, flat fish that appears to be mostly head and very little tail. It tends to grow quite large, about 8 to 10 feet across the flat side, and has a habit of lying almost motionless near the surface of the water. This trick has earned it the popular name of "floater."

Ocean sunfish are found in warm and temperate waters, but they seem to be considered food fish only in California, where commercial fishermen occasionally bring them in. The average size is 20 to 24 inches across, and two will serve four to six people. Both the skin and the flesh are tough and leathery, and special preparation is required.

OCEAN SUNFISH ITALIAN

Sunfish	Salt, pepper
Olive oil	Lemon juice
2 crushed cloves garlic	White wine
1 cup tomato puree	

First, split the fish in two very carefully and cut the flesh away from the skin. Put the flesh into a kettle with a little boiling water and simmer slowly for an hour to release the fat and the excess gelatinous material. Heat olive oil in a large skillet, add the garlic and the pieces of sunfish meat. Salt and pepper to taste, sprinkle with lemon juice, pour on a little white wine, and simmer slowly for a few minutes. Add the tomato puree and continue cooking until the fish is tender.

129

Pollock

A RELATIVE of the haddock and the cod, pollock is one of the great sources of fillets for frozen fish sales. It is a well-flavored white fish of good texture that holds up well under freezing. You will find it marketed throughout the country as "ocean-fresh fillets," "deep-sea fillets," and other similar labels. In New England it was once called "Boston bluefish," but somehow the name failed to stick.

You may prepare pollock in any of the ways given for haddock or cod.

Pompano

MANY people—I am not among them—think that pompano is the finest fish caught in American waters.

Most of the catch obtained off Florida and in the Gulf is consumed locally. Some is shipped north and sold to luxury restaurants. It is not a cheap fish. Pompano is thin, with a deeply forked tail and a beautiful silvery skin.

BROILED POMPANO

You may broil either a whole pompano or fillets. The fish should be well oiled or buttered, and the broiling rack should be piping hot and oiled before the fish is placed on it. Broil the fish about 3 inches from the flame or charcoal. Season to taste after cooking. For detailed procedure see "Cooking Methods."

Serve with lemon wedges, lemon butter, anchovy butter, or parsley butter.

POMPANO SAUTE MEUNIERE

Roll the fish in flour and follow directions for sauté meunière under "Cooking Methods."

BAKED POMPANO

Clean the fish, place it on an oiled baking dish or pan and

dot heavily with butter, season with salt and pepper, and add a few slices of lemon. Bake at 425° for about 20 minutes, depending upon the size of the fish. Test with a fork. When the fish flakes easily, it is done.

Serve with lemon butter, anchovy butter, or Hollandaise sauce. My favorite is a good Béarnaise, with a side dish of very crisp julienne potatoes, and grilled tomato.

POMPANO EN PAPILLOTE

This is one of the most elegant ways of preparing pompano. You may use either the whole fish or fillets. For each serving you will need 1 fillet or small whole fish, a heart-shaped piece of parchment that is big enough to wrap the fish in, 2 tablespoons of sauce duxelles (see index), and 3 mushroom caps.

Mushroom caps	Cooking parchment
Butter	Salt, pepper
Fillets or small whole fish	Sauce duxelles
Chopped parsley	

Sauté the mushrooms lightly in butter. Butter the fish well. Place the fish on the parchment, toward one edge. Season to taste, top with the sauce duxelles and the mushroom caps, dot with butter, and sprinkle with chopped parsley. Fold the parchment over the top of the filling and crimp the edges together securely. Bake in 425° oven until the paper is browned and puffed. Serve with shoestring potatoes and lemon wedges.

VARIATION

Place a thin slice of broiled ham on the parchment and top with the fish. Dot with butter, add 2 or 3 shrimp, a little chopped parsley, and, if available, a bit of chopped truffle. Proceed as above.

Porgy or Scup

THIS fish is found in nearly all Atlantic Coast waters and sometimes in the Gulf. There are a number of different varieties of the fish, all very popular as game fish. It has great commercial value, but is more readily obtainable in coastal markets than inland because it is so seldom filleted. It usually weighs from ¾ to 2 pounds.

SAUTEED PORGY

Follow the directions for sauté meunière under "Cooking Methods."

PAN-FRIED PORGY

Roll the fish in seasoned flour, crumbs, or corn meal and fry in butter or oil. Serve with tartar sauce (see index).

Redfish

THE redfish or red drum is a valuable commercial fish used extensively in Southern cookery. On the West Coast it is known as spot bass. In both the West and South it is regarded as a fairly good game fish.

Something of a gourmet in its own right, the redfish likes shrimp and crab, occasionally varying its diet with mullet and minnows. Redfish comes whole, in steaks, and in fillets. The fish vary in size from about 2 to 25 pounds.

BROILED REDFISH

You may broil steaks, fillets, or whole fish according to directions on page 15. Serve with lemon or parsley butter or with a sauce Italianne (see index), diable (see index) or Provençale (see index).

PAN-FRIED REDFISH

Use steaks or fillets for pan frying. Dust the fish with flour, dip in beaten egg, and roll in crumbs or corn meal. Sauté in butter or oil until nicely browned on both sides and cooked through. Salt and pepper to taste, and serve with lemon wedges, lemon butter (see index), or tartar sauce (see index). I like plain boiled potatoes with plenty of butter and cole slaw with this particular dish.

STUFFED BAKED REDFISH

This is a rather elaborate Southern recipe. I found it in an old handwritten cook book that had been carefully copied and thoroughly indexed by a fine old Louisiana cook. Even though I have toned down the recipe to some extent, it is still a rich dish and a pleasant curiosity.

1 pound lean veal	1 teaspoon dried tarragon
1 pound lean pork	6 tablespoons butter
2 medium onions	3 eggs
1 stalk celery	1 cup crumbs
2 sprigs parsley	1 5-pound redfish
1 teaspoon salt	2½ cups red wine
1 teaspoon black pepper	Salt pork
Dash of cayenne	Beurre manié
1 teaspoon paprika	Boiled potatoes
Dash of nutmeg	Mushrooms
Parsley	

Grind twice, or pound in a mortar, the veal, pork, onions, celery, and parsley. Add salt, pepper, cayenne, paprika, nutmeg, and tarragon. Sauté the mixture well in the butter and mix in the eggs and crumbs.

Clean the redfish and prepare it for stuffing. Fill it with part of the mixture, reserving the rest for a garnish. Sew up the fish and place it in an oiled baking pan. Cover the fish with strips of salt pork and add 2 cups of red wine to the pan. Bake at 350° for 30 minutes, basting every 10 minutes.

While the fish is baking, form the rest of the stuffing into small balls and sauté them in butter until nicely browned. Add the rest of the wine to the pan and poach the forcemeat balls until they are cooked through.

Remove the fish from the oven and place it on a hot platter. Combine the juices from the fish and the forcemeat balls, reduce slightly, taste for seasoning, and thicken with beurre manié (see index). Surround the fish with the forcemeat balls and boiled potatoes, and garnish with sautéed mushrooms and parsley. Serve the sauce separately.

BAKED REDFISH CREOLE

4 slices bacon	1 bay leaf
3 tablespoons butter	2 cloves
2 large onions	½ teaspoon thyme
1 clove garlic	Salt, pepper
3 cups cooked or canned tomatoes	4 or 5 pound redfish
	Sliced hard-cooked eggs
Olives	

Try out the bacon until crisp. Drain on absorbent paper and set aside. Add the butter to the bacon fat. Chop the onions and garlic and sauté them in the butter and bacon fat until tender. Rub the tomatoes through a sieve or put them through a food mill and add them to the onions and garlic. Add the bay leaf, cloves, thyme, and salt and pepper to taste. Simmer this for 30 minutes.

Clean the fish, but leave the head and tail intact. Salt and pepper the interior of the fish and place it in an oiled baking pan. Pour the sauce over the fish and bake in a 425° oven for 25 minutes, or until the fish flakes easily when tested with a fork. Baste often during the cooking.

Remove the fish to a hot platter and garnish it with the bacon slices, sliced eggs, and black olives. Pour the sauce around it. If the sauce seems too thick, dilute it with a little red wine.

With this serve saffron rice, garlic bread, and a salad of mixed greens dressed with garlic and oil. Amazingly enough, a *rosé* wine seems to be an excellent accompaniment.

CREOLE COURT BOUILLON

Follow the recipe for New Orleans court bouillon (see index), substituting redfish for red snapper.

POACHED REDFISH

You may poach either a whole redfish, a large piece, or fillets. Cook in a court bouillon (see index), and serve with any of the sauces used for similar fish: Hollandaise (see index), Béarnaise (see index), Mornay (see index), or oyster, shrimp, or lobster sauce (see index).

COLD REDFISH

Serve poached redfish cold with sauce rémoulade (see index), Béarnaise (see index), Mornay (see index), or oyster, vinaigrette sauce (see index).

COLD REDFISH BAYOU

1 3-pound piece of redfish	¼ cup chopped green pepper
1 sliced onion	¼ cup chopped celery
Salt, pepper	1 teaspoon dry mustard
¼ cup chopped green onion	1 tablespoon lemon juice
1 envelope gelatin	

Poach the redfish in boiling water with the sliced onion and salt and pepper. Cook for about 15 minutes. Remove it from the broth, and when it is cool enough to handle, skin it and take out the bones. Add these to the broth, and let it cook down one third.

Break the fish into small pieces and mix them with the green onion, green pepper, and celery. Moisten the mustard with the lemon juice, and blend it into the fish and vegetable mixture. Soak the gelatin in ¼ cup of cold water and stir it into 2 cups of the boiling fish broth. Mix the fish into the broth and gelatin, pour it all into a mold or loaf pan, and chill thoroughly.

When ready to serve, slice the fish loaf and arrange the slices on a bed of green. Serve with a sauce rémoulade (see index) or with vinaigrette sauce (see index).

Red Snapper

THIS colorful Gulf Coast fish has become widely known as choice food. It is a magnificent fish, 2 or 3 feet long and weighing up to 30 pounds. To see one resting on the ice in a market showcase is most attractive, and the fine flavor is just as appealing to the appetite.

Red snappers weighing around 5 pounds are often sold whole. The larger ones are cut into steaks and fillets. The meat is excellent prepared in almost any manner.

Other species of snapper, smaller and less colorful, are caught in the Gulf region, but are usually marketed locally. These include the yellowtail of Key West, the gray snapper, the muttonfish and the schoolmaster. All are fine eating.

In general, snapper may be prepared according to any of the recipes suggested for sea bass (see index).

BROILED RED SNAPPER

Follow directions for broiling under "Cooking Methods."

SAUTEED RED SNAPPER

Follow directions for sautéing under "Cooking Methods."

VARIATIONS

1. Just before removing the fish from the pan, add chopped garlic and parsley in equal proportions.

2. When the fish is almost cooked, add to the pan 1 tea-

spoon of fresh or dried tarragon and ½ cup of white wine. Swirl this around for a few seconds and pour it over the fish. Parsley is a pleasant addition.

FILLET OF RED SNAPPER AMANDINE

4 fillets of red snapper	Butter
Flour	½ cup blanched almonds
Salt, pepper	¼ cup melted butter
1 tablespoon lemon juice	

Dip the fillets in flour, season with salt and pepper, and sauté in butter until nicely done and brown. Meanwhile, chop the almonds and brown them in melted butter. Remove the fillets to a hot platter, and add the almonds to the pan in which the fish was cooked. Add the lemon juice, heat the mixture through, and pour over the fillets.

VARIATION

Add ¼ cup of dry white wine to the pan juices along with the almonds and the lemon juice. Quickly bring to a bubbling boil and pour over the fillets.

RED SNAPPER STUFFED WITH SEAFOOD

1 4-pound red snapper	1 cup chopped raw shrimp
Salt, pepper	1 cup chopped green onions
Butter	1 cup chopped raw oysters
Flour	½ cup chopped celery
1 cup dry bread crumbs	Bacon

Wash and clean the fish for stuffing. Season the inside with salt and pepper, rub it with butter, and sprinkle with flour. Mix the bread crumbs, shrimp, onions, oysters, celery, and season to taste. Add a lump of butter to the mixture, and stuff the fish lightly. Sew it up and arrange it on well-greased baking pan.

Sprinkle the fish with salt and pepper. Score the skin in two or three places and strip with bacon. Place the fish in a 350° oven and bake for about 40 minutes, or until the flesh flakes easily when tested with a fork. Baste often during the cooking.

BAKED STUFFED RED SNAPPER

1 4-pound red snapper	4 cups dry bread crumbs
Salt, pepper	1 cup minced cucumber
Butter	½ cup chopped toasted
1 large onion, chopped	almonds
1 clove garlic, minced	1 teaspoon thyme
White wine or sherry	

Prepare the fish for baking. Rub the inside with salt, pepper and butter. Sauté the chopped onion and minced garlic in butter until they are soft, and then add them to the bread crumbs, cucumber and almonds. Season all with salt, pepper and thyme, and moisten, if you wish, with white wine or sherry. Stuff the fish lightly, and sew it up.

Place the fish on a well-greased baking pan, season it with salt and pepper, and add a little white wine or sherry to the pan. Bake the fish in a 350° oven for 40 minutes, or until the fish flakes easily when tested with a fork. Baste occasionally with the pan juices, adding more wine and butter if necessary.

BAKED SNAPPER FLORIDA

This fine dish calls for a red snapper weighing 5 to 7 pounds. I first tasted it in the South, and the experience was memorable.

First clean and split the fish, leaving the head intact. Then prepare the following stuffing:

Bacon fat	2 cloves garlic
1 medium onion	2 cups dry bread crumbs
1 large green pepper	Fresh dill or dill seeds
3 beaten eggs	

Sauté in the bacon fat the onion, pepper, and garlic, all finely chopped. Add the bread crumbs, a touch of fresh dill or a few dill seeds, the beaten eggs, and another tablespoon of bacon fat.

Bacon fat or strips
1 cup red wine

Stuff the fish, and sew or secure it with toothpicks. Arrange it in an oiled baking pan, brush it with the bacon fat or strip it with bacon. Pour the red wine in the pan and bake at 400° for 35 minutes, or until the fish flakes easily when tested with a fork. Remove the fish to a hot platter.

| 3 tablespoons flour | ½ cup red wine |
| ½ cup tomato paste | Salt, pepper |

Chopped parsley

Blend the flour with the pan drippings, add the tomato paste and red wine. Stir constantly until the mixture is smooth and thick. Season the sauce with salt, pepper and chopped parsley, and serve with the fish.

This delicious dish should be accompanied by plain boiled potatoes and a chilled *rosé* wine.

POACHED RED SNAPPER

For one of the most elegant fish dishes in the country, poach a good-sized red snapper according to the directions for poaching fish under "Cooking Methods." Use a mild court-bouillon (see index), and serve with a sauce mousseline (see index) or sauce Béarnaise (see index).

Cold poached red snapper, jellied or plain, is very delicate. Serve with a good olive oil mayonnaise or rémoulade (see index). For a spectacular summer dish, serve a cold poached red snapper on a platter with cold lobster, the whole garnished with cold jumbo shrimp and greens. Sauce verte is the ideal accompaniment (see index).

QUENELLES MADE WITH RED SNAPPER

The finest quenelles are made with a combination of red snapper, sea bass and pickerel. The snapper gives them a body and flavor approximating the qualities of the famous French quenelles.

½ pound filleted red snapper	6 egg yolks
¼ pound sea bass	Salt, pepper
¼ pound pickerel or pike	Nutmeg
2 pounds beef kidney fat	8 egg whites
1½ quarts very heavy, rich cream	

Pound the fish in a mortar or grind it several times until it is pureed. Also grind or pound beef kidney fat until it is creamy. Combine the kidney fat and the fish, and then work in 1 quart of the cream, to which you have added the egg yolks. Season to taste with salt, pepper and a little nutmeg. Blend with the stiffly beaten egg whites, and then force the mixture through a fine sieve. Put the mixture in a bowl, set the bowl in ice, and work it with a wooden spoon, gradually adding 1 pint of extra-heavy cream. The mixture must be quite stiff so that you can mold it into egg-shaped pieces.

Poach the quenelles in boiling salted water for a few minutes and let them dry on a paper towel. They may be dropped into sauce at once, or they may be kept in the refrigerator and reheated in sauce later.

Quenelles may be served in a white wine sauce (see index), and they may also be served Lyonnaise: To sauce Espagnole (see index) add ⅓ cup of Madeira, and ½ cup each of sliced green olives, sliced sautéed mushrooms and sliced sautéed sweetbreads. Garnish, if you wish, with sliced truffles, and serve with toast points dipped in chopped parsley.

River Herring

THERE are two species of river herring along our Atlantic coast, the alewife or branch herring found chiefly in the North, and the blueback, whose range extends south to Florida. Like the salmon, river herring come into fresh-water streams to spawn. They are small and bony, weighing on the average about ½ pound. They are seldom sold fresh, but support a large industry engaged in preserving them in salt, curing them in vinegar, smoking and canning them.

The river herring may be prepared in any of the ways given for sea herring or for sardines (see index).

Sablefish

SOMETIMES miscalled Alaska black cod, sablefish is an extraordinarily good Pacific Coast fish that has been greatly neglected. It has a peculiar gelatinous fat—I find it delicate and very tasty.

Especially when it is kippered or smoked, the sablefish has few rivals. The smoked meat can be eaten raw or may be cooked in various fashions.

The fish is sold whole, in steaks and fillets, and in cured forms.

BROILED SABLEFISH

You may broil the whole fish, steaks, or fillets. Brush the

fish well with oil and follow the directions for broiling under "Cooking Methods." Serve with lemon butter (see index), white wine sauce (see index), or mustard sauce (see index).

DEVILED SABLEFISH

Broil sablefish steaks until not quite done. Press crisp buttered crumbs on top and finish cooking, browning the crumbs well. Serve with sauce diable (see index).

SAUTEED SABLEFISH

Use steaks or fillets. Flour the fish well and sauté according to the directions under "Cooking Methods." Serve with lemon butter (see index) or lemon quarters.

SABLEFISH A L'ANGLAISE

Dip sablefish steaks or fillets into flour, then into beaten egg, and roll in crumbs. Sauté in butter until the fish is cooked through and the crumbs browned. Serve with sauce soubise (see index) or a tomato sauce with curry added (see index).

BAKED SABLEFISH

Bake the whole fish, a section of the fish, or steaks. Place the fish on an oiled baking dish, dot with butter, and season with salt and pepper. Bake at 400°, allowing 6 minutes per pound.

KIPPERED SABLEFISH

You may eat the kippered fish plain or use it in any of the recipes given for finnan haddie (see index).

BAKED SABLEFISH CREOLE

When I was a child we often had this fish with an imitation Creole sauce.

2 to 3 pound piece of sablefish	2 medium onions
Salt, pepper	1 or 2 cloves garlic
⅔ cup red wine	6 tablespoons butter
6 to 8 tomatoes	Chopped parsley

Place the fish in an oiled baking dish, season, and add the

wine. Bake at 400° for about 25 minutes, basting with the wine frequently.

Peel, seed, and chop the tomatoes. Chop the onions and garlic, and sauté them in butter until they are just soft. Add the tomatoes and simmer until the mixture is thoroughly soft and well blended. Season to taste and serve poured around the fish. Top with chopped parsley.

POACHED SABLEFISH

Poach the fish in boiling salted water or in a highly seasoned court bouillon (see index). Serve with Hollandaise sauce (see index), sauce Mornay (see index), white wine sauce (see index), shrimp sauce (see index), or oyster sauce (see index).

CURRIED SABLEFISH

Poach sablefish and arrange it on a bed of rice. Serve with curry sauce prepared from the bouillon (see index). Pass chutney and crisp French-fried onions.

SMOKED SABLEFISH

Serve the smoked fish as you would smoked salmon (see index).

BROILED SMOKED SABLEFISH

Brush with oil and broil as you would fresh sablefish. Serve with lemon quarters.

SMOKED SABLEFISH IN CREAM

Smoked sablefish	Dash of lemon juice
1¾ cups thick cream	Black pepper
3 egg yolks	Chopped parsley

Remove the skin and arrange the fish in a gratin dish or oval baking dish. Put the fish in the oven to heat while you are making a heavy cream sauce.

Pour 1½ cups of thick cream in a pan and let it come just to a boil. Remove it from the stove and gradually stir in 3 egg yolks beaten with ¼ cup of heavy cream. Place it over a low heat and stir until thickened but do not let it boil. Add a dash of lemon juice.

141

Pour this sauce over the fish, sprinkle with freshly ground black pepper and chopped parsley, and run under the broiler flame to glaze.

Sprinkle with grated Swiss cheese before running under the broiler flame.

Salmon

SALMON has an international reputation, richly deserved, as gourmet food. Like beef, it is also popular among people of plain taste, and it is eaten even by some members of that minority of Americans who dislike fish in general. Both fresh and quick-frozen salmon are readily obtainable. Smoked, kippered, salted, canned and potted salmon may be purchased nearly everywhere.

The bulk of the salmon eaten in this country now comes from the Columbia River, Puget Sound and Alaska. There was once a time when salmon was also plentiful along the Eastern seaboard, but our forefathers fished the rivers so ruthlessly that the eastern catch has become commercially insignificant. Nearly all eastern salmon offered in the markets comes from Canada's Atlantic seaboard. In New York especially, smoked Nova Scotia salmon is sold as an expensive delicacy.

The decline of salmon fishing in the East has at least set an example for the West Coast. Eager to prevent its own extinction, the Far Western salmon industry has co-operated with the government in efforts to perpetuate the great "runs" of salmon that appear each year in western rivers. The migrations are not so large as they once were, but they are still awe-inspiring spectacles.

The salmon of the North Pacific is basically a salt-water fish. It spends most of its life span in the open sea, then returns unerringly to the fresh-water stream where it was born. There it spawns and dies. Its fingerlings migrate again to the sea, renewing a mysterious and fascinating cycle.

The mature salmon is a magnificent fish varying in size from 6 to 60 pounds, or even more. Vigorous and game, it is a spectacular jumper of rapids during its final journey to the spawning ground. It often migrates as far as 200 miles inland.

There are several varieties of Pacific salmon—Chinook is perhaps the best known—and the meat varies in color from very pale pink to reddish. Eastern salmon is usually paler than the western salmon found in the markets, and some people contend that the flesh is not so firm.

I was brought up near Astoria, Oregon, which is the center of the Columbia River fishing industry, and salmon was a steady part of our family diet. We never tired of it. My father, who had been a "covered wagon child" during the pioneer days, used to tell us how the Indians smoked and cured salmon for their winter food—and when I was a child, I too saw them spearing and smoking the salmon. Their recipe was beautifully simple. Having speared the fish, they cleaned it, split it, and put it between the branches of a sapling, often spiraea wood. Then they tied the twigs so as to hold the salmon in a sort of cage of wood. This they hung over the fire and slowly cooked and smoked the fish at the same time. This was known to me, when I was small, as Indian "barbecued" salmon. I can recommend it highly. For sauce, try lemon butter.

For broiling, sautéing or cutlets you may buy salmon steaks sized according to the fish. I suggest you have steaks cut 1 to 1½ inches thick. Some places sell fillets of salmon cut from the tail. For baking or cooking in a court bouillon, the best choice is a center cut or a half or whole fish. In our family we used a baby's bathtub for cooking any whole salmon that was beyond the size of our fish boiler. If you have a revolving spit with your outdoor grill or in front of your fireplace, it is no trick to spit and roast the whole fish. In my opinion, a whole salmon revolving on a spit is a pretty wonderful sight.

Fresh Salmon

BROILED SALMON

Whether this is done over charcoal or under gas or electric flame, the procedure is the same. The fish should be about 2 inches from the heat unit.

Brush the steaks or fillets well with oil and squirt with a little lemon juice. If you like herb flavors, you will find that rosemary, dill or tarragon are all delicious when cooked with salmon. Rub in a little of the herbs before you oil the fish. Place the fish in an oiled broiling pan which has been preheated and broil for approximately 5 minutes. Baste the fish

143

with the oil in the pan and turn and broil for approximately 5 minutes more or until the fish flakes easily with a fork. Salt and pepper and remove to a hot platter. Serve with plenty of lemon, plain boiled potatoes and a cucumber salad.

VARIATION

If you prefer a rich sauce with the already rich salmon, serve a Hollandaise (see index) or a Béarnaise (see index).

SAUTEED SALMON

Sauté your steaks in a mixture of butter and a small amount of oil. Because salmon is such an oily fish, not much lubrication is required. Flour the steaks lightly, brown on one side and turn with a large spatula. Salt and pepper the fish and continue cooking until the flesh flakes easily when tested with a fork. Do not overcook. Sprinkle with chopped parsley and serve with lemon. Pour the pan juices over the fish if you wish.

This needs no sauce with it. It is rich, oily and flavorful.

BAKED STUFFED SALMON

Choose any of the fish stuffings given in the section on stuffings. Salt the interior of the fish lightly and stuff it well. Use small metal skewers stuck through the edges to secure the salmon; lace with light twine. Place the fish in a lightly oiled pan and oil the surface of the skin. Bake at 350°, allowing approximately 10 minutes per pound, or bake until it flakes easily from the bone when tested with a fork.

You may bake a whole fish, half a fish, or a center cut. You can also bake salmon steaks and fillets (see "Cooking Methods").

POACHED SALMON

You may poach the whole fish, or half of it or a small piece. Prepare a court bouillon and, if you are going to make a cold dish, add some extra bones and heads of fish to make a rich broth. Wrap the fish in cheesecloth or thin cotton, leaving a length of the material protruding on either end to use as handles. Allow approximately 8 minutes per pound for poaching. Remove the fish and let it cool out of the court bouillon. Reduce the broth and strain.

SAUTEED SALMON WITH CREAM

4 salmon steaks
Flour
4 tablespoons butter
Salt, pepper

⅓ cup sherry
1 cup heavy cream
Beurre manié
Chopped parsley

Dust the steaks lightly with flour and sauté them in butter until nicely browned on both sides. Salt and pepper to taste. When the salmon is done remove it to a hot platter. Add the sherry to the pan and let it took down for a minute or two. Add the cream and beurre manié (see index) and stir until nicely thickened. Add chopped parsley, taste for seasoning, and pour over the salmon.

SALMON SAUTE FLORENTINE

4 salmon steaks
Flour
4 tablespoons butter
Salt, pepper

3 cups finely chopped
   spinach
1 clove garlic
1 teaspoon tarragon
Lemon juice

Dip the steaks in flour and sauté in butter until they are done. Season to taste. Serve them on a bed of chopped cooked spinach which has been flavored with garlic, tarragon and lemon juice. Surround with slices of boiled potato browned and crisped in butter and mixed with sliced mushrooms.

SAUTEED SALMON WITH CURRY SAUCE

½ cup finely chopped onions
6 tablespoons butter
4 salmon steaks or fillets
1 cup sour cream

Flour
2 tablespoons curry powder
Salt, pepper

Sauté the chopped onions in 2 tablespoons of butter until just soft. Remove them from the pan and add the remaining butter to the pan. Dust the salmon with the flour mixed with about 2 teaspoons of the curry powder. Season with salt, pepper. Sauté the steaks very quickly just until they flake when tested with a fork. Remove to a hot platter. Return the onions to the pan and reheat. Add the rest of the curry powder and blend well. Gradually stir in the sour cream and heat but do not boil. Check seasoning. Pour sauce over the salmon and serve with rice.

SALMON SAUTE WITH MUSHROOM PUREE

½ pound mushrooms
8 tablespoons butter
Salt, pepper
2 cups sauce velouté (see index)

4 salmon steaks
Flour
8 anchovy fillets
Lemon slices

Chop the mushrooms very fine and sauté them in 4 tablespoons of butter until they are thoroughly cooked and almost a puree. Salt and pepper to taste and combine with the sauce velouté. Dust the salmon steaks with flour and sauté in the remaining butter until they are nicely browned and flake easily when tested with a fork. Serve with the sauce poured around the fish. Garnish with anchovy fillets and slices of lemon.

BREADED SALMON STEAK NICOISE

4 salmon steaks
2 eggs, beaten
Bread crumbs
⅓ cup of olive oil
Salt, pepper

Anchovy fillets
Lemon slices
1 cup of tomato puree
1 clove of garlic
Ripe olives

Dip the salmon steaks in the beaten eggs and roll well in bread crumbs. Sauté them quickly in the olive oil until nicely browned and crisp. Salt and pepper to taste and arrange them on a hot platter topped with anchovy fillets and lemon slices. Serve with a hot tomato puree flavored with garlic and garnished with ripe olives.

NOTE: If the puree is too thick, thin it with red wine.

PLANKED SALMON

For this spectacular dish, you will want a whole salmon weighing anywhere from 3 to 12 pounds. (It would be wise to consider the size of your plank in choosing your fish.) Clean and wash the fish as for baking, being sure to leave the head intact. This will give you a juicer, more flavorful dish and also a handsomer one.

Oil the plank well and place it in a cold oven. Bring the heat up to 400°. Remove the plank and arrange the fish on it. Brush it well with butter, and salt and pepper to taste. Return the plank with the fish to the oven and bake. Plan on approximately 10 minutes per pound for cooking your fish, but to be sure of its state of doneness, test with a fork to see if it flakes easily. Shortly before you consider the fish done, remove the plank from the oven. Using a pastry tube, pipe a border of Duchess potatoes to decorate around the edge of the plank. Then pipe strips of the potatoes from this border to the fish in the center, like the spokes of a wheel, leaving spaces between to be filled with other vegetables. Brush the potatoes with butter, return plank to the oven and bake until the fish is done and the potatoes browned.

When the fish is done, fill the spaces between the potatoes with any vegetables you choose: small grilled tomatoes; tiny cooked green peas; tiny onions steamed in butter and glazed; bundles of cooked French green beans. Garnish the fish with rings of green pepper and lemon slices. Whisk to the table with a flourish and serve with any sauce you prefer.

SALMON WITH PUNGENT STUFFING

4 to 6 pounds salmon, dressed for cooking	Salt
	4 tablespoons oil
4 strips salt pork	

STUFFING

2 to 3 cups dry bread crumbs or zweiback crumbs	2 tablespoons olive oil
	¼ cup chopped parsley
1 cup ground cooked ham	1 teaspoon dried or 1 tablespoon fresh tarragon
½ cup finely chopped onion	
4 tablespoons butter	Salt, pepper

Make the stuffing first. Combine the crumbs and the ham. Sauté the onions in butter and oil until soft, add the other ingredients and blend thoroughly. If the stuffing is too dry, add ⅓ cup of sherry or vermouth.

Wash the salmon and rub both inside and out with salt. Stuff it rather loosely, and either sew up the sides, or run skewers through and lace with twine. Place the stuffed fish on a lightly oiled pan and top with salt pork slices. Bake at 350° for 40 to 50 minutes, or until the fish flakes easily when tested with a fork. Serve plain or with Hollandaise sauce (see index).

BAKED SALMON, OREGON FASHION

4 to 6 pounds salmon	3 to 6 sprigs parsley
Salt	Salt, pepper
Lemon	4 tablespoons olive oil
2 green peppers, seeded and cut in fine strips	4 strips salt pork
2 large onions, thinly sliced	2 cups tomatoes (cooked or canned)
4 large tomatoes, peeled and sliced	

Wash the fish and rub it with salt and lemon. Stuff it with the green peppers, onions, tomatoes and parsley. Salt and pepper lightly. Place the fish in a lightly oiled baking pan and top with slices of salt pork. Surround it with cooked (or canned) tomatoes and bake in a 350° oven for 40 to 60 minutes, basting occasionally with the pan juices. Remove the fish to a hot platter, blend the pan juices and taste for seasoning. Serve the sauce separately. Plain boiled potatoes and French peas are excellent with this dish.

NOTE: If you like, you can add chopped garlic and red wine to the cooked tomatoes to make a more flavorful sauce.

BAKED SALMON SCANDINAVIAN

6 to 8 pounds salmon	½ cup crumbs
1½ pounds fillet of whitefish or sole or haddock	4 tablespoons olive oil
3 eggs	4 slices salt pork
1 cup cream	Sauce velouté (see index) seasoned with chopped fresh dill and parsley
1 teaspoon salt	
1 tablespoon chopped fresh dill	

Put the whitefish through the fine blade of the grinder twice. Pound it in a mortar or work it over with a wooden spoon, mixing in the eggs and cream until the whole is well blended and smooth. Work in the salt, the fresh dill and the crumbs. Stuff the salmon with this mixture and either sew it up or secure it with skewers and twine. Place the fish on an oiled baking pan and top with salt pork strips. Bake in a 350° oven for about 1 hour or until the fish flakes easily when tested with a fork. Serve with a sauce velouté seasoned with chopped fresh dill and parsley.

BAKED SALMON SLICES IN SOUR CREAM

2 salmon steaks (2 inches thick)	1 tablespoon lemon juice
1 teaspoon salt	1 tablespoon chopped fresh dill or tarragon, or 1 teaspoon dried tarragon
2 cups sour cream	
1 onion finely chopped	Parsley

Arrange the steaks in a baking dish and salt lightly. Mix all the other ingredients except the parsley with the sour cream and pour it over the fish. Bake at 350° for about 35 minutes. Sprinkle with chopped parsley and serve with crisp shoestring potatoes.

BAKED SALMON SLICES WITH MUSHROOMS
AND SEAFOOD

2 salmon steaks (1½ inches thick)
Oil
½ pound mushrooms, sliced
4 tablespoons butter
1 pint sour cream
½ pound shrimp, finely chopped
Salt, pepper
Fennel or tarragon
1 teaspoon salt

Brush the salmon well with oil and place one steak on the bottom of a baking dish. Sauté the mushrooms in butter until just soft, add the chopped shrimp and let it cook for 1 minute. Spread this mixture on the steak in the pan, salt and pepper to taste and top with the second steak. Mix the herbs and 1 teaspoon of salt with the sour cream and pour it over the fish. Bake at 350° for 45 minutes or until the fish is done.

BRAISED SALMON BURGUNDIAN

6 to 8 pounds salmon
2 medium onions, thinly sliced
2 stalks celery, cut in strips
1 carrot, cut in thin strips
3 sprigs parsley
1 leek, cut in strips
5 tablespoons butter
Salt
1 quart (or more) red wine
1 teaspoon thyme
1 bay leaf
18 small white onions
3 tablespoons butter
1 pound mushrooms

Place the sliced onions, celery, carrot, parsley and leek in the bottom of a large fish cooker or braising pan with 5 tablespoons of butter and let cook over a medium flame until wilted down. Salt the salmon inside and out and place it on this bed of vegetables. Add red wine to half the height of the fish in the pan and put in the thyme and bay leaf. Let just come to a boil. Cover the fish with a piece of cooking parchment and place it in the oven for about 40 minutes or until the salmon is cooked through. Meanwhile, brown the small onions in 3 tablespoons of butter and let them cook through in a covered pan. Sauté the mushrooms lightly in butter and season to taste.

Baste the fish in the oven from time to time. When it is cooked, arrange it on a hot platter and surround it with the onions and mushrooms. Strain the sauce, and if you wish it thickened add beurre manié. Taste for seasoning and serve it separately. Plain boiled potatoes go well with this dish.

BRAISED SALMON IN WHITE WINE

Red wine is an important ingredient in the previous recipe. Is there really much difference when you use white wine? Definitely yes. The whole principle is different, the trimmings are different, and so is the flavor.

Finely cut onions, celery, carrot, leek, parsley (see previous recipe)	White wine
	½ pound mushrooms
	1 pound shrimp
Butter	1 cup cream or Hollandaise
5 to 7 pounds of salmon	sauce (see index)
Fish stuffing (see index)	Beurre manié (see index)

Prepare the vegetables and smother them in butter as in the preceding recipe. Stuff the fish with the fish stuffing and sew it or secure with skewers and twine. Place it on the bed of vegetables and add white wine to half the height of the fish. Bring it to a boil, cover the fish with parchment paper and place in a 350° oven.

Sauté the mushrooms in butter. Baste the fish during the cooking and about 5 minutes before it is done add the shrimp to the pan juices. When the fish flakes easily, remove it to a hot platter and surround it with the shrimp and mushrooms. Strain the sauce and reduce it to 1 cup. Add the cream and thicken with beurre manié. If you prefer, you may serve this with Hollandaise sauce.

BRAISED SALMON A L'AMERICAINE

Here we are back to an old friend, sauce à l'Américaine (see index), which, except for Hollandaise, is probably the greatest fish sauce in the world.

Prepare one recipe of shrimps à l'Américaine (see index) and let it stand for an hour or so. Meanwhile prepare braised salmon in white wine as in the preceding recipe (see index). When the salmon is cooked, remove it to a hot platter, and surround it with the shrimps à l'Américaine. This dish is sometimes served with the Hollandaise sauce or the white wine sauce from the pan juices, but to my taste it actually doesn't need anything in addition to the sauce à l'Américaine.

Be sure to serve rice with this.

PAPRIKA SALMON

1 tablespoon paprika	4 salmon steaks
Flour	6 tablespoons butter
Salt	½ cup white wine

1½ cups sour cream

Mix a little paprika with the flour and dip the salmon steaks in the mixture. Sauté them quickly in butter until the fish flakes easily. Season with salt. Remove the steaks to a hot platter. Add the wine to the pan, stir it around to mix well, and let it cook down to ¼ cup. Add the sour cream and additional paprika, blending it well, and heat through but do not let it boil. Taste for seasoning and pour over the salmon steaks. Serve with rice.

SALMON PIQUANTE

1 clove garlic, finely chopped	2 tablespoons lemon juice
1 small onion, finely chopped	3 tablespoons Worcestershire
5 tablespoons butter	sauce
4 salmon steaks	½ cup tomato sauce
Flour	1 garlic dill pickle, chopped

Salt, pepper

Sauté the garlic and onion in butter until just soft. Dust the fish with flour and add to the pan. Cook until they are nicely browned and just cooked through. Add the lemon juice, the Worcestershire sauce and the tomato sauce to the pan and let it cook down for a minute. Remove the salmon to a hot platter. Add the pickle to the sauce and taste for seasoning—it may need a little more Worcestershire sauce. Pour the sauce over the fish steaks.

NEW ENGLAND BOILED SALMON IN EGG SAUCE

There is a tradition in classic New England cuisine that the Fourth of July opens the season for eating new potatoes, new peas and summer salmon. The new potatoes must be the small ones, cooked in boiling water until just tender, then drenched with butter, salt, pepper, and a fine sprinkling of chopped parsley. The peas are smothered in wet lettuce leaves, with a large lump of butter, and cooked just long enough to make them tender without dulling their brilliant green. The salmon:

4 to 6 pounds salmon	3 peppercorns
Salt	1 bay leaf

2 slices lemon

EGG SAUCE

2 cups sauce béchamel (see   2 hard-cooked eggs
   index)

GARNISH

Lemon slices   Parsley

Wash the salmon and wrap it in a piece of cheesecloth, leaving the ends long enough so that you can easily lift it in and out of the pan. Heat 2 to 3 quarts of water mixed with salt and the other seasonings. Bring it to the boiling point and let it boil for 15 minutes. Reduce the heat until the water is barely simmering, add the salmon and simmer it for 15 to 20 minutes, or until it flakes easily. It generally takes 6 to 8 minutes per pound. Do not overcook it or it will be mushy.

Serve the salmon with egg sauce made by mixing coarsely chopped hard-cooked eggs with the sauce béchamel. If you like it that way, make your béchamel with some of the fish stock. Garnish the platter with lemon slices and parsley.

POACHED SALMON WITH VARIOUS SAUCES

Poach any salmon, from 1 pound to an entire fish, in any of the court bouillons. Allow about 6 minutes per pound of fish. It is wise to test to be sure the center of the fish is cooked. Serve poached salmon with:

1. Hollandaise sauce
2. Sauce Béarnaise
3. Sauce villeroi
4. Béchamel or velouté made with fish stock
5. Egg and parsley sauce
6. Sauce rémoulade
7. Sauce gribiche
8. Duxelles
9. Lobster sauce
10. Oyster sauce

Plain boiled potatoes, with butter and parsley, and peas are customary with salmon. I also like a puree of spinach or a puree of spinach mixed with sorrel.

COULIBIAC OF SALMON

This roll of salmon, a Russian dish, is one of the most unusual I have encountered. It is wonderful for buffet service, for it slices well and is easy to eat with a fork. With spinach or a salad it is a meal in itself.

For the crust use either a bread recipe or the following brioche recipe:

BRIOCHE

1 yeast cake or envelope yeast	4 or more cups flour
1 tablespoon sugar	4 eggs
⅔ cup milk	4 ounces butter

Pinch of salt

Dissolve the yeast and sugar in a little warm milk. Mix this with 2 cups of flour and additional milk to make a sponge. Set in a warm place to rise until double in bulk.

Mix the additional flour, the eggs, melted butter and salt with the sponge. Knead it for about 10 minutes or until it is satiny and smooth. Use the dough hook on your electric mixer if you have one. Set it aside in a warm place to rise again.

Now for the filling:

2 pounds salmon fillets cut in small strips	Paprika
½ pound cod or sole cut in strips	Chives
	Fennel
5 tablespoons butter	1 cup buckwheat groats or rice
Salt, pepper	
6 shallots	1 egg
½ pound mushrooms	2 cups rapidly boiling water
4 tablespoons butter	3 tablespoons butter
	3 hard-cooked eggs
	1 egg for brushing dough

Sauté the strips of fish lightly in butter for about 2 minutes. Salt and pepper to taste. Sauté the shallots and mushrooms, and add the herbs and seasonings. Mix the buckwheat with a slightly beaten egg, place in a skillet over medium heat and stir until each kernel is separate. Add the boiling water, cover tightly, and let steam for 20 minutes over very low heat.

Roll out the bread or brioche dough to a 14 by 20 inch oblong about ½ inch thick. Butter the dough and place layers of fish, buckwheat, sliced hard-cooked eggs and seasonings in the center. Then fold it over and tuck in the ends so that the dough seals in the mixture. Brush with beaten egg, sprinkle with crumbs (if you wish) and paprika, and let rise in a warm place for 20 to 30 minutes. Bake at 375° for 30 or 40 minutes or until nicely browned and cooked through.

Slice at the table and serve with Hollandaise sauce (see index) or with melted butter and chopped parsley.

NOTE: This may be prepared with boiled rice instead of the buckwheat kasha. Add chopped parsley and butter to the rice before mixing it with the fish.

SALMON ROLL

1½ pounds salmon cut in thin strips 3 inches long
½ cup olive or peanut oil or melted butter
4 tablespoons grated onion
3 tablespoons chopped parsley
Salt, pepper
Biscuit dough
Hollandaise sauce (see index)

Mix the salmon strips well with the shortening and flavorings. Prepare the biscuit dough and roll out to ¼ inch thickness. Spread it with the seasoned fish, roll and secure the ends. Slash the top diagonally. Bake at 375° for 30 to 35 minutes or until the roll is nicely browned and cooked through. Serve with Hollandaise sauce.

VARIATION

Roll and butter the biscuit dough. Cover with paper-thin slices of smoked salmon and sprinkle with freshly ground pepper and lemon juice. Roll and cut in thin wheels. Bake at 425° until nicely browned—about 15 minutes. These are delicious with cocktails.

SALMON PIE

2 pounds salmon cut in cubes
Salt, pepper
Paprika
½ pound shrimp
2 tablespoons finely chopped onion
3 tablespoons chopped parsley
¼ cup sherry or Madeira
2 cups sauce velouté
Rich pie crust
Beaten egg yolk

You can use either fillets or a large piece of salmon for this recipe. Remove the bones and skin, cut into cubes and dust with salt, pepper and paprika. Place the fish, the shrimp, onion and parsley in a casserole. Combine the sherry or Madeira with the sauce and pour over the fish mixture. Put a support in the center to hold up the crust, or else build the fish up in the center and pour the sauce around it. Cover with a rich pastry. (It is wise to roll it out about 1 hour ahead and chill it in the refrigerator.) Cut little leaves and decorations from the leftover pastry and decorate the crust. Brush well with beaten egg yolk and bake in a 450° oven for 15 minutes. Reduce the heat to 375° and cook for another 10 to 15 minutes or until the top is nicely browned.

SALMON PILAFF

2 large onions, chopped
4 tablespoons butter
1 cup rice
1½ pounds salmon cut in small
    pieces

Fish broth or white wine
    to cover
1 tablespoon curry powder
1½ teaspoon salt

Sauté the chopped onion in butter. Add the rice and cook 5 minutes or until lightly browned. Place in a casserole or baking dish with the salmon. Cover to 1 inch above the mixture with fish broth or white wine that has been brought to a boil with the curry powder. If the liquid is not salted, season to taste.

Bake at 350° covered for about 45 minutes or until the rice is tender and the liquid completely absorbed. If the liquid is absorbed before the rice is cooked, add more. Serve with chutney, crisp fried onions and chopped almonds.

SALMON EN BROCHETTE

2 pounds salmon cut in 1½ inch
    cubes
4 tablespoons lemon juice
Fresh dill

1 teaspoon salt
½ teaspoon pepper
1 pound mushrooms
½ cup of olive or peanut oil

Mix the salmon and seasonings and let it stand for 3 to 6 hours. When you are ready to broil it, place a mushroom cap on the end of each skewer, then 2 salmon cubes, another mushroom, more salmon, and end with a mushroom cap. Brush well with oil and broil, turning several times during the process, or bake at 375°, basting with the marinade. Serve with plain boiled potatoes and fresh dill. (If you can't get fresh dill, serve dill pickles.)

SALMON SOUFFLE

4 tablespoons butter
3 tablespoons flour
¾ cup milk
    Salt
1 cup flaked cooked salmon

Juice of half a lemon
6 eggs separated
Pinch of fresh dill or ½
    teaspoon tarragon

Make a heavy cream sauce with the butter, flour and milk. Season to taste. Add the salmon, lemon juice and the dill or tarragon and let it cool for a few minutes. Gradually add 5 of the 6 egg yolks, slightly beaten. Beat the egg whites until stiff and fold them into the mixture. Pour into a buttered soufflé dish. Bake at 375° for 35 to 45 minutes or until lightly browned. Serve with a Hollandaise sauce (see index). (Use the extra egg yolk in making the sauce.)

Canned Salmon—Hot Dishes

Following are some recipes particularly suited to canned salmon, as well as to cooked fresh salmon.

QUICK SALMON SOUFFLE

1 can condensed mushroom or cream of celery soup	5 egg yolks
1½ cups flaked salmon (fresh, canned or smoked)	6 egg whites
	Butter

Combine the undiluted soup with the salmon and egg yolks, slightly beaten. Taste for seasoning. (If you use smoked salmon, be sure you do not use any additional salt without tasting first.) Fold in the stiffly beaten egg whites and pour the mixture into a buttered soufflé dish. Bake at 375° for 35 to 45 minutes.

QUICK SALMON CURRY

1 onion, finely chopped	1½ tablespoons curry powder
3 tablespoons butter	Heavy cream or vermouth or white wine
1 cup flaked salmon	
1 can green pea or cream of celery soup	

Sauté the onion in butter until lightly browned. Add the salmon, the soup and curry powder, and blend well. Heat to the boiling point. If the mixture is too thick, add several tablespoons of cream or vermouth or white wine. Serve with rice and chutney.

SCALLOPED SALMON

1 pound can of salmon	½ cup melted butter
2 tablespoons lemon juice	½ teaspoon salt
2 tablespoons chopped onion	½ teaspoon pepper
1½ cups coarse cracker crumbs	1 cup milk or other liquid

Combine the salmon, lemon juice and onion. Blend the crumbs, butter and seasoning. Pile in alternate layers in a buttered baking dish and add just enough milk (or fish broth or tomato juice) to moisten the crumbs. Dot with butter and bake in a 350° oven for about 30 minutes or until nicely browned.

1. To the salmon and lemon juice, add ½ cup of finely diced celery, ½ cup of finely diced onion, ½ cup of finely chopped parsley and 1 teaspoon of freshly ground black pepper. Mix with cracker crumbs, butter and salt, and add just enough milk to moisten. Pile in a casserole and dot with butter.

2. To the salmon, add ½ cup of finely diced onion, 1 clove of garlic, grated, ¼ cup of finely diced green pepper and 1 tablespoon of chili powder. For liquid use ½ cup of chili sauce diluted with 2 tablespoons of Worcestershire sauce, a dash of tabasco and 2 tablespoons of sherry or red wine. Proceed as above.

3. With the basic mixture include layers of peeled sliced tomatoes sprinkled with chopped garlic and parsley. Add tomato juice with a dash of cayenne. Top the casserole with anchovies and dot with butter. Poke large ripe olives into the crumbs after 25 minutes of baking.

4. Mix the salmon with the crumbs and ½ cup each of finely diced celery, onion and parsley. Add 12 to 14 mushroom caps, 3 chopped hard-cooked eggs, 3 tablespoons of sherry and salt to taste. Moisten with milk, top with buttered crumbs and sprinkle with grated Parmesan cheese.

5. Brown eggplant slices in butter. Alternate layers of the eggplant, the salmon mixture, the crumbs and sliced peeled tomatoes. Top with buttered crumbs and moisten with tomato juice. Sprinkle with grated Parmesan cheese.

SALMON CUTLETS

1 can salmon (16 ounces)	1 teaspoon paprika
2 cups creamy mashed potatoes	Flour
1 tablespoon grated onion	1 egg
1½ teaspoons salt	Bread crumbs
Fat for frying	

Bone, flake and mash the salmon. Combine it with the potatoes and seasonings and form into cutlets. Roll the cutlets in flour, dip in beaten egg and roll in crumbs. Chill for one hour. Fry in deep fat heated to 390 degrees. Serve with egg sauce or Hollandaise sauce.

KEDGEREE

Kedgeree (or cadgery) may be made with either fresh

cooked salmon or canned or smoked salmon. (This dish is often made with other fish, such as cod, haddock, finnan haddie.)

1 pound salmon	¼ cup chopped parsley
4 hard-cooked eggs	1½ cups sauce béchamel
2 cups cooked rice	(see index)

1 or 2 tablespoons curry powder

Flake the salmon and slice the eggs. Place alternate layers of rice, fish, eggs, parsley and béchamel (which has been mixed with the curry powder) in the top of a double boiler or in a mold. Place over hot water and heat thoroughly.

You may wish to serve additional béchamel with curry as a sauce.

VARIATION

Omit the curry and use tomato sauce spiced with chili powder. Or instead of the béchamel use heavy cream—enough to moisten the mixture.

SALMON MOUSSE

See index for halibut mousse.

Smoked Salmon—Hot Dishes

SMOKED SALMON A LA BERNARD

4 to 6 medium potatoes	Butter
1 small onion	Pepper
1 pound smoked salmon	Chopped parsley

Peel and cut the potatoes into quarters. Peel and slice the onion thin. Barely cover with unsalted water and boil until just turning tender. Place the salmon on top of the potatoes and continue cooking until the potatoes are soft and the salmon heated through. Serve in bowls with the broth from the bottom of the pan, a dab of butter and a grind of fresh pepper. Sprinkle with chopped parsley.

SMOKED SALMON ROLLS

½ recipe of pastry	Finely chopped green onion
6 to 8 ounces thinly sliced	Freshly ground pepper
smoked salmon	Beaten egg

Prepare the pastry and roll out into a 9-inch circle. Cover the top with strips of the salmon and add seasonings. Cut the circle into wedge-shaped pieces and roll each one tightly, beginning at the outside edge. Brush the rolls with beaten egg and bake at 425° for about 15 minutes. Serve hot with cocktails.

Cold Salmon Dishes

GRAVAD LAX (SWEDISH MARINATED SALMON)

4 to 5 pounds salmon, dressed
    weight, bone removed
⅔ cup salt
½ cup sugar

1 tablespoon coarsely
    ground black pepper
Bit of saltpeter
Fresh dill

Cut the salmon into two even pieces. Mix the salt, sugar, pepper and saltpeter together and rub the salmon well with this mixture. Line the bottom of a deep pan or casserole with dill branches, place a piece of salmon on them, skin side down, sprinkle the top with the spices and add more dill sprigs. Place the second piece of salmon on this, skin side up. Put a board and a weight on top and place it in the refrigerator for 24 hours or more.

This dish is not cooked. The action of the spice and seasonings gives it an unusual texture and a remarkably good flavor. It is excellent sliced thin and served with black bread as a cocktail snack, or it is a pleasant addition to a luncheon plate of cold meat and salad. It should then be served with a vinaigrette sauce (see index).

COLD POACHED SALMON

The ultimate in summer dining is cold salmon. New York restaurants proudly advertise it, especially as the "season's first." It is a spectacular dish for a buffet supper.

Poach the salmon in a highly spiced court bouillon (see index). It is wise to use a cheesecloth or cotton wrapper for the fish so that you can lift it from the broiler without breaking it. (There are long fish boilers which are especially adapted to this form of cookery. If you do much fish cooking they are a fine addition to your kitchen. Hotel supply people handle them.) When the fish is done remove it from the bouillon and set the bouillon aside to cool. While the fish is cooling, carefully remove the skin and trim the fish so that it looks inviting. If you are serving a whole fish, you may want to leave the head and tail on it. This gives it a classical appearance. Arrange your fish on a large platter and garnish with sliced cucumbers, tiny tomatoes or sliced tomatoes, greens—parsley or masses of watercress—and thin slices of lemon with scalloped edges or cut into any fancy shapes you wish.

Serve the salmon with any of these sauces:

1. Mayonnaise	4. Gribiche
2. Rémoulade	5. Verte
3. Vinaigrette	6. Tartar

Cucumber salad is the traditional accompaniment, and a salad of string beans in vinaigrette sauce garnished with tiny artichoke hearts is another excellent addition.

VARIATIONS

1. Salmon steaks may be poached in court bouillon and chilled and served in the same way. They make an attractive platter if they are of fairly even size. Naturally they take much less cooking time than a large piece of fish.

2. Spiced salmon is another fine cold dish. After poaching the fish, reduce the court bouillon to half its volume. Flavor to taste with vinegar, herbs and seasonings; pour this over the salmon and let it stand for 24 hours. Drain and serve with a mayonnaise. The pickle should be highly spiced and quite well laced with vinegar.

SAUMON FROID AU CHAMBERTIN

Whole salmon with head	3 envelopes gelatin
Red wine court bouillon	Salt, pepper
(see index) (6 cups clari-	
fied bouillon)	

Prepare about 4 quarts or more of red wine court bouillon, using heads and bones of fish. (The amount you need will depend on the size of your salmon.) Wrap the fish in cheesecloth or place it on a rack and poach it until it flakes easily. This should take about 6 minutes per pound of fish. Remove the fish carefully to a large board or platter and let it cool. Take off the skin, cutting sharply at the tail and stripping it up to the head.

Reduce the bouillon to about 2 quarts. Clarify it with the white of an egg and the shell and strain it through a linen napkin. Dissolve the gelatin in ¾ cup of cold water and prepare an aspic, using 6 cups of the hot bouillon stirred into the gelatin. While the aspic is cooling, prepare the garnshes:

1 cup cooked small peas	Mayonnaise
1 cup finely cut cooked snap beans	Small tomatoes
	Ripe olives
1 cup finely diced cooked carrots	15 hard-cooked eggs
	Salt, pepper
1 cup finely diced cooked potatoes	Cucumbers, sliced
	Lemons, sliced

Mix the cooked vegetables with enough mayonnaise to bind them stiffly. Peel and scoop out the tomatoes and stuff them with the vegetable salad. Brush the tops with a thin layer of the aspic and top each one with a ripe olive. Cut the eggs in half horizontally and remove the yolks. Mash and mix with salt, pepper, chopped ripe olives and mayonnaise. Heap this mixture into the whites, or pipe it through a pastry tube. Glaze the tops with aspic. Brush the salmon with aspic, giving it a thick coating. It is sometimes better to give it a first heavy coating, then let it set thoroughly, and give it another coating. Decorate the fish with thin cucumber slices, lemon slices, and quarters of ripe olives and hard-cooked egg yolk.

You may arrange the platter as elaborately as you wish, for this is a show piece. Surround the salmon with the stuffed tomatoes and the stuffed eggs. Serve with either mayonnaise or sauce verte (see index).

SALMON CUTLETS IN ASPIC

6 salmon steaks	Fresh tarragon leaves, if available
White wine court bouillon (see index)	Hard-cooked eggs
2 envelopes gelatin	Cucumber

Poach the salmon steaks in the bouillon just long enough for them to cook through. Remove them to a dry towel or absorbent paper and take off the skin. Arrange the steaks in a deep platter or in individual serving dishes. Decorate them with tarragon leaves and hard-cooked eggs, or any other garnish you may prefer.

Prepare an aspic by dissolving the gelatin in ½ cup of cold water and combining it with 4 cups of hot clarified bouillon. Allow it to cool. When it is partly congealed, brush the decorated salmon slices with this mixture and place them in the refrigerator to chill. When the glaze is firm, pour enough of the rest of the gelatin mixture over the slices to cover them. Chill until ready to serve. Serve with a mayonnaise or sauce verte (see index).

161

MOLDED SALMON LOAF

4 salmon steaks
White wine court bouillon
(2 cups clarified)
1 egg white and shell
1 envelope gelatin
1 cucumber, seeded and cubed
Greens

1 medium onion, thinly
sliced
12 stuffed olives
3 hard-cooked eggs
2 pimientos cut in strips
Mayonnaise

Cook the salmon steaks in court bouillon until they are just cooked through. Cool them and cut them into small cubes. Reduce the bouillon to 2 cups, clarify it with the egg white and shell, and strain it through a napkin. Dissolve the gelatin in ¼ cup of cold water or broth and combine it with the hot bouillon. Let it cool until it starts to set.

Pour a thin layer of the gelatin mixture in bread pan or small mold and put it in the refrigerator to solidify. Arrange sliced olives, halved hard-cooked eggs and rings of onion on the bottom of the mold. Toss the salmon cubes with the cubed cucumber, the pimiento and more onion rings and arrange this mixture in the mold. Cover with the remaining gelatin and chill in the refrigerator. Unmold on a bed of greens and serve with either a mayonnaise or a sauce verte (see index).

SALMON STEAKS PARISIENNE

4 thick salmon steaks (about
2 inches, center cuts)
White wine court bouillon
(see index) (3½ cups
clarified)

1 egg white and shell
2 envelopes gelatin
Sauce verte (see index)
Asparagus tips
Hard-cooked eggs

Poach the salmon in the court bouillon until it is just cooked through. Remove to cool. Cook the bouillon down to about 4 cups. Clarify it with the egg white and shell and strain through a napkin. Dissolve the gelatin in ½ cup of cold water or bouillon and add the rest of the broth. Let it cool until almost set.

Remove the skin from the salmon steaks. When the jelly is almost set, combine 1 cup of it with 1½ cups of sauce verte. Give the salmon steaks a liberal coating of this mixture. Spread the jellied bouillon in the bottom of a rather deep platter, arrange the salmon on top of this and decorate with asparagus tips and hard-cooked eggs. Serve with additional sauce verte (see index).

Cold Canned Salmon

Canned salmon comes in various grades. Some very choice cuts are put up in cans, and there are some very inferior grades. These days, because of the requirements of Federal law, you can usually judge the quality from the labels. Good grades of salmon may be served in one piece, chilled, with a mayonnaise and cucumber salad. Garnish it any way you choose. Be sure to remove the skin, which is often unsightly.

Here are several salad recipes suitable for either canned or fresh-cooked salmon.

SALMON MAYONNAISE

2 cups cold flaked salmon	Cucumber or cooked
Mixed greens	peas in vinaigrette
Mayonnaise	sauce (see index)

Arrange the salmon on a bed of greens. Top with mayonnaise and decorate with sliced cucumbers or cold cooked peas that have marinated in a vinaigrette sauce. Serve with additional mayonnaise.

SALMON CELERY SALAD

2 cups cold salmon	Greens
1 cup finely diced celery	¼ cup chopped parsley
Mayonnaise	Hard-cooked eggs

Combine flaked salmon and celery and bind them with mayonnaise. Heap the mixture on a bed of greens, sprinkle liberally with chopped parsley, and decorate with sliced or quartered hard-cooked eggs.

SALMON SALAD BOATS

6 cucumbers	1 cup cooked peas
Greens	½ cup chopped green onion
1½ cup cold flaked salmon	2 chopped hard-cooked eggs
½ cup finely diced celery	Mayonnaise

Cut a piece, the long way, from each cucumber, remove the seeds and make the cucumbers into boats. Arrange them on beds of greens. Combine all the other ingredients, binding them together with mayonnaise, and fill the cucumbers with this mixture.

Use tomatoes or avocado halves for the boats.

Cold Dishes with Smoked Salmon

SMOKED SALMON CORNUCOPIAS

Roll perfect slices of smoked salmon into small cornucopias and secure them with toothpicks. Fill them with a mixture of cream cheese combined with freshly grated horseradish. Serve for hors d'oeuvre.

CANAPE DANOIS

This is merely a round or square of fried toast with a layer of smoked salmon topped with a thin slice of ham and decorated with olives. Serve it as a first course with a little horseradish sauce (horseradish mixed with sour cream).

SMOKED SALMON APPETIZERS

The finest quality of smoked salmon has practically no salt content and has a very delicate flavor. This is expensive, but worth it. Serve thin—very thin—shavings of this fish delicacy, and allow several to each portion. The usual and certainly the best accompaniments are freshly ground black pepper, capers, and thin slices of Spanish or red Italian onion in an olive oil and lemon dressing. Pumpernickel or rye bread and butter sandwiches go with this.

SMOKED SALMON SANDWICHES

These may be used for luncheon or supper sandwiches or cut into small bits to serve with cocktails. Smoked salmon calls for rye or pumpernickel or a heavy whole wheat bread. It also needs plenty of butter—preferably unsalted. Try these combinations:

1. Smoked salmon, coarse black pepper
2. Smoked salmon, cream cheese, sliced onion
3. Smoked salmon, onion, ham
4. Smoked salmon, cream cheese, sliced egg, sliced onion

Other Salmon Dishes

SALT SALMON AND SALMON BELLY

Both these preserved parts of salmon, as well as salmon

tips, are very salty. Soak them for several hours or overnight before cooking. They are all primarily breakfast or luncheon dishes. Steam or poach them until they are tender and flaky, and serve with a sauce béchamel to which you have added chopped parsley and chopped hard-cooked eggs.

SALMON CHEEKS

These tiny delicacies—they are about the size of a fifty-cent piece—are hard to come by. If you live near the canneries or in the salmon district, possibly you can get some. To my taste, the cheeks are the very best part of the fish. They should be lightly dipped in flour and sautéed in butter. Serve them with lemon and finely chopped parsley.

Cheeks are often kippered and put in tins or glasses for cocktail tidbits. They are remarkably good.

KIPPERED SALMON

Kippered salmon is fish that has been cooked while it was being smoked. It has a pleasant flavor and is a most attractive luncheon dish with salad. Or it may be heated for a breakfast or supper. Flaked and mixed with horseradish, chopped fresh dill and sour cream, it makes a wonderful spread for sandwiches or canapés.

SALMON ROE

The roe of salmon, like that of similar fish, is a delicacy of which many people are very fond. Try it sautéed or poached. (See index for shad roe.)

Sand Dabs

UNFORTUNATELY this delightful morsel is not available outside the state of California. I can think of no other fish that is so delicately, subtly flavored.

BROILED SAND DABS

To broil these delicate fish, anoint them well with butter and cook quickly. The meat must not harden or dry out or the perfect texture will be destroyed. Season to taste and serve with a delicate sauce.

To my taste, the best way a sand dab can be cooked is sauté meunière. (See index).

BAKED SAND DABS

Helen Evans Brown says in her *West Coast Cook Book* that sand dabs are excellent cooked in parchment, as follows:

Cut heart-shaped pieces of cooking parchment, big enough to hold filleted, skinned pieces of sand dab. Butter the paper well and place a fillet on each piece of parchment, a little to one side. Season with salt and pepper. Add a thin slice of ham, 2 or 3 mushroom caps which have been lightly cooked in butter, and a sprinkling of chives and parsley. Fold the parchment over and crimp the edges together. Bake at 425° until the paper is puffy and brown.

Sardines

No doubt there are many children—and possibly some adults —who think that sardines are caught in cans. The fresh fish are available also, and may be prepared in a variety of ways. For myself, I prefer them tinned.

Actually, there is no one fish named "sardine." The term refers to any tiny fish with weak bones that can be preserved in oil. They are probably called sardines because they were first prepared in this manner on the island of Sardinia. In the Mediterranean and in the English Channel the pilchard is used for sardines. The Norwegian sardine is the brisling or sprat. Our East Coast variety is an infant alewife or herring, while the West Coast version, as in the Mediterranean, is the pilchard.

The sardines of Maine and California would be "tops" if the packers seasoned them well and used good oil. Since this is not the case, I recommend the fine Portuguese and the incomparable French sardines, whole, and skinned and boned. Try also the smaller Norwegian fish.

Sardines are the perfect emergency food. If your shelves are stocked with these, and good canned salmon and tuna, you need never worry about feeding the unexpected guest.

Fresh Sardines

Either the pilchard of the West or the infant alewife or herring of the East cooks well and makes a tasty dish.

GRILLED SARDINES

Split and bone the fish. Dip them in milk and crumbs and sauté them in butter very quickly until nicely browned on both sides. Serve with a tartar sauce (see index), a lemon-flavored vinaigrette sauce (see index), or a mustard sauce (see index).

FRIED SARDINES

Wash and clean the fish. Dip them in flour, in beaten egg, and then in corn meal or crumbs. Fry until nicely brown and crisp in deep hot fat heated to 375°. Remove to absorbent paper and season to taste. Serve with tartar sauce or tomato sauce. Fried parsley (see index) as an accompaniment is a "must."

BAKED SARDINES

Bone the fish or not, as you choose. Arrange the sardines in a buttered baking dish or pan and top with finely cut shallots or green onions. (About 4 to a fish.) Season to taste, dot with butter, and barely cover with white wine. Bake at 425° for 12 to 15 minutes.

Serve with plain boiled potatoes and grilled tomatoes.

SARDINES IN ESCABECHE

This recipe is suitable for any small fish. It makes an outstanding first course or luncheon dish.

36 fresh sardines	1 teaspoon freshly ground
⅔ cup olive oil	black pepper
Flour	½ teaspoon thyme
Salt, pepper	¾ cup chopped parsley
2 small carrots	½ cup wine vinegar
1 medium onion	⅔ cup water
1 clove of garlic	Pimiento
1 bay leaf	Green pepper

Clean the sardines but leave their heads and tails intact. Heat the oil in a skillet. Dust the fish with flour, and salt and pepper them to taste. Sauté them in the oil just long enough to brown. Remove to a hot dish.

Add thinly sliced carrots and onion to the oil and let them cook until almost tender. Add garlic, bay leaf, black pepper, thyme and parsley. Pour the wine vinegar and water over this and bring it to a boil. Add the sardines and simmer for about 5 minutes. Let the fish cool in the sauce and chill thoroughly before serving. Decorate with strips of pimiento and green pepper.

Serve with a cucumber salad for contrast.

Canned Sardines

Few simple meals are tastier than a can of fine sardines, lemon, good bread and sweet butter, and a glass of chilled white wine or beer. But here are some suggestions for "dolling up" the tinned variety.

GRILLED SARDINES

Carefully remove the fish from the tin. (There is a new permanent key for sardine cans that has a good lifter as part of the gadget.) Arrange the sardines in a shallow pan or rack and pour the oil over them. Run them under the broiler flame just long enough to heat through. Serve on pieces of fried toast with lemon wedges.

This makes a good first course as well as a good luncheon or supper dish.

VARIATIONS

1. Sprinkle the sardines with a little curry powder and chopped parsley and give them a squeeze of lemon juice. Grill them and serve them on toast with chutney.

2. Arrange sardines on a baking sheet, sprinkle with lemon juice and grated Swiss Gruyère or Switzerland Swiss cheese. Broil until the cheese melts. Serve on fried toast.

3. Grill sardines with curry powder and serve on a bed of scrambled eggs.

4. Arrange grilled sardines on fried toast. Cover with a sauce Mornay and run under the broiler flame for a minute or two.

SARDINE PUFFS

1 can skinned and boned
    sardines
2 tablespoons onion juice
⅔ cup grated Gruyère or
    Cheddar cheese

1 teaspoon freshly ground
    black pepper
2 egg whites, stiffly beaten
    Bread

Mash the sardines with a fork. Add the onion juice, cheese and pepper and blend thoroughly. Fold in the beaten egg whites. Toast slices of bread on one side. Spread the sardine mixture on the untoasted side and place under the broiler flame or in a 450° oven. Cook until they puff and brown lightly. Serve for a first course or as a cocktail snack.

SARDINE TURNOVERS

Sardines	Grated onion
Pastry or puff paste	Chopped parsley
Lemon juice	Beaten egg yolk

Roll pastry or puff paste out thin and cut into circles large enough to accommodate a whole sardine with some room to spare. Place a sardine to one side of each circle. Sprinkle with lemon juice, a bit of grated onion, and chopped parsley. Fold the pastry over and crimp the edges. Brush the top with beaten egg yolk. Bake at 450° until the pastry is puffed and brown—about 12 to 15 minutes. Serve hot with cocktails or as a first course for luncheon or dinner.

SUMMER SUPPER IN A HURRY

For a perfect summer meal prepared in a rush, open 1 or 2 tins of fine sardines, a tin of solid-pack tuna, and perhaps a tin of crabmeat or the frozen lobster meat that comes in tins. Arrange these delicacies on a large platter with hard-boiled eggs, wedges of tomato, and plenty of sweet onions sliced to transparent thinness. Accompany this with a bowl of mayonnaise, some good pumpernickel bread and sweet butter. Serve chilled white wine or beer.

This same dish may be served to a large group as a first course at dinner if you plan to follow it with a rather light meat course.

SARDINE SALAD

Arrange a bed of greens and make a sunburst of sardines in the center. Garnish with halved hard-cooked eggs, onion rings, pimiento strips, and capers. Serve with a bowl of mayonnaise.

For 2 servings, use 1 large can of sardines, 4 eggs and 1 onion.

For 6 servings, use 3 cans of sardines, 12 eggs, and 2 large onions.

169

NORWEGIAN SARDINE APPETIZER

2 pounds cream cheese	Salt, pepper
⅓ cup lemon juice	Paprika
3 to 4 cans sardines	Onion juice

This is strictly a spread and a wonderful one.

Mash the cream cheese well with a fork. Beat in the lemon juice, bit by bit, and then beat in the well-mashed sardines. Season with salt, black pepper and paprika, and blend the mixture thoroughly. (If you are going to eat it all during one sitting, add a little onion juice; if you plan to keep some, omit the onion to avoid a stale taste.)

Spoon the mixture into a well-oiled mold and chill thoroughly. Unmold on a large plate and surround with pumpernickel fingers and crackers. Let people do their own spreading.

This is a favorite dish of mine for parties. I vary the seasonings, but the basic flavors must be sardine and lemon.

Sculpin

THIS is a bony fish with a large meaty head. Although it is common in Atlantic waters it does not seem to be well known in the eastern area of the country. On the Pacific Coast, however, some sculpin is sold commercially in California markets, usually whole. I am sure that if you try it you will find it an excellent food fish.

BROILED SCULPIN

Follow the directions for broiling under "Cooking Methods."

BAKED SCULPIN

Follow the recipe for baked striped bass (see index).

Sea Bass

THIS popular game fish is a member of a large family of fishes that includes the groupers and the jewfish. Varieties are caught on both coasts, and the Atlantic sea bass is commercially important in the Middle Atlantic region.

The sea bass usually sold in Eastern markets lurk around sunken ships and pilings just off shore, a habit that makes trawl-fishing difficult. As a result, some of the commercial catch is taken in fishpots.

Market sizes range from about ½ pound to 5 pounds, and the fish is sometimes cut into steaks or fillets. Cooked and on the table, sea bass clearly resembles its relatives. It can be prepared in any of the ways suggested for striped bass.

(See also California black sea bass.)

SEA BASS ITALIAN

Butter	1 teaspoon salt
⅔ cup each of finely cut onion, carrot, celery	1 teaspoon pepper
	1½ cups red wine
Several sprigs of parsley	½ cup water
Sprig of thyme	1 whole sea bass
1 bay leaf	3 tablespoons butter
2 cloves garlic	3 tablespoons flour
Juice of 1 lemon	

Butter a good-sized saucepan or Dutch oven. Add all the vegetables and herbs, salt and pepper, wine and water. Bring it to a boil. Place the cleaned fish on the bed of vegetables, cover the pan, and simmer for 15 to 18 minutes, or until the fish is cooked.

While the fish is cooking, melt the butter in a pan and blend in the flour. Remove the fish to a hot platter, strain the bouillon and add it gradually to the mixed butter and flour. Stir until thickened. Taste for seasoning, add the juice of a lemon and serve with the fish. Baked rice and asparagus are good with this dish. Also a bottle of *rosé* wine.

SAUTEED SEA BASS

The small sea bass are delicious when sautéed and served with a tartar sauce or a rémoulade. I shall always remember a hot summer day when we sat down to a platter heaped with them—they had been caught that morning and were as delectable as any fish could be.

Clean the sea bass, roll in flour, dip in egg, and then in dry bread crumbs. Sauté quickly in butter or olive oil, browning well on both sides. Salt and pepper to taste. Serve crisp and

171

hot with your favorite sauce. Boiled potatoes and grilled tomatoes are an ideal accompaniment.

SEA BASS FILLETS PACIFIC

Sea bass caught on the Pacific Coast are larger than the Eastern variety and more often sold as fillets.

Marinate 2 good-sized fillets in lemon or lime juice for an hour. Dip them in flour, again in the lemon or lime juce, and roll them in sesame seeds. Sauté them in olive oil until nicely browned on both sides and cooked through. Season to taste with salt and pepper. Serve with lemon butter (see index).

SEA BASS AMANDINE

Split a good-sized sea bass and rub it well with butter. Sprinkle with sliced blanched almonds and salt and pepper. Place in an oiled baking dish or pan and bake at 400° for 20 to 25 minutes. Baste during the cooking with the butter in the pan.

HELEN EVANS BROWN'S BROILED
SEA BASS SESAME

1 sea bass (3 or 4 pounds)	2 ounces whiskey or brandy
2 cloves garlic	2 ounces lemon juice
1 tablespoon salt	½ cup butter, melted
2 tablespoons soy sauce	1 cup or more of sesame seeds

Slivers of ginger (if desired)

Split the fish and remove the backbone. Grind the garlic very fine or pound it in a mortar with the tablespoon of salt. Or you may crush it and mix it in a bowl with a heavy wooden spoon. Rub this mixture on the fish and let it stand for at least 1 hour—2 or 3 will make it much better. Prepare a basting sauce with the soy sauce (use more than 2 tablespoons if you like the flavor), the whiskey or brandy, the lemon juice, and melted butter. Paint the fish with this mixture before and during the broiling process. This dish is much better if charcoal-broiled; in this case you should place it in a hinged broiler so that it can be turned. If you broil it in the oven, cook it skin side down.

Broil until pleasantly browned and then sprinkle heavily with sesame seeds. Continue broiling until the seeds are well toasted. Serve on a hot platter with wedges of lemon or lime.

Slivers of ginger (fresh or preserved) may be added to the basting sauce if you like the zest they give.

Sea Trout

AMONG the fish that bear this name are the California corbina, the white sea trout, the spotted weakfish or spotted sea trout, and the weakfish or gray sea trout. The weakfish is sought along the Middle Atlantic Coast by both anglers and commercial fishermen. Its name implies no lack of strength, but tenderness of flesh.

All sea trout like warm weather. At times they venture north, and when they are caught in unusually low temperatures, their flavor and texture are badly affected.

Since they are small, sea trout are usually sold whole, although you may find some fillets cut from larger fish.

SEA TROUT SAUTE MEUNIERE

Follow directions under "Cooking Methods."

BROILED SEA TROUT

Clean and split the fish, sprinkle with seasonings, and broil according to the directions under "Cooking Methods."

VARIATION

Follow directions for bass flambé (see index).

SEA TROUT BROILED OUTDOORS

Broil a whole sea trout over charcoal, basting it with a white wine and butter sauce. When almost done, brush well with a spicy barbecue sauce (see index) and let the fish glaze. Serve with additional barbecue sauce.

SEA TROUT SAUTEED WITH ALMONDS

See directions for sea bass amandine.

PAN-FRIED SEA TROUT

Dip small whole fish or fillets in flour, then in beaten egg, and roll in any of the following: buttered crumbs, corn meal, cracker crumbs, sesame seeds, crumbs mixed with chopped nuts, or cornflakes. Pan fry quickly in butter or oil until brown and crisp and cooked through. Serve with lemon or sauce rémoulade (see index).

SEA TROUT SAUTEED WITH TARRAGON

Sea trout	¼ cup chopped parsley
Flour	¼ cup chopped tarragon
Butter	½ cup white wine

Use either fillets or whole sea trout. Clean the fish and flour lightly. Sauté in butter until nicely browned on both sides. Season to taste and remove to a hot platter. Add the chopped parsley and tarragon to the pan. Add the wine and let it cook down for 1 minute. Pour this over the fish. Serve with boiled potatoes and sautéed mushrooms.

BAKED SEA TROUT

Follow the directions for striped bass (see index).

BAKED SEA TROUT CALIFORNIA

Sea trout	Basil leaves, fresh or dried
Sliced onions	2 cups tomato puree
Chopped parsley	½ cup red wine
Salt, freshly ground pepper	

Clean the fish and stuff with onion slices, parsley and basil. Arrange on an oiled baking pan. Make a sauce with tomato puree and red wine seasoned with basil, salt and pepper. Pour this over the fish. Bake at 400° for about 20 minutes, basting twice during the cooking process.

Serve with green noodles tossed with butter and grated Parmesan cheese. This exotic dish takes to a fine *rosé* wine.

BAKED SEA TROUT SCANDINAVIAN

2 small sea trout	Sour cream
Parsley sprigs	Salt
Fresh dill	Capers
Butter	Paprika

Clean and stuff the sea trout with parsley sprigs and fresh dill. Sprinkle with salt. Arrange them on an oiled baking dish, dot them with butter and bake at 400° for 15 minutes, or until almost done. Cover the fish with sour cream that has been seasoned with chopped dill and salt. Return to the oven to finish cooking the fish and heat the cream thoroughly.

Sprinkle with capers and a dash of paprika.

Shad

THIS great gastronomic delight is native to Europe and to our Atlantic Coast. In the 1870's it was transplanted to the Pacific Coast, where it has flourished ever since. As a matter of fact, East Coast shad is now overfished, and some of the Pacific catch is shipped across the continent and sold in Eastern markets. The shad is in season from early January, when the first of the southern catch arrives, until May when the northernmost supply is at its height.

Shad has such an intricate bone structure that boned fillets are most desirable for general use. A stuffed baked shad, however, offers so much pure eating joy that the task of extracting all the bones is worth the effort. There was a time when people felt that shad should be slowly cooked for hours to dissolve the bones. If you care to eat fish that has been overcooked and is tasteless, you may try it.

BROILED SHAD

Unless you are an expert, don't try to bone shad for broiling. It is a tedious job that requires skill. Either use the boned fillets or a split shad. In my opinion, it is wiser to leave the skin on the fillets. Place the fish skin side down, and broil according to the directions under "Cooking Methods." Serve with parsley butter.

SAUTEED SHAD

Roll boned shad in flour and proceed as for sauté meunière, page 16. Serve with lemon wedges or tartar sauce (see index).

VARIATION

Dip pieces of shad into flour, then in beaten egg, and in rolled bread crumbs. Sauté in butter or oil until nicely browned. Serve with lemon butter (see index) or rémoulade (see index).

BAKED SHAD

Split a shad or buy a whole boned shad. Place it on a flat oiled baking dish or pan. Dot with butter, and salt and pepper to taste. Bake at 400° for 20 minutes or until the fish flakes easily when tested with a fork. Baste several times during the cooking process. Serve with herb butter (see index) or lemon butter (see index).

BAKED STUFFED SHAD

1 split, boned shad	½ teaspoon thyme
2 large onions, sliced	2 tablespoons finely chopped
4 tablespoons butter	celery leaves
1 cup bread crumbs	1 teaspoon salt
¼ cup finely chopped parsley	1 egg, well beaten

Sauté the onions in the butter until they are soft. Add the other ingredients and mix well. Stuff a split, boned shad with this mixture and sew it up or secure it with string. Place it in an oiled baking dish or pan and bake at 400° for 30 to 40 mnutes—depending on the size of the fish. Serve it with boiled parsley potatoes and fresh green peas. The fish needs no sauce, but if you must have one, use Hollandaise (see index) or tartar sauce (see index).

VARIATIONS

1. Sauté 1 onion in butter until just soft. Add ½ pound of chopped mushrooms and cook for 5 minutes. Season to taste and mix with ¼ cup of chopped parsley and ½ cup of crumbs. Stuff the fish, sew it or tie it with string. Cover the fish with rashers of bacon and bake as above. Serve with a sauce duxelles (see index).

2. Sauté 2 onions in butter until soft. Add 1 clove of garlic, 1 green pepper, and 4 ripe tomatoes, all chopped. Season and mix well. Stuff the fish with this and sew or tie securely. Place it on an oiled baking dish, dot with butter, season with salt and pepper, and pour 1 cup of white wine over it. Bake as above, basting often. Use the juices in the pan and additional wine to make a white wine sauce (see index).

3. Split a shad and place it in the following marinade: 1 cup of olive oil, 2 cloves of garlic, crushed, 1 sliced onion, 1 bay leaf, 1 teaspoon of salt, 1 teaspoon of ground pepper, ¼ cup of lemon juice, enough white wine to cover. Let it stand for 12 hours. Prepare a stuffing with the following: 1 small chopped onion sautéed in 4 tablespoons of fat, 1 cup of dry bread crumbs, salt, pepper, ¼ cup of chopped parsley, ½ cup of sliced toasted almonds, enough of the marinade to moisten. Mix this thoroughly and stuff the fish with it. Place it on an oiled pan or baking dish and bake at 400° for 30 to 40 minutes. Heat the marinade separately and use as a basting sauce. Serve with the pan juices.

NOTE: In France, shad is often served with sorrel—more commonly known in this country, where it grows wild, as "sour grass." To some extent sorrel is cultivated here as a vegetable. It is delicious in soups; or it may be cooked in the same way as spinach; or it may be combined with spinach and made into a puree.

If you like the taste of sorrel, try stuffing a shad with a sorrel puree, or baking a shad on a bed of the puree.

SHAD BAKED IN CREAM

Split a shad and place it on an oiled baking dish. Dot with butter and sprinkle with salt and pepper. Bake at 400° for 20 minutes. Add ¾ cup of heavy cream and bake for 10 more minutes, basting with the cream during the process. Serve with plenty of chopped parsley and the pan juices.

Shad Roe

This is one of our finest treats. Strangely enough, it is practically unknown in France, where the shad is greatly appreciated, and it is not done well in England. It seems to be a dish that has but two extremes—wonderful and horrible. The mistreatment of roe may almost always be attributed to overcooking. It should never be dry, never tasteless.

Roe are usually sold by the pair. They are apt to be expensive except at the end of the season, when they become plentiful. I believe that the only way to cook shad roe is as follows:

SMOTHERED SHAD ROE

For 2 pair of roe, melt 6 ounces of butter—¾ of a cup—in a covered skillet. When the butter is melted and warm, but not hot, dip the roe in it and arrange them in the pan. Cover and simmer over a low flame for about 12 to 15 minutes, turning once. Season to taste with salt, pepper, and chopped parsley. Serve with lemon wedges and the butter from the pan. Accompany this dish with crisp bacon and boiled potatoes. This is a dinner that deserves to be enhanced by a good bottle of Chablis or a fine Meursault.

BROILED SHAD ROE

Personally, I think that to parboil and then broil shad roe is to make it unfit for human consumption. If you must broil it, do so without parboiling. Brush it well with butter and baste often during the process. Even then, it tends to become dry and uninteresting.

SHAD ROE SOUFFLE

2 pair shad roe	4 tablespoons flour
Salt	¾ cup milk
1 tablespoon lemon juice	Pepper
2 tablespoons melted butter	4 egg yolks, slightly beaten
4 tablespoons butter, for sauce	6 egg whites, beaten stiff

Poach the shad roe in boiling salted water for 10 minutes. Remove, and when cool enough to handle, break up into small bits. Add the lemon juice and melted butter. Prepare thick white sauce: Melt the 4 tablespoons of butter, blend in the flour, add a little of the water in which the shad roe was cooked and about ¾ cup of milk. Stir until thick and smooth. Season to taste and cool slightly.

For the soufflé, add the egg yolks to the white sauce. Mix the shad roe through it. Beat the egg whites until stiff and fold these into the mixture. Pour it into a buttered soufflé mold and bake at 375° for 30 to 40 minutes, or until the soufflé is puffy and brown. Serve with lemon butter (see index) or shrimp sauce (see index).

SHAD ROE EN PAPILLOTTE

Partially cook 6 rashers of bacon. Cut 6 pieces of cooking parchment in heart shapes—about 9 by 11 inches—and butter them. Place a piece of shad row on one side of each piece of parchment. Brush well with softened butter, season to taste with salt, pepper, and chopped parsley. Top with a rasher of bacon. Fold the parchment over this and crimp the edges together, making an air-tight package. Bake on a buttered pan

178

at 400° for 15 to 20 minutes or until the paper is brown and puffy.

CANNED SHAD ROE

This is excellent when sautéed quickly in butter.

Sheepshead

THE sheepshead, a relative of the porgy, abounds in Florida, Gulf and California waters. It is no relative of the fresh-water sheepshead, which belongs to the croaker family.

The smaller sheepshead are the ones usually found in Southern markets. Occasionally a 20 to 25 pounder is available. Sheepshead are sold either whole or filleted.

BROILED SHEEPSHEAD

Either the whole sheepshead or the fillets may be broiled. Follow directions for broiling under "Cooking Methods." Serve with lemon, lemon butter, or parsley butter (see index).

SAUTEED SHEEPSHEAD

For sautéing the whole fish or the fillets, see the directions for sauté meunière (see index), or for sauté à l'Anglaise (see index). Serve with lemon butter (see index), lemon quarters, or sauce rémoulade (see index).

BAKED SHEEPSHEAD

Clean and split the fish. Dot with butter, season with salt and pepper, and sprinkle with parsley. Place on an oiled baking dish or pan and bake at 425° for 20 to 25 minutes, or until the fish flakes easily when tested with a fork.

BAKED STUFFED WHOLE SHEEPSHEAD OR FILLETS

Prepare your favorite fish stuffing (see index). Clean a whole fish, stuff it and tie securely. If you are using fillets, spread them with the stuffing, roll, and tie securely. Dot with butter, sprinkle with salt and pepper and bake at 425° for

25 to 28 minutes, depending on the size of the fish. Baste frequently with the juices in the pan.

Skate

ABUNDANT on both coasts, the skate is regarded by most people as something odd and uneatable that floats in on the tide. Children are fascinated by them, and dogs like to roll on top of them, apparently preferring them to any other type of dead fish. The fact is that, despite its strange look, the skate is good eating. Especially on the East Coast, it is beginning to be more popular.

The wings are the part generally used for cooking. The flesh is very gelatinous and the flavor is delicate and distinctive. I have eaten it since I was a child, in both English and French versions. If you have never tried it, you owe it to yourself to make the experiment.

In eating skate, you do not cut through the meat as you do with other fish. You scrape along the wings with your knife and fork. This gives you the full benefit of the long strips of delicious flesh.

SKATE BEURRE NOIR

This is the best-known fashion of serving skate. If you buy large wings, cut them into serving-size pieces. If you buy the small ones, cook them whole.

Prepare a court bouillon of vinegar, salt and water. Poach the wings in the bouillon and drain them thoroughly. Place them in a serving dish. Melt and brown butter, add a little wine vinegar and plenty of capers. Pour this over the fish.

SKATE WITH TOMATO SAUCE

Prepare skate wings as above. Serve with sautéed onions and a rich tomato sauce (see index).

COLD SKATE REMOULADE

Prepare skate wings in court bouillon, using white wine (see index). Remove to a deep platter. Let the bouillon cook down to half its volume and pour it over the fish. Cool and chill in

the refrigerator. Serve with sauce vinaigrette (see index) or
rémoulade (see index).

The meat of the skate may be scraped from the bones and
used in a salad combined with finely chopped celery and
onion. Moisten with mayonnaise and serve on a bed of greens.
You will find that this dish is a welcome change from the
usual fish salad.

Smelt

COLUMBIA RIVER smelt, which are related to Eastern smelt,
are the best I have tasted. They are fat, rich and mildly
flavored. Their oil content is so high that Indians used to dry
them in large quantities and then burn them for light, a prac-
tice that led to their being known as "candlefish."

During my childhood the smelt run in the Columbia River
and its tributaries resembled an orgy. The word that the fish
were running attracted thousands of people, many of whom
had never baited a hook. The smelt were so abundant that the
channel of a small stream would glisten with the silver of their
bodies. I have watched entire families—men, women and
children—dragging the fish from the water with nets, bird
cages, gunny sacks and even old dresses knotted together.
The squirming fish were dumped into boxes, and the sight of
so many smelt and so much waste was far from appetizing.
For a long time I disliked the fish and only in recent years
have I become fond of them.

The smelt is sometimes called the "king" of the small fishes.
Its relationship to the salmon gives it a distinctive flavor and
good texture. Sometmes the smelt is excessively oily, or it
may absorb unpleasant flavors of the river. When this happens, the only thing to do is discard the fish.

In New England, as on the Pacific Coast, the smelt is a mi-
grating salt-water fish. The Great Lakes smelt is a transplant
from New England. It has flourished in fresh water, but has
retained the migratory habits of its marine ancestors. During
the spawning seasons, it runs up the streams and rivers of the
Great Lakes region. In all locations, coastal and inland, the
spawning season of the smelt is variable, and a run may last
a week or so.

Most people like smelt cooked crisp in butter or oil, and some people like them crisp enough to eat the bones. As a matter of personal preference I recommend boning the fish.

BROILED SMELT

Split and clean the smelt. Brush them well with butter, dip in cream, and roll in crumbs until they are well coated. Broil over charcoal, basting with butter during the broiling process. (You may skewer them, if you wish, and make your task easier.) Salt and pepper to taste.

SAUTEED SMELT

Split and clean the smelt and bone them if you wish. However, it is a simple job to do this after they are cooked—just remove the head and backbone at one time.

Dip the fish in flour and sauté them quickly in butter or oil. Season to taste and serve with tartar sauce (see index) or sauce rémoulade (see index).

VARIATIONS

1. Split the smelt at the back and remove the bone. Dip the fish in beaten egg and then in finely rolled crumbs. Sauté in butter and add ½ cup of buttered toasted almonds to the pan. Season to taste.

2. Bone the smelt as above and then marinate them in lemon or lime juice for 1 hour. Roll them in flour and sauté in olive oil very quickly. Season to taste and serve with lemon or lime butter (see index).

3. Split the smelt at the back and remove the bone. Dip the fish in beaten egg and then in finely rolled crumbs. Sauté in butter and add ½ cup of buttered toasted almonds to the pan. Season to taste.

4. Dip the fish in milk and roll in seasoned corn meal. Sauté in butter or olive oil. Serve with a tomato sauce (see index).

5. Split the fish and remove the bones. Spread with mustard, dip in crumbs, sprinkle with dry mustard, salt and cayenne. Sauté in butter or oil and serve with a sauce diable (see index).

FRIED SMELT

You may bone the fish or not, before frying. Heat fat in

your deep fryer to 370°. Dip the smelt in crumbs, then in beaten egg, and then in crumbs again. Dry for 3 to 5 minutes. Drain, season to taste, and serve with tartar sauce (see index) or sauce rémoulade (see index). Always serve fried parsley (see index) with smelt.

VARIATIONS

En Brochette. Skewer the smelt S-shape by running the skewer through the head, then through the middle, and then through the tail. Or you may make loops of them by running the skewer just through the heads and tails. Dip the skewered fish in flour, then in beaten egg, and roll in crumbs. Fry as above.

Curried. Mix 1 cup or more of corn meal with 1 teaspoon of salt and 1½ tablespoons of curry powder. Beat 2 eggs very light and add 1 teaspoon of freshly ground pepper and 1 teaspoon of curry powder. Dip the smelt in flour, then in the beaten egg, and roll in the seasoned corn meal. Fry as above. Serve with rice heavily laced with curry. Chutney goes well with this.

Rolled. Split and bone the smelt and lay them out flat. Place an anchovy fillet on each fish, sprinkle with a little salt and pepper and some chopped parsley. Roll them up and fasten on brochettes. Dip in flour, then in beaten egg, and roll in crumbs. Fry as above. Serve with anchovy butter (see index).

Piquant. Clean the smelt but do not bone them. Dip them in flour, then in beaten egg, and roll them in crumbs mixed with finely chopped garlic, salt and cayenne. Fry as above and serve with a tomato sauce (see index).

BAKED SMELT AU GRATIN

Oil	Salt, pepper
Chopped onion, carrot, and celery	Butter
	White wine
Smelt	Buttered crumbs
Grated Parmesan cheese	

Oil a large flat baking dish or pan. Cover the bottom with the chopped vegetables. Clean the smelt and arrange them on top. Sprinkle with salt and pepper and dot with butter. Add enough wine to the pan to half cover the fish. Bake at 400° for 10 to 15 minutes or until the smelt are just cooked through. Remove the pan from the oven, sprinkle the top with buttered crumbs and grated Parmesan cheese. Run under the broiler flame for a few minutes.

Cold Smelt

BAKED SPICED SMELT

We often used to have this dish when the smelt run was on. It was a great favorite at our home. The fish should be very cold, and are delicious accompanied by potato salad, pickled beets and rye bread. Beer to drink with it, too.

36 to 48 smelt	½ cup olive oil
2 large onions, thinly sliced	½ cup wine vinegar
2 cloves garlic, chopped	1 tablespoon salt
2 grated or chopped carrots	1 teaspoon paprika
2 bay leaves	1 tablespoon of allspice,
8 peppercorns	cloves and cinnamon
5 lemon slices	bark mixed
	2 cups water
1 cup white wine	

Clean and arrange the fish in a large baking dish. Combine all the other ingredients and bring to a boil. Simmer for 15 minutes. Pour this sauce over the fish and bake at 400° for 12 to 15 minutes. Let the smelt cool in the pickle and serve chilled.

SMELT ORIENTAL

This is another delicious cold dish. It may be used as hors d'oeuvre or part of a buffet supper.

36 smelt	3 cups tomato puree
Olive oil	4 cloves garlic
Salt, pepper	Juice of 2 lemons
Paprika	3 tablespoons chopped parsley

Clean the fish, dip them in olive oil and arrange on an oiled baking dish. Brush again with oil and sprinkle with salt, pepper, and paprika.

Mix the tomato puree with the finely chopped garlic, the lemon juice, and the parsley. Cover the smelt with this mixture and bake at 400° for 12 to 15 minutes. Let the fish cool in the sauce. Serve very cold and garnish with lemon slices, chopped parsley, and hard-cooked egg.

Sole and the Flounder Family

THERE is no genuine sole in American waters, but more fish called sole is served in our restaurants than any other kind. We tend to apply the name "sole" to any white fish that comes in fillets, with the result that the average diner has only the haziest idea of what fish he is eating. Generally, he is eating one of the abundant members of the flounder family—the dab, the gray sole, the yellowtail, the winter flounder, the lemon sole.

In Eastern cities you can easily obtain true Channel sole imported from England, Belgium, the Netherlands, and Denmark. It comes frozen, of course, and demands a fine price. Its texture is quite different from that of the so-called "American sole."

In the fish markets of seaboard towns, a great percentage of the flounders and sole are sold in fillets, and even greater quantities are sold as frozen fillets all over the country. However, the fish is also often sold whole. The most common American flounder is a flat fish, darkish gray on top and white on the bottom, with its two eyes on top.

Any of these recipes will fit any type of flounder and will be just as appropriate to the true Channel or Dover sole. It is difficult to tell you just how much to buy since fillets vary so much in size, as does the whole fish. If you figure on about a half pound per person, you will always have plenty. Some people contend that a pound of fish will serve three, but I find this skimpy.

GRILLED SOLE

This, naturally, is the simplest way to prepare a whole sole or fillets. A charcoal fire is perfection, but gas or electricity does nearly as well. Dip the fish in flour or bread crumbs, as you wish, and give it a good bath of melted butter or oil. Broil or grill slowly, about 3 inches from the flame, just long enough to set the flesh and give it a little color. Baste it with butter or oil while it is cooking. Salt and pepper before removing from the grill.

Serve the broiled sole with some of the pan drippings, or with lemon or lemon butter. If you prefer a sauce, serve Hollandaise (see index), Béarnaise (see index), tomato (see index), or mustard (see index). Anchovy butter (see index), parsley butter (see index), and caviar butter (see index) are also all excellent with the grilled fillets.

If you want to save yourself the work of cleaning a broiling pan, line it with metal foil before you put in your fish.

1. Start the grilled fish in the oven at 425° and cook it for about 8 or 10 minutes. Then brush with butter and crumbs and run under the broiler to brown nicely.

2. Serve the grilled sole with steamed clams and mussels.

SAUTEED SOLE

When you sauté either the whole fish or the fillets, you have a choice of many interesting ways to garnish and sauce the fish.

SOLE MEUNIERE

Dredge the fish or fillets well with flour. Sauté quickly in butter or oil until nicely browned and just flaky. Turn once during the cooking process and salt and pepper to taste. Remove to a hot platter, add the butter from the pan and a goodly sprinkling of lemon juice and chopped parsley. This simple method of preparation seems to bring out the true flavor of the fish about as well as any other way.

1. After dishing on to the hot platter, sauce with some beurre noisette (see index) and garnish with lemon slices.

2. Add anchovy butter and lemon and garnish with strips of anchovy.

3. Peel, seed and chop ½ pound of very ripe tomatoes. Let them cook down in 4 tablespoons of butter until they are a paste. Season with a little grated garlic, 1 teaspoon of salt and 1½ tablespoons of curry powder. Add ½ cup of white wine and allow the mixture to simmer for ½ hour. Serve poured over the sautéed sole.

4. Sauté slices of eggplant or summer squash until golden brown. Season well with salt and pepper. Place sautéed sole on these slices, surround with freshly steamed rice and serve with a tomato sauce (see index).

SOLE A LA TSAROVITZ

3 cups mashed potatoes
3 egg yolks
1 teaspoon paprika
1 tablespoon each of chopped
parsley, chives, chervil

Salt
6 tablespoons butter
4 large fillets of sole

Boil or bake the potatoes, mash them smoothly and combine with the egg yolks and the seasonings. Beat them well, form into thin flat cakes and cook them in butter on a griddle or in a frying pan until they are nicely browned on both sides. Sauté the fillets as in the preceding recipe. Top the potato cakes with the sautéed fish and serve with the following sauce, made in the pan in which the fillets were cooked:

1 tablespoon chopped shallot
or green onion
½ cup white wine or dry vermouth

½ cup tomato paste
¼ cup sauce Espagnole
(see index) or beurre
manié (see index)
Salt, pepper

Add the shallot to the pan in which the fish was sautéed and let it cook for a few minutes. Add the white wine, swirl it around a bit, then add the tomato puree and blend well. Add the thickening agent (either sauce Espagnole or beurre manié) and stir until it is nicely blended and thick. Taste for seasoning and pour over the fish.

VARIATION

Instead of the tomato sauce, garnish the fillets with sautéed mushroom caps and serve with a Hollandaise sauce (see index).

FILLETS A LA CECILY

6 fillets of sole
1 cup sauce duxelles (see
index)
Flour
1 egg
Bread crumbs

Butter or oil
2 cups cooked buttered
spinach
Grated Parmesan cheese
Beurre noisette (see
index)
Lemon slices

Choose long fillets for this dish. Spread each one well with the duxelles and fold over once. Dip the folded fillets in flour, beaten egg and crumbs, and sauté in butter or oil until nicely browned on both sides. Arrange the fillets on a bed of cooked buttered spinach, sprinkle with grated cheese and run under the broiler for a minute to brown on top. Serve with beurre noisette poured over the fish and a garnish of lemon slices.

SOLE GAVARNI

5 or 6 green and red peppers	4 tablespoons butter
Olive oil	Salt, pepper
1 pound sliced mushrooms	6 fillets of sole
1 clove garlic	Flour

6 tablespoons butter

Cut the peppers in thin strips and sauté in olive oil until just soft. Sauté the mushrooms and garlic in butter, and salt and pepper to taste. Dredge the fillets in flour and sauté in butter until browned. When the fish is cooked, serve it on a bed of the mushrooms topped with the sautéed peppers.

SOLE A L'INDIENNE

1 onion	Broth
Butter or oil	4 fillets cut in small pieces
1 cup rice	Flour
1 tablespoon curry powder	6 tablespoons olive oil

Curry sauce

Sauté the onion, chopped, in butter or oil until tender, add the rice and brown quickly. Add the curry powder and enough boiling broth (or water) to cover 1 inch above the rice. Bake in a 350° oven until the rice is tender and the liquid absorbed, adding more liquid if it cooks away too quickly.

Cut the fillets in small pieces, dredge them with flour and sauté them in olive oil until nicely browned and just cooked through.

Prepare a curry sauce with 1½ cups of sauce béchamel flavored to taste with curry powder. Unmold the rice, arrange the sole around it, and cover with the curry sauce.

Thin French-fried onions are excellent with this dish.

SOLE A LA PIÉMONTESE

1 cup corn meal	½ teaspoon salt
3 cups water	1 tablespoon lemon juice
1 teaspoon salt	6 fillets of sole
4 tablespoons butter	Flour
4 tablespoons grated cheese	6 tablespoons butter or oil
2 cups cooked chopped spinach	Parsley
1 teaspoon tarragon	½ cup white wine

½ cup tomato puree

Prepare a polenta by bringing to a boil the 3 cups of water and stirring in the corn meal and 1 teaspoon of salt. When it is thick, add the butter and cheese and let it cook over hot water for 1½ hours.

Cook the spinach, chop and season with tarragon, salt and lemon juice.

Flour the fillets and sauté them in butter or oil until nicely browned. Pour the polenta on the bottom of an oval serving dish, top with the spinach, and cover with the fillets. Sprinkle with chopped parsley. Make a sauce by adding the wine and tomato puree to the pan juices, blending them well. Pour this over the fish.

FILLETS WITH PILAFF, ITALIAN

6 large fillets of sole	6 zucchini or summer
Flour	squash
Rice pilaff or rice ring	18 mushroom caps
6 tomatoes	Butter
	Salt, pepper
Tartar sauce	

Cut the fillets into small julienne strips and roll in flour.

Prepare a rice pilaff or rice ring according to your own recipe. Sauté the vegetables in butter until they are nicely browned and just cooked through. Salt and pepper to taste. Sauté the sole strips very quickly in butter and season to taste.

Set the pilaff or ring in the center of a platter, decorate it with the strips of fish and surround it with the sautéed vegetables. Serve with a tartar sauce.

VARIATION

Mix a great quantity of chopped parsley and tiny cooked peas with the rice.

This is a delightful dish for a buffet supper since the entire meal is right there on the platter. You can vary the vegetables as you wish.

GINGER-FRIED FLOUNDER

Make the following batter:

3 eggs	2 tablespoons soy sauce
3 tablespoons cornstarch	3 tablespoons chopped
1 tablespoon grated ginger	green onion
(fresh or preserved)	3 tablespoons sherry

Mix thoroughly. Cut fillets of flounder in strips, dip in the batter, and fry in shallow or deep fat.

189

FILLETS CASSIS

1 tablespoon finely chopped basil	Crumbs
	Butter or oil
1 cup concentrated tomato puree	Salt
	8 ounces spaghetti
Freshly ground black pepper	6 tablespoons butter
6 fillets of sole	1 cup grated Cheddar or imported Swiss cheese
Flour	
2 eggs, beaten	Parsley

Pepper

Mix the basil and the tomato puree and add freshly ground pepper. Spread each fillet well with this mixture and fold over. Dip the fillets in flour, in beaten egg and in crumbs, and sauté in butter (or oil), being careful when you turn them not to drip the tomato filling all over the pan. Salt them to taste. When they are nicely browned and cooked through, serve them on a bed of spaghetti that has been boiled, drained, and mixed with butter and grated cheese.

You may serve this with a tomato sauce if you wish, but I think it needs nothing more than a little chopped parsley and some freshly ground pepper.

NOTE: For a change, when you mix your spaghetti and cheese, sauté it in butter until it is lightly browned. Turn it with the aid of spatulas, brown the other side, and turn it out on a serving dish with the brown showing. This is a fine treat.

FILLETS PAYSANNE

½ pound mushrooms coarsely chopped	Salt, pepper
	6 fillets of sole
4 tablespoons butter	Paprika
4 tablespoons olive oil	Flour
½ cup shredded almonds	4 tablespoons butter
6 sour or dill pickles	4 tablespoons olive oil
¼ cup capers	Salt, pepper

Chopped parsley

Cook the mushrooms in the butter and olive oil. Add the almonds, blanched and cut in small pieces. When slightly browned add the pickles and capers and season to taste.

Sprinkle the fillets with paprika and dredge in flour. Sauté in butter and oil until nicely browned and salt and pepper to taste. Arrange the fish on a platter and cover with the mushroom and almond mixture. Combine the juices of the two pans and pour over the fish. Sprinkle with chopped parsley.

FILLETS OF SOLE ST. JACQUES

4 fillets of sole	½ pounds scallops
Flour	2 cloves garlic
6 tablespoons butter	Chopped parsley
Salt, pepper	Sauce Béarnaise (see index)

Cut the fillets into small strips, approximately 3 inches long by ¾ to 1 inch wide. Roll them in flour and sauté in butter just long enough to color them. These small pieces are very easy to overcook, so be careful. Salt and pepper to taste.

Roll the scallops in flour and sauté in butter. Add the garlic, finely chopped, and chopped parsley, and season to taste.

Heap the scallops in the center of a hot platter and arrange the fillets around the edge. Or arrange the fillets in individual shells and use the scallops for topping. Sprinkle with chopped parsley and serve with a sauce Béarnaise.

POACHED SOLE, FILLETS AND WHOLE FISH

Poaching is usually done in one of the court bouillons—preferably those with white wine, for most of the appropriate sauces include white wine broth. Occasionally a recipe calls for a red wine sauce, and some use vermouth. In some cases the fillets are poached in undiluted white wine with the addition of flavoring agents.

Sole—or fish of the flounder family, as the case may be—requires very little poaching to make it palatable and juicy. The delicate flesh is very fragile and should be watched carefully or it may be overcooked and become dry and crumbly.

ESCABECHE OF FLOUNDER

2 pounds fillets or steaks	⅓ cup orange juice
Lemon or lime juice for dipping	⅓ cup olive oil
Flour	¼ cup minced green onions
Butter	Dash of tabasco or cayenne
1 clove garlic	Salt to taste
3 tablespoons lemon or lime juice	Ripe olives
	Quartered limes or lemons

Dip the fish in lemon or lime juice, rub with flour, and sauté in butter until golden brown. Arrange in a deep dish (about 2 inches deep) in a symmetrical fashion. Remove any skin and bone, if it is steak.

Make a sauce by crushing the garlic and adding the lemon or lime juice, orange juice, olive oil, minced onions, tabasco or cayenne, and salt to taste. Pour this over the fish, and let it stand in the refrigerator for 24 hours or more. To serve as a first course or one of the dishes at a buffet supper, garnish with ripe olives and quartered limes or lemons.

NOTE: You may add fresh coriander (sometimes called Chinese parsley) to the sauce. Also try ground cumin seed or toasted coriander seeds.

STUFFED SOLE A LA BORDELAISE

1 large flounder (or sole) Fish stuffing 1 pound shrimp	White wine court bouillon (see index) Sauce Bordelaise (see index)

Make an incision in a large sole or flounder, and with a sharp, pointed knife loosen the flesh from the bones. (Or ask your fish dealer to do this for you.) Stuff the fish with a fish stuffing (see index), and poach it with shelled shrimp in white wine court bouillon. When cooked, place the fish on a hot platter, surround it with the shrimp, and cover it with sauce Bordelaise. Serve with plain boiled potatoes and a cucumber salad.

NOTE: If the fish are small, use two. This recipe is very flexible and can easily be increased or reduced.

SOLE WITH SHRIMP SAUCE

2 medium sized soles or flounders White wine court bouillon (see index)	2 pounds shrimp 2 cups sauce velouté (see index) prepared with the broth
Grated Parmesan cheese	

Poach the soles or flounders in the court bouillon. After the fish has been cooking about 2 minutes, add the shrimp, cleaned and de-veined. When they are done, place the fish on a hot serving dish or gratin dish.

Select the 12 largest and best-looking shrimp and set them aside to use as a garnish. Chop the rest of the shrimp very fine or put them through a food chopper, using the finest blade. While you are doing this, let the bouillon reduce to

1½ cups. Strain it and correct the seasoning. Prepare 2 cups of sauce velouté, using the bouillon as a base, and when it is smooth and thick add the chopped shrimp. Pour the sauce over the fish, garnish with whole shrimp, sprinkle with grated Parmesan cheese and brown quickly under the broiler.

NOTE: You may prepare this dish with fillets instead of whole fish.

FILLETS OF SOLE BENEDICTINE

Brandade de morue
6 fillets of sole

Court bouillon
Chopped parsley

This has a delightful combination of flavors and is a wonderful dish for a buffet party. It's so good, in fact, that it's worth keeping secret as a "specialty of the house."

Prepare a brandade de morue (see index). Poach the fillets in a simple white wine court bouillon (see index). When done, arrange them on top of the brandade and sprinkle with chopped parsley. When you serve them, surround the fish with grilled whole tomatoes or sautéed zucchini.

FILLETS OF SOLE CLOVISSE

6 fillets of sole
White wine court bouillon
2 cans minced clams (7 ounces each)

Sauce velouté (see index)
12 mushroom caps
Chopped parsley

Poach the fillets in the court bouillon just long enough for them to cook through—about 3 to 4 minutes. Remove them to a baking dish or gratin dish. Add the juice from the clams to the court bouillon and let it reduce to 1½ cups of liquid. Prepare 2 cups of sauce velouté, using the broth as a base. When it is thick, add the minced clams and taste for seasoning. Pour the sauce over the fillets and garnish with sautéed mushroom caps and chopped parsley. Run the dish under the broiler just long enough to brown lightly.

NOTE: Naturally, you may use fresh minced clams for this dish. If you do, use several whole poached clams as a garnish.

FILLETS OF SOLE ESPAGNOLE

3 heads of Boston lettuce
6 tablespoons butter
½ cup consommé or stock
6 fillets of sole

Sherry or marsala
Brown sauce (see index)
Mushrooms
Tomatoes

193

Clean the lettuce heads and cut them in half. Sear them in hot butter for a few minutes, add the consommé, cover and let them simmer until tender—about 10 minutes. Season to taste.

Poach the fillets in sherry or marsala—just enough to cover them. Be careful not to overcook. Baste several times, spooning the wine over them as it cooks down. Season to taste.

Prepare 2 cups of brown sauce, using the cooking liquids reduced to half. Arrange the braised lettuce on a platter, top with the fillets and mask with the brown sauce. Serve garnished with sautéed mushrooms and grilled tomatoes.

FILLETS OF SOLE CASANOVA

1 pound mushrooms	Garlic
2 cups shredded celery root	6 fillets of sole
Salt, pepper	Beurre manié (see index)
2 teaspoons curry powder	1 cup cream
Butter	Grated Parmesan cheese

Chop the mushrooms stems, combine them with the shredded celery root, cover with cold water and bring to a boil. Add seasoning and simmer until the celery root is tender. Add the curry powder.

Sauté the mushroom caps in butter with just a touch of garlic. Season to taste.

Poach the fillets in the curry broth with the celery root and mushroom stems. When they are done, place the fillets in a gratin or baking dish, and top with the celery root. Thicken the curry broth with beurre manié, add the cream gradually, and stir until smooth and well blended. Taste for seasoning and pour over the fish. Surround with the sautéed mushroom caps, sprinkle with grated Parmesan cheese, and brown quickly under the broiler.

FILLETS OF SOLE CREOLE

6 fillets of sole	2 medium onions, thinly
Court bouillon	sliced
1½ cups sauce velouté (see	½ pound mushrooms, sliced
index)	6 tablespoons butter
3 large tomatoes, peeled and	Chopped parsley
diced	

Poach the fillets in court bouillon and remove to a hot gratin dish or serving dish. Reduce the bouillon to 1 cup and strain. Using it as a base, prepare 1½ cups of sauce velouté.

Sauté the vegetables in butter until lightly browned but not mushy. Season to taste. Top the fillets with the vegetable mixture, cover with the sauce, sprinkle with chopped parsley, and run under the broiler for a few minutes.

FILLETS OF SOLE NICOISE

2 cloves garlic, chopped	6 fillets of sole
4 tablespoons olive oil	2 cups tomato juice
1 cup concentrated tomato puree	¼ cup vermouth or red wine
12 anchovy fillets	1 teaspoon basil
	18 ripe olives

Chopped parsley

Sauté the garlic in olive oil, add the tomato puree and 6 anchovy fillets, chopped. Season to taste.

Poach the fillets in the tomato juice and the vermouth (or wine) flavored with basil. Remove the fish to a hot platter and reduce the liquid to 1 cup very quickly. Combine it with the tomato puree and allow it to cook down and blend nicely. Taste for seasoning and pour over the fish. Garnish with the 6 remaining anchovy fillets and the olives. Sprinkle with chopped parsley.

FILLETS OF SOLE MACONNAISE

This is a trick dish that is amusing to serve for a large buffet supper or dinner party when you wish to have a very handsome table arrangement.

12 fillets of sole	
Red wine court bouillon (see index)	1½ cups of sauce Espagnole (see index)
White wine court bouillon (see index)	12 large mushroom caps
1½ cups of sauce velouté (see index)	4 tablespoons butter
	Chopped parsley
	12 anchovy fillets
	Paprika

Poach half of the fillets in the red wine court bouillon and half in the white. Remove them to a hot dish. Prepare a sauce velouté with the white wine broth and a brown (Espagnole) sauce with the red. Taste for seasoning.

On a large round or oval platter, arrange the fillets, alternating the two varieties and topping each one with its own kind of sauce. Decorate each white wine fillet was a mushroom cap sautéed in butter and a little chopped parsley.

Decorate each red wine fillet with an anchovy fillet and a sprinkling of paprika. This is a handsome dish.

SOLE AU VERMOUTH

6 fillets of sole	½ cup butter
1¼ cups dry vermouth	3 tablespoons cream
4 egg yolks	Salt

Poach the fillets in just enough dry vermouth to cover them. When they are just cooked through, remove them to a flat baking dish or gratin dish. Reduce the cooking liquid over a brisk flame until it is practically a glaze.

Put the egg yolks and the butter cut in small pieces into the top of a double boiler. Cook over hot water and beat with a wire whisk or electric beater until thickened and smooth. Add the cream and the reduced cooking liquid, and salt to taste. Take care that the water never boils, or you will have scrambled eggs instead of a smooth sauce. Pour the sauce over the fillets and run under the broiler to glaze.

NOTE: The many herbs and flavorings in the vermouth make extra seasonings unnecessary in this dish.

FILLETS OF SOLE MARGUERY

6 fillets of sole	24 shrimp
White wine	36 mussels
Sauce au vin blanc	

Poach the fillets in enough white wine to cover them. Remove to a baking dish. Shell and clean the shrimp and poach in the same wine for 3 minutes. Keep hot. Steam the mussels until they open (see index for "Mussels Mariniere"), and extract the meat. Reduce the white wine and prepare the sauce as given in variations under Basic Sauce Béchamel. Cover the fillets with the white wine sauce, surround them with the shrimp and mussels, and run under the broiler for a minute to glaze.

NOTE: This is one of the most famous recipes for sole, having been created in the old Restaurant Marguery in Paris. It is not a difficult dish, and the combination of flavors makes it remarkably good.

FILLETS OF SOLE DUXELLES

6 fillets of sole
White wine
Sauce duxelles (see index)
18 small mushroom caps

4 tablespoons butter
Salt, pepper
¼ cup port wine
Chopped parsley

Poach the fillets in white wine to cover. Remove to a flat baking dish or gratin dish. Reduce the wine and make the sauce duxelles. Sauté the mushrooms lightly in butter and season to taste. Remove to a hot plate and keep hot. Rinse the pan in which the mushrooms were cooked with port wine and pour it over the fish. Cover with the sauce, top with the sautéed mushroom caps, and run under the broiler to glaze. Sprinkle with chopped parsley.

FILLETS OF SOLE WITH LOBSTER

2 lobsters (1½ pounds each)
Salt
4 fillets of sole (about equal size)

White wine
Sauce béchamel (see index)
¼ cup cognac or whiskey
½ cup heavy cream

Grated Parmesan cheese

Cook the lobsters in boiling salted water for about 8 to 10 minutes. When cool enough to handle, split them and remove all the meat from the bodies and claws. The pieces of claw meat should be removed carefully so as to keep them perfect. Set these aside and chop or grind the rest of the lobster meat very fine.

Poach the fillets of sole in white wine. Remove them to a piece of absorbent paper or cloth. Reduce the wine to half and use it as a base for preparing 2 or 3 cups of béchamel. Combine the chopped lobster meat and the sauce béchamel, add the cognac (or whiskey), and gradually stir in the heavy cream. Continue stirring until the mixture is thoroughly blended and heated through. Line each half lobster shell with a little of the sauce. Place a fillet in each half shell, cover with additional sauce, top with a piece of claw meat, sprinkle with cheese, and glaze under the broiler.

FILLETS OF SOLE MORNAY

6 fillets of sole
White wine or vermouth

Sauce Mornay (see index)
Grated Parmesan cheese

Poach the fillets in white wine or vermouth, and when they are done put them in a flat baking dish or gratin dish. Reduce the wine to half and add it to the sauce Mornay. Pour this over the fish, sprinkle with grated cheese, and run under the broiler to glaze.

FILLETS IN SHELLS

6 croustades	Freshly ground black
Butter	pepper
6 fillets	½ cup grated American or
White wine	Switzerland Swiss
8 ounces noodles (green or	cheese
white)	Sauce Mornay (see index)
Salt	Grated Parmesan cheese
Butter	
Garlic	

Prepare 6 croustades from large loaves of bread. The croustades should be about 6 inches long and 4 inches wide and fairly deep—3 inches at least. Toast them, butter them well, and keep hot.

Next, poach 6 fillets which you have folded in half in white wine until they are flaky and cooked through.

Third, cook the noodles in boiling salted water until just tender. Drain them and sauté lightly in butter with a touch of garlic and some coarsely ground pepper. Add grated Swiss cheese.

Fourth, prepare a sauce Mornay and add the reduced wine broth to the sauce.

Fifth, fill the croustades with the noodle mixture, top each one with a folded fillet and cover with sauce Mornay. Sprinkle with grated Parmesan cheese and glaze for a minute under the broiler.

This, with a green vegetable and such as green beans, with plenty of butter, and a salad, makes a remarkably good supper for a large group of people. It take a little extra trouble to prepare, but it is attractive and the individual loaves make it convenient to serve. A white wine, dry and flinty—such as a fine Chablis—is excellent with it.

FILLETS IN BLANKETS

4 fillets of sole	Salt
White wine or vermouth	Butter
Sauce Mornay (see index)	4 individual omelets
2 cups cooked spinach	Chopped parsley

Poach the fillets in white wine or vermouth and keep them hot in the warming oven or over low heat. Use the liquid to make a sauce Mornay. Cook the spinach and flavor with salt and butter.

Prepare omelets according to your favorite recipe. When they are ready to roll, add to each a bit of the sauce, a little spinach and a fillet. Then roll and top with more spinach and sauce. Sprinkle with chopped parsley.

SOLE MIRABEAU

This is the original version of the fillets in blankets. It is simple to make although it sounds involved.

6 fillets of sole	6 eggs
White wine or vermouth	Salt, pepper
2 cups sauce Mornay (see index)	6 tablespoons butter
2 cups cooked, buttered spinach, *en branche*	

Fold the fillets in half and poach them in enough white wine or vermouth to cover. Cook only until they flake easily with a fork. Remove them from the broth and keep warm. Reduce the cooking liquid and add to the sauce Mornay.

Cook the spinach, drain it, and butter and season to taste.

Prepare a large soufflé omelet with 6 eggs. Beat the yolks and whites separately, and fold the whites into the yolks. Season and cook in a skillet in which you have melted 6 tablespoons of butter. While it is cooking, make a soufflé mixture:

4 tablespoons butter	3 egg yolks
4 tablespoons flour	4 egg whites
½ cup milk	Salt, pepper
½ to ¾ cup grated Parmesan cheese	

Melt the butter, blend in the flour, add the milk and grated cheese. Cool slightly, season to taste, and add the slightly beaten egg yolks, then fold in the stiffly beaten whites.

When the soufflé omelet is deep and puffy, slide it onto a large baking dish, and with a sharp knife and a spatula, remove the center part of the omelet. Cover the bottom with a layer of the sauce Mornay. Then add a layer of spinach, then the fillets, and cover the entire top with a thin layer of the soufflé and Parmesan cheese mixture. Bake for about

10 minutes in a 425° oven until the soufflé mixture is puffy and lightly browned. Serve with additional sauce Mornay.

OMELET STUFFED WITH SOLE

Here is a quick version of the recipes above. For each serving make two small plain omelets. Place an omelet on each dish, top with a fillet of sole which has been poached in court bouillon, cover this with the second omelet and over all pour a good cheese sauce (see index).

FILLETS OF SOLE BONNE FEMME

Butter
2 shallots, finely chopped
¼ pound mushrooms, chopped
4 fillets of sole

Chopped parsley
1 glass white wine
Beurre manié (see index)
Lemon juice

Salt, pepper

Melt enough butter in a large saucepan to oil the bottom of the pan well. Add the shallots and half the mushrooms, place the fillets on top and cover with the rest of the mushrooms. Season to taste and sprinkle with a little chopped parsley. Add the wine and cook over a fairly quick fire for about 10 minutes, basting often. Remove the fish to a serving dish. The liquid should have reduced to less than half its original volume. If not, cook it rapidly until it is reduced. Thicken with a little beurre manié, add a few drops of lemon juice, and taste for seasoning. Pour over the fillets and sprinkle the top with chopped parsley.

FILLETS OF SOLE IDAHO

4 large Idaho potatoes
4 small fillets of sole
1 pound shrimp
White wine

Sauce velouté (see index)
Butter
Salt, pepper
Paprika

Chopped parsley

Bake the potatoes. Fold the fillets and poach with the shelled shrimp in white wine. Reduce the cooking liquid. Prepare the sauce velouté and add the wine broth to the sauce. Chop the shrimp and add half of it to the sauce.

Cut an even slice from the top of each potato and scoop out the meat. Beat it well with plenty of butter, salt, pepper and paprika. Place a little of the plain chopped shrimp in the bottom of each potato shell, then a folded fillet, then a covering of the sauce, and top with a little of the potato puree. Put the pieces of potato shell that you cut off back on and reheat the potatoes in a hot oven. Serve with additional sauce.

If you bake several extra potatoes, you can stuff them with the leftover mixture. Cut these extra potatoes in half, heap the fluffed-up potato puree in the halves, sprinkle with paprika and chopped parsley, and arrange them around the whole potatoes bubbling with the shrimp mixture. This is a trick dish, but it is very attractive and has a good flavor.

FILLETS OF SOLE WITH SCALLOPS MORNAY

4 fillets of sole	Sauce Mornay (see index)
½ pound scallops	Paprika
White wine	Toast points

Poach the fillets and the scallops in white wine and season to taste. Remove from the liquid and keep hot. Reduce the wine broth and use it to make the sauce Mornay, which should be well seasoned. Place the fillets in a flat baking dish. Add the scallops to the sauce and pour it over the fish. Run under the broiler to glaze, sprinkle with paprika, and serve garnished with fried toast points.

DEEP-FRIED SOLE

Fillets of sole should be fried at a temperature of 365° and only until they are delicately browned. Otherwise you will have a dish that resembles sawdust and that has no more flavor than the breading materials. It is much more difficult to fry fish well than to grill or poach it.

Fish fillets for frying should be dredged with flour, dipped in a mixture of well-beaten eggs and milk, then rolled in crumbs or corn meal until they are thoroughly covered. Then they should be carefully lowered into the hot fat. When cooked, drain on absorbent paper. Salt and pepper.

For the average frying you will want 2 eggs beaten with about ¾ cup of milk. Corn meal is exceedingly popular with many people as a covering for fish because of the added flavor it gives. Others use cracker crumbs, bread crumbs, prepared cereals, and various mixes for pancakes and foodstuffs. But whatever you use, be sure the pieces of fish are thoroughly covered.

FRIED FILLET OF SOLE

Follow the directions above and serve with a tartar sauce (see index), sauce Béarnaise (see index), or with wedges of lemon.

JULIENNE OF SOLE

These are also called goujons of sole (From *goujon*—a tiny fresh-water fish popular in France.). Cut the fillets into small strips and cook as you do whole fillets. These make a most unusual appearance on a platter—the small strips, golden brown, piled high, with a garnish of parsley and a bowl of sauce. They taste wonderful, too. Serve them with cocktails and have a bowl of tartar sauce at hand for dunking. Pass plenty of paper napkins.

VARIATIONS

1. Serve fried fillets with French-fried parsley and a good tomato sauce (see index). French-fried parsley is simple: Merely dip a bunch of parsley into the hot fat and fry for about 2 minutes, or until crisp. The flavor is unforgettably good.

2. Serve fried fillets on a bed of onions fried in butter until soft. Make a sauce by frying 1 chopped onion and ½ pound of chopped mushrooms in plenty of butter. Add 4 chopped dill or sour pickles, some chopped parsley, and a good slug of lemon juice. Heat this well, season to taste and pour over the fillets on the bed of onions. Sprinkle with paprika.

3. Fry julienne of sole and arrange on a mound of rice. Serve with a sauce made with 1½ cups of sauce velouté (see index) flavored with 1 tablespoon of curry powder and 3 tablespoons of chutney. Top with grated coconut.

ROLLED FILLETS

Spread fillets with anchovy butter (see index) or herb butter (see index), roll and fasten with toothpicks. Roll in flour, dip in a beaten egg and milk mixture, roll well in crumbs and fry according to the directions above.

CURRIED ROLLS OF SOLE

1 cup coconut or almond milk (see recipe below)
4 onions, soaked in 2 cups milk
2 onions
1 apple
2 tomatoes
4 tablespoons butter
Salt
2 tablespoons curry powder
Salt
1 cup white wine
4 fillets of sole, spread with butter and chopped parsley
Rice pilaff
Flour

Peel 4 onions and slice fairly thin. Separate the slices into rings and cover them with 2 cups of plain milk. Set aside to soak for about 2 hours.

Prepare coconut or almond milk by soaking ⅔ cup of grated coconut or ground almonds in 1 cup of milk.

Chop 2 onions, the unpeeled apple, and tomatoes. Melt the butter in a skillet and cook the onion until just soft. Add the apple, tomatoes, curry powder, and salt to taste. Cook slowly until the vegetables are tender. Add the wine and simmer for ¼ hour; then add the coconut or almond mixture and simmer for 15 minutes more. Force the sauce through a fine sieve, return it to the stove and let it cook down for a few minutes until well blended and thickened. Add a little cream if necessary. Taste for seasoning.

Spread the fillets with butter and chopped parsley and secure with toothpicks. Ten minutes before serving, add them to the sauce and let them poach until just cooked through. Turn them several times.

Take the onion rings from the milk, dip them in flour and deep-fry them. Serve the curry dish with rice pilaff and the crisp fried onions.

STUFFED SAUTEED FILLETS

4 fillets of sole
Fish forcemeat (see index)
Flour
2 eggs, beaten
½ cup milk
Crumbs or corn meal
6 grilled tomatoes
6 tablespoons butter
3 ounces sherry
½ cup tomato puree
1 cup sauce béchamel (see index)
Salt, pepper

Spread the fillets with forcemeat, roll and secure with toothpicks. Dust with flour, dip in beaten egg and milk, and roll well in crumbs or corn meal. Sauté the rolls in butter until nicely browned. Remove to a hot platter. Rinse the pan well with sherry, add the tomato puree and the sauce béchamel, blend thoroughly and let it come to a boil. Taste for seasoning. Surround the fillets with grilled tomatoes and serve the sauce separately.

STUFFED FILLETS

4 fillets of sole	White wine
Fish forcemeat (see index)	1 cup cream
Mirepoix (carrots, onions, celery)	Beurre manié (see index)
	Salt, pepper
4 tablespoons butter	1½ cups mashed potatoes
2 eggs	

Spread the fillets with the forcemeat, roll them and secure with toothpicks. Chop the vegetables very fine and steam them in butter until soft. Add the fillets and enough white wine to cover the bottom of the pan. Poach the fish, basting with the wine. They should cook in about 8 minutes over slow heat. Remove them to a hot plate. Strain the cooking liquid, add the cream, and return to the stove to cook down for a few minutes. Thicken slightly with beurre manié. Season to taste.

Mix the seasoned mashed potatoes with the eggs and blend well. Arrange small rosettes of the potatoes (piped through a pastry tube, using the large rosette end) on a serving dish. Place the fillets in the center and cover with the sauce. Dust with paprika and run under the broiler to brown the potatoes and the sauce.

HERBED ROLLED FILLETS

1½ cups finely chopped mushrooms	Flour
4 tablespoons butter	2 eggs beaten with ¾ cup of milk
Salt, pepper	Crumbs
½ cup chopped chives	Butter
½ cup chopped parsley	3 to 4 tablespoons flour
½ cup chopped onion	1 cup (about) white wine
8 fillets of sole	1 cup cream
Grated Parmesan cheese	

Sauté the mushrooms in 4 tablespoons butter until well cooked. Add the chopped chives, parsley and onion, and season to taste. When thoroughly blended and cooked, remove from the fire and spread the mixture on the fillets. Roll the fillets and secure with toothpicks. Dip each fillet in flour, then

204

in beaten egg and milk, and roll in crumbs. Sauté in butter until nicely browned and cooked through. Remove to a hot platter. Add 3 or 4 tablespoons flour to the pan and mix well with the juices. Add the wine and cook to reduce the liquid a bit. Add the cream and stir until well blended and thickened. Pour the sauce around the fillets, sprinkle with grated Parmesan cheese, and run under the broiler to glaze.

ROLLED FILLETS WITH SHRIMP SAUCE

Fish forcemeat (see index)
Tarragon
8 fillets of sole
½ pound shrimp

White wine
Sauce béchamel (see index)
Salt, pepper
Grated Parmesan cheese

Prepare a fish forcemeat and flavor it heavily with tarragon. Spread each fillet with the forcemeat, roll and secure with toothpicks. Poach the fillets and the shelled and cleaned shrimp in white wine, basting often so as to cook evenly. This should take about 8 minutes. Remove the cooked fish to a hot serving dish. Remove the shrimp and chop very fine. Prepare a sauce béchamel, using the reduced cooking liquid as a base. Salt and pepper to taste and add additional tarragon. Add the chopped shrimp and pour over the fillets. Sprinkle with grated Parmesan cheese, and run under the broiler to glaze for a minute or two.

FILLETS STUFFED WITH SALMON

½ pound salmon
2 eggs
½ cup chopped parsley
Salt, pepper
6 fillets of sole
White wine

1½ cups sauce velouté (see index)
12 mushroom caps
6 artichoke hearts
Butter
Sautéed potatoes

Grind the salmon and mix with the eggs and parsley until it is smooth and pasty. Season to taste with salt and pepper and spread on the fillets. Roll and secure with toothpicks. Poach the fillets in white wine, basting well, until the fish is just cooked and flaky. Remove the fillets to a baking dish. Prepare a sauce velouté, using the cooking liquid. Sauté the mushrooms and artichoke hearts in butter and season to taste. Pour the sauce over the fish, surround with the artichoke hearts, top with the mushrooms and garnish with sautéed potatoes.

ROLLED FILLETS OF SOLE NICOISE

8 fillets of sole	Court bouillon
Chopped parsley	½ pound shrimp
Shallots or green onions	24 clams
Anchovy fillets	Sauce velouté (see index)
Grated Parmesan cheese	

Sprinkle the fillets heavily with chopped parsley and chopped green onion or shallot. Lay several anchovy fillets on each one. Roll and secure with toothpicks. Poach in a court bouillon (see index). About 3 minutes before the fillets are done add the shelled and cleaned shrimp to the bouillon. Remove the fillets to a hot platter.

Steam the clams until they open (see index). Take the meat from the shells. Prepare a sauce velouté (1¼ cups), using the reduced court bouillon as a base. Add the clams and shrimp to the sauce and pour over the fillets. Sprinkle with grated Parmesan cheese and glaze under the broiler for a few minutes.

TOAD IN THE HOLE

6 large Idaho potatoes	Crumbs
6 fillets of sole	6 tablespoons butter, or
Fines herbes	more
Salt, pepper	½ cup cream
Flour	1 teaspoon paprika
2 eggs, beaten with ¾ cup of milk	Egg yolks

Bake the potatoes. Sprinkle the fillets with the herbs and season to taste. Roll and secure with toothpicks. Dip in flour, beaten egg and milk, and roll in crumbs. Sauté in butter until golden brown.

When the potatoes are baked, cut the tops off and scoop out most of the pulp. Mash and whip with butter, cream, seasonings and paprika. Place a fillet in each potato, surround with the whipped potato and put the potato shell back on. Serve any leftover potato filling in a separate dish.

OPEN-FACE SOLE SANDWICHES DE LUXE

Poach 1 fillet of sole for each serving. Spread a slice of toasted bread with Smithfield deviled ham, top with a fillet, and pour sauce Béarnaise over all.

Omit the ham and spread the toast with tarragon-chive butter.

Cold Fillets

COLD JELLIED FILLETS WITH FINE HERBS

8 fillets of sole
1½ cups chopped herbs (dill, parsley, chives, tarragon)
Salt, pepper
White wine court bouillon (see index)

Egg white
2 envelopes gelatin
1½ cups mayonnaise
Black olives
4 cups (or more) potato salad
Hard-cooked eggs

Spread the fillets well with the herbs and sprinkle with salt and pepper. Roll and secure with toothpicks. Cook in court bouillon just until cooked through. Be very careful not to overcook. Remove the toothpicks.

Let the bouillon cook down to a little less than a quart—about 3 cups. Strain and clarify with egg white. Melt the gelatin in ½ cup of water, and when it is thoroughly dissolved combine with the boiling bouillon. Let it cool until it is thick and syrupy. Combine 1 cup of the jelly with 1 cup of mayonnaise and taste for seasoning. Mask the fillets with this mixture and chill well until firm. Decorate with slices of ripe olives and brush with another coat of the jelly. Chill.

Arrange a bed of highly seasoned potato salad on a platter. Make a row or circle of the glazed fillets on top and decorate with hard-cooked eggs and olives. Serve with additional mayonnaise.

JELLIED FILLETS OF SOLE NICOISE

4 hard-cooked eggs
12 to 15 anchovy fillets
½ cup chopped parsley
1½ cups chopped onion
8 fillets of sole
White wine court bouillon (see index)
Egg white

2 envelopes gelatin
1 cup tomato puree
1 teaspoon basil
Sliced hard-cooked eggs
Olives
Greens
Onion rings
French dressing
Tomato mayonnaise

Chop 4 hard-cooked eggs and the anchovy fillets. Combine with the chopped parsley and onion. Spread each fillet with this mixture and fold over. Poach in court bouillon until just cooked through. Remove with a spatula, being careful that you do not break the fish. Reduce the liquid to about 3 cups, strain, and clarify with egg white. Melt the gelatin in ½ cup of cold water and combine with the boiling bouillon. Chill until thick and syrupy, but not set.

Cover each cooked fillet with a highly seasoned tomato puree to which you have added the basil. Decorate with slices of hard-cooked egg and sliced olives. Cover with some of the jelly and chill. When set, brush again with jelly and chill.

Arrange a bed of greens on a platter and place the fillets on top. Decorate with onion rings which have been marinated in a French dressing. Garnish with hard-cooked egg slices and serve with tomato mayonnaise.

VARIATION

Prepare the fillets of sole as above but omit the greens. Make a rice salad by combining 3 cups of cold cooked rice, 1 cup of chopped cooked shrimp, ½ cup each of chopped onion, green pepper and parsley, and salt and pepper to taste. Make a sauce vinaigrette (see index) and add chopped pickles and herbs. Pour this over the rice mixture. Arrange the rice salad on a platter, and place the fillets on top in the shape of a fan. Put rows of chopped jellied bouillon between the fillets. Garnish with sliced pickles and hard-cooked eggs. This is an easy but spectacular dish for a supper party.

JELLIED FILLETS WITH TARRAGON

8 fillets of sole	2 envelopes gelatin
Fish forcemeat (see index)	3 to 4 cups salade Russe
Fresh tarragon leaves	(see index)
White wine court bouillon	Green mayonnaise
(see index)	Small tomatoes
Egg white	Sliced cucumbers

Spread the fillets with highly seasoned forcemeat and fresh tarragon leaves. Roll and secure with toothpicks. Poach in court bouillon until just cooked through. Chill. Reduce the bouillon, strain, and clarify with egg white. Melt the gelatin in ½ cup of cold water and combine with the boiling bouillon. Cool until thick but not solid. Pour the jelly into 8 molds or one large mold and place in the refrigerator to chill until a thin layer has formed on the bottom and sides. Pour off the rest of the jelly and arrange the fillets, topped with additional tarragon leaves, in the mold. Pour the rest of the jelly over this and chill until firm. Arrange the molds of fillets on a platter with a mound of salade Russe in the center. Surround with tiny tomatoes and cucumber slices. Serve with sauce verte (see index).

WHEEL OF SOLES

This is another spectacular buffet dish.

12 fillets of sole	Chopped parsley
Court bouillon (see index)	Hard-cooked eggs
Egg white	Chopped onion
2 envelopes gelatin	Chili sauce
2 cups mayonnaise (and a little extra)	

SALADE ORIENTALE

5 cups cold cooked rice	½ cup chopped pimiento
12 chopped anchovies	Sauce vinaigrette mixed
½ cup chopped parsley	with ¼ cup chili sauce
1 cup chopped green onion	

Trim the fillets until they are of equal size and are each pointed at one end. Poach them in court bouillon until they are just cooked through. With a spatula, or with a pair of them, remove the fish carefully to a platter to cool. Reduce the bouillon to 3 cups, strain and clarify with egg white. Dissolve the gelatin in ½ cup of cold water and add to the boiling bouillon. Cool. When it is syrupy, combine 2 cups of the jelly with an equal amount of thick mayonnaise. Chill.

Mix the salade Orientale and chill. When ready to serve, place the salade on a large round serving dish and top with the fillets arranged in the form of a wheel. Sprinkle the fillets heavily with chopped parsley.

Halve each hard-cooked egg horizontally and remove the yolk. Mash it and mix with a little mayonnaise, some chopped parsley, chopped onions, and a dash of chili sauce. Fill the egg whites with this mixture piped through a pastry tube. Decorate the platter with the stuffed eggs in the center and between the fillets.

No additional dressing is needed for this dish, but you may serve a bowl of mayonnaise with it of you wish.

Spanish Mackerel

THE ichthyologist Mitchell, writing in 1815 in his *Fishes of New York*, gave the Spanish mackerel this brief but favorable biography: "A fine and beautiful fish; comes in July."

The Spanish mackerel, is a handsome wanderer. It loves the warm seas of the south, and in the summer it migrates to the cool northern waters. Then it heads south again before cold weather sets in. Smart fish.

A fine sport, Spanish mackerel gives a good battle. It is vigorous and sometimes grows to 50 to 75 pounds in weight. In the markets, however, the average weight of the fish sold is about 2 pounds, and it usually comes whole. A choice dish, it is readily bought in the Atlantic Coast area, but unfortunately is rare along the Pacific Coast.

BROILED SPANISH MACKEREL

The Spanish mackerel either split or filleted makes a magnificent dish when broiled and served with lemon butter, tartar sauce or any of the favorite fish sauces. (See index.)

SAUTEED SPANISH MACKEREL

Sauté fillets of Spanish mackerel or small whole fish according to directions for sauté meunière under "Cooking Methods."

BAKED SPANISH MACKEREL

This fish is particularly adapted to baking, either plain or stuffed. It varies in size from 1 to 4 pounds. If you have a large number to serve, you may need to plan on baking 2 mackerel.

Place the fish on an oiled pan or baking dish, dot with butter and season with pepper and salt. Bake at 400° and allow about 9 minutes per pound of fish. Baste frequently.

Serve with parsley butter, lemon butter, maître d'hôtel butter or tomato sauce. (See index.)

BAKED STUFFED SPANISH MACKEREL I

Choose 4 mackerel small enough for individual portions. Make the following mixture:

½ cup soft bread crumbs	1 cup sliced green olives
1 tablespoon grated onion	¼ cup melted butter

Combine all the ingredients, stuff the fish and sew them up securely. Place them on an oiled sheet or pan and surround then with 1½ cups of ripe olives (the dried Italian or Greek ones are best). Brush the fish lavishly with olive oil and sprinkle with pepper. Bake at 400° for 25 to 30 minutes or until the fish flakes easily when tested with a fork. Serve with the olive garnish, steamed potatoes and a cucumber salad.

BAKED STUFFED SPANISH MACKEREL II

6 tablespoons butter	½ teaspoon salt
½ cup finely chopped green onions or scallions	1 teaspoon freshly ground black pepper
¼ cup parsley	½ cup fine crumbs

Blend the butter, herbs, salt and pepper and gradually work in the crumbs. Stuff 2 medium or 1 fairly large mackerel and sew up securely. Place the fish in an oiled baking dish or pan, dot with butter and sprinkle with salt and pepper. Bake at 400° for 25 minutes and serve with parsley potatoes and a tomato and cucumber salad. This will serve four people.

BAKED STUFFED SPANISH MACKEREL III

1 clove garlic, chopped	½ cup crumbs
1 medium onion, chopped	8 anchovy fillets, chopped
2 green peppers, chopped	1 teaspoon coarsely ground black pepper
6 tablespoons oil or fat	
4 large tomatoes, peeled, seeded, and chopped	1 teaspoon fennel seeds
	2 tablespoons capers

Sauté the garlic, onion and green pepper in the oil until soft. Add the tomatoes and let them cook down for about 20 minutes. Add the rest of the ingredients, mix well and stuff a good-sized Spanish mackerel. Sew it securely. Place the fish in a well-oiled baking dish and brush with olive oil. Bake at 400° for 25 minutes, basting frequently. Serve with a tomato sauce (see index).

Spot

THIS is an Atlantic Coast member of the croaker family, and, like its relatives, can play little tunes with the aid of its air bladder. Spot is not well known and is rarely found in the markets at this time. This is regrettable, since it is an attractive fish.

Prepare spot according to the directions for sea trout or butterfish.

Squid

ALSO called poulpe, inkfish and cuttlefish, this elongated ten-armed cousin of the octopus was once a "poor man's" dish, and was eaten only by the Italians, the Spaniards and the Orientals. Squid is now becoming "chic." It is served in the most elegant restaurants.

The Spaniards and the Italians like the squid stewed in its own ink, and so do I. But for most dishes you should slit the belly and remove the bone, which, incidentally, has a number of commercial uses—canary food, for one thing. Wash the squid well under running cold water.

FRIED SQUID I

Cut the tentacles into small pieces, dust them with flour, and dip in beaten egg and crumbs or in batter. Fry quickly in oil heated to 375°. Drain on absorbent paper and salt and pepper to taste. Serve with tartar (see index) or mustard sauce (see index).

These are excellent as part of a "mixed fry" in the Italian style. Use a selection of small bits of fish, all fried and served with a highly seasoned sauce.

FRIED SQUID II

Cut the tentacles in small pieces and dust well with flour. Sauté in plenty of olive oil. It's wise to cover the pan, for the small pieces of squid may fly out and hit you in the face.

Salt and pepper well and serve with puree of spinach lightly flavored with garlic.

BAKED SQUID

Clean the squid and soak it in milk for an hour. Roll it well in buttered bread crumbs, and arrange it in an oiled pan or baking dish. Season with salt and pepper and dot with butter. Bake at 500° for 12 minutes. Serve with a sauce diable (see index), tartar sauce (see index), or tomato sauce (see index).

SAUTEED STUFFED SQUID

1 medium onion, chopped	½ cup ripe olives
4 tablespoons olive oil, and more	2 cups buttered crumbs
2 chopped cloves garlic	1 teaspoon salt
4 tomatoes, peeled, seeded and chopped	1 teaspoon freshly ground black pepper
	Oregano

6 squid

Sauté the onion in 4 tablespoons of olive oil. Add the garlic, tomatoes, and ripe olives. Simmer for 15 minutes. Add the buttered crumbs, salt, pepper, and a good pinch of oregano. Clean and stuff the squid with this mixture and sauté them in plenty of olive oil until the tentacles are crisp and the stuffing thoroughly cooked. Serve, if you wish, with a tomato sauce (see index).

SQUID, ITALIAN STYLE

6 small squid	Pinch of fennel
2 cloves garlic	Juice of 1 lemon
½ cup olive oil	1 cup red or white wine
	Salt, pepper

Wash the squid well, split and remove the cartilage or bone. Place them in a baking pan or large kettle with the garlic, olive oil, fennel, lemon juice, wine, and salt and pepper to taste. Cover and steam on top of the stove or in a slow oven for 45 minutes or until the squid is tender.

Striped Bass

STRIPED bass, sometimes known as rockfish, is a great favorite with anglers on both coasts and an important commercial fish on the East Coast. It is not yet a household food in the same sense as mackerel and cod, but its popularity is growing. Occasionally you may see an exceptionally large striped bass in your market, but on the average the fish runs 15 to 18 inches long. Some is sold filleted, some frozen.

BROILED STRIPED BASS

Either fillets or the whole split fish may be broiled according to the recipes on pages 7-8. Serve with lemon butter or Hollandaise sauce, cucumber sauce with sour cream, tartar sauce, oyster sauce, or lobster sauce (see index).

VARIATIONS

1. (Flambé). Broil a whole striped bass. When it is done, arrange it on a large metal platter on a bed of dried fennel or thyme. Top with a mixture of dried herbs—fennel, thyme, parsley. Add cognac and ignite. Let the herbs burn down so that their flavors permeate the whole fish. You may vary the dried herbs as you wish, but fennel and thyme seem to me to be the perfect combination.

2. Split a whole striped bass and remove the backbone. Oil the broiler pan well, and place the fish on it, skin side down. Oil the fish well, and broil it for 10 minutes. Cover it with paper-thin slices of lemon, salt and pepper it to taste, and continue broiling for 5 to 7 minutes more, or until the fish flakes easily when tested with a fork. Remove the lemon slices and add herb butter—chopped parsley, and other herbs to taste, kneaded into butter.

STUFFED STRIPED BASS I

Split a whole striped bass and remove the backbone. Stuff it with thin slices of onion, tomato, green pepper, and plenty of chopped parsley. Salt and pepper to taste, add some fresh or dried tarragon to taste and dot heavily with butter. Sew the fish together or secure with skewers and twine. Flour it lightly, butter it well, and season to taste. Place it in an oiled baking dish and add 1 cup of red wine. Bake at 400° for 25 to 35 minutes, depending upon the size of the fish. Baste with the wine while it is cooking. Serve with a tomato sauce well flavored with the wine and some garlic.

STUFFED STRIPED BASS II

Prepare a stuffing mixture of the following:

1 pound crabmeat
¼ cup chopped chives or
   green onion
¼ cup chopped parsley
4 tablespoons melted butter

3 tablespoons chopped
   celery
½ cup crumbs
¼ cup heavy cream
Salt, pepper

Stuff the fish and sew it up or fasten it with skewers and twine. Oil and season it and place it on an oiled baking dish or pan and bake at 400° for 25 to 35 minutes. Serve with a sauce rémoulade (see index) which you have mixed with ½ cup of crabmeat.

STUFFED STRIPED BASS III

Striped bass
2 slices salt pork, cut in small
   pieces
4 tablespoons butter
½ cup finely chopped onion
¼ cup finely chopped celery
¼ cup finely chopped green
   pepper

½ cup finely rolled crumbs
1 teaspoon fennel or thyme
½ cup toasted chopped
   almonds
Salt, pepper
Bacon strips

Cook the salt pork in the butter. Add the onion, celery and green pepper. Sauté until just soft. Mix in the crumbs, fennel or thyme, and toasted chopped almonds (the canned ones are excellent). Stuff the fish and sew it up or fasten it with skewers and twine. Season to taste, place in an oiled baking dish and top with strips of bacon. Bake at 400° for 25 to 35 minutes. Serve with a tomato sauce (see index) or a cucumber and sour cream sauce (see index).

STUFFED STRIPED BASS IV

Prepare an omelet *fines herbes* with 4 or 5 eggs and a mixture of herbs. Stuff the fish with the omelet and sew it up. Make a bed of shallots or green onions on the bottom of an oiled baking dish or pan. Add enough white wine to cover these. Place the fish on top, oil it and season it to taste. Bake at 425° for 25 to 35 minutes, basting often. Remove the fish to a hot platter and strain the liquid in the pan. Correct the seasoning, and add ½ cup of heavy cream mixed with 2 or 3 egg yolks. Stir until the sauce is thickened, being careful that it does not boil. Serve with the fish.

BAKED STRIPED BASS

Split a whole fish and place it on an oiled baking pan or dish. Dot with butter and salt and pepper to taste. Bake at 425° for 20 to 25 minutes. Serve with parsley butter (see index).

STRIPED BASS SAUTE

You may sauté either a small whole striped bass or the fillets. Follow directions for sauté menuière under "Cooking Methods." The fish may be served in this manner with any of the following sauces:

1. Tomato sauce
2. Sauce Provençale
3. Sauce duxelles

STRIPED BASS EN PAPILLOTE

First, see the instructions given in the recipe for pompano en papillote (see index) for cutting and folding parchment paper for baking.

1 striped bass, filleted, or 2 pounds fillets
White wine sauce
¼ cup chopped mushrooms, sautéed
¼ cup chopped shallots, sautéed
½ cup finely chopped cooked shrimp
Truffles or mushroom caps

Cut a striped bass into fillets or buy the fillets. Cut these into portions small enough to fit a piece of parchment 8 by 11 inches. Prepare a white wine sauce and add to it the mushrooms, shallots and shrimp. When the sauce is cool, spread it over half of each piece of paper. Place a piece of fillet on top of the sauce, and top each fillet with another spoonful of sauce and a slice of truffle or a mushroom cap. Fold the paper over and crimp it securely.

Bake at 425° for 15 or 20 minutes or until the paper is well puffed. Serve at once in the paper. When you pierce the paper to get at the fish, a mouth-watering odor pours out—one reason why this method of serving fish is so delightful.

POACHED STRIPED BASS

Poach a striped bass in boiling salted water or in a court bouillon (see index) and serve it with any of the following sauces:

1. Hollandaise sauce
2. Sauce mousseline
3. Shrimp sauce
4. Lobster sauce
5. Oyster sauce
6. Sauce velouté
7. Parsley sauce

STRIPED BASS CURRY

Poach 2 pounds of filleted striped bass in boiling salted water until it flakes easily when tested with a fork. Remove and cool. Prepare a curry sauce (see index). Flake the fish and mix it with the sauce. Heat thoroughly. Serve in a ring of saffron rice and pass chutney, chopped toasted almonds, chopped hard-cooked eggs, sliced cucumbers, and thinly sliced bananas in a vinaigrette sauce. The secret of this dish is to be sure not to overcook the fish. It is wonderful for a buffet dinner.

CHINESE SWEET AND SOUR STRIPED BASS

Poach a good-sized striped bass in boiling salted water. Arrange it so that it stands on its split side, complete with head and tail, on a deep platter. Cover with either of the following sweet and sour sauces:

SWEET AND SOUR SAUCE I

2 ounces butter
1 cup dark brown sugar
¼ cup sherry
¼ cup soy sauce
¾ cup wine vinegar
2 tablespoons cornstarch
¼ cup water
1 tablespoon chopped ginger

Melt the butter in a skillet and add the sugar, wine, soy sauce, and vinegar. Mix the cornstarch and water and stir it in. Continue stirring until the sauce thickens. Add the ginger and serve. Add more vinegar if you like more tartness.

SWEET AND SOUR SAUCE II

This is an Americanized version of the sauce:

1 clove garlic	¼ cup soy sauce
4 tablespoons butter	¼ cup chopped ginger
¾ cup brown sugar	3 tablespoons cornstarch
1 cup water	2 small white onions
¾ cup vinegar	2 small ripe tomatoes
¼ cup sherry	1 green pepper
½ cup pineapple cubes	

Chop the garlic and sauté it in the butter. Add the sugar, the water, the vinegar, and wine. Add the soy sauce and ginger and taste for seasoning. Mix the cornstarch with a little water and add it to the sauce, stirring constantly until it is thickened. Add the onion cut in quarters, the tomatoes cut in quarters, the green pepper shredded, and the pineapple cubes. Let it all cook for 3 minutes. Serve with the fish.

COLD STRIPED BASS

Follow any of the recipes for cold salmon or cold halibut (see index).

STRIPED BASS SALAD

Poach 3 pounds of striped bass fillets in boiling salted water until the fish flakes easily. Cut the cooked fillets into dice, or flake with a fork. Combine with 1 cup of finely chopped celery and 1 cup of mayonnaise or Russian dressing. Arrange on a bed of water cress. Decorate with additional mayonnaise, quartered hard-cooked eggs, strips of pimiento, green pepper, and ripe olives.

Sturgeon

THIS fine fish used to be plentiful on the West Coast, in the Great Lakes and in some Eastern rivers. Now it is scarce indeed. Fishing for sturgeon is prohibited by law in many states, and you will rarely see a freshly caught specimen in the market. Its scarcity is a pity, for besides being delicious in itself, the American sturgeon is a source of excellent caviar.

Of all varieties, including the giants of the Columbia and Sacramento rivers, none compares in flavor and texture to the lake sturgeon. A considerable amount of smoked sturgeon is sold throughout the country. It is very expensive, but when you buy it, you may console yourself with the thought that you are paying for a great delicacy.

BRAISED STURGEON

1 large onion
2 carrots
2 stalks of celery
4 sprigs of parsley
A pinch of thyme
Salt and pepper
6 tablespoons butter

Mushroom stems or
  peelings
1½ cups white wine
5 to 6 pound piece of
  sturgeon
3 tablespoons butter
2 tablespoons freshly
  grated horseradish
1 teaspoon sugar

2 tablespoons vinegar

Chop the onion, carrots, celery, and parsley very fine. Add the thyme, salt and pepper to taste, and sauté in 6 tablespoons of butter until soft. Transfer to a large braising pan or Dutch oven. Add the juices from the pan, a few mushroom stems or peelings, and the wine. On a rack over this arrange the piece of sturgeon and steam it in a 350° oven for about 1 hour. The container—braising pan or Dutch oven—must be sealed tightly. When the fish is cooked remove it to a hot platter and baste with the liquid from the pan.

Now, put the pan juices and the vegetables through a food mill, a fine sieve, or into a Waring Blendor. Add 3 tablespoons of butter, the horseradish, and the sugar dissolved in the vinegar. Blend thoroughly, taste for seasoning, and pour over the fish. Serve with wild rice and mushrooms.

STURGEON SCANDINAVIAN

5-pound cut of sturgeon
Anchovy fillets
Bacon
White wine court bouillon
  (see index)

Beurre manié (see index)
1 tablespoon anchovy paste
¼ cup chopped sour
  pickles

Bone the sturgeon and replace the bone with anchovy fillets and pieces of bacon. Tie the fish securely.

Prepare a white wine court bouillon and soak the fish in it for 2 hours. Bring it to a boil. Remove all to a 400° oven and bake for 25 minutes. Put the fish on a hot platter. Strain the sauce and thicken with beurre manié. Add the anchovy paste and the finely chopped pickles. Pour the sauce over the fish.

STURGEON STEAK SAUTE MEUNIERE

Dip sturgeon steaks in flour, and season them with salt and pepper. For every 2 pounds of steak, melt 4 tablespoons of butter in a large skillet. Sauté the steaks gently, browning them nicely on both sides. Baste with butter during the process. Remove the fish to a hot platter and pour the butter over it. Sprinkle with chopped parsley and serve with lemon wedges and Béarnaise sauce (see index).

BRAISED STURGEON, SWEET AND SOUR

4-pound piece of sturgeon
Larding pork
3 onions
3 carrots

2 cups white wine
Salt, pepper
Bouquet garni: leek,
  stalk of celery, bay
  leaf, thyme

Skin the sturgeon and tie it with pieces of larding pork. Place it on a rack in a braising pan or Dutch oven over the onions and carrots, thinly sliced. Add the wine, salt and pepper to taste, and the bouquet garni. Cover and cook in the oven at 350° for about 1 hour. Remove the fish to a hot platter and make the following sauce:

¼ cup vinegar
½ cup brown sugar
3 tablespoons cornstarch
Pineapple chunks

Soy sauce
Green onions
Green peppers

Put the pan juices through a food mill or fine sieve. Return to the heat; add the vinegar, brown sugar, and the cornstarch mixed with a little of the broth. Stir until thickened. Season with soy sauce. Add thinly sliced green onions and green peppers, and chunks of pineapple. Cook them just until well glazed.

Rice is a "must" with this dish.

COULIBIAC OF STURGEON

See index for coulibiac of salmon.

STURGEON STEAKS WITH CREAM

2 inch thick steaks
Salt pork or bacon
Onion, finely chopped
2 cups white wine
Cognac

Butter
½ cup heavy cream
Beurre manié (see index)
Salt, pepper

Skin the steaks and tie them with salt pork or bacon. Arrange them on a bed of finely chopped onion and pour the wine over them. Butter the steaks well and cover the pan with

220

a piece of buttered paper. Bake at 350° for about 1 hour or until the fish is tender and flaky. Remove the fish to a hot platter. Add heavy cream to the pan juices and reduce for 5 minutes. Put the sauce through a food mill or fine sieve and thicken if necessary with beurre manié. Taste for seasoning. Add a dash of cognac and pour over the fish.

My choice of accompaniment for this dish is wild rice or a rice pilaff baked in the oven with strong consommé. For salad, cucumbers in a sweet-sour sauce are ideal.

Caviar

True caviar, which is always gray, is the roe of the sturgeon and is the most expensive food in the world. The best quality caviar is priced around $40 a pound. The gray roe of the whitefish and the red caviar, which comes from the salmon, are less expensive, but could never be called cheap.

Nowadays the finest caviar comes from Iran and the Soviet Union. Its quality is judged by the largeness of the eggs—the sevruga and the sterlet are regarded as the finest of all. Another test of quality is the amount of salt. The less salt, the better the caviar.

In the past, really excellent caviar came from the Great Lakes region and from the mouth of the Columbia River, but the present output is very small as a result of years of wholesale slaughter of sturgeon.

TO SERVE CAVIAR

Caviar is the perfect hors d'oeuvre. If you have the finest with practically no salt in it, store it at around 28° until you are ready to use it. About 2 ounces, or 2 good-sized spoonfuls, are considered an ample serving. My contention is that there is no better way to serve it than straight, with nothing save perhaps a little lemon juice, and some toast or dark bread.

Serve it in a glass bowl placed in another bowl full of chopped ice. Or, if you prefer, use a silver bowl. On very elaborate occasions, caviar is sometimes served in ice carved into the figure of a swan or some other design. There are even special caviar bowls on the market for those who can afford to serve this great delicacy often.

The drink usually associated with caviar is vodka, straight, although many people prefer champagne. This is entirely a matter of personal taste.

If you wish to embellish the caviar serving there are certain accompaniments that are considered *de rigeur*. Besides the usual lemon, they include chopped hard-cooked egg—yolks and whites chopped separately; chopped raw onion; sour cream. Any or all of these are good, but I am definitely of the opinion that they are not needed unless the roe is exceedingly salty.

The perfect after-theater supper, or the perfect celebration of any special event, is certainly as much fresh caviar as you can afford, along with toast, sweet butter, and champagne.

CAVIAR CANAPES

To serve caviar as canapés: Arrange a bowl of the roe surrounded by small bowls of chopped onions, chopped egg—whites and yolks separate—quarters of lemon, and sour cream. Have plenty of hot toast fingers, and let the guests spread their own canapés. Or arrange fingers of toast topped with caviar on a platter along with small dishes of the condiments, and pass the platter. Be certain the canapés are fresh. There is no food less interesting than tired flabby dabs of food on cold, dank toast.

BLINIS WITH CAVIAR

This is one of the most popular hot hors d'oeuvre in Europe. It should be made with the true caviar and served with sour cream. Often, however, you will find it served with the red caviar or herring.

1 package yeast	½ cup butter
¾ cup milk	3 egg yolks
1 teaspoon sugar	½ teaspoon salt
4 cups flour	⅓ cup cream, whipped
3 egg whites, stiffly beaten	

Dissolve the yeast in ¼ cup of warm milk. Add the sugar. Add ½ cup of lukewarm milk and 2 cups of flour. Make a paste of this, cover, and put in a warm place to rise until it is double its bulk.

Cream together the butter, egg yolks, and salt. Combine this with the sponge when it is risen, and beat thoroughly. Let it rise again for 1 hour. Finally add the whipped cream and the stiffly beaten egg whites and let rise again for 15 minutes. Bake into small pancakes about 3 inches in diameter in a buttered pan or griddle.

222

Serve the cakes very hot with melted butter, caviar, and sour cream. From 3 to 6 pancakes will make a serving.

CAVIAR OMELET

This is sheer luxury, but exceedingly delicious luxury. Prepare an omelet in your usual fashion. Fold in about 2 tablespoons of chilled caviar and serve with a dollop of sour cream on top.

TO SERVE RED CAVIAR

Red caviar, or salmon roe, is not so delicate as the caviar of the sturgeon, but it is excellent in appetizers. It may be used for canapés with chopped onion, sour cream, and chopped egg. Or make this dip of red caviar:

RED CAVIAR DIP

1 pint sour cream
¼ cup cream or milk
1½ cups red caviar
1 small grated onion

1 teaspoon freshly ground pepper
1 tablespoon lemon juice
Chopped hard-cooked egg

Dilute the sour cream with cream or milk. Add the caviar, grated onion, black pepper, and lemon juice. Heap in a bowl and sprinkle the top with chopped hard-cooked egg. Serve with raw vegetables, toast or bread sticks.

RED CAVIAR CHEESE

Cream ½ pound of cream cheese. When it is light and fluffy, add ½ cup of red caviar, 1 tablespoon of grated onion, and 1 teaspoon of freshly ground black pepper. Season to taste with lemon juice and beat thoroughly with a fork. Serve with crackers or toast.

CAVIAR EGGS

This is a delightful hors d'oeuvre. For 6 servings:

6 hard-cooked eggs
6 tablespoons caviar (red or black)
1 tablespoon chopped chives or green onion

1 tablespoon chopped parsley
1 tablespoon mayonnaise or sour cream
1 teaspoon freshly ground black pepper

Shell the eggs, cut them in halves, and remove the yolks. Mash these well and combine with the caviar, chives or green onion, parsley, mayonnaise or sour cream, and pepper. When it is thoroughly whipped together, heap it into the whites with a spoon, or pipe it in, using the rosette end of a pastry tube.

For a first course, serve 2 halves per person. Arrange them on greens and pass a Russian dressing. Or double the recipe and serve it as a salad course with water cress, Russian dressing, and crisp French bread.

Surf Perch and Sea Perch

SOMETIMES called striped or blue perch, the surf perch is a small Pacific fish. I like it cooked simply and served with a good sauce, such as an olive sauce, or sweet-sour sauce (see index).

The sea perch of the Atlantic is sometimes sold as frozen fillets, and these fillets can be cooked according to the recipes for ocean perch (see index). New England anglers, fishing off the rocks, often catch sea perch. It is a very bony fish to cook whole; however, it may be prepared in the same ways as the Pacific surf perch.

BROILED SURF PERCH

Broil the fish whole, following the directions under "Cooking Methods."

SAUTEED SURF PERCH

Follow the directions for sautéing under "Cooking Methods."

Swordfish

THIS continues to hold its place among the most popular fish marketed in the United States. Swordfish is caught on both the Atlantic and Pacific coasts and in most coastal waters around the world. For years we have imported it in large quantities, sometimes bringing in more poundage than is caught in American waters. Swordfish is a fine game fish and is eagerly sought by anglers.

The meat of the fish is firm, oily, and well-flavored. It is sold mainly in steaks, sometimes in fillets. Usually it is served broiled with a variety of sauces, but it is also often baked or sautéed. The flesh tends to be dry if not basted often.

BROILED SWORDFISH

Swordfish steaks are large and will usually serve several people. The size of the steak—it can be cut from ½ to 2 inches thick—will depend on the number of servings you wish.

Brush the fish well with butter or oil and place it on an oiled rack about 2 inches from the flame. Baste with more butter or oil during the cooking process, and turn once. Be careful not to let the flesh become too dry.

Season to taste with salt and pepper and serve with lemon wedges, lemon butter, tarragon butter, parsley butter, or beurre noisette (see index). Excellent accompaniments are sautéed potatoes and a tart salad, such as celery in French dressing made with plenty of dry mustard.

VARIATIONS

1. Baste the fish with a mixture of melted butter, white wine, and dried or fresh tarragon.

2. Marinate the fish for 1 hour in a mixture of lemon juice, chopped onion, olive oil, and basil. Baste with this sauce while broiling. Season and serve with crisp julienne potatoes and slices of raw onion and cucumber in vinaigrette sauce (see index).

PLANKED SWORDFISH STEAKS

This is a festive dish for a dinner party.

Select 1 or 2 large steaks—about 5 to 6 pounds—for 6 people. Broil them as above, but remove them just before they are done. Arrange them on a hot hickory or oak plank and surround with a border of duchess potatoes and vegetables, as follows:

Mash or puree 8 large boiled or baked potatoes. Season to taste with salt and pepper, add ¼ pound of butter, and the yolks of 3 eggs beaten with a little cream. The potatoes must be stiff enough to force through a pastry tube. Using the large rosette end of the tube, make a border of the potatoes around the edge of the plank. Then make strips, like spokes, of the potatoes running from the fish in the center out to the potato border. Fill the spaces between the spokes with green peas, julienne beets, tiny grilled tomatoes, and snap beans.

Sprinkle the top of the whole plank with paprika, dot with butter, season with salt and pepper, and run it under the broiler flame to brown slightly. Sprinkle with chopped parsley.

A sweet-sour cucumber salad is delicious with this, and needless to say, the addition of some good chilled *vin rosé* will make this dinner party one your guests will never forget.

BARBECUED SWORDFISH STEAK

This is an outstanding fish dish when cooked over charcoal and basted with a good tart sauce. But it's almost as good cooked indoors as outdoors.

Use your own special barbecue sauce, or try this version:

BARBECUE SAUCE

½ cup soy sauce
2 cloves garlic, chopped
4 tablespoons tomato sauce or catsup
2 tablespoons lemon juice
¼ cup chopped parsley

1 teaspoon finely powdered oregano
½ cup orange juice
1 teaspoon freshly ground pepper

Mix these ingredients together and soak the swordfish steak in it for 2 hours before cooking. Brush or baste the fish with the sauce during the broiling. Serve with braised kidney beans, a hearty salad of greens, tomatoes and onion rings, and a red wine.

SWORDFISH STEAK WITH PEPPER

2 inch thick steak
Flour
2 teaspoons freshly ground black pepper

Oil
Butter
Salt
¼ cup white wine or sherry

Dredge the steak with flour and grind the pepper onto the surface. Press the pepper into the flesh of the fish with the heel of your hand. Brush with oil and sauté in 5 tablespoons of butter until nicely browned on both sides. Turn once during the cooking. Salt to taste and remove the steak to a hot platter. Add a little more butter to the pan, and the wine. Swirl it around and pour it over the fish. Serve with lemon quarters, plain boiled new potatoes, and beets dressed with sour cream and dill.

VARIATION

Swordfish Steak with Rosemary. Follow the recipe above, but substitute dried or fresh rosemary for the pepper. The rosemary gives a rare and unusual flavor to the fish.

BAKED SWORDFISH STEAK

2 steaks, 1 inch thick	Butter
Flour	Salt, pepper
Oil	1 cup white wine
Fresh dill	1 cup cream
Sliced onions	3 egg yolks

Dust the steaks with flour and brush with oil. Place one in the bottom of a well-oiled baking dish. Spread it with a layer of dill and then a layer of onion slices. Dot with butter and season with salt and pepper. Top with the second steak, and dot this with butter and seasonings. Pour ½ cup of white wine into the pan and bake at 425° for about 25 minutes. Baste the fish several times during the cooking.

Remove the fish to a hot platter. Add ½ cup of wine to the pan, bring it to a boil, and gradually stir in the cream mixed with the egg yolks. Stir until well thickened and smooth. Pour the sauce over the fish.

BAKED SWORDFISH WITH MUSHROOMS

2 steaks, 1 inch thick	2 tablespoons chopped
Butter	shallots or onions
Crumbs	Salt, pepper
3 tins of "broiled in butter"	½ cup white wine
chopped mushrooms	1 cup cream
Beurre manié (see index)	

Place one steak in the bottom of an oiled baking dish. Spread the steak with butter and top with crumbs. Open 2 tins of chopped mushrooms and drain, saving the juice. Spread the mushrooms over the steak. Add chopped shallots or onions, salt and pepper to taste, and dot with butter. Top with the second steak, dot this with butter and season with salt and pepper. Add the wine to the mushroom liquid and pour over the fish. Bake at 425° for about 25 minutes, basting with the pan juices.

Remove the fish to a hot platter. Open the third tin of mushrooms and add them to the pan juices. Add 1 cup of cream and thicken with beurre manié. Taste for seasoning and pour over the fish. Serve with crisp sautéed potatoes and braised endive. A chilled *vin rosé* is the perfect complement.

BAKED SWORDFISH CASTILIAN

4 green peppers, shredded	1 teaspoon oregano
Olive oil	1 tablespoon chili powder
Salt, pepper	2 tablespoons chopped
1 teaspoon lemon juice	parsley
3 medium onions, chopped	Fresh coriander or
3 cloves garlic, chopped	cilantro
2 cups stewed or canned	1 thick swordfish steak
tomatoes	Butter

Sauté the shredded peppers in olive oil, season to taste, and add 1 teaspoon of lemon juice. Sauté the onion and garlic in oil. Add the tomatoes, oregano, chili powder, parsley, and coriander (or cilantro, if available). Simmer for 25 minutes.

Place the steak in an oiled baking dish. Dot it with butter, and season with salt and pepper. Bake at 425° for 20 minutes, or until done. Pour the sauce over the fish, top it with the green peppers and return to the oven for 5 minutes to blend thoroughly. Serve with rice and sautéed eggplant.

Tautog (Blackfish)

THIS is a good game fish that is well known to sportsmen on the North and Middle Atlantic Coast. In New England it is known as tautog, and elsewhere it is called blackfish, or sometimes black porgy or salt-water chub. It is usually caught near shore, since it is a fish that likes rocks and ledges. It is also fond of snooping around piers and old wrecks.

The tautog or blackfish is taken commercially from Cape Cod to Delaware Bay. The average fish weighs 2 to 3 pounds and is 12 to 18 inches long. The flesh is white, juicy and has a pleasant flavor.

SAUTEED TAUTOG

Clean and split the fish and sauté according to directions under "Cooking Methods."

BROILED TAUTOG

Broil according to directions under "Cooking Methods."

BAKED TAUTOG

Bake tautog as you would striped bass (see index).

Tuna and Related Fish

THIS is a fish that I think is better canned than fresh. There are many varieties of tuna on both coasts, and all are robust game fish. The albacore, which has the true white meat, is the one used for the finest pack tuna fish and for the most delicate dishes. The others are not so white, varying in color from a sort of amber to a purply red. Bonito is an important Pacific member of the family, all members of which are related to the mackerel.

Small tuna weigh 10 to 15 pounds, large ones up to 600 pounds. The fish is sold whole, in steaks, and in fillets.

Some smoked tuna is found here and there on the markets, but other varieties of smoked fish are more popular.

Fresh Tuna

GRILLED TUNA WITH VARIOUS SAUCES

Marinate 1 inch thick tuna steaks in olive oil flavored with garlic and lemon juice. Soak the fish for 1 hour before cooking. Grill the steaks over charcoal or in the broiler, basting well with additional oil. Cook for 8 to 10 minutes, turning once. Season the steaks with salt and pepper, remove them to a hot platter and serve with any of the following sauces: Hollandaise (see index), Béarnaise (see index), lobster (see index), shrimp (see index), lemon butter (see index), or parsley butter (see index).

VARIATION

Marinate the fish in your favorite barbecue sauce, and brush it with the sauce while it is grilling. Serve with sautéed potatoes and plenty of garlic bread to dunk into the sauce.

TUNA SAUTE AMANDINE

4 pounds tuna steaks	Flour
½ pound almonds	Salt, pepper
6 tablespoons butter	2 tablespoons chopped parsley

Lemon wedges

Use 1 inch thick tuna steaks. Blanch and sliver the almonds, or open a tin of the chopped buttered almonds. Melt the butter, flour the fish lightly and brown quickly in the butter. Salt and pepper them to taste. When you have turned the steaks, add the almonds and chopped parsley. Add more butter to the pan if necessary. Remove the fish to a hot platter, pour the almonds and butter over the top, and surround with lemon wedges.

Serve with plain boiled potatoes.

SAUTEED ALBACORE WITH TARRAGON AND WHITE WINE

1 albacore steak	1 teaspoon dried, or 1 tablespoon fresh, tarragon
4 tablespoons butter	
⅔ cup dry white wine	

Choose a good-sized albacore steak—about 1 inch thick or thicker. Melt the butter in a skillet, add the steak and brown lightly on both sides over a fairly brisk heat. Add the white wine, in which you have soaked the tarragon while the steak is browning. Let the wine cook down rapidly and spoon it over the fish. Remove the fish to a hot platter and pour the wine sauce over it.

Serve with tiny new potatoes smothered in butter and small glazed onions.

FRIED FINGERS OF TUNA

These are delicious for a luncheon dish. If you have the patience to cut the fingers very small, you can serve them as an appetizer with a good dunk sauce.

Cut tuna steaks into small fingers about 3 inches long and ½ inch through. Marinate these in oil for 1 hour. Dip them in flour, then in beaten eggs, and roll them in crumbs or corn meal. Fry in deep hot fat heated to 370°. They will take 2 to 3 minutes at the most. Drain on absorbent paper, season with salt and pepper, and serve with tartar sauce (see index), sauce rémoulade (see index), or sauce diable (see index).

(see index), sauce rémoulade (see index), or sauce diable (see index).

VARIATIONS

1. Mix grated Parmesan cheese and a good deal of chili powder in with the crumbs. Roll the fish in this, fry, and serve with a hot Mexican sauce.

2. Mix the crumbs well with sesame seeds. Roll the fish in this, fry, and serve with sauce diable.

3. Roll the fish in sesame seeds alone, fry, and serve with a sweet-sour sauce (see index).

HELEN EVANS BROWN'S BAKED ALBACORE

4 pounds albacore steaks or fillets	½ cup olive oil
1 large onion, chopped	1 teaspoon salt
1 green pepper, chopped	1 teaspoon freshly ground black pepper
4 or 5 stalks of celery, chopped	1 teaspoon oregano
6 sprigs of parsley, chopped	1 cup red wine
1 large clove of garlic, chopped	1 No. 2½ can of tomatoes

Sauté the onion, pepper, celery, parsley, and garlic in the olive oil. Season with salt, pepper, and oregano and add the wine and tomatoes.

Place the fish on a well-oiled baking dish and pour the sauce over it. Bake at 350° until the internal temperature of the fish registers 140°, or until the fish flakes easily when tested with a fork. Baste frequently during the cooking.

Serve it in the dish in which it was baked and pass plenty of sourdough bread with garlic butter, or—if you live on the East Coast—garlic bread.

MARINATED ALBACORE

4 pound piece of albacore or other tuna	1 carrot thinly sliced
2 cups red wine	Heaping teaspoonful of dried basil or several leaves of the fresh basil
2 cloves of garlic, chopped	
1 or 2 leeks, cleaned and chopped	1 teaspoon salt
1 or 2 stalks of celery, chopped	4 tablespoons butter
	Beurre manié (see index)

Make a marinade of the wine, vegetables, and seasonings. Soak the fish in this for 6 hours. Remove the fish from the marinade and strain it. Melt butter in a skillet, add the vegetables from the marinade and cook until they are just soft.

Oil a baking dish, place the vegetables on the bottom and top with the fish. Dot it with butter and pour the wine around it. Bake at 400° for 25 or 30 minutes, basting often during the cooking process. Remove the fish to a hot platter. Force the sauce through a fine sieve, return it to the stove and thicken with beurre manié. Taste for seasoning.

Serve with spaghetti or macaroni cooked until just tender and flavored with garlic, olive oil, and basil. This is a wonderful dinner for people on a meatless diet.

POACHED TUNA WITH VARIOUS SAUCES

Since albacore has the lightest meat, it is, of course, the best of the various tunas for poaching.

Poach a 3 or 4 pound piece of tuna in court bouillon (see index) until the fish flakes easily when tested with a fork. Serve with a sweet-sour sauce (see index), a sauce Béarnaise (see index), or an oyster sauce (see index).

COLD POACHED TUNA

Serve the poached fish cold with a good olive oil mayonnaise, a sauce rémoulade (see index), or a Russian dressing (see index).

Canned Tuna Fish

The finest canned tuna is the albacore, or all white meat solid pack. There are some excellent brands of canned tuna put up in this country, but I must say that—as with the sardines—the very best canned tuna comes from France. The olive oil used by the French packers makes the fish a richer, tastier dish. If the fine Oregon and California canneries would substitute olive oil for the vegetable oils they now use, and add more flavor, their product would be superb.

Tuna flakes, tuna hunks, and tuna bits in cans are excellent for salads and other dishes in which the fish must be cut up.

I am not going to tell you how you can achieve miracles with a can of tuna, cream of mushroom soup, and cornflakes. To my mind, such dishes merely ruin the taste of good canned tuna—of which I am very fond. There *are* delicious ways to serve this product.

CANNED TUNA AS HORS D'OEUVRE

I think one of the finest first courses or luncheon dishes is a good tin of tuna, with some capers, some homemade mayonnaise, and crisp French bread and butter.

TUNA AS A COCKTAIL SPREAD

1 No. 1 tin of tuna, mashed
½ cup capers
2 tablespoons mayonnaise
1 teaspoon paprika
2 tablespoons onion juice
3 egg whites, stiffly beaten

Blend all ingredients. Spread on fingers of toast and place under the broiler flame until lightly browned and puffy.

CURRY OF TUNA FISH

1 large onion, chopped
1 unpeeled apple, chopped
2 cloves garlic, chopped
6 tablespoons oil or butter
1½ tablespoons curry powder
½ cup water
1 cup tomato puree
Salt
½ cup white wine
1½ cups canned tuna

Sauté the onion, apple and garlic in oil or butter. Add the curry powder and blend well. Add the water and let it cook down. Gradually stir in the tomato puree and blend thoroughly. Taste for seasoning. Stir in the wine and add the tuna fish. Heat thoroughly. Serve with rice, chutney, French-fried onions, and chopped hard-cooked egg.

TUNA FISH PLATE

For each serving, arrange a bed of shredded greens, topped with 1 small can of solid pack tuna broken into pieces. Garnish with paper-thin slices of onion, sliced hard-cooked egg, and capers. Serve mayonnaise separately.

TUNA FISH SAUCE FOR SPAGHETTI

This is an authentic Italian recipe. It is simple, but delicious.

¼ pound dried mushrooms
3 cloves garlic, chopped
¼ cup olive oil
1½ cups tomato sauce or
strained canned tomatoes
1 teaspoon basil
Salt, pepper
½ tin of tuna bits
Chopped parsley

Soak the mushrooms in water for 2 hours. Sauté the garlic in olive oil for a few minutes. Add the tomatoes and simmer until thick. Add the mushrooms and basil, season to taste with salt and freshly ground black pepper, and add the tuna. Cook for 10 minutes. Serve over spaghetti or other pasta, and top with freshly ground pepper and chopped parsley.

SCALLOPED TUNA FISH

1½ cups cracker crumbs	1 teaspoon salt
1 cup celery, chopped fine	1 teaspoon freshly ground
1 cup onion, chopped fine	black pepper
2 cloves garlic, chopped fine	1½ cups tuna bits
1 green pepper, chopped fine	½ cup melted butter
½ cup parsley, chopped	2 eggs, lightly beaten

Use rather coarse cracker crumbs. Combine them with the chopped vegetables, seasonings and tuna. Add the melted butter and beaten eggs. Blend well and pour into a buttered casserole. Dot the top with butter and bake at 375° for 25 or 30 minutes.

TUNA FISH OMELET

Use ½ cup of flaked tuna for each omelet. Heat the fish in a little olive oil or butter, and season with onion juice and freshly ground black pepper. Make omelets according to your usual method and fold the hot tuna fish into them. Garnish with chopped parsley, or parsley and chives mixed.

SALADE NICOISE

This will make a salad for 3 or 4 people, or a first course for 6 people.

Arrange greens on a large platter. Open 2 tins of solid pack tuna fish and place the fish in the center of the platter. Around the edge arrange fillets of anchovies (about 3 tins), 6 small or 3 large tomatoes cut in wedges, 6 hard-cooked eggs quartered, and strips of green pepper and pimento. Garnish with chopped parsley and ripe olives and serve with sauce vinaigrette (see index) or sauce gribiche (see index).

TUNA SALAD SUPREME

This will make a salad for 6 people.

Grate 2 heads of raw celery root. Add 2 No. ½ cans or 1

No. 1 can of tuna fish bits, 2 chopped hard-cooked eggs, 6 chopped green onions, and blend with a vinaigrette sauce (see index) to which you have added 1 tablespoon of prepared mustard, 1 teaspoon of chopped parsley and 1 teaspoon of tarragon. Serve on endive spears or chicory. Garnish with ripe olives and pimiento strips.

OLD-FASHIONED TUNA SALAD

Combine 1½ cups of tuna bits with ½ cup of finely chopped celery, 8 chopped green onions, 2 tablespoons of capers, and enough mayonnaise to bind the salad. Serve in a nest of romaine or lettuce. Garnish with mayonnaise, ripe olives, tomato wedges, and sliced hard-cooked eggs.

TUNA SALAD BUFFET PLATE

Make a good French potato salad: Pour white wine and olive oil over hot sliced potatoes; add slivered almonds, chopped chives, onions, and parsley; add a dash of vinegar and chill it well.

Make a Russian salad with finely cut cooked vegetables: peas, carrots, string beans, and potatoes bound together with mayonnaise.

Arrange greens on a long platter. In the center place a smoked whitefish, the tuna from 3 large cans, skinless and boneless sardines from 3 cans. Spoon the French potato salad and the Russian salad around the fish. Garnish with paper-thin slices of onion, quartered hard-cooked eggs, and wedges of tomato. Serve with a bowl of mayonnaise and a dish of fresh horseradish mixed with sour cream and dill.

Hard Swedish bread and a bottle of chilled *rosé* wine will make this a summer buffet of exceptional flavors.

Whitebait

THESE minnowlike fish are much discussed. Some experts say they are a mixture of various infant fish, while others claim they are a definite species. Who knows, who cares and what can we do about it? They are wonderful eating.

When you sample whitebait for the first time, you may find it disconcerting to have a whole plateful of eyes staring up at you. I did. This initial reaction soon passes, and they become one of your favorite delicacies. They are often served with the tiny oyster crabs, and when offered in this fashion at a smart restaurant, they are definitely on the expensive side.

SAUTEED WHITEBAIT

Use 1 to 1½ pounds of whitebait for 4 servings. Soak them in ice water for an hour or two. Drain them on a towel and roll in corn meal. Sauté them very quickly in olive oil, shaking the pan often to move the fish around, and shifting them carefully with a wooden spoon. Salt and pepper to taste and serve with a rémoulade (see index) or tarter sauce (see index).

VARIATIONS

1. Serve with sautéed oyster crabs as a garnish.
2. Dust with flour instead of corn meal.

FRIED WHITEBAIT

Prepare whitebait as above and fry in deep fat heated to 375°. The fish will take about 15 seconds to cook—at the most a half minute. Drain on absorbent paper and season to taste.

VARIATION

Let the fish cook until very crisp. Sprinkle with a little cayenne and dry mustard and squeeze lemon juice over them.

WHITEBAIT PANCAKES

Wash and dry a pound of whitebait. Mix with the following:

3 eggs, lightly beaten	⅓ cup grated Parmesan
¼ cup chopped parsley	cheese
1 finely chopped garlic clove	1 teaspoon sweet basil
	Salt, pepper

Add enough flour to hold the fish and egg mixture together —about 1 cup. Form into small cakes. Dust them lightly with flour and fry in olive oil until browned on both sides. Serve with a rémoulade (see index) or tartar sauce (see index).

WHITEBAIT ITALIAN

1½ pounds whitebait	1 teaspoon salt
Corn meal	1 tablespoon paprika
Olive oil	4 eggs
2 teaspoons grated onion	4 tablespoons cream
½ cup grated Parmesan cheese	

Wash the whitebait and roll them in corn meal. Sauté in olive oil until just barely cooked through. Add the grated onion, salt, and paprika. Beat the eggs well, and add the cream and grated Parmesan cheese. Gently pour over the whitebait. Run under the broiler flame for 3 or 4 minutes to set the eggs.

Whiting

WHITING, or silver hake, are caught off the coast of New England, New York and New Jersey, and as far south as Virginia. They are most plentiful in the spring and the fall. The frozen product is shipped throughout the country and has a ready market, especially in "fish and chips" shops.

The flesh is white and delicately flavored. It adapts well to nearly all forms of preparation. The average whiting is about 12 to 14 inches long, but occasionally one may reach 24 inches and weigh as much as 8 pounds. One small whiting is usually considered a portion.

GRILLED WHITING

Have small whiting—one per portion—split and dressed. Sprinkle with salt and pepper, brush with melted butter or oil, and grill about 4 inches from a medium flame. Baste often with butter or oil. Serve sprinkled with chopped parsley.

VARIATIONS

1. Serve with Hollandaise sauce (see index) or sauce Béarnaise (see index).

2. Sprinkle the split whiting heavily with sesame seeds.

3. Grill as above, sprinkle with fried crumbs and serve with lemon wedges.

4. Mix together ½ cup of oil, ½ cup of chopped parsley, 1 tablespoon of paprika and 1 teaspoon of salt. Baste the fish with this mixture while it is cooking.

WHITING SAUTE MEUNIERE

Choose 1 small whiting per person and have it dressed. Cook according to directions for sauté meunière under "Cooking Methods."

FRIED WHITING

The usual method is to remove the backbone from the whiting before frying in deep fat. Dip the fish in flour, then in beaten egg and milk, then roll well in crumbs or corn meal. Fry in fat heated to 365°. Drain on absorbent paper, and season to taste. Serve with tartar sauce (see index) or lemon wedges.

VARIATIONS

1. (Mediterranean). Sauté 6 green peppers, cut in strips, in 6 tablespoons of olive oil until just tender. Season to taste, add 1 teaspoon of wine vinegar and swirl it around the pan. Deep-fry 4 whiting according to the directions above. Arrange them on a bed of the peppers and serve with rice pilaff and a tomato sauce.

2. Serve the fried fish with sautéed onion rings and deep-fried parsley (see index).

3. Serve the fried fish on a bed of eggplant slices, which have been dipped in flour and sautéed in olive oil until nicely browned. Garnish with sautéed green peppers and grilled tomatoes. This combination of flavors is delicious.

POACHED WHITING

Poach whiting in boiling salted water just until it flakes when tested with a fork. Be very careful not to overcook. Serve it with:

1. Melted butter, lemon, boiled potatoes, parsley.
2. Hollandaise sauce, boiled potatoes, parsley.
3. Tomato sauce, sautéed potatoes.
4. Black butter, capers, lemon juice.

238

STUFFED ROLLED WHITING

6 whiting fillets
   Fish forcemeat (see index)
1½ cups sauce velouté (see
   index)

Lemon juice
½ pound mushrooms
4 tablespoons butter
¼ cup chopped parsley

Stuff the fillets with the forcemeat, roll and pin with toothpicks. Poach them in boiling salted water until just cooked through. Arrange them on a hot platter, cover with sauce velouté flavored with a little lemon juice, surround with mushroom caps sautéed in butter, and sprinkle with parsley.

WHITING CREOLE

6 small whiting
2 tablespoons butter
1 onion, chopped
½ cup chopped celery
½ cup chopped green pepper

½ cup chopped pimiento
3 cups canned tomatoes
1 tablespoon cornstarch
2 tablespoons water
Salt, pepper

Chopped parsley

Melt the butter, add the onion and let it brown lightly. Add the celery, pepper and pimento and sauté for a few minutes. Add the tomatoes, bring it to a boil and simmer for 1 hour. Mix the cornstarch and water, add it to the sauce and stir until thickened. Season to taste and add parsley. Put the fish in the sauce and let them cook for about 7 minutes or until they flake easily.

Yellowtail

THE Pacific Coast yellowtail is a juicy fish with a rather heavy texture, but with a really pleasant flavor. It is a good game fish, always plentiful in the spring and early summer. Yellowtail is sold in the markets whole, or as fillets or steaks.

BROILED YELLOWTAIL

For broiling, select steaks 1½ to 2 inches thick. It is a good idea to marinate them before broiling. Try a marinade of olive or peanut oil and white wine or sherry. Soak the steaks for 1 hour, and baste them with this sauce during the broiling process. Follow the general directions for broiling under "Cooking Methods." Serve with lemon butter, parsley butter, anchovy butter, or a dill sauce.

BAKED YELLOWTAIL

Yellowtail steaks	Chopped chives or green
Salt, pepper	onions
Tarragon	Butter
Parsley	1 cup white wine

Arrange the steaks in an oiled baking dish. Season to taste with salt and pepper. Sprinkle with chopped tarragon, parsley, chives or green onions. Dot with butter and add 1 cup of wine to the pan. Bake at 425° for about 25 minutes, or until the fish flakes easily when tested with a fork. Baste with the pan juices during the cooking process. Serve with tarragon butter mixed with the juices from the pan.

FRESH-WATER FISH

Bass

THE name "bass" can mean somewhat different things to different people. When you think of catching or eating a bass, the way you picture the fish in your mind depends upon where you live or possibly upon the memory of your youthful experiences as an angler.

Bass is usually described by a qualifying word, such as small-mouthed, large-mouthed, spotted, striped, black, white, rock, calico, not to mention many local names, or to reckon with the fact that some of the qualifying terms apply to the same fish or to other fishes that are not bass at all. To add to the confusion, there are some marine fishes called bass.

To simplify the matter of fresh-water bass, I shall make only these generalizations: Bass are members of a large voracious family of fishes that includes the sunfish and the crappie; most bass are good game fishes, they are abundant, widely distrubted, and well adapted to pond culture.

The small-mouthed bass, a lively game fish, is found in the streams and lakes of the Northern and Central states. It averages 3 to 4 pounds. The spotted bass, somewhat smaller, inhabits the same general area.

The large-mouth bass, sometimes called a black crappie, prevails in the Central and Southern states. Less lively than its small-mouthed relative, it usually weighs about 3 pounds but has been known to attain very impressive weights.

The rock bass, sometimes called red-eyed or goggle-eyed, is a common game fish in the Great Lakes region, Mississippi Valley, and in Eastern and Southern states. It is thick-bodied, meaty, and averages about 10 inches in length. It likes shadowy spots and is actually not much of a fighter.

BROILED BASS

Small whole bass or larger ones split can be broiled and served with lemon butter (see index), tartar sauce (see index), or any of the favorite fish sauces. Follow the directions for broiling on page 15.

PAN-FRIED BASS

Small bass may be pan-fried as you would crappies (see index).

BAKED BASS

Clean and wash the bass, place it on an oiled baking dish, dot with butter and season with salt and pepper. Bake in a 400° oven and allow about 9 minutes per pound of fish. Test for doneness with a fork. Baste the fish frequently during the cooking process.

Serve with parsley butter (see index), lemon butter (see index), or your favorite fish sauce.

Bluegill Sunfish

MOST states prohibit commercial fishing of the bluegill sunfish, reserving it for the benefit of sportsmen. It is a delightful pond fish, highly prolific, and has been artificially propagated over a wide area. The flesh is firm, flaky and of good flavor. A bluegill rarely weighs over 1 pound, but it is game for its size and fairly amusing as a sport fish.

Occasionally you may hear anglers refer to the bluegill and to other sunfishes as "bream," a name that is also applied sometimes to such unrelated salt-water fishes as ocean perch or rosefish, and to porgy or scup. At any rate, the bluegill sunfish and any fresh-water fish called bream may be cooked by following the recipes for crappies (see index).

Bowfin

THE bowfin is a prehistoric holdover. It sometimes breathes air, a faculty it developed in the Devonian period when severe droughts made life tough for fish. In fact, it is claimed that when droughts occur in the South, live bowfin can go underground and breathe air.

The bowfin is practically never prepared fresh. It needs much careful attention and skilled cookery. Smoked bowfin is superb. It should be approached with a good appetite.

Buffalo Fish

THERE are different varieties of this fish in the Middle West—the common buffalo, sometimes called the redmouth and the bigmouth; the round or prairie buffalo, also called the rooter; and the small-mouthed buffalo.

The fish is less bony than the carp and has an excellent flavor. Many people prefer it to carp, feeling that the somewhat musty taste of the latter is unpleasant.

A great deal of smoked buffalo fish is available in the East and Middle West. It is more delicate than smoked carp and a delicious change in the smoked fish field.

You may prepare buffalo fish in the same way you prepare carp.

Burbot

THE burbot is the one fresh-water member of the cod family. It has a slight beard and fins that resemble those of the cusk. Burbot liver oil is one of the most valuable sources of vitamin A, and the fish itself is fine eating. It is found in northern waters.

Prepare burbot in any of the ways suggested for cod or haddock.

Carp

THIS fish has a splendid literary background. There are many references to it in fables and stories, and its long history includes an Asiatic origin followed by plantings in Europe and America. American carp have been known to weigh as much as 60 pounds, and I have seen even larger ones in Europe. I remember especially a magnificent carp that I saw fished out of a pond on an estate in France. After it had been cooked and wonderfully decorated, it was placed on a plank. It was so large that it took two maids, carrying it between them, to bring it to us.

Carp are sometimes transported to market in tanks. Some are sold filleted, and pieces are occasionally available, but the usual thing is to find the carp whole. It is a very scaly fish and should be carefully prepared. Some people object to its rather muddy flavor. This can be overcome by the seasoning and by bleeding the fish completely before cleaning it.

CARP FILLET, SPENCER METHOD

Evelene Spencer, who was a government food expert many years ago, developed a form of fish cookery that has been known since as the Spencer Method. Any fillets may be cooked this way, but I think that it applies particularly well to the carp. The following recipe is for four people:

Cut 4 fillets of carp in serving portions. Fill a shallow pan with salted milk and a large flat plate with dry bread crumbs. Dip the fillets into the milk and then into the crumbs, being sure that the crumbs cover both sides of the fish. Lay the fillets on a well-buttered baking sheet and pour 3 tablespoons of melted butter or bacon fat on each one. Heat the oven to 550°, and place the pan near the top of the oven. Bake for 10 to 12 minutes. Remove the fillets to a hot platter and serve with quarters of lemon or tartar sauce (see index).

This method is intended to achieve a fine crust on the outside and tender moist fish inside. You'll find it is amazingly good.

OVEN-BRAISED CARP FILLETS PROVENCALE

2 medium onions	Dried thyme
Oil	1 teaspoon salt
4 carp fillets	1 teaspoon ground black
Flour	pepper
2 cloves garlic	1 cup red wine
½ cup chopped parsley	Tomato puree (about 1 cup)
	18 to 20 ripe olives
Steamed rice	

Chop the onions fairly coarse and place them on a well-oiled baking pan. Dip the fillets in flour and arrange them on the bed of onions. Sprinkle with chopped garlic, chopped parsley, thyme, salt, and pepper. Add the red wine to the pan, and then drizzle olive oil all over the fish. Top each fillet with 3 tablespoons of tomato puree. Bake at 425° for 15 to 18 minutes, basting often with the wine in the pan. Remove to a hot serving platter. Blend the sauce in the pan with 3 or 4 more tablespoons of tomato puree and add the ripe olives. Pour the sauce around the fish and serve the steamed rice.

CARPE AU BLEU

The small fish are sometimes cooked like trout, in a vinegar and water boullion. Serve them with melted butter, or a sauce gribiche (see index), or vinaigrette (see index), and a boiled potato.

ALSATIAN CARP WITH SAUERKRAUT

4 pounds sauerkraut	Flour
4 cloves garlic	Butter or bacon fat
1 tablespoon coarsely ground pepper	Grated Gruyère or Cheddar cheese
1 quart beer	Sour cream
4 carp fillets	Buttered crumbs

Steam the sauerkraut mixed with the garlic, black pepper, and beer for 4 to 6 hours in a covered dish over low heat.

Flour the fillets and sauté them in butter or bacon fat until they are nicely browned on both sides.

Arrange a layer of the sauerkraut in the bottom of a well-buttered baking dish, then add a layer of grated cheese, then a layer of the fish covered with sour cream; repeat these layers and top with a layer of the kraut. Add 2 cups of beer or liquid from the sauerkraut, sprinkle with grated cheese and buttered crumbs. Dot with butter and bake at 350° for 30 minutes.

CARP HAWAIIAN

1 large coconut	Sesame or peanut oil
1 cup milk	2 tablespoons curry powder
1 large onion	1 teaspoon ground ginger
2 cloves garlic	Salt

3-pound carp

Open the coconut and, if possible, preserve the milk. Grate the meat very fine and soak it in the coconut liquor or in 1 cup of milk.

Chop the onion and garlic and sauté in 4 tablespoons of oil until nicely colored and soft. Add the curry, ginger, and salt to taste. Place the fish in a well-oiled baking dish and pour this mixture over it. Add the coconut and milk. Cover the pan with buttered paper or foil and bake at 425° for 25 minutes. Serve with rice and crisp French-fried onions.

BAKED CARP, HUNGARIAN STYLE

4-pound carp	2 large onions
Salt, pepper	4 to 6 tablespoons fat
Paprika	Oil

Sour cream

Clean and prepare the carp for baking. Season the inside with salt, pepper, and 1 tablespoon of paprika.

Slice the onions very thin and sauté them in fat until they are just tender but not colored. Spread them on the bottom of a well-oiled baking dish and place the carp on top. Brush the fish with oil, sprinkle heavily with paprika, cover with sour cream, and sprinkle again with paprika. Bake at 350° for 35 to 40 minutes or until the fish flakes easily when tested with a fork.

Serve with buttered noodles mixed with poppy seed and sprinkled with a little grated cheese.

BRAISED CARP MEXICAINE

4 to 6 pound carp	½ cup chicken broth or
2 medium onions	white wine
2 cloves garlic	Salt
5 tablespoons olive oil	Sesame seeds
2 tablespoons chili powder	Chopped buttered
	almonds

Clean, scale, and split the fish and remove the backbone.

Chop the onions and garlic and sauté them in the oil until soft and lightly colored. Add the chili powder and the broth or wine, salt to taste, and blend well.

Place the fish on a well-oiled baking dish or pan, spread the chili-onion mixture over the flesh of the fish and brush with oil. Bake at 425° for 15 to 18 minutes. Sprinkle with sesame seeds and the chopped almonds. Run under the broiler for 3 or 4 minutes to brown the seeds and nuts. Serve with corn-meal mush crisply fried with salt pork or bacon.

CARPE DE CAHORS

This is a delicious recipe from my friend Madame Pannetrat, who with the aid of her daughter and granddaughter runs an amusing *bistro* in Paris—Aux Bonnes Choses. In this small place, which contains only 5 or 6 tables, Madame fixes delicious and sometimes exciting dishes. This, I think, is one of the most attractive.

3-pound carp	Chopped shallots or
3-egg omelet *fines herbes*	scallions
(parsley, chives, tarragon,	Salt, pepper
or your own choice)	1 cup white wine
	1 cup cream
3 egg yolks	

Clean and split the carp.

Prepare the omelet *fines herbes*, and roll it into the fish as stuffing. Sew up the carp and place it on a bed of chopped shallots or onions in a well-oiled baking dish. Salt and pepper the fish and add the wine. Bake at 400° for 25 or 30 minutes or until the fish flakes easily when tested with a fork. Remove the fish to a hot platter and take out the string or thread which you used to secure it. Strain the pan juices and force the onion through a fine sieve. Reduce the juices slightly and add the cream mixed with the egg yolks; stir until thick but do not let it boil. Taste for seasoning and pour the sauce around the fish.

PATE CHAUD DE CARPE

This is an elaborate dish for a buffet party or a magnificent first course for a special dinner party at which you wish to display your prowess as a cook.

Puff paste	1 teaspoon rosemary
4-pound carp	½ cup cream
Salt, pepper	4 egg yolks
1 medium onion	⅓ cup mixed chopped
1 carrot	herbs (chives, parsley,
Parsley	and the like)
2 cups white wine	1 cup dry bread crumbs
4 tablespoons butter	

249

Prepare a recipe of puff paste—if you do not know how, consult a basic cook book or Anne Seranne's *Delectable Desserts*.

Clean the carp and place it on a well-oiled baking dish. Salt and pepper to taste and add the sliced onion, the sliced carrot, a few sprigs of parsley and the wine. Bake at 400° for 20 minutes, basting frequently. When the fish is cool enough to handle, remove the bones and the skin and add them to the liquid in the pan. Reduce the liquid to 1 cup. Strain and return to the stove. Add the cream mixed with the egg yolks and cook over low heat, being sure it does not boil, until the sauce is thickened.

Mix the rosemary, the chopped herbs, the bread crumbs and blend in the butter.

Roll out the puff paste and cover the bottom of a round pan or pie tin with a layer of the paste. Add the crumbs and herb mixture. Sprinkle with salt and pepper. Add the fish, cut into good-sized pieces, and top these with the sauce. Cover all with a crust of puff paste. Cut 2 vents in the top and bake at 450° for 12 minutes. Reduce the heat to 350° and continue baking until the paste is nicely browned and cooked through.

Cut into wedges or squares and serve very hot.

CARPE A LA CHAMBORD

This is a simplification of one of the most elaborate dishes in all cookery. Over the years many variations of it have been created, but this I feel is the best.

4 to 6 pound carp	4 tablespoons butter
Salt pork	Red wine and water or
2 medium onions	fish broth
3 carrots	Sauce Espagnole (see
3 stalks of celery	index) or beurre
	manié (see index)

FISH FORCEMEAT

1 pound of pike or other	4 egg yolks
white fish	Salt, pepper
1 cup soft bread crumbs	Thyme
Milk, about ½ cup	Tarragon
1 egg	Heavy cream

Prepare the forcemeat by grinding the pike several times or pounding it in a mortar. Soak the bread crumbs in milk until they have thoroughly absorbed all of it. Add this to the pike.

Add the egg and egg yolks, the seasonings and enough heavy cream to make a fine mixture. Work this all in a mortar or blend it with a heavy wooden spoon in a bowl.

Clean and scale the carp and stuff it with the forcemeat. Sew it up securely, and cover it with strips of salt pork, tying them well around the fish.

Chop the onions, carrots and celery all rather fine and cook them in the butter for 8 minutes. Place this mixture in the bottom of a well-buttered fish cooker or Dutch oven and put the fish on top. Now pour in a mixture of red wine and fish broth or water—⅔ wine to ⅓ water or broth. Fill up to ⅔ the thickness of the fish. Cover and bake at 400° for 20 minutes or until the fish flakes easily. Remove the fish to a hot platter dressed either with a bed of rice or a croustade that is large enough to be a base for the whole fish.

Reduce the sauce, strain it through a fine sieve and check for seasoning. Thicken it with a little sauce Espagnole or beurre manié. Serve the sauce separately.

Garnish the fish generously with cooked mushroom caps; quenelles, if you feel like taking the trouble to make them; truffles, if available; crawfish. This is a classic dish. It will win you a round of applause when it reaches the table.

MARINATED CARP

3 to 4 pound carp	Salt, pepper
1 large onion	⅔ cup white wine
¼ cup chopped parsley	Beurre manié (see index)
1 piece of chopped fresh ginger or 1½ teaspoons powdered	2 egg yolks
	4 tablespoons cream
3 tablespoons oil	1 tablespoon lemon juice

Clean the carp and place it in a steamer or fish boiler. Chop the onion, and add it and the parsley, ginger, and oil to the fish. Cover and let it stand for 3 hours. Turn the fish from time to time.

Add salt and pepper to taste and the wine, and poach the fish until it flakes easily when tested with a fork. When it is done, remove it to a serving dish. Thicken the sauce with beurre manié. Stir in the egg yolks mixed with the cream and blend well, but do not let it boil. At the last minute, stir in the lemon juice. Pour the sauce over the fish and serve with Lyonnaise potatoes heavily laced with parsley.

SWEET AND SOUR CARP, CHINESE FASHION

4 to 5 pound carp
¾ cup pineapple juice
½ cup wine vinegar
½ cup sugar

3 tablespoons cornstarch
1 tablespoon soy sauce
⅓ cup each green onion,
    green pepper and pine-
    apple

½ cup water

Clean and scale the fish. Place it on a rack over hot water so that the fish does not touch the water. Cover and steam until it flakes easily—about 25 minutes or so. Arrange the carp on a serving dish in the form of an S, using a skewer to hold it in place if you need to. Top it with the following sweet-sour sauce:

Cook together the pineapple juice, the vinegar, the sugar, and water; thicken with cornstarch. Season with soy sauce. Add green onion, green pepper, and pineapple cut in thin slivers, and cook these in the sauce just long enough for the onions and pepper to turn bright green.

COLD CARP WITH VARIOUS SAUCES

Serve poached carp cold with:

1. Mayonnaise
2. Sauce rémoulade
3. Sauce verte

Garnish cold carp with cucumbers, tomatoes, salade Russe, olives, truffles, greens. Or, if you like, you may put the cold carp in an aspic. (See salmon in aspic).

SWEET AND SOUR CARP, JEWISH FASHION

This is one of the oldest recipes for carp. Sometimes it is made without the addition of the vinegar and raisins, but it is almost invariably served cold.

4 to 5 pound carp
⅔ cup olive oil
3 or 4 shallots
2 large onions
4 tablespoons flour
1 pint white wine
1 pint water
1 teaspoon salt
Few grains cayenne
Bit of nutmeg

1 bay leaf
Pinch of thyme
2 cloves garlic
¾ cup olive oil
2 tablespoons chopped
    parsley
½ cup seedless raisins
½ cup currants or sultana
    raisins
⅓ cup wine vinegar
2 tablespoons brown sugar

Cut the carp into 2-inch slices. Heat ⅔ cup of olive oil in a large skillet or deep Dutch oven. Chop the shallots and onions and add them to the oil. When they are soft add the flour and blend thoroughly. Gradually stir in the wine and water, and continue stirring until thickened. Add salt, cayenne, and nutmeg. Bring this to a boil, then add the pieces of fish, the bay leaf, thyme, and garlic, crushed. Simmer for about 20 minutes. Remove the carp and arrange it on a long deep serving dish.

Now reduce the sauce over a medium flame to ⅓ of its volume. With a whisk or electric mixer at medium speed, or in the Waring Blendor, beat in ¾ cup of olive oil as you would if making mayonnaise. When thoroughly blended, add the parsley, raisins, currants, wine vinegar, and brown sugar. Pour this sauce over the carp and chill thoroughly.

POACHED CARP WITH VARIOUS SAUCES

Poach whole carp in court bouillon (see index). Serve with:

1. White wine sauce
2. Hollandaise sauce
3. Sauce duxelles
4. Shrimp sauce
5. Lobster sauce
6. Sauce Béarnaise

POTTED CARP

This is an old Central European dish that has a flavor entirely different from that of most fish dishes.

4 carrots	4 carp fillets
8 gingersnaps	Flour
½ cup sherry	Salt, pepper

Butter

Cut the carrots in thin slices and parboil until they are just tender. Soak the gingersnaps in the wine. Butter a large skillet that can be covered. Dip the fillets in flour and arrange them in the pan. Salt and pepper lightly, top with the carrots and the water in which they were cooked, and the sherry-gingersnap mixture. Cover, bring to a boil, and simmer for 15 to 20 minutes. Serve with steamed rice and a crisp green salad.

GEFUELLTE FISH

For 36 medium-sized patties:

6 to 8 medium onions	Salt, pepper
8 pounds fish (buffalo, whitefish, carp, pike, or a mixture) including heads and bones	6 eggs
	3 slices bread (soaked in water or milk)
	4 or 5 carrots

1 bay leaf

Chop 2 of the onions very coarse, place them in a large pot, add the fish heads and bones, water to cover, and bring to a boil. Add 1 or 2 tablespoons of salt and simmer while you prepare the fish.

Grind the cleaned and skinned fish and the rest of the onions. Mix them together, chop them in a large bowl, or pound in a mortar, until they are thoroughly blended. Salt and pepper to taste. Beat the eggs slightly and add to the mixture. Add the bread, which has soaked for an hour or so, and pound again until thoroughly smooth.

Scrape the carrots and cut them in rather thick slices. Shape the fish mixture into egg-sized quenelles and drop them with the carrot slices into the boiling broth. If the broth has cooked down too much, add more water. Simmer for 1 to 1½ hours.

Remove the fish balls from the broth and let them cool slightly. Strain the broth and clarify it with egg white and shells, if you wish. Chill the broth and the fish overnight in the refrigerator. Serve garnished with a slice of carrot and the jellied broth as a sauce. Grated horseradish and beet salad go with this dish.

NOTE: I learned to make this dish from Minnie Bernard, who makes the most delicious gefuellte fish I have ever eaten.

SMOKED CARP

Smoked carp is served a great deal for an appetizer, for luncheon dishes, or with salad. It has a rather nice texture, not so delicious as smoked sturgeon or so delicate as smoked whitefish.

Catfish

EVEN though you may never have eaten catfish, you most certainly know someone who has. Commercially, over 10,000,000 pounds are consumed each year, and many millions more are carried home by individual anglers. Despite the impressive quantities, catfish remains an inland dish. It is rarely sold in coast markets.

Common sorts of catfish are the channel cat, blue cat, spotted or fiddler cat, yellow or goujon, and the differently designed bullhead or horned pout. These vary in size from

1 to 50 pounds or more, but none equals the European cat-fish, which, in full sail, may weigh over 400 pounds.

For flavor, the best American catfish is the spotted or fiddler cat, which runs around 5 pounds and is found everywhere in the Mississippi Valley—as far south as Mexico and as far north as the Great Lakes. Catfish must be skinned before cooking. Draw a sharp knife around the fish just in back of the gills and strip off the skin by hand or with tweezers.

Catfish are oily and lend themselves to many different forms of cookery. They are sold whole or skinned and dressed.

SAUTEED CATFISH

Small-size catfish may be sautéed as for sauté meunière under "Cooking Methods."

PAN-FRIED CATFISH

Use either the whole fish or pieces of fish. It is customary to use lard or oil for frying in this manner—which actually is not pan-frying, but semideep-frying. Dip the fish in milk, then in crumbs or corn meal. Cook rapidly in the skillet in fat about 1 inch deep. Season to taste.

FRIED CATFISH

Deep-fried catfish is probably the most usual method of preparation. Use either the whole fish or pieces of fish.

Heat the fat in your deep fryer to 370°. Beat 2 eggs lightly. Roll out bread or zwieback crumbs or use corn meal. Dip the fish in flour, then in beaten egg, and roll in the crumbs. Fry for 3 to 5 minutes, depending on the size of the fish. Drain and season to taste. Serve with tartar sauce (see index), rémoulade (see index) or mustard sauce (see index).

POACHED CATFISH

Catfish may be poached in salted boiling water or in a court bouillon (see index). Serve it with lemon butter (see index) or with Hollandaise (see index), Béarnaise (see index) or lobster sauce (see index).

It may be served cold with mayonnaise (see index) or rémoulade (see index).

CATFISH HEAD SOUP

This a great favorite in the South.

2 or 3 good-sized catfish heads	A few sprigs of parsley
1 onion stuck with 1 clove	6 cups water
1 carrot	1 tablespoon salt
1 leek	½ teaspoon thyme

Wash the catfish heads well, and let the tap water run over them. Place them in a saucepan with the onion stuck with a clove, the carrot, leek, and parsley. Add the water and bring it to a boil. Add the salt and thyme and simmer for 45 to 60 minutes. Remove the heads and take the meat from the bones. You may use this in the soup or serve it the next day in a souffle or creamed fish dish—any of your favorite ways of using leftover fish.

Strain the broth and taste for seasoning. Serve any of the following ways:

1. Add 1 cup of finely chopped carrots and string beans cooked for 12 minutes in boiling salted water.

2. Add ½ cup of finely broken noodles. Cook these in the broth for 12 minutes.

3. Add the meat from the catfish heads and chopped parsley and grated cheese.

4. Prepare a recipe of fish forcemeat (see index), and drop small balls of it into the boiling broth. Let them poach for 15 minutes, or until the tiny dumplings are cooked through.

NOTE: Catfish may be used in any of the fish stews or in the bouillabaisse (see index).

Chub

THE varieties of chub, which is a member of the whitefish family, are known mainly for their excellence as smoked fish. The fish resembles whitefish, of course, but is smaller and thinner. The flesh is extremely soft.

Prepare chub as you would whitefish.

Crappies

CRAPPIES are seldom taken commercially because of state prohibitions. An excellent pan fish, they are caught frequently by sportsmen. They propagate readily, and in sections where fish is scarce they are sometimes planted in ponds and used for individual family consumption.

The crappie is a small fish, seldom weighing more than a pound or exceeding a foot in length. The white crappie, also known as the chinquapin or white perch, is found in New England and down the Mississippi Valley. The black crappie, also known as the strawberry bass, is found in almost the same section.

BROILED CRAPPIES

The usual portion is one crappie to a person. Oil the fish well, or brush it with melted butter, and broil according to the directions under "Cooking Methods."

CRAPPIES SAUTE MEUNIERE

See directions for sauté meunière under "Cooking Methods."

PAN-FRIED CRAPPIES

When pan frying crappies, it is probably better to remove the heads and tails of the fish. Clean them well, run the fins, and wash thoroughly. Dip them in flour, then in milk, and roll them in crumbs or corn meal. Sauté in butter, oil, or bacon fat until the fish is lightly browned and crisp. Serve with tartar sauce (see index) or lemon wedges.

Lake Herring

THESE small fish, plentiful in the Great Lakes region, are no relation to the herring of the sea but resemble whitefish. They are popularly known as "ciscoes."

Some of the lake herring catch is sold salted, and much of it is smoked. The smoked fish is exceedingly good; the texture is delicate. Altogether, lake herring is deservedly popular and is one of the most important fresh-water catches.

Lake herring sold fresh in the market average ½ to 1 pound. Any of the recipes for small trout and smelt (see index) can be followed in preparing them.

Pike and Pickerel

AMONG the well-known varieties of pike are the common pike, the pickerel, and, most of all, the huge muskellunge. All varieties are popular as sport fish.

The pike is a fierce and voracious fish, even devouring small waterfowl and mammals, and it puts up a strong fight when hooked. Like many fish popular with anglers, it has special local names: lake pickerel, grass pike, jack pike, great Northern pike. It is abundant from New York to the mouth of the Ohio River and thence northward to Alaska. Some varieties of pike often weigh up to 25 pounds, but the average market weight is 1½ pounds to 10 pounds.

Eastern pickerel, called chain pickerel in the North and jack pickerel in the South, is well known to anglers east of the Alleghenies. It can grow to 8 pounds, but the average size is a 22-inch fish weighing 2 to 3 pounds.

There are innumerable ways of cooking pike, but it has often seemed to me that not enough care is taken to bring out its fine flavor and texture.

BROILED PIKE

You may broil either the steaks, the fillets, or the boned and split whole fish. Pike is a lean fish, however, and I do not believe broiling is the best method of preparing it. If you do broil it, be sure to lubricate it well during the cooking with butter or oil. Follow the general rules for broiling under "Cooking Methods." Serve with lemon butter, parsley butter, or maître d'hôtel butter (see index).

BAKED STUFFED PIKE

5 to 6 pound pike
2 cups cracker crumbs
½ cup chopped celery
½ cup chopped onion
¼ cup chopped green pepper
½ cup crabmeat

3 eggs
1 teaspoon salt
Heavy dash of cayenne
1 teaspoon dry mustard
½ cup melted butter
Strips of salt pork

Make a stuffing of the crumbs, chopped vegetables, crab-meat, eggs, seasonings, and melted butter. Clean the fish and stuff it with this mixture. Sew it up and place on an oiled baking dish or pan. Top with strips of salt pork and bake at 350° for about 40 minutes, or until the fish flakes when tested with a fork. (If you use a thermometer, the temperature will register about 140° when the fish is done.)

Serve with a crabmeat sauce (see index), saffron rice, and cooked chopped spinach seasoned with garlic, nutmeg and butter.

BRAISED STUFFED PIKE

5-pound pike
½ cup chopped onion
4 tablespoons butter
½ pound ground smoked ham
2 cups dry bread crumbs
½ cup chopped parsley
½ teaspoon thyme
1 teaspoon salt
1 teaspoon freshly ground
     pepper

3 eggs
4 tablespoons melted butter
Strips of salt pork
White wine
Beurre manié (see index)
2 egg yolks
Lemon juice
Parsley

Clean the fish and prepare for stuffing. Sauté the chopped onions in 4 tablespoons of butter until soft. Combine them with the ham, crumbs, parsley, thyme, salt, pepper, 3 eggs, and 4 tablespoons of melted butter. Stuff the fish with this mixture and sew it up. Place it in a shallow baking pan with enough white wine to cover the bottom of the pan well. Top the fish with strips of salt pork and bake at 350° for 45 minutes. Baste occasionally, and cover the pan after the first 15 minutes of cooking. When the fish is done, remove the salt pork and arrange the stuffed pike on a platter.

Strain the pan juices and thicken with beurre manié. Stir in the slightly beaten yolks of 2 eggs and continue stirring until well blended. Do not let the sauce boil. Check for seasoning, add a dash of lemon juice and plenty of chopped parsley. Pour the sauce over the fish.

QUENELLES I

These have been great favorites in France for many years. They are not simple to make, and they must be done properly or they are not good.

3 cups soft bread crumbs	1 grind of fresh pepper
1 cup boiling milk	¼ teaspoon nutmeg
1 pound of pike	1 cup creamed butter
1 teaspoon salt	2 eggs
	4 or 5 egg yolks

Pour the boiling milk over the bread crumbs and let the crumbs soak until the milk is entirely absorbed. Mix them well with a wooden spoon until they are practically a paste. Place this over the lowest flame on your stove and dry it out, working it all the time with the wooden spoon. Spread it out on a flat pan and let it cool thoroughly.

Put the pike through the fine grinder twice. Then work it in a mortar, or put it in a heavy bowl and work it with a wooden spoon. Add salt, pepper, and nutmeg and blend thoroughly. Turn it out on a board, combine it with the crumb mixture and mix well with your hands. Return it to the mortar or bowl, add the creamed butter and continue blending until it is smooth and thoroughly mixed. Gradually work in 2 whole eggs and 4 or 5 additional egg yolks. Put the mixture through a fine sieve or a food mill and work it again with a wooden spoon until it has a smooth and silky texture.

Form into flat oval cakes about the size of an egg or a little larger, and arrange them in a buttered skillet so that they barely touch one another. Cover them with boiling salted water and poach gently for about 10 minutes. Remove the cooked quenelles to absorbent paper. Serve them with a rich cream sauce (see index), a shrimp sauce (see index), a lobster sauce (see index), sauce Mornay (see index), or Hollandaise (see index).

VARIATIONS

1. Arrange the quenelles on a bed of spinach, top with sauce Mornay, sprinkle with grated cheese and run under the broiler flame for a few minutes.

2. Prepare a white wine sauce (see index). Add small

sautéed onions, sautéed mushrooms and chopped parsley. Add the quenelles to the sauce and heat thoroughly.

QUENELLES II

This recipe for quenelles may be a little simpler than the one above.

½ cup hot water	6 ounces chopped kidney
¼ cup butter	fat
½ cup flour	Salt, pepper
¼ teaspoon salt	Nutmeg
2 eggs	3 egg whites
1 pound of pike	½ cup butter
	½ cup heavy cream

Put ½ cup of hot water and ¼ cup of butter in saucepan. When the butter is melted and the water boiling, add flour and salt sifted together and stir with a wooden spoon until the mixture leaves the sides of the pan and forms a ball in the middle. Remove from the fire and continue beating with the spoon, or put in an electric beater. Add 2 eggs, one at a time, and continue beating until the mixture is waxy and smooth. Cool.

Put the fish through the fine grinder several times or pound it in a mortar. Work it well in a heavy bowl with a wooden spoon. Gradually add about 6 ounces of finely chopped kidney fat and the pâte à choux (the butter, flour, and egg mixture which you have prepared before). Season with salt, pepper, and nutmeg. Work in the whites of 3 eggs and ½ cup each of butter and heavy cream. Work the mixture thoroughly until it is smooth and satiny. Chill for 24 hours.

Form into small oval cakes and poach as in the preceding recipe. Serve with the rich sauce and garnish with fried toasts.

PIKE PUDDING OR MOLD

1 pound pike fillets	1 egg
1 cup heavy béchamel sauce	3 egg yolks
Salt, pepper	

Grind the fish very fine. Then pound it in a mortar or give it a second grinding. Beat it with a wooden spoon until it forms a paste. Blend in the heavy béchamel (see index). Gradually work in 1 whole egg and the yolks of 3 more. Force the mixture through a fine sieve or a food mill. Season it to taste and pour it into a well-buttered earthenware casserole with straight sides. (A copper or glass oven dish with fairly straight sides will do.)

Place the casserole in a pan of hot water and bake at 350° for 25 or 30 minutes, or until just set. Unmold on a hot platter and surround with shrimp sauce (see index) or sauce Béarnaise (see index). Garnish with cooked shrimp and sprigs of parsley.

MOUSSE OF PIKE

See index for halibut mousse.

POACHED PIKE

Pike lends itself to poaching even better than most fish. It can be poached whole or in pieces of 3 to 4 pounds. Wrap the fish in cheesecloth, poach in a white wine court bouillon (see index) just until the fish flakes easily when tested with a fork. Serve it with Hollandaise (see index), Béarnaise (see index), duxelles (see index), or shrimp sauce (see index), or with anchovy or lemon butter (see index).

VARIATIONS

1. Prepare a court bouillon as follows:

Chop fine 8 to 10 shallots or 12 green onions, 2 cloves of garlic, 1 leek, 2 or 3 carrots and plenty of parsley; add 1 tablespoon of salt, 1 teaspoon of pepper, 1 bay leaf, and a heaping spoonful of thyme. Cover with white wine and let stand for 3 hours. Put the court bouillon on the stove, add the fish and slowly bring it to a boil. Poach just long enough to cook the fish through—about 25 minutes for a 5-pound pike. Remove the fish to a hot platter.

Strain the bouillon through a fine sieve or food mill. Reduce it quickly to 2 cups. Add 1 cup of heavy cream and 4 or 5 egg yolks. Stir well until thickened, being careful that the mixture does not boil. Cream 4 to 5 tablespoons of butter with a little flour and add it to the sauce. Stir until smooth, taste for seasoning and pour over the fish.

Serve with plain boiled potatoes and follow with a dish of braised celery topped with bits of marrow poached in boiling salted water.

2. Poach pike in boiling salted water with the addition of plenty of fresh dill, parsley, and an onion stuck with 2 cloves. When the fish is cooked, remove it to a hot platter. Make a

sauce velouté (see index) with some of the broth, season it with chopped fresh dill, parsley, and 1 tablespoon of lemon juice. Pour the sauce over the fish.

COLD PIKE WITH VARIOUS SAUCES

Cold pike is one of the most delicate and flavorful of the white fish. A delightful supper dish in summer is a whole cold pike garnished with cucumbers, tomatoes, salade Russe, stuffed eggs flavored with anchovy and sardines, and olives.

To prepare the fish, poach it in a court bouillon until it is just tender—about 6 minutes to the pound. Chill it, and when cool skin it, leaving the head and tail intact. You may make an aspic of the broth, if you wish, and mask the fish with it. Or simply place the cold poached pike on a platter of greens and garnish to suit your own taste. Serve it with a well-flavored olive oil mayonnaise (see index), sauce verte (see index), or sauce rémoulade (see index).

If you wish to be really elaborate, you may make an aspic of the court bouillon (see index). Combine some of the aspic with mayonnaise to make a chaudfroid (see index) and cover the fish with this. Chill until the chaudfroid is set, then mask it with aspic and chill again. Decorate with truffles, pickled mushrooms, capers—anything you like. For suggestions for decorating fish in aspic, see recipe for Cold Halibut.

IZAAK WALTON'S RECIPE FOR ROASTING A PIKE from THE COMPLEAT ANGLER

Mr. Walton's comment on this recipe for roasting pike is ample proof that he enjoyed the cooked results of his angling as much as the angling itself. He wrote: "This dish of meat is too good for any but anglers, or very honest men; and I trust you will prove both, and therefore I have trusted you with this secret."

Here is the recipe:

"First, open your pike at the gills, and if need be, cut also a little slit towards the belly; out of these take his guts and keep his liver, which you are to shred very small with thyme, sweet marjoram, and a little winter-savory; to these put some pickled oysters, and some anchovies, two or three, both these last whole (for the anchovies will melt, and the oysters should not); to these you must add also a pound of sweet butter,

263

which you are to mix with the herbs which are shred, and let them all be well salted (if the pike be more than a yard long, then you may put into these herbs more than a pound, or if he be less, then less butter will suffice): these being thus mixed with a blade or two of mace, must be put into the pike's belly, and then his belly so sewed up as to keep all the butter in his belly, if it be possible, if not, then as much of it as you possibly can; but take not off the scales: then you are to thrust the spit through his mouth out at his tail; and then take four, or five, or six split sticks or very thin laths, and a convenient quantity of tape or filleting: these laths are to be tied round about the pike's body from his head to his tail, and the tape tied somewhat thick to prevent his breaking or falling off from the spit: let him be roasted very leisurely, and often basted with claret wine and anchovies and butter mixed together, and also with what moisture falls from him into the pan: when you have roasted him sufficiently, you are to hold under him (when you unwind or cut the tape that ties him) such a dish as you purpose to eat him out of; and let him fall into it with the sauce that is roasted in his belly; and by this means the pike will be kept unbroken and complete: then, to the sauce which was within, and also that sauce in the pan, you are to add a fit quantity of the best butter, and to squeeze the juice of three or four oranges: lastly, you may either put into the pike with the oysters two cloves of garlick, and take it out whole, when the pike is cut off the spit; or to give the sauce a *haut-gout* let the dish (into which you let the pike fall) be rubbed with it: the using or not using of this garlick is left to your discretion."

Pike Perch

IN spite of the name, pike perches are not related to pike. They are, rather, members of the same family as the yellow perch. There are three well-known varieties: blue pike perch, yellow pike perch—also called wall-eyed pike, and sauger or sand pike. These are excellent food fishes with firm white flesh.

Yellow pike perch are found plentifully in streams along the Middle Atlantic seaboard, westward to the Mississippi Valley and north through the Great Lakes region to Hudson Bay. There is a large commercial catch each year, and a sizable amount is caught and cooked by sportsmen. The sauger is found farther west in the Missouri Valley region. The blue pike perch likes deep water and is caught mainly in the Great Lakes.

Most of the perch caught are small fish weighing around 1 pound to 1½ pounds, although occasionally larger ones are marketed. A large proportion of the commercial catch is filleted, but the fish are also sold whole.

PIKE PERCH SAUTE MEUNIERE

The fish may be cleaned and split, or if small enough, they may be sautéed whole. Follow directions for sauté meunière under "Cooking Methods." Fillets may be treated in the same manner.

VARIATIONS

1. After removing the fish to a hot platter, add blanched almonds to the pan and toss them about until they brown. Pour the almonds and the pan juices over the fish and serve with lemon wedges.
2. Sauté mushroom slices with the fish.
3. Add chopped parsley and white wine to the pan juices, bring to a boil and pour over the fish.

PAN-FRIED PIKE PERCH

Follow directions for pan-frying crappies.

OVEN-FRIED FILLETS OF PIKE PERCH

Follow directions for oven-frying fillets of whitefish.

BAKED PIKE PERCH

Clean and wash the fish. Oil a large flat baking dish and cover the bottom with chopped green onions. Arrange the fish on top, dot them with butter and sprinkle with salt and pepper. Add enough white wine to cover the bottom of the pan. Bake at 400° for 10 or 15 minutes or until the fish are just cooked through. Baste during the cooking process, and add more wine and butter if needed.

265

Just before the fish are done, sprinkle the top with bread crumbs and grated Parmesan cheese.

BAKED PIKE PERCH FILLETS

The fillets may be baked in the same manner as the whole fish, but the cooking time will be less.

Sheepshead

THE sheepshead is the only fresh-water relative of the drums and the croakers—the fish that are heard as well as seen. They love to play tunes, and you may hear their entertaining music on still nights.

The flesh of the sheepshead is white, lean, and tender, with an excellent flavor. You will find sheepshead on the market in the Middle West and the South, whole and filleted. They come in sizes from 1 to 12 pounds, though some sheepshead have been known to weigh 60 pounds.

Cook sheepshead as you would drum, croaker, or weakfish.

Suckers

WHEN I was about eight years old, my neighborhood contemporaries were always running off on fishing excursions and coming home with suckers—and I was never much impressed. I still think the sucker is a dull fish, a sort of underwater vacuum cleaner. It is plentiful, however, in country streams and many people enjoy eating it. In fact, there is a good commercial market for suckers.

The sucker is not a fat fish, and needs the lift of a good sauce to make it palatable.

BROILED SUCKER

Suckers must be lubricated well with oil or butter before broiling. Follow the general directions under "Cooking Methods." Serve with lemon butter (see index) or anchovy butter (see index).

PAN-FRIED SUCKER

Small-sized suckers may be pan-fried whole. Clean them and soak for about ½ hour in milk with salt and pepper added. Roll them in crumbs and sauté in butter or bacon fat until nicely browned and cooked through. Serve with a tartar sauce (see index) or rémoulade (see index).

BRAISED SUCKER

2 large onions	2 cups tomato puree or
2 cloves of garlic	strained canned
6 tablespoons olive oil	tomatoes
1 tablespoon chili powder	4 pounds of sucker
	Salt, pepper

Oregano

Chop the onions and garlic and sauté them in the olive oil. Add the chili powder and tomato puree. Place the fish on a well-oiled baking dish or pan, season to taste with salt, pepper, and oregano. Cover with the sauce and bake at 350° for 18 to 20 minutes or until the fish flakes easily when tested with a fork. Serve with saffron-flavored rice.

POACHED SUCKER

Poach suckers in a court bouillon (see index) until they are just flaky and tender. Serve them with a Hollandaise sauce (see index), or with a shrimp (see index) or lobster sauce (see index), or sauce velouté (see index) made with the reduced court bouillon.

COLD POACHED SUCKER

Mask the cold poached sucker in mayonnaise (see index) or rémoulade (see index). This is a nice change for a hot summer day when the neighborhood fisherman brings you part of his catch.

Trout

THIS is the glamor fish. They are beautiful, they are perfectly meated, and in many places they are scarce.

Since I am not an ichthyologist, I am not going into a discussion of all the different varieties of trout. I recommend all of them indiscriminately. I do remember particularly, however, a mess of tiny mountain trout caught in a cold Oregon stream, cooked with bacon over a campfire and served up for breakfast less than an hour after they had been taken from the water. The combined flavors of wood smoke, bacon and delicate trout could not have been duplicated in a modern kitchen by even the most experienced chef. But if outdoor simplicity can work miracles with trout, so can sophistication. I recall with drooling tastebuds the incomparable truite en chemise at the station restaurant in the Gare de l'Est in Paris—one of the truly great restaurants of the world.

The recipes here are for the small trout—mountain trout, Dolly Vardens, small-sized brook or speckled trout, all those running from 8 to 12 inches. These are usually served whole with head and tail intact. Simply wash and clean them. As for the amount of trout per serving, that depends on individual taste. Certainly, at least one per person, and of the smaller fish, two or three. But suit yourselves.

If the trout you intend to cook is one of the larger varieties, try the salmon recipes. You'll find that they apply perfectly.

TROUT SAUTE MEUNIERE

This, of course, is the classic preparation for trout. See directions for sauté meunière under "Cooking Methods."

VARIATION

Sauté the trout, and just before removing it from the pan, add ½ to 1 cup of heavy cream. Let it come to a boil and cook for 2 minutes. Remove the trout to a hot platter. Correct the seasoning, reduce the cream a bit, and pour it over the fish. Sprinkle with chopped parsley.

TROUT AMANDINE, IN THE MANNER OF RESTAURANT CASENAVE IN PARIS

½ pound shelled almonds	Flour
6 tablespoons butter	Salt, pepper
4 trout	Chopped parsley

Blanch the almonds. Leave half of them whole and cut the rest into slivers. Melt the butter in a skillet. Dip the trout in flour, and when the butter is bubbly but not burning, add the trout and the almonds. Spoon the nuts around in the butter so that they will brown well. Turn the trout once—they will take only a few minutes to cook. Salt and pepper to taste. Remove the trout to a hot platter and sprinkle with chopped parsley. Pour the golden-colored almonds and the butter from the pan over the fish. With this serve new potatoes in their jackets, and some lemon butter (see index) or lemon wedges, if you like.

BROOK TROUT, OUTDOORS METHODS

If you catch trout early and can have them for breakfast that same morning, you are the most fortunate of men. To cook 6 trout:

Try out 6 to 12 rashers of bacon, depending on your appetite. When the bacon is crisp, remove it to a paper or plate. Dip the trout in flour or corn meal and sauté them quickly in the bacon fat. Do not add salt until the fish are cooked and you have tasted them; the bacon fat may add enough seasoning. Serve the trout with the bacon rashers and toast made over the fire. Steaming campfire coffee is a "must," of course.

TRUITE EN CHEMISE

This delightful way to serve trout and other small fish will always bring cheers from your guests. For 6 people:

½ pound mushrooms	6 French pancakes, made
4 tablespoons butter	without sugar
Salt, pepper	6 trout, sauté meunière
3 tablespoons flour	(see "Cooking
4 tablespoons heavy cream	Methods")
	Browned butter

Lemon juice

Chop the mushrooms very fine. Sauté them in the butter until they are soft and well cooked. Sprinkle with salt, pepper and flour. Add the heavy cream and stir until the mixture is thick.

Prepare the French pancakes without sugar. They should be about 6 inches in diameter, well browned, thin and tender. If you do not have your own recipe, you will find the recipe for French pancakes or crepes in any basic cook book.

Sauté the trout meunière, according to the directions on page 16. Spread each pancake with the mushroom mixture, place a trout on top of this and roll up the pancake so that the head sticks out one end and the tail the other. Arrange these rolls in a baking dish—an oval one is perfect. Cover with a little browned butter and lemon juice. Heat for just a moment or two in the oven and serve. Delicious with a good green salad and a brittle white wine.

TROUT A L'ANGLAISE

12 trout	4 tablespoons butter
2 eggs	3 tablespoons olive oil
2 cups crumbs	Flour

Salt, pepper

Clean and wash the trout. Beat the eggs lightly, and crush or roll the crumbs.

Heat the butter and olive oil in a large skillet. Dust the trout with flour, sprinkle with salt and pepper, dip in the egg, and then in the crumbs. Sauté quickly in the hot fat. Remove to a hot platter and serve with a tartar sauce (see index), devil sauce (see index), or rémoulade (see index). Boiled potatoes and peas seem to be a good but rather homely accompaniment.

VARIATION

French-fried Trout. Prepare the fish as above, but fry it in deep hot fat heated to 370°. Cook for just a few minutes to let the fish brown and get crisp on the outside. Serve with tartar sauce (see index) or rémoulade (see index).

CHARCOAL-BROILED TROUT

I have had all sorts of trout broiled over coals: wrapped in wet newspapers; wrapped in clay (and they were not too bad this way); and held over the coals after being impaled on a stick—which works very well if you do it right.

I really feel, however, that there are only two ways of doing the job and doing it well.

I: Clean the trout, dip them in flour, and then in melted butter. Salt and pepper them and arrange securely in a wire grill. Grill over hot coals for about 4 to 6 minutes, depending upon the size of the fish. Brush with butter during the cooking (a good-sized pastry brush or a small paintbrush is excellent for doing this). The trout should have a nice crispy coating—

be careful not to overcook them. Serve with potatoes sautéed over the outdoor fire or baked under it, and cole slaw.

II: Arrange trout in an S-shape on long skewers, or make rings of the fish by running the skewers through the head and tail. Dip these in flour, then in melted butter, and sprinkle with salt and pepper. Broil them over the coals until just cooked through, brushing with butter during the process. Serve with lemon or lime wedges and melted butter, or with a Hollandaise sauce (see index).

TROUT EN PAPILLOTES

For 6 people:

6 trout	Salt, pepper
Butter	Oil

FILLING

2 carrots	2 stalks celery
2 small white onions	4 to 6 tablespoons butter
2 shallots or green onions	Salt, pepper

Prepare the filling by chopping the vegetables fine and sautéing them in the butter until soft. Salt and pepper to taste.

Split and clean the trout, and stuff each one with a little of the mixture. Dot with butter, and place about 3 inches from the broiler flame. Broil for 4 minutes. Salt and pepper the fish when you remove them.

Have ready 6 heart-shaped pieces of cooking parchment large enough for the trout. Place a fish on each piece of parchment, near one edge. Fold the rest of the paper over the fish and crimp the edges together so that the fish is sealed in. Oil the paper. Place these on a buttered baking sheet and bake at 425° until the parchment is inflated and browned.

VERY DRESSY STUFFED TROUT

This is a spectacular dish for special occasions.

12 good-sized trout	Chopped tarragon
2 medium onions	Chopped parsley
Butter	3 large onions
Salt, pepper	6 tablespoons butter
½ pound raw white-meated fish	2 cups dry white wine
	1 cup very heavy béchamel (see index)
2 egg yolks	½ pound butter
3 egg whites	

Clean the fish and prepare them for stuffing. Leave the heads intact.

Chop the onions and sauté them in butter until they are soft and golden. Salt them lightly. Grind the white-meated fish several times; salt and pepper it to taste. Add it to the onions and blend the two together with a wooden spoon. Add the egg yolks and egg whites, slightly beaten, and season with tarragon and parsley. Stuff the fish with this mixture.

Chop 3 large onions and sauté them in 6 tablespoons of butter until soft. Force them through a sieve or food mill. Cover the bottom of a baking dish with this onion puree and arrange the trout on top. Dot them with butter, add the wine, and bake at 450° for 8 to 10 minutes, just until the fish are cooked.

Remove the fish to a hot platter. Force the sauce through a sieve or food mill and combine it with 1 cup of very heavy béchamel and ½ pound of butter. Blend thoroughly and pour over the fish. Sprinkle with chopped parsley. Serve with julienne potatoes and a good green salad.

TROUT SMOTHERED IN MUSHROOMS

8 trout	1½ cups (and 2 tablespoons) heavy cream
1 pound mushrooms	
6 tablespoons butter	Butter
1 clove garlic	Beurre manié
1 teaspoon salt	Fried toast
1 teaspoon freshly ground black pepper	Parsley

Clean and wash the trout. Chop the mushrooms very fine and sauté them in butter until they are soft. Season with minced garlic, salt, and pepper. Add 2 tablespoons of cream and let it cook down.

Arrange the trout on a well-oiled baking dish and top them with the mushrooms. Dot with butter and bake at 425° for 10 minutes, or until the fish are just cooked through. Remove them to a hot platter. Add 1½ cups of heavy cream to the pan, heat, and blend thoroughly. Add beurre manié and stir until nicely thickened. Taste for seasoning and pour over the trout. Garnish the platter with pieces of fried toast heavily sprinkled with chopped parsley.

TRUITE AU BLEU

This, I am told, was originally an outdoor meal, and the

trout were cooked as soon as caught. In fact, they are supposed to be alive, or practically alive, when they are plunged into the boiling water. Many restaurants have tanks of trout so that they can pull them out and pop them into the cauldron on order.

Prepare a court bouillon of 3 parts water to 1 part vinegar. Add 6 peppercorns, a part of a bay leaf, and 1 teaspoon of salt to each quart of liquid. Bring this to a boil. Plunge in the trout and poach them just long enough to cook them through —about 4 minutes for the average fish. Serve them hot with melted butter and boiled potatoes, or chill them and serve cold with mayonnaise.

The vinegar in the water turns the skin of the fish a vivid metallic blue, hence the name *"truite au bleu."*

POACHED TROUT

Trout are delicious if they are poached lightly in a court bouillon (see index). They need only from 4 to 6 minutes cooking. It is better to poach them in a flat dish so that they are barely covered. It is difficult to remove them from a deep pan. Serve the poached trout with beurre noisette (see index), shrimp sauce (see index), sauce Béarnaise (see index), or Hollandaise sauce (see index).

COLD TROUT IN JELLY

6 trout
White wine court bouillon (see index)
White of egg and egg shells

1½ envelopes gelatin
Green onion, leek, chives, tarragon leaves, hard-cooked eggs

Poach the trout in the bouillon and remove them to a platter. Reduce the bouillon to 3 cups and clarify with the lightly beaten egg white and shells. Strain. Soak the gelatin in ⅓ cup of water and combine it with the boiling broth. Chill until it is thick and syrupy.

The fish may be decorated as elaborately as you choose. Or you may prefer to serve them plain, simply masked with the jelly. If you want a spectacular dish, remove about half of the skin from the chilled, cooked trout. Then make a flower design on the flesh. Use the green stems of onions, leeks, or chives, green tarragon leaves, and make tiny flowers cut out of hard-cooked egg.

Pour enough of the jelly over the decorated (or plain) trout to mask it thoroughly. Put the platter with the fish and a bowl of the rest of the jelly in the refrigerator to chill. Just before serving, chop the rest of the jelly very fine and garnish the fish platter with it. Serve with mayonnaise (see index) or rémoulade (see index).

VARIATION

Reduce the broth to 1 cup and add 1 cup of red wine or port wine. Add 1 envelope of gelatin to make a jelly.

COLD TROUT WITH DILL SAUCE

Poach 6 or 8 trout in court bouillon (see index) for 5 minutes, or until they are just cooked through. Chill thoroughly. Remove part of the skin from the top of the trout, leaving the heads and tails intact. Sprinkle with finely chopped dill, parsley, and chives. Arrange alternate slices of cucumber and hard-cooked egg on each fish. Serve with a sour cream sauce made with 1½ cups of sour cream, 1 tablespoon of fresh dill, 1 teaspoon of grated onion, 1 teaspoon of dry mustard, and ½ cup of finely chopped hard-cooked egg. Season to taste with salt and pepper.

PICKLED TROUT

1 bottle white wine	1 teaspoon freshly ground
6 peppercorns	pepper
1 carrot, thinly sliced	¼ cup wine vinegar
4 small white onions	12 trout
2 cloves	½ cup olive oil
1 bay leaf	12 thin lemon slices
1 teaspoon tarragon leaves	1 medium onion, thinly
Pinch of thyme	sliced
1 teaspoon salt	

Prepare a court bouillon with the wine, peppercorns, carrot, small onions (two with cloves stuck in them), bay leaf, tarragon, thyme, salt, pepper, and vinegar. Bring it to a boil and let it boil for 15 minutes. Add the trout and poach about 5 minutes, or until they are just cooked through. Remove the fish to a serving dish.

Add the olive oil, lemon slices and sliced onion to the broth. Reduce it to 1 cup and when cool, pour it over the trout. Chill for 24 hours before serving.

These may be served with their own marinade for the sauce, or with mayonnaise. A salad of cucumbers, tomatoes stuffed with cucumbers, or salade Russe are good additions.

SMOKED TROUT

This is a rare treat if you can come by it. Skin the trout, cut it into long fillets, and serve with lemon for a truly distinctive hors d'oeuvre.

CANNED SMOKED TROUT

I have not yet found a variety of canned smoked trout that I like. However, many people enjoy it for a snack. Serve it plain with lemon wedges.

Whitefish

ONE of the most important fresh-water food fishes, whitefish comes from the Great Lakes, from small lakes in many sections of the country, and from very far north in Canada. The supply has been noticeably reduced by overfishing and also by the activity of an eel called the lamprey, which attaches itself to the fish and chews off the flesh. The Fish and Wildlife Service of the government is now dealing effectively with this problem.

Whitefish available in the markets weighs from 2 to 6 pounds and is sold whole or in fillets. Smoked whitefish is sold widely in the East and Middle West as well.

Whitefish roe can be lightly salted and made into a caviar that is excellent if well prepared. There used to be a great deal of this in the markets, and you may find it today from time to time.

BROILED WHITEFISH

You may broil either the fillets or the whole fish, split or round. Follow the directions for broiling under "Cooking Methods."

Serve with lemon butter (see index), Maître d'hôtel butter (see index), or parsley butter (see index).

WHITEFISH SAUTÉ MEUNIÈRE

The small fish may be sautéed whole, or you may use fillets. Follow directions for sauté meunière under "Cooking Methods."

VARIATIONS

1. Sprinkle the fish heavily with sesame seeds after sautéing and put them in a hot oven or under the broiler flame to brown the seeds.

2. Add buttered almonds, chopped or slivered, to the pan while the fish are cooking.

3. Add small mushroom caps while the fish are cooking.

OVEN-FRIED FILLETS OF WHITEFISH

Soak the fillets in salted milk for 1 hour. Roll them in crumbs and arrange on a well-oiled baking dish. Pour melted butter over them and bake at 500° for 10 minutes.

Serve with a tartar sauce (see index), sauce gribiche (see index), or with lemon (see index) or parsley butter (see index).

BAKED WHITEFISH

Clean a 4 or 5 pound whitefish. Rub with oil, butter, or fat and season with salt and pepper. Place it in a well-oiled baking dish and bake at 400° for about 25 minutes or until the fish flakes easily. Baste frequently during the cooking. Serve with parsley potatoes and grilled tomatoes.

BAKED STUFFED WHITEFISH

Prepare the fish for stuffing. Leave the head and tail on. Prepare a stuffing (see index), stuff the fish and sew it up. Place it on a well-oiled baking dish, strip it with bacon or dot it with butter, and sprinkle with salt. Bake at 400° for 25 to 35 minutes, depending on the size of the fish. Transfer the fish to a hot platter with the aid of two spatulas.

Serve with lemon wedges, lemon butter (see index), or anchovy butter (see index). Accompany the stuffed fish with boiled new potatoes heavily sprinkled with parsley and tiny green peas cooked with a little onion.

1. Make a fish forcemeat (see index) to use as stuffing. Sew up the whitefish. Chop 8 to 10 shallots or small green onions and place them in the bottom of a well-oiled baking dish. Top these with the fish, dot it with butter, sprinkle with salt and pepper and pour 1½ cups of white wine over all. Bake at 400° for 25 to 35 minutes, basting frequently. Remove the fish to a hot platter.

Force the pan juices through a sieve or blend them in a Waring Blendor. Add ½ cup of heavy cream mixed with 2 egg yolks. Stir over a medium heat until the mixture thickens slightly, but do not let it boil. Taste for seasoning and pour over the fish. Serve with rice and a spinach puree.

2. Sauté slices of Spanish onion in butter until soft but not colored. Stuff the whitefish with slices of the onion alternated with sliced, peeled tomato, thinly sliced mushrooms and chopped parsley. Salt and pepper to taste and dot with butter. Sew up the fish and place it on a well-oiled baking dish. Brush it with oil, sprinkle it with salt and pepper, and bake at 400° for 25 to 35 minutes. Serve with a tomato sauce and buttered noodles or macaroni.

CHINESE FISH CAKES

1½ pounds whitefish	1 tablespoon ginger
½ cup raw, fat pork	(optional)
1 cup water chestnuts and/or	Almonds (optional)
bamboo shoots	2 tablespoons soy sauce
	2 tablespoons cornstarch

1 tablespoon sesame oil

Grind the fish very fine. Grind the pork, which should be rather fat. Chop the water chestnuts or bamboo shoots, and the ginger and almonds, if you use them. Mix all together and add the soy sauce, cornstarch and sesame oil. Form into small cakes and fry in hot deep fat. Serve with the following:

SWEET-SOUR SAUCE

¾ cup pineapple juice	3 tablespoons cornstarch
½ cup vinegar	⅓ cup each green onion,
½ cup sugar	green pepper and pine-
1 tablespoon soy sauce	apple
½ cup water	

Cook the pineapple juice, vinegar, sugar, soy sauce, water. Add cornstarch mixed with a little water. Stir until thickened. Add strips of green onion, green pepper, and pineapple, and cook in the sauce just long enough to turn the vegetables a vivid green color.

HELEN EVANS BROWN'S CHINESE STEAMED WHITEFISH

This is cooked in the typical Chinese manner. The fish is stuffed and arranged on the dish in which it is to be served. Then the dish is set on a rack over hot water, a lid is clamped on tightly, and the fish steams until it is done. If you want the fish to be really handsome, arrange it in an S-shape with the split, stuffed side underneath. You can secure it with the aid of a long skewer. Here is the recipe:

1 cup ground Virginia ham	½ cup chopped water
¼ cup sherry	chestnuts
1 tablespoon soy sauce	3 or 4 pound whitefish
2 tablespoons grated ginger	¼ cup soy sauce
6 minced green onions	½ cup sherry
¼ cup of water	

Prepare a stuffing with the ham, ¼ cup of sherry, 1 tablespoon of soy sauce, grated ginger, onions, and water chestnuts. Stuff the fish and sew it, or secure it with skewers or toothpicks. Arrange it on the serving dish and place the dish on a rack in a large steamer. Pour over the fish ¼ cup of soy sauce, ½ cup of sherry, and ¼ cup of water. Pour hot water in the bottom of the steamer, being careful not to get any in the serving dish. Cover tightly and steam until the fish is tender—about 25 minutes.

Serve with rice.

POACHED WHITEFISH

This delicate fish takes very well to poaching. Be careful not to overcook it, and remove it from the boiler very gently. The old method of wrapping fish in cheesecloth is excellent; it's a good idea to leave long ends of the cloth that you can use as handles when you lift the fish. Of course, a real fish boiler with a rack solves the problem.

Poach the fish in a court bouillon (see index) or in a mixture of milk and water—perfect with this type of fish. Follow the directions for poaching fish under "Cooking Methods."

There is a wide variety of sauces to use with poached white-fish. Personally, I like an oyster or shrimp sauce, but Hollandaise and Béarnaise go well with it, too. Serve plain boiled potatoes and a puree of spinach mixed with a little grated garlic, grated Parmesan cheese, and butter.

COLD WHITEFISH

A whole poached whitefish that has been chilled makes a very good buffet dish or a good dish for any summer meal. Or you may serve it as a first course at dinner, followed by game or a red meat. This combination gives you a chance to serve a nice contrast of wines.

Garnish the whitefish with cucumbers in sour cream and dill, and hard-cooked eggs stuffed by adding caviar to the yolks. If you use the fish as a luncheon dish, serve a real French potato salad made with a white wine and olive oil dressing, with the addition of a few slivered almonds and onion. An outstanding dressing for cold poached whitefish served as a salad or hors d'oeuvre course is mayonnaise mixed with lemon juice, finely chopped hard-cooked egg, caviar, grated onion, and just a touch of sherry or Madeira.

SMOKED WHITEFISH

Smoked whitefish is one of the greatest of fish delicacies. The meat, being delicate and fat, lends itself to the smoking process as readily as sturgeon, salmon, or eel. I enjoy it served with cocktails or as a first course.

To serve with cocktails: Remove the skin and arrange the whole fish, with head and tail intact, on a bed of water cress. Garnish with wedges of lemon and have several fish knives available. On another plate arrange some buttered strips of pumpernickel and let people help themselves. If you want to do something especially fancy, accompany this with a bowl of caviar and some finely chopped onions.

To serve as a first course: Place a section of smoked white-fish on a bed of water cress. Garnish with a lemon wedge, some chopped onion and parsley. Thin sandwiches of buttered pumpernickel are a "must."

SUNDAY BREAKFAST SPECIAL

Friends of mine who are famous for entertaining beautifully in their elegant New York apartment serve a Sunday breakfast that is a delight. Their handsome oval table is dominated by a huge platter of smoked whitefish, smoked salmon, and smoked sturgeon with thinly sliced Bermuda onion and lemon wedges. When the guests are seated, a big dish of fluffy scrambled eggs is brought in, steaming hot, and hot rolls are passed. This is a superb combination of flavors.

WHITEFISH ROE

The fresh roe of whitefish is very good when sautéed or poached. See directions for cooking shad roe.

Yellow Perch

MANY people think that the yellow perch is one of the best flavored of fresh-water fishes. A small greenish-golden fish easily obtainable in markets in the Middle West, it is caught commercially in rather large quantities in the Great Lakes, and anglers take it in unrecorded quantities from lakes, streams and ponds of the interior. It has been transplanted successfully to lakes in the Far West.

The yellow perch seems to flourish best in lakes. It likes shallow water and the company of its kind. Seldom exceeding 12 inches in length or 1 pound in weight, it is a relative of the sauger and pike perches and can be cooked in the same way.

SHELLFISH

Abalone

This univalve, native to the waters of California, has been popular for many years among the Chinese-Americans of the Far West, who dried and canned it in large quantities. Now that other Americans have learned to appreciate it, the supply is very small. No fresh abalone can be purchased outside California, but small amounts of canned abalone, including some imported from Mexico, are available in certain Eastern shops.

The fresh abalone meat needs tenderizing before cooking. Most of that bought in California markets is ready to use; if it has not been tenderized, you must soften the meat by pounding with a mallet. Never overcook abalone. It will be tough and disappointing.

ABALONE SAUTE

Have the abalone sliced thin and tenderized. Melt butter in a skillet and cook the fish for 45 to 55 seconds, turning once. Salt and pepper to taste.

BREADED ABALONE

Bread slices of abalone in flour, then dip them in eggs beaten with water, and roll them in crumbs. Sauté in butter as in the recipe above.

FRIED ABALONE

Slice and tenderize abalone and cut into thin strips. Heat fat or oil in a deep fryer to 370°. Dip the pieces of abalone into beer batter for frying (see index) and fry until delicately browned. Salt and pepper to taste.

ABALONE CHOWDER

This is made in the same way you make clam chowder,

except that the abalone is cooked in chicken broth until tender and then ground. The ground abalone is added to the potatoes while they are cooking.

STUFFED ABALONE

(From Helen Evans Brown's *West Coast Cook Book*)
For each serving:

1 lobster tail, sliced	Butter
2 tablespoons crabmeat	1 abalone steak
3 or 4 shrimp	Sauce béchamel

Sauté the lobster tails, the crabmeat and shrimp in butter for 2 or 3 minutes. Sauté the abalone steaks lightly for about 45 seconds, or even less. Brush the cooked steak with sauce béchamel flavored with sherry. Dip the shellfish in the sauce and place on top of the abalone. Roll each steak and fasten with a toothpick. Brush with more sauce and run under the broiler to brown lightly.

CANNED ABALONE, CHINESE STYLE

4 or 5 large Chinese black mushrooms	4 green onions
	½ cup sliced celery
1 cup chicken stock	1 tablespoon soy sauce
1 pound can of abalone	1 tablespoon sherry
5 water chestnuts	2 tablespoons cornstarch

Soak the mushrooms in water for 2 or 3 hours, then cut them in strips. Cook them in a cup of chicken stock with the juice from the canned abalone, the sliced water chestnuts, the onions, split and cut into 1-inch length, and the celery. After 5 minutes, add the sliced abalone, the soy sauce and sherry. Mix the cornstarch with 2 tablespoons of water and stir it in. Stir until the sauce is thickened. Serve with rice.

This will serve 4 to 10 people, depending on whether it's a Chinese or American meal.

Clams

WE in America are fonder of clams than are the people of other nations. And fortunately for us, our shoreline is well supplied with them.

Clams come in a variety that is often confusing to the inlander. Two main species make up the bulk of East Coast clamming—the soft or long-necked clam (*Mya arenaria*) and the hard or little-necked clam (*Venus mercanaria*). Many New Englanders will assure you that the soft clam is the only "real" or "true" clam. The exclusiveness of this claim may possibly be attributed to the fact that *Mya* is abundant north of Cape Cod but scarce to the south. New Englanders refer to the hard clam by its Indian name, quahog, while other Easterners more often call it the "littleneck" or "round clam." The species begins to be abundant south of the Cape, is especially plentiful on the North Carolina and Florida shores, and occurs all the way to Texas.

The Pacific Coast has some 30 varieties of clams, dominated by the razor clam, the famous Pismo clam, and the large mud clam. There is also that odd, gargantuan member of the clam family called the geoduck, goeduck or gweduc (pronounced *gooey-duck*). It has an excellent flavor, but sad to say, is not obtainable in the markets.

Like the razor clam, New England's soft clam is a tide-flat dweller with a long tubelike siphon. It is a deep burrower and is taken by digging. The hard or littlenecked variety generally lives in deeper water, is not so active in its burrowing, and is taken by long-handled rakes or tongs and by dredging.

In my opinion, the razor clam—correctly prepared—is unsurpassed in flavor and texture. When I was a child and living near the Oregon coast, I used to dig them by the bucketful in the early morning when the tide was out. My mother sautéed them in butter, cooked them as delicately light fritters, or made them into magnificent chowder. You may now buy the Pacific Coast razor clam, minced, in tins (the brand name Pioneer is a favorite). The tinned variety is fine for soups and soufflés and for the clam appetizer that is so widely popular these days.

In the East, the distinct flavor of the hard clam or quahog makes it the preferred ingredient in Boston clam chowder and in that entirely dissimilar soup—not so highly regarded by connoisseurs—Manhattan clam chowder. Several regional varieties of clams are popular on the half shell, but perhaps the best known is the "cherrystone," which is actually a small quahog. Clams served on the half shell must be very cold. Care should be taken when they are opened that no drop of the wonderful juice is lost, and anyone who does not drink the juice from the shells is losing half the enjoyment of eating clams. Raw clams are usually served with cocktail sauce, which in my opinion really ruins their delicate flavor. I prefer lemon juice and a little freshly ground pepper or horseradish. Others insist that lime juice is far better with clams than lemon.

CLAM APPETIZERS

1 clove of garlic
7-ounce tin of minced clams
Parsley
¼ pound cream cheese
Sour cream

Mince the garlic very fine or put it through a garlic press. Mix with the clams, the cream cheese and enough sour cream to thin it down for dunking. Taste for seasoning and add chopped parsley.

This makes an excellent dunk for crisp raw vegetables. It is also good with bread sticks or very small corn sticks.

VARIATIONS

1. Try a spread instead of a dunk. Drain the clams and work them into the cream cheese. Then add just enough of the clam juice to make a smooth spread. Flavor with a little grated onion, salt and pepper.
2. Drain the clams and mix with cottage cheese and a dash of Worcestershire sauce.
3. Drain the clams, mix with sour cream, a tablespoon of chopped fresh dill, a tablespoon of chopped parsley, a little onion juice, and salt and pepper. You may add some cream cheese to this to make a stiffer paste, if you prefer.
4. Mince tiny white pickled onions and combine with cream cheese and minced clams, drained. Salt and pepper to taste.

CLAM CHOWDER

See index.

CLAM SOUP

This may be made with any type of clam. It is best, to my taste, with either littlenecks (known as quahogs in New England) or razor clams.

2 cups milk	½ cup heavy cream
1 cup minced clams	Salt, pepper
2 egg yolks	3 tablespoons butter
	Paprika

Scald the milk. Grind the clams and save their liquor. Beat the egg yolks with the cream, stir them into the clams and clam juice, and add to the hot milk. Continue stirring over a low flame until the clams are just heated through and the cream and egg yolks well blended in. Correct the seasoning and serve in small bowls with a lump of butter and a dash of paprika added at the last minute.

STEAMED CLAMS

For this popular dish, figure an average of 20 clams per person. You may increase or decrease this amount according to the appetites of the diners. Place the clams, which have been thoroughly scrubbed, in a large kettle with ½ inch of salt water at the bottom. Cover the kettle tightly and steam just until the clams open. This should take from 6 to 10 minutes. Discard any clams that do not open. Serve at once with large bowls of melted butter and cups of the broth. (Taste the broth for seasoning.)

STEAMED CLAMS A LA MARINIERE

This recipe is usually used for preparing mussels, but clams may be prepared in any way that you cook mussels.

6 to 7 dozen clams	1 cup (approximately)
1 large onion	white wine
Parsley	4 tablespoons butter
Thyme	Freshly ground pepper
Bay leaf	2 tablespoons butter

Scrub the clams well and put them in a large kettle with the chopped onion, parsley, thyme, and bay leaf. Add the wine and 4 tablespoons of butter, and grind a little black pepper over all. Cover tightly and steam until the clams open. Discard any that do not open. Remove the clams to a large serving dish, or to individual serving dishes. Put the sauce through a fine sieve, taste it for seasoning, and reheat, adding 2 tablespoons more of butter and a little chopped parsley. Pour this sauce over the clams.

1. Some people like 2 or 3 cloves of garlic chopped and added to the mixture in the pan.

2. If you like a thicker sauce, stir a half cup of sauce velouté (see index) into the broth after it has been strained.

STEAMED CLAMS ON TOAST

2 dozen steamed clams (see index)	2 cloves garlic
4 slices bread	4 tablespoons chopped parsley
½ cup butter	Lemon wedges

Remove the steamed clams from their shells. Check the broth for salt. Toast the bread and trim the crusts. Melt the butter with the garlic, finely chopped, and the parsley. Arrange the clams on the hot toast, pour some of the sauce over them, and serve at once with additional sauce and wedges of lemon.

STUFFED CLAMS

24 steamed clams (see index)	½ cup thick béchamel (see index)
1 tablespoon each of chopped onion, parsley, tarragon	Salt, pepper
½ cup buttered crumbs	Cayenne
1 tablespoon sherry	

Remove the steamed clams from their shells. Chop very fine and combine with the chopped seasonings, crumbs, and just enough béchamel sauce to bind them. Add the sherry, salt and pepper, and a few grains of cayenne. Fill the clam shells with this mixture, dot with butter and crumbs and brown very quickly under the broiler.

(NOTE: For certain clam, oyster and other seafood dishes in the shell, it is a good idea to have some inexpensive pie plates or cake pans which you can fill with rock salt. Heat the pan filled with salt, and place the clams in their shells on the hot salt. Then return the pans to the oven or under the broiler. Serve the food right in the salt-filled pans.)

1. Steam clams as for clams marinière. Reduce the liquid to ⅓ cup. Add ⅓ cup of heavy sauce velouté. Season with cayenne, chopped parsley. Add chopped clams and stuff the mixture into the shells. Top with buttered crumbs and small cubes of bacon. Bake at 400° until the bacon is crisp.

2. Use 24 clams on the half shell. Sprinkle with chopped chives, parsley and garlic. Top with bacon. Bake in a 425° oven until the bacon is crisp.

3. Top 24 clams on the half shell with a lump of anchovy butter, made by creaming together ½ cup of butter with 2 or 3 teaspoons of finely chopped anchovies and 1 teaspoon of finely chopped onion. Sprinkle with buttered crumbs and broil for 3 or 4 minutes.

4. Use 24 clams on the half shell. Combine 1 cup of bread crumbs with the clam liquor, ⅓ cup of white wine, 1 tablespoon each of chopped onion, parsley, green pepper. Salt and pepper to taste. Cover the clams with this mixture, pour melted butter over it, and sprinkle with grated Parmesan cheese. Bake at 400° until nicely browned.

CLAM HASH

During the summer months when we lived at the shore near the mouth of the Columbia River, we used to feast almost daily on clams, and we ate them in many different ways. Clam hash was one of the favorites, and although it was never made the same way twice, it always tasted ambrosial. This is an approximation of it:

6 tablespoons butter	Salt, pepper
1 tablespoon finely minced onion	Nutmeg
	4 egg yolks
1½ cups finely diced cooked potatoes	4 tablespoons grated Parmesan cheese
1½ to 2 cups minced clams	Heavy cream

Melt the butter in a heavy skillet and cook the onion until it is just transparent. Add the finely diced potatoes and the clams and press them down with a spatula. Salt and pepper lightly and add a few flecks of nutmeg. Let the hash cook for about 10 minutes and stir with a fork or spatula, mixing in some of the crust which forms on the bottom. Press down again. Beat the egg yolks well, combine with the grated cheese and about 6 tablespoons of heavy cream. Pour this over the hash very gently, and cover tightly for a few minutes until the egg is set.

CLAM FRITTERS

2 eggs, separated	1 teaspoon salt
2 cups minced clams (fresh or canned)	½ teaspoon pepper
	Few grains cayenne
1 cup cracker crumbs or toasted bread crumbs	Milk or clam juice

Beat the egg yolks until light and lemon-colored. Gradually add the clams, the crumbs and seasonings. Add enough liquid —clam juice or milk—to make a rather heavy batter. Fold in the stiffly beaten egg whites. Drop the batter by spoonfuls into hot butter or oil and sauté 4 or 5 minutes, turning once.

VARIATIONS

1. Beat 2 eggs until light. Add 1 cup of mixed milk and clam juice, and ¾ cup of flour sifted with a teaspoon of baking powder. Stir in 1 cup of minced clams and season with salt and pepper. Drop by spoonfuls into hot butter or oil and sauté for 4 or 5 minutes, turning once.

2. Beat 2 eggs, stir in 2 cups of minced clams, ⅔ cup of bread crumbs which have been browned in butter, ½ teaspoon of salt, ½ teaspoon of paprika, and 2 tablespoons of chopped parsley. With your hands, form the mixture into cakes— round, cutlet-shaped or oval. Roll these in flour and crumbs and sauté them in butter or oil until nicely browned. Serve with lemon wedges.

Or you may deep fry them for 4 or 5 minutes in fat heated to 365°. Drain on absorbent paper.

CLAM SOUFFLE

3 tablespoons butter	2 tablespoons chopped
3 tablespoons flour	parsley
½ cup clam juice	Salt, pepper
½ cup cream	Nutmeg
⅔ cup minced clams	6 egg whites
4 egg yolks	

Melt the butter in a saucepan, add the flour and brown lightly. Stir in the clam juice and the cream and continue stirring until the mixture thickens. Add the minced clams and remove from the stove. Cool slightly. Beat the egg yolks into this mixture, one by one, add the chopped parsley and the seasonings. Beat the egg whites until stiff and fold them in. Pour into a well-buttered soufflé dish. Bake at 375° for 30 to

35 minutes, according to the state of runniness you prefer in a soufflé.

To be really elegant, serve this soufflé with a sauce mousseline (see index).

SCALLOPED CLAMS

½ cup butter (and more)
½ cup toasted bread crumbs
1 cup cracker crumbs
Salt, pepper
Paprika

2 cups minced clams
2 tablespoons finely minced onion
2 tablespoons finely minced parsley

⅓ cup cream

Melt ½ cup of butter and mix it with the bread and cracker crumbs. Add salt and pepper to taste and a dash of paprika. Set aside ⅓ cup of this mixture for the top of the casserole. With the rest mix the clams, the onion and parsley. Pour it into a well-buttered baking dish and top with the remaining crumb mixture. Dot with butter and pour the cream over all. Bake in a 375° oven for 20 to 25 minutes.

CLAM PIE

2 quarts clams in shells
2 cups white wine
1 carrot
1 onion
1 bay leaf
1 teaspoon freshly ground pepper
2 cups sauce velouté (see index)

1 pound mushrooms
5 tablespoons butter
Salt, pepper
3 tablespoons sherry or Madeira
1 recipe of rich pastry
Beaten egg yolk

Steam the clams in the white wine with the carrot, onion, bay leaf and pepper (see index for Steamed Clams). Remove from the shells. Prepare a sauce velouté (see index), using some of the clam broth. Sauté the mushrooms in butter, and season to taste with salt and pepper. Combine the mushrooms, the clams and the sauce and add the sherry or Madeira. Taste for seasoning. Pour into a deep baking dish and top with pie crust rolled ¼ inch thick. Decorate with leaves cut out of additional crust, brush with beaten egg yolk mixed with a little water, and bake at 450° for 15 minutes. Reduce the heat to 350° and bake until nicely browned.

CLAM TART

Pastry for 1 pie crust	1½ cups clam juice and
4 strips of bacon	cream, mixed
2 tablespoons minced onion	Salt, pepper
4 eggs	Nutmeg

1 cup minced clams, drained

Line a 9-inch pie tin with the pastry and chill in the refrigerator for several hours. Sauté the bacon until crisp and drain on absorbent paper. Sauté the onion in the bacon fat until just soft. Beat the eggs, combine with the liquid and add seasonings to taste. Remove the pie shell from the refrigerator. Sprinkle crumbled bacon and the onion on the bottom, then add the clams. Pour the custard mixture over all. Bake in a 450° oven for 10 minutes. Reduce the heat to 350° and continue baking until a knife inserted in the center comes out clean. Serve hot.

VARIATION

You may sprinkle the tart with grated Parmesan cheese before baking it.

CLAMS WITH RICE, SPANISH STYLE

1 medium onion	Salt, pepper
1 clove garlic	Pinch of saffron
1 slice smoked ham	18 to 20 small clams
1 cup cooked tomatoes	1 cup washed rice
1 pint clam broth (fresh or	
canned)	

Chop the onion and the garlic very fine and shred the ham. Combine these with the tomatoes and the clam broth and simmer for 20 minutes. Season to taste and add the saffron. Wash the clams, scrubbing them well. Arrange them in a large casserole with the rice. Pour the sauce over this and bake in a 350° oven until the rice is cooked and the liquid nearly all absorbed.

CLAM PAN ROASTS

In reality, pan roasts are nothing more nor less than sautés, a most delicate and delicious way to serve clams. There seem to endless variations on this theme, and I include only the few that are my favorites. For a plain pan roast:

¼ pound butter	Paprika
1 pint drained clams	Buttered toast
Salt, pepper	Chopped parsley

Melt the butter in a skillet or chafing dish. Add the drained whole clams from which you have trimmed the tough little-necks. Cook them just long enough to heat through and plump up. Season to taste with salt, pepper and paprika, and serve on rounds of toast—buttered (or on fried toast), and top with parsley.

VARIATIONS

1. Add a spoonful of Worcestershire sauce and a dash of French mustard to the pan when the clams are cooked.

2. Add finely chopped chives, fennel, parsley or tarragon to the clams as they cook.

3. Add ½ cup of white wine or champagne to the pan and let it cook for just a minute after the clams have puffed.

4. Add butter, ⅓ cup of sherry, ⅓ cup of chili sauce and a little grated onion. Cook the clams in this mixture and serve them on garlic fried toast with the sauce poured over.

5. Chop 1 small green pepper and 1 onion very fine and sauté them in ⅔ cup of butter until soft. Add the clams and cook until they are plump and heated through. Salt and pepper to taste and add a few grains of cayenne. Serve on toast.

CLAMS SAUTE

Clams should be dipped in flour or beaten egg and crumbs and then sautéed in plenty of butter.

1. *Razor clams:* Clean the clams, and either use whole, or use only the tender digging foot—if clams are plentiful. Dip in flour, or in egg and crumbs, and sauté quickly in plenty of butter. Salt and pepper to taste and serve with lemon wedges.

2. *Soft clams:* Clean and dip in flour, or egg and crumbs, and sauté lightly until delicately browned. Add chopped parsley and lemon juice, salt and pepper.

3. *Littleneck clams:* The procedure is the same.

FRIED CLAMS

These to clam lovers are as tank wine is to lovers of good Burgundies! Murder!

⅔ cup corn meal, or more	¾ cup cream
⅔ cup flour, or more	Clams
2 eggs	Fat or oil heated to 365°
	Salt, pepper

Combine the corn meal and the flour. Beat the eggs and mix with the cream. Dip the clams into the liquid mixture, roll in the flour and corn meal, and fry in the hot fat 1 or 2 minutes, depending on size. Drain on absorbent paper and sprinkle with salt and pepper.

BATTER-FRIED CLAMS

2 eggs, separated	1 tablespoon lemon juice
1 tablespoon olive oil	About 2 cups of small
1 cup sifted flour	clams
⅓ teaspoon salt	Fat or oil heated to 365°
½ cup milk	Salt, pepper

Beat the egg yolks until light and lemon-colored. Beat in the olive oil, the sifted flour and salt, the milk and lemon juice. Beat the egg whites until stiff and fold them in. Add the clams. Let stand for 2 hours. Drop by spoonfuls into hot fat and fry 4 or 5 minutes or until golden-brown. Drain on absorbent paper and salt and pepper to taste.

VARIATION

Substitute 1 tablespoon of brandy or whiskey for the lemon juice.

GREEN NOODLES WITH CLAMS

1 quart clams in shell	½ cup chopped parsley
1 medium onion	(Italian, if possible)
1 stalk of celery	1½ tablespoons chopped
1 carrot	basil
1 cup white wine or vermouth	Salt, pepper
½ cup olive oil	8 ounces green noodles
3 cloves garlic	(white will do)
	Grated Gruyère cheese

Wash the clams well. Cut the onion, celery and carrot into fine strips, and put them in a large kettle. Add the wine and the clams. Cover tightly and steam until the clams open. Remove the clams from their shells and strain the broth. Heat the olive oil and the garlic, finely chopped, add the parsley, basil, and salt and pepper to taste. Reduce the clam broth by half, add it to the olive oil mixture and let it come to a boil. Taste for seasoning. Add the clams, chopped.

294

Cook the noodles and drain. Pour the clam mixture over the noodles and top with the grated cheese.

Combine the sauce with ½ cup of tomato puree and cook until well blended. Thin with a dash of white wine or vermouth. Serve the same way.

SPAGHETTI WITH CLAM SAUCE

Use the preceeding recipe but substitute spaghetti for the noodles.

Conch

THIS southern shellfish has a fine flavor, but its toughness presents the same problem as the Pacific Coast abalone. There are several ways to tenderize it. One is to pound it with a sharp-edged instrument, or as the average housewife does, with the edge of a plate. Another way is to parboil it and then pound until the flesh is tender. Still another method, followed by Sloppy Louie, the famous New York fish dealer and restaurateur, is to immerse live conch in boiling water. As soon as the live conch (pronounced *konk*, by the way) is affected by the heat and retreats into its shell, take it from the water, drain, and shell it. It must be shelled at almost the instant it releases its muscles, or it will still require beating or parboiling.

CONCH FRITTERS

6 conchs	2 cloves garlic
½ cup chopped onion	1 teaspoon salt
½ cup chopped tomato	1 cup rolled cracker crumbs
(peeled and seeded)	¼ cup chopped parsley
3 eggs	

Grind the conch meat and combine it with the onion, tomato, chopped garlic, salt, parsley, crumbs, and the yolks of the eggs beaten lightly. Beat the 3 egg whites until stiff. If the batter seems stiff thin it with cream, then fold in the egg whites. Drop the mixture by spoonfuls on a well-buttered pan

295

or griddle. Cook until nicely browned and turn to brown the other side. Serve with lemon butter (see index).

STEWED CONCH

4 conchs	1 teaspoon basil, or more
2 onions	1 teaspoon salt
3 cloves garlic	2 cups tomato puree
6 tablespoons olive oil	1 cup red wine

Tenderize the conchs. Chop the onions and garlic and sauté them in oil. Add basil and salt, the tomato puree and wine and simmer for 30 minutes. Dilute the sauce with a little more wine if it gets too thick. Add the conch and cook just until it heats through and is tender. Taste for seasoning and serve on rice.

FRIED CONCH

For 4 people, tenderize 4 conchs. Cut them into thin slices. Dip them in flour, then into beaten egg, and roll in crumbs or corn meal.

Heat the fat in your deep fryer to 370°, and fry the strips of conch for about 3 minutes or until nicely browned and crisp on the edges. Remove to absorbent paper and season to taste. Serve with tartar sauce (see index).

Crab

CRAB is second to shrimp as the shellfish most preferred by Americans, and the supply is varied and fairly abundant. The magnificently flavored Pacific Coast crab—the Dungeness—is now brought frozen to the East. The giant king crab is flown fresh from Alaska and is also shipped frozen. Crab caught in the Gulf and in the north and south Atlantic is sent in refrigerated tins to all parts of the East and far inland. In addition, the famous stone crabs from Cuba often appear in our markets, and quantities of soft-shelled crabs are shipped all over the East.

There is general misunderstanding about soft-shelled crabs. They are not a distinct soft-shelled species—they are the same blue crabs (*Callinecte Sapidus*) found all along the Atlantic Coast. It is the habit of the crab to shed its shell many times before maturity, and the soft-shelled crab is one caught just as it has shed one shell and before it has grown a new and larger one.

On the Pacific Coast, most crabs are sold whole and freshly cooked. In the East, with the exception of the soft-shelled, crab is usually sold already cleaned and shelled in 1 or ½ pound tins. There are many different grades of this crabmeat on the Eastern market. The larger choice lump crabmeat is hard to find in retail shops, for most of it is bought by the better restaurants and clubs. But various other qualities are generally available. Some markets carry the leg meat, which has excellent flavor and is delicious for salads and for deviled crab. The giant crab legs (from claw tip to claw tip, these gargantuan crustaceans sometimes measure almost 9 feet across) are sent from Alaska frozen and ready to broil.

Crabmeat is expensive; however, there is no waste, and a pound will serve 4 people well.

If you are cooking live crabs—which is unlikely unless you go crabbing—boil them in sea water or in a mild court bouillon, allowing 8 minutes for each pound of crab. When the crab is cool, remove its back and the spongy parts under the shell. Then remove the apron and spit the body so you can take out the meat. Crack the claws and take the meat from them.

I have vivid memories of the preparation of the crabs that we caught on the Pacific coast when I was young. The system followed by my mother and most of our neighbors was to remove the back and clean the crab before plunging it into the boiling sea water. Supposedly the flavor was much better if the crab was cleaned first. These crabs—the Dungeness variety —were cooled and then used for many special dishes. My favorite was, and still is, a feast of cracked crab and mayonnaise freshly made with good olive oil, flavored with lemon juice, mustard, salt, pepper and a touch of tarragon. With good bread and butter and a bottle of chilled white wine, this is the absolute ultimate for a summer luncheon.

CRABMEAT VINAIGRETTE

Arrange 1 pound of crabmeat (either Dungeness or blue crab) on romaine or lettuce. Cover with the vinaigrette sauce (see index) and sprinkle with fresh or dried tarragon.

CRABMEAT COCKTAIL OR CRABMEAT
AS A FIRST COURSE

Most restaurants insist on smothering crab with a hot tomato sauce that kills its elegant flavor. If more of them would only learn to send you a choice of different sauces for crabmeat, I'm sure the dining-out public would be pleased. Here are a few suggestions.

1. Serve fine lump or leg crabmeat on a bed of water cress or romaine. Top with a sauce rémoulade (see index).

2. Arrange crabmeat on a bed of shredded Boston or leaf lettuce and serve with a Russian dressing. Garnish with hard-cooked egg slices. This is popular at "21."

3. Serve large lump crabmeat—or the choicest Dungeness crab legs—garnish with paper-thin slices of peeled tomato and very thinly sliced onions. Pass a bowl of well-flavored olive oil mayonnaise and capers. This is a favorite recipe of William Palmer, well-known Jamaica hotel operator.

CRAB LEGS PALACE COURT

This is one of the most famous first course specialties in the country. It has been one of the outstanding dishes at the Palace—that magnificent hotel in San Francisco—for generations. It was a favorite on the old Wednesday luncheons and is truly an American classic.

Start with a bed of shredded lettuce—preferably leaf or Boston lettuce. Then add a large artichoke heart filled with salade Russe (a mixture of cooked tiny peas, finely diced cooked carrot, finely cut cooked snap beans and diced cooked potatoes bound together with mayonnaise). Arrange 5 or 6 large crab legs on the salade Russe and top with a Thousand Island dressing or a Russian dressing. Surround the base of the artichoke with finely chopped hard-cooked egg and garnish with strips of green pepper or pimiento.

CRAB LOUIS

This is another dish that comes from the Pacific Coast. Helen Evans Brown says it was served at Solari's in San Francisco in 1914. If I'm not mistaken, the father of the West Coast writer Richard L. Neuberger served it in his

Bohemian Restaurant in Portland, Oregon, at that time, too. At any rate, the old Bohemian served the finest Louis I have ever eaten.

It is very easy to make this superb dish. Begin with a bed of finely shredded lettuce. Heap plenty of crabmeat on top and garnish with quartered hard-cooked eggs and quartered tomatoes. Pour a Louis dressing over all. We always made our Louis dressing with 1 cup of mayonnaise (a good homemade mayonnaise made with olive oil and lemon juice), ⅓ cup of heavy cream, whipped, ¼ cup of chili sauce, 2 tablespoons of grated onion, 2 tablespoons of chopped parsley, and a few grains of cayenne.

AVOCADO STUFFED WITH CRABMEAT

This is a very popular first course in Florida and in the West. My favorite sauce for this is made with ½ cup of good mayonnaise, ½ cup of stiffly whipped cream, ⅓ cup of chili sauce and 1 tablespoon of grated onion.

SAUTEED CRABS WITH ALMONDS

4 tablespoons butter	Salt, pepper
1 pound crabmeat	⅓ cup heavy cream
⅔ cup almonds, blanched and split in half	3 tablespoons chopped parsley
3 tablespoons butter	

Melt 4 tablespoons of butter in a medium skillet, add the crabmeat and toss lightly until it is delicately browned. While this is cooking, sauté the almonds in 3 tablespoons of butter over a rather brisk flame until they brown lightly. Salt and pepper to taste and add to the crabmeat. Finally add the cream and the chopped parsley and let it cook up and boil for 2 minutes. Serve on rice or rounds of fried toast.

VARIATIONS

1. Add 3 tablespoons of sherry just before serving.
2. Omit the almonds and add 3 tablespoons of chives or finely chopped green onion. Cook these with the crab and then add 3 tablespoons of tomato puree or chili sauce to the pan before adding the cream.
3. Add ½ cup of cream and 1 tablespoon of curry powder to the crabmeat and serve on rice with crisp French-fried onions.

4. Combine the crab with ½ pound of mushrooms which have been sautéed in 6 tablespoons of butter and flavored with lemon juice. Add ⅓ cup of cream and let it cook down for 3 or 4 minutes.

5. This variation is called **Crabmeat Marseillaise.** To the sautéed crabmeat add an equal amount of mussels which have been opened (see mussels) and removed from their shells. Add 1 cup of heavy cream, and let it cook down slightly.

POLLY HAMBLET'S DEVILED CRAB
(DEVILED CRAB I)

This is the recipe for the deviled crab that I ate as a child. It was the first one I ever tasted and has been my favorite ever since. Originally I had it made with Dungeness crab, but many times since I have had it made with blue crabs and even with king crab. It never fails to please me.

1 pound crabmeat	½ teaspoon salt
1½ cups rolled cracker crumbs	Few grains of cayenne
¾ cup finely diced celery	2 tablespoons chopped
¾ cup chopped onion	parsley
½ cup butter, melted	1 tablespoon chopped
¼ cup milk	green pepper
1 teaspoon dry mustard	

Combine the crabmeat with the crumbs, celery and onion and moisten with melted butter and milk. Season with mustard, salt, cayenne, parsley and green pepper. Mix thoroughly, pile into shells or a casserole, and bake in a 350° oven for about ½ hour.

DEVILED CRAB II

The average deviled crab in New York is made with a cream sauce base. It has other seasonings, but the creaminess is the dominant quality.

1 pound crabmeat	Few grains of cayenne
2 cups sauce velouté	2 tablespoons chopped
(see index)	parsley
2 egg yolks	2 tablespoons finely
1 teaspoon dry mustard	chopped green pepper
Buttered crumbs	

Combine the crabmeat, the sauce, slightly beaten egg yolks and the flavorings. Heap into individual shells or ramekins or in a large baking dish. Dust with buttered crumbs and brown quickly in a 425° oven.

1. Add 3 tablespoons of sherry to the mixture before putting it in the shells.

2. Add 2 tablespoons of grated onion to the sauce before adding the crabmeat.

DEVILED CRAB III

½ cup red wine
1 tablespoon chili sauce
1 teaspoon dry mustard
1 tablespoon Worcestershire
    sauce
Dash of tabasco
6 tablespoons finely chopped
    onion

2 tablespoons chopped
    green pepper
4 tablespoons butter
4 tablespoons chopped
    parsley
1 pound crabmeat
Salt
Buttered crumbs

Combine the wine and the seasonings and cook for 3 or 4 minutes. Cook the onion and green pepper in the butter for 2 minutes. Add the parsley and combine with the sauce and the crabmeat. Salt to taste, pile into shells, top with buttered crumbs and dot with butter. Bake at 425° just long enough to brown.

CRABMEAT IN CREAM

Add 1 pound of crabmeat to 2 cups of béchamel (see index) or sauce velouté (see index). Serve on toast, in patty shells, or in croustades.

VARIATIONS

1. Add ¼ cup of sherry or Madeira to the sauce.

2. Use half crabmeat and half shrimp, clams or mussels. Add 4 tablespoons of sherry or Madeira to the mixture.

3. Combine ¾ pound of crabmeat with ½ pound of sliced sautéed mushrooms. Add to the sauce and flavor with 3 tablespoons of brandy or whiskey.

4. This variation is called **Hongroise**. Add 1 tablespoon of Hungarian paprika to the sauce.

5. (Indienne). Add 2 tablespoons of grated onion and 1 tablespoon of curry powder to the sauce. Serve on rice with a garnish of toasted almonds and crisp French-fried onions.

6. Pile creamed crab in a baking dish or in individual ramekins. Sprinkle with finely chopped almonds and crumbs and dot with butter. Brown quickly in a 425° oven.

CRABMEAT MORNAY

Combine 1 pound of crabmeat with 1¾ to 2 cups of sauce Mornay (see index). Serve with croustades or in ramekins.

VARIATIONS

1. Heap the crabmeat Mornay in shells or ramekins and top with grated cheese and buttered toasted crumbs. Run under the broiler flame for a few minutes to brown.

2. (Florentine). Cover the bottom of a casserole with finely chopped cooked spinach. Top with crabmeat and cover with sauce Mornay. Sprinkle with paprika and buttered crumbs and brown quickly under the broiler or in a hot oven.

3. Poach some small oysters in their own liquor and a little white wine until the edges curl. In a baking dish arrange a layer of crabmeat and then a layer of the oysters. Top with sauce Mornay, sprinkle with crumbs and grated cheese and brown quickly under the broiler flame.

4. Stuff large mushroom caps with crabmeat and arrange in a flat baking dish. Top each mushroom with sauce Mornay and sprinkle with crumbs. Brown quickly under the broiler flame or bake in 450° oven for 10 or 12 minutes.

5. Heat the crabmeat in 3 tablespoons of butter. Add 1 tablespoon of grated horseradish, 1 teaspoon of dry mustard, 4 tablespoons of chopped parsley and 2 tablespoons of grated onion. Arrange in the bottom of a baking dish and top with sauce Mornay. Sprinkle with buttered crumbs and brown quickly under the broiler flame.

CRABMEAT SOUFFLE

3 tablespoons butter	Nutmeg
1 tablespoon grated onion	Juice of ½ lemon
4 tablespoons flour	1½ cups crabmeat
¾ cup milk	4 egg yolks
Salt, pepper	6 egg whites

Melt the butter in the upper part of a double boiler, add the onion and cook for 2 or 3 minutes. Add the flour and mix well. Gradually stir in the milk until the mixture has thickened. Season to taste with salt, pepper and nutmeg, and the lemon juice. Remove from the fire, add the crabmeat and stir in the slightly beaten egg yolks. Beat the egg whites until stiff. Fold in one half of them and blend well. Then fold in the second half very lightly. Pour into a buttered soufflé dish and bake in a 375° oven for 35 to 45 minutes or until the soufflé is light and puffy.

Serve with a sauce Mornay (see index) or a sauce béchamel (see index) with a little crabmeat and 4 tablespoons of sherry added.

CRAB CAKES

This famous Southern dish has changed a great deal from the early days, possibly because we have lost much of the quality and distinction of the good regional cooking of the eighteenth and nineteenth centuries. It is my personal opinion that these popular cakes, considered great delicacies in Maryland, are a bit on the heavy side. But they have a great public.

4 tablespoons butter	1 teaspoon dry mustard
1 medium onion, chopped	4 tablespoons chopped
1 cup bread crumbs	parsley
1 pound crabmeat	Heavy cream
3 eggs	Flour
1 teaspoon salt	

Melt the butter in a skillet and cook the onion until just transparent. Add the crumbs and blend well. Mix with the crabmeat, the beaten eggs and the seasonings. Add just enough cream to make the mixture hold together. Shape into large flat cakes. Roll each cake in flour and fry in butter or oil until nicely browned on both sides and cook through. Serve with tartar sauce (see index) or with lemon butter (see index).

PILAFF DE CRABES

This is a recipe from a small Martiniquaise restaurant in Paris that specializes in all the dishes of the Indies.

6 strips of bacon, finely cut	1 pound crabmeat
2 medium onions, finely chopped	⅓ cup dark rum
	1 pint white wine
1 clove garlic, finely chopped	1 tablespoon chopped
½ pound smoked ham, cut in thin strips	parsley
	Pinch of sugar
3 tablespoons tomato puree	¼ cup heavy cream

Let the bacon try out in a large skillet. Add the onions and garlic and allow them to just color. Add the ham and heat through. Add the tomato puree, the crabmeat, and pour the rum over this and ignite. When it has flamed, add the wine, parsley and sugar and let it all simmer for 15 minutes. Finally stir in the heavy cream. Serve with a rice pilaff.

CRAB A L'AMERICAINE

If live crabs are available in your part of the country, use them in this recipe and eat the crab from the shell, cracking the claws at the table. If you cannot get crab in the shell, follow the note at the end of the recipe. First, the sauce:

SAUCE AMERICAINE

3 tablespoons butter	3 tablespoons chopped
1 small onion, finely chopped	parsley
6 shallots, or green onions, finely chopped	1 tablespoon fresh or 1 teaspoon dried tarragon
5 large, or 8 medium tomatoes, peeled, seeded, chopped	1½ teaspoons thyme
	½ bay leaf
1 clove garlic, peeled and chopped	Salt
	4 tablespoons tomato puree

Melt the butter in a skillet, add the onions and let them cook for a few minutes but do not let them brown. Add the shallots, the tomatoes, the garlic and seasonings and salt to taste. Let this all simmer for 1 hour or until well blended and thick. Add the tomato puree. Now, for the rest of the recipe:

3 Dungeness crabs or 6 rather small blue crabs	1½ cups white wine
	¼ cup cognac or whiskey
½ cup olive oil	Few grains cayenne

Wash the crabs and remove their backs. Crack the claws, and cut the crabs in half with a sharp knife. Heat the olive oil in a large kettle, add the pieces of crab and sear quickly, turning with a wooden spoon and fork so that the flesh of the crab comes in contact with the hot oil. Add the white wine, the brandy, and the sauce and let it all simmer for 20 or 25 minutes. Add the cayenne, and taste for seasoning. Serve with a rice pilaff and plenty of large paper napkins or bib-like aprons. This is not a dainty dish to eat and you must use your fingers.

NOTE: If you are making this dish with crabmeat already taken from the shell, prepare the sauce in the same way. Then sauté the crabmeat—1½ pounds—in the olive oil for 3 minutes. Add the brandy or whiskey and the wine. Combine with the sauce and cook up for just a few minutes before serving.

CRABMEAT AND RICE

1½ cups rice
1 pound crabmeat
1 cup cooked green peas
6 tablespoons butter

½ cup finely chopped
  parsley
3 tablespoons grated onion
2 finely chopped pimientos
  Salt, pepper

Grated Parmesan cheese

Cook the rice in your usual way. When it is drained and fluffy add the crabmeat, the cooked green peas, the butter and the flavorings. Season to taste and toss lightly until it is well mixed. Place in a casserole or copper baking dish, sprinkle liberally with grated cheese, dot with butter and heat in a 425° oven for 10 minutes—or until it is thoroughly heated through. Serve with a tomato sauce, if you wish, although I prepare mine plain.

CRABMEAT CREOLE

2 small onions
¼ cup olive oil
1 large or 2 small green
  peppers
4 tomatoes, peeled and
  chopped

1 stalk celery
½ cup white wine
1 clove garlic, crushed
3 tablespoons tomato paste
  Salt, pepper
1 pound crabmeat

Peel and slice the onions thin. Sauté them in the olive oil until just soft but not browned. Add the peppers, finely shredded, and the tomatoes. Chop the celery fine and add that. Cover and simmer for 25 to 30 minutes or until the vegetables are soft and well blended. Add the garlic, the tomato puree and salt and pepper to taste. Finally add the crabmeat and cook until it is thoroughly heated. Serve with rice.

QUICHE DE CRABES

Pastry for a 9-inch shell
Egg white
About 1½ cups crabmeat
1 tablespoon finely chopped
  celery
2 tablespoons finely chopped
  parsley

¼ cup white wine or 2
  tablespoons sherry or
  dry vermouth
  Salt, pepper
5 eggs
1½ cups milk
  Paprika

Line a 9-inch pie tin with a rich pastry and chill it for at least 1 hour. Brush the bottom of the crust with white of egg. Fill it with a mixture of the crabmeat, celery, parsley, wine and seasonings. Mix the eggs and milk together thoroughly and pour over the crabmeat mixture. Sprinkle lightly with paprika and bake at 450° for 10 minutes. Reduce the heat to 350° and continue baking until the custard is set, about 20 minutes. Serve for a first course or for the main course at luncheon.

Soft-shelled Crab

The smaller the soft-shelled crab and the earlier it is caught in the molting process, the tenderer and the better flavored it will be. Usually soft-shelled crab is bought already cleaned at the market, but here is the process in case you must do it yourself: With the aid of a small sharp-pointed knife, fold back the covering at the points of the back, and remove all the spongy bits you find there. Turn the crab over and remove the small apron on the front.

Two or three soft-shelled crabs are usually ample for one portion. There are, of course, some people with heavy appetites who can eat a dozen at a sitting.

SOFT-SHELLED CRABS MEUNIERE

8 to 12 soft-shelled crabs, cleaned	Salt and pepper
Flour	6 or more tablespoons chopped parsley
6 to 8 tablespoons butter	Lemon slices

Dip the crabs in flour and cook them in hot butter until they are delicately browned and crisp on the edges. Salt and pepper to taste. Add chopped parsley and transfer to a hot platter. Pour the pan juices over the crabs and serve with lemon slices.

VARIATIONS

Sautéed Crabs Amandine. Add ½ cup of blanched sliced almonds to the pan with the crabs and cook them until they are lightly browned. Pour over the crabs.

Soft-shelled Crabs in Cream. After removing the sautéed crabs to a platter add 3 tablespoons of flour to the pan and stir until lightly browned. Add 1½ cups of heavy cream and stir until thickened and well blended. Add 4 tablespoons of Madeira or sherry. Taste for seasoning. Pour the cream sauce over the crabs and serve with fried toasts.

BROILED SOFT-SHELLED CRABS

12 soft-shelled crabs, cleaned
Flour
½ cup butter or more

½ cup chopped parsley
2 teaspoons paprika
1 teaspoon salt

Dust the crabs lightly with flour. Arrange them on a broiling rack or in a flat broiling dish. Cream the butter with the various seasonings. Dot the crabs liberally with the butter mixture, and broil about 3 inches from the flame, basting often and turning once during the cooking. These will take from 5 to 8 minutes to cook, depending upon the size of the crabs. Serve with the sauces from the broiling pan poured over them.

FRIED SOFT-SHELLED CRABS

Heat fat for frying in your French fryer to 375°. Dip cleaned crabs in flour, then in beaten egg, and then in dry crumbs (bread or cracker). Fry for 4 or 5 minutes or until nicely browned. Remove to absorbent paper and salt and pepper to taste. Serve with tartar sauce (see index) or sauce rémoulade (see index).

SOFT-SHELLED CRABS À L'AMERICAINE

Prepare a sauce à l'Américaine (see index). Sauté the crabs in olive oil with a finely chopped clove of garlic. Add the sauce and let it all simmer for about 10 minutes. Serve with rice.

CURRIED SOFT-SHELLED CRABS

4 onions, finely chopped
5 tablespoons butter
1 unpeeled apple, coarsely
  chopped
2 tomatoes, coarsely chopped

2 tablespoons curry powder
1 cup white wine (or more)
½ cup ground almonds
  mixed with 1 cup heavy
  cream

Salt, pepper

Sauté the chopped onions in butter until they are just creamy colored. Add the apple and the tomatoes. Cover and simmer for 1 hour or more. Put through a puree or a coarse sieve. Add the curry powder and the white wine. Return to the stove and cook for 10 minutes. Then add the almonds and cream and let it all come to a boil. Taste for seasoning.

12 soft-shelled crabs
6 tablespoons butter
Flour

Dip the crabs in flour and brown quickly in butter. Add them to the sauce and let them cook for 10 more minutes. Serve with rice.

King Crab or Alaska Crab

These giant land crabs were known before the last war as Japanese crabs, and great quantities of them were shipped into this country in cans. It was excellent canned crab for creamed dishes, soups and curries. Now it is a product of Alaska—the fishing beds having come under our supervision since the war. This delectable and expensive delicacy is obtainable frozen—usually precooked in its shell—and also as cleaned crabmeat. One of the giant center claws is a generous portion. In my opinion it is as fine as any crabmeat I have ever tasted.

KING CRAB SALAD

Cut the meat into good-sized lumps and combine with mayonnaise. Garnish with chopped hard-cooked eggs and capers. Serve on a bed of greens.

BROILED KING CRAB LEGS

Remove just enough of the tough shell of each leg so that you can baste the meat inside freely. You should also consider the diner and allow enough room for him to get in with knife and fork. Brush the meat well with butter and broil over charcoal or under the broiler flame just long enough to heat it through. (Remember these crabs are precooked.) Baste during the cooking with melted butter and lemon juice or dry sherry. Take care that you do not overcook. Serve with additional melted butter.

CRAB LEGS REMOULADE OR MAYONNAISE

Serve the crab legs in the shell after you have thoroughly

thawed them. Pass the rémoulade (see index) or mayonnaise and lemon wedges.

KING CRAB A L'AMERICAINE

Leave the meat in the shells, but cut each shell in half and sauté very quickly in olive oil. Combine with sauce à l'Américaine (see index) and serve as you do lobster à l'Américaine.

KING CRAB NEWBURG

See index for lobster Newburg.

KING CRAB THERMIDOR

See index for lobster thermidor.

KING CRAB SOUFFLE

See index for crabmeat soufflé.

Stone Crabs

This delicacy is found mainly in the South around Key West, Miami and Palm Beach. The larger claws of the crab are served in the shell, and the rest of the meat—from the small claws and the body—can be used the same way as any other crabmeat.

STONE CRAB LEGS BEURRE NOIR

Cook the crabs in a court bouillon (see index) for 20 minutes. Remove the large claws and serve them, 2 to 4 to a person, with beurre noir and wedges of lemon. (For beurre noir, see index). Save the other parts of the crab for salad or for:

CRABMEAT SAUTE FLORIDA

Pick the meat from the crab and sauté 2 cups of it in ¼ pound of butter, tossing it lightly. Salt and pepper to taste and add 4 tablespoons of lime juice and ¼ cup of chopped parsley. Serve on fried toast.

Add 4 tablespoons of sherry or Madeira.

Crawfish or Crayfish

THESE are the beloved écrevisses of the French. They are rare in Eastern markets but sold in large quantities in Portland, Oregon, Seattle, New Orleans, and in the states of Wisconsin and Minnesota.

As a young boy, I often fished for crawfish in the Necanicum River in Oregon, using a piece of liver on a string. Later, I also enjoyed great plates of them, along with many glasses of beer, at Jake's Crawfish Parlor in Portland. Jake's crawfish were cooked to perfection in a spiced court bouillon. Years afterward, in more sophisticated days, I ate the fabulous and famed gratin d'écrevisses in the great restaurants of France. I have eaten them, too, at the Swedish festivals in August when crawfish are the special dish, accompanied, of course, by aquavit and beer.

In some parts of the country you will find crawfish in the markets the year round. In other areas you must check with your local fish dealer to find when they will be available.

It is hard to tell you just how many crawfish will make a serving. One person can easily eat 10 to 12, but many people may want more than a dozen.

ECREVISSES BORDELAISE

24 to 36 crawfish	4 or 5 tablespoons butter
2 carrots	Salt, pepper
2 onions	2 cups white wine
2 stalks celery	1½ cups tomato puree

Wash the crawfish well. It is wise to tear off the tiny wing in the center of the tail. This loosens and brings with it the small black intestine.

Prepare a mirepoix by cutting the carrots, onions, and celery in fine julienne strips. Melt the butter in a large kettle and cook the vegetables in it until they are wilted. Salt and pepper to taste, add the wine, and let it cook for a few minutes. Add the crawfish and cook them just long enough to color their shells—about 5 minutes. Add the tomato puree. Bring it up to a boil and let it blend with the other seasonings. Taste for seasoning, and pour into a big tureen or bowl. Serve with plenty of saffron rice and a good stout salad of greens.

GRATIN D'ECREVISSES IN THE FRENCH MANNER

36 crawfish
Court bouillon or salted
  water
½ cup creamed butter
Sauce velouté (see index)

Duchess potatoes, or rice,
  or a croustade
Grated Gruyère or
  Parmesan cheese

Clean the crawfish and cook in a court bouillon (page 16) or in salted water. When they are cool enough to handle, remove the meat from the tails, and any meat from the bodies. Keep several of the shells for garnish. Grind the rest of the shells, or pound them in a mortar. Blend them with the creamed butter and force the mixture through a fine sieve.

Prepare a sauce velouté. Stir the crawfish butter into the sauce to color it and give it flavor. Add the crawfish meat and cook just long enough to heat it through.

Pour the crawfish mixture on a flameproof serving dish and surround it with a border of Duchess potatoes or rice. Or pour it into a large croustade, which you have made by hollowing out a loaf of bread and toasting it in the oven. Sprinkle the top with grated Gruyère or Parmesan cheese and decorate it with the whole shells. Run the dish under the broiler flame just long enough to melt the cheese and glaze the top.

COLD CRAWFISH, SPICED

Wash and clean the crawfish, being sure to pull off the tiny wing in the center of the tail. Cook them in a spicy court bouillon (see index) for about 5 minutes—no more. Cool the crawfish in the court bouillon and let them stand in it for several hours. Serve cold with bread and butter—preferably rye bread—and either beer or a dry white wine, well chilled.

CRAWFISH REMOULADE

This is one of my favorites as a first course.

To serve 4 people, cook 36 crawfish in a court bouillon (see index), and let them cool. When cool enough to handle, remove the meat from the tails. Chill it. To serve, arrange the crawfish meat on a bed of greens and accompany with a well-seasoned sauce rémoulade (see index).

Lobster

LIKE Europeans, we are blessed with two types of shellfish called lobster. The "homard," or lobster with claws, comes from the northern waters around Maine and Nova Scotia. The spiny, or rock lobster, is caught in southern waters, but is only a distant relative of the homard. Both varieties are superb eating, and the homard, especially, is one of the great delicacies of the sea.

The northern European homard is very much like ours, and their Mediterranean langouste resembles our rock lobster, although, to my taste, the Mediterranean variety has much sweeter meat. European lobster is not sold in our markets, but frozen rock lobster tails shipped from South Africa are now generally available and are very popular.

Our native lobsters can be bought whole and already boiled in most markets—or as cooked lobster meat in frozen tins. If you prefer to cook your own, as most people do, you buy a live lobster. Never cook a dead one. The larger the lobster the more likely it is to be tough. The small lobster is the true delicacy.

Some people object to plunging a lobster into boiling water or bouillon while it is still alive. Don't let this process affect your appetite. Lobsters are most insensitive creatures. Killing them in hot water is almost instantaneous and certainly as merciful as any other method. True, they wriggle. It would be helpful if more American fish dealers would adopt the French custom of trussing the beasts with string when they sell them. This makes the task of popping the lobster into the pot much simpler.

The easiest way to prepare lobster is to boil it. It can be served hot with melted butter and lemon juice, or cold with mayonnaise or any other cold sauce.

BOILED LOBSTER

For a 1 to 1½ pound lobster use 3 quarts of water and about 3 tablespoons of salt. Or you may use ocean water. Bring the water to a rolling boil. Grab the lobster from behind the head and plunge it into the water. Cover and let it simmer for 5 minutes for the first pound, and 3 minutes more for each additional pound. Remove the lobster from the water and place it on its back. Using a large heavy knife and a hammer or mallet, split it in half from end to end starting at the head. Remove the stomach and intestinal vein.

Do not discard the green liver, or tomalley. It is delicious. In female lobsters you may find a pinkish red deposit—the roe—often called lobster coral. This is one of the choicest bits and can be eaten with the lobster or used in sauce.

The claws should be cracked with a nutcracker so the meat can be easily extracted at the table.

BROILED LIVE LOBSTER

This is one of the favorite dishes in the United States. Personally, I think it is rather dull, and unless superbly done with a wood or charcoal fire, not worth the money. However, here is the method:

Use a 1½ or 2 pound lobster for each person. You can ask your fish dealer to split and clean the lobster. To do it yourself, first kill the lobster by inserting a sharp knife between the body and tail shells; this cuts the spinal cord. Then place the lobster on its back, and with a heavy sharp knife and mallet, split it. Cut right through the back shell separating the two halves. Remove the stomach and the intestinal vein that you will find running down the tail section close to the back. Leave the liver, which is the grayish-looking meat in the body cavity (it turns green after cooking). Butter each half lobster well. Have bowls of melted butter handy. You will need it during the cooking process and will serve it with the lobsters later. Preheat your broiler for 10 minutes.

Place your lobster halves on the broiler rack, flesh side to the flame, and broil until they are cooked through. Baste frequently with the melted butter. The cooking time should be about 12 to 15 minutes. Salt and pepper to taste and serve on very hot plates with plenty of melted butter and lemon wedges. Shoestring or French-fried potatoes are the accepted accompaniment.

LOBSTER A L'AMERICAINE

This is probably the most famous of all lobster dishes. It has been called by many names and was originally lobster Provençale, a dish native to the south of France where the people have used tomatoes in sauces for generations. It has also been called homard armoricaine by those who thought the dish originated in Armorique. It is now generally conceded that the first lobster à l'Américaine, as we now know it, was prepared at the restaurant of Noel Peters in the Passages des Princes—not a favorite spot today, but once exceedingly fashionable.

3 pounds of lobster	3 tablespoons chopped parsley
½ cup olive oil	
3 tablespoons butter	1 tablespoon chopped fresh, or 1 teaspoon dried, tarragon
1 small onion, finely chopped	
6 shallots, finely chopped	
1 clove garlic, peeled and chopped	1½ teaspoons thyme
	½ bay leaf
6 ripe tomatoes, peeled, seeded and chopped	1½ cups white wine
	3 tablespoons tomato puree
	Cayenne pepper
	Salt

¼ cup cognac

Wash the lobster, or lobsters, well. With a very sharp heavy knife, cut medallions of the tail, cutting through the markings in the tail. Cut the body in half, clean it, and save the liver and coral, if any, for the sauce. Remove the claws.

Heat the olive oil and add the pieces of lobster. Toss them around in the oil until the shells have turned red and the meat is seared. Remove the meat and shells to a hot platter. Add the butter to the pan with the olive oil and sauté the onions and shallots until lightly colored. Add the garlic, the tomatoes, the herbs and the white wine and let it simmer for 30 minutes. Add the tomato puree and season to taste. Pour the cognac over the lobster pieces and ignite. Then put them in the sauce, cover and simmer for about 20 minutes. At the last, stir in the liver and lobster coral.

Serve with a rice pilaff.

NOTE: The meat of the lobster may be removed from the shells before adding it to the sauce. If you do this, be sure to put the shells in for the added flavor they give to the sauce. Personally, I feel that taking lobster meat from the shell before serving makes no sense unless it is going into a tart, or soufflé, or some other form of preparation that actually requires it.

314

CHAUSSON OF LOBSTER A L'AMERICAINE

1 pound of puff paste
Lobster à l'Américaine (see
   preceding recipe)

Beaten egg
Heavy cream
Butter

Chopped parsley

A chausson is a large turnover made of puff paste. Use your favorite recipe for the paste and chill it for 2 hours. Then roll it out in a circle about ⅓ inch thick. Spread the center with lobster à l'Américaine (without the shells), and save some of the sauce. Now, fold one part of the circle two thirds of the way over the lobster mixture. Take the other end of the pastry and pull that over the first fold. Now you should have two thicknesses of pastry over the center part. Seal the edges with a little cold water, brush the pastry well with beaten egg and put in a 450° oven. Bake for 10 minutes and reduce the heat to 350°. Continue baking until the pastry is cooked— about 30 to 35 minutes.

Serve the chausson in slices with the remaining sauce, which you have heated with a little heavy cream and a good pat of butter. Garnish with chopped parsley.

LOBSTER OMELET

Sauté lobster meat lightly in butter with a little chopped onion and parsley. Fold the mixture into individual omelets and garnish with broiled mushroom caps.

LOBSTER FRA DIAVOLO

This is the Italian version of lobster à l'Américaine. In fact, it might even be the original. The following recipe will serve two people.

2 lobsters (1 to 1½ pounds
   each)
6 tablespoons olive oil
4 sprigs of parsley
1 teaspoon thyme or oregano
1 small onion, finely chopped

1 clove garlic, finely
   chopped
Pinch of cloves
Pinch of mace
Salt, pepper
2 cups cooked tomatoes

¼ cup brandy

Split the live lobsters and cook them in hot olive oil until the color has turned. Continue cooking gently for about 10 minutes. Add the seasonings, and the herbs and tomatoes. Cover and cook for about 15 minutes, stirring often. Arrange a ring of rice on a serving dish. Put the lobster halves in the center and pour the sauce over them. Add the brandy and blaze just before serving.

CIVET OF LOBSTER

This is really still another version of lobster à l'Américaine.

1 lobster (about 2 pounds)
2 tablespoons butter
2 medium onions
2 cloves garlic
4 or 5 ripe tomatoes
½ teaspoon thyme
½ teaspoon tarragon

2 tablespoons chopped parsley
Salt, pepper
3 tablespoons olive oil
½ cup white wine
¼ cup cognac or whiskey
Liver and intestines of the lobster

Cut the lobster in small pieces as for lobster à l'Américaine. Remove the claws. Reserve the liquid, liver and intestines. Butter a shallow skillet or saucepan. Chop the onions and garlic and peel, seed and chop the tomatoes. Put them all with the herbs in the saucepan. Place the pieces of lobster on this bed of vegetables, salt and pepper to taste and brush well with olive oil. Add the white wine and cognac, cover and bring to a boil. Let it boil vigorously for about 2 minutes. Remove the pieces of lobster to a hot platter. Add the liver, intestines, liquid and a little more parsley to the saucepan and let it cook down for a few minutes. Taste for seasoning and pour the sauce over the pieces of lobster. Serve with rice.

LOBSTER FRANCO-AMERICAN

This, too, is a version of lobster à l'Américaine.

2 lobsters (about 2 pounds each)
⅓ cup olive oil
2 medium onions, finely chopped
2 cloves garlic, finely chopped
2 tablespoons chopped pimiento

1 cup tomato sauce or tomato soup
¼ cup cognac
2 tablespoons meat glaze
⅓ cup sherry or Madeira
2 tablespoons cognac

Plunge the lobsters into boiling water for 1 minute to kill them. Cut them in half, and save the liquid and liver and intestines. Put the olive oil in a large ovenproof pan and heat over a flame. Add the onions, garlic, the lobster halves and season to taste. Add the tomato sauce and let it cook with the other ingredients for 4 minutes. Pour ¼ cup of cognac into the pan, cover it and place it in a 400° oven for approximately 18 minutes. Remove the lobsters to a hot platter and keep warm.

Strain the sauce through a fine sieve. Reheat it, add the liver, intestines and liquid from the lobsters, a little meat glaze, the sherry or Madeira, 2 tablespoons of cognac and the pimiento. Pour the sauce over the lobster.

LOBSTER AU GRATIN

3 cups cooked lobster meat
6 tablespoons butter
¼ cup cognac
¼ cup white wine
½ cup heavy cream
Hollandaise sauce (see index)

Sauté the lobster in butter just long enough to heat it. Add the cognac and ignite. Add the white wine and cream and cook for 5 minutes. Pour into a casserole, top with Hollandaise sauce and run under the broiler long enough to glaze. Serve with rice.

LOBSTER IN CREAM, FRENCH STYLE

This is very delicate and flavorful.

2 lobsters (1 to 1½ pounds each)
6 tablespoons butter
Salt, pepper
Paprika
⅓ cup sherry
Cream to cover
Beurre manié (see index)

Cut the lobsters as for lobster à l'Américaine. Melt the butter in a large skillet, add the lobster and let it just color. Season to taste, add the sherry and let it cook down a little. Add just enough hot cream to cover the lobster, clap on a lid and let it simmer for 20 minutes. Remove the pieces of lobster, take the meat from the shells and put it in a serving dish. Thicken the sauce with beurre manié and taste for seasoning. Pour the sauce over the lobster. This may be served in patty shells or croustades or with rice or toast points.

VARIATIONS

Lobster in Cream, Mornay. When the lobster is cooked and removed from the cream, add 1 cup of grated cheese (Gruyère or Cheddar) and a few grains of cayenne to the

317

sauce. Stir until the cheese is well blended and the sauce thickened. Place the lobster meat in an ovenproof dish, pour the sauce over this, and top with more grated cheese and a sprinkling of bread crumbs. Brown under the broiler.

Lobster Curry. While the lobster is cooking in the cream, sauté 3 tablespoons of chopped onion in 3 tablespoons of butter. When the onions are soft, add 3 tablespoons of flour and 1 tablespoon of curry powder. Blend well and add ½ cup of white wine. Continue stirring until the sauce is thickened. Arrange the lobster meat in a serving dish and pour the curry sauce over it. Serve with rice.

Lobster Hungarian. Add 1 tablespoon of paprika to the sauce just before pouring it over the lobster meat.

LOBSTER ARCHDUKE

1 lobster (about 2 pounds)	½ cup sherry or port, or
3 tablespoons butter	both
3 tablespoons olive oil	¼ cup whiskey
⅓ cup whiskey	Salt, pepper
	Cayenne

Heavy cream

Cut the lobster in sections as for the preceding recipes. Melt the butter and add the oil. Sear the lobster in the hot fat. Add ⅓ cup of whiskey and flame. Add the wine and the additional whiskey and season with salt, pepper and cayenne. Cover and simmer for about 15 minutes. Remove the lobster and add a few tablespoons of heavy cream to the pan. Cook down for several minutes and pour over the lobster. Serve with rice.

LOBSTER NEWBURG, FRENCH VERSION

There are two different theories about the preparation of a Newburg. The French is a little more deft than the American, so I give it first.

1 lobster (2 to 3 pounds)	¼ cup brandy or whiskey
2 tablespoons butter	1½ cups heavy cream
2 tablespoons olive oil	½ cup bouillon (fish or
Salt, pepper	meat stock)
⅔ cup white wine	Beurre manié (see index)

Cut the lobster in sections. Heat the butter and oil and sear the lobster, seasoning it to taste while it is cooking. When the shell has turned red—in about 3 minutes—remove the lobster and add the white wine and spirits to the fat. Let this cook down to half its volume. Add the cream, the lobster and the bouillon. Cover and simmer for 30 minutes. Remove the lobster and take the meat from the shell and arrange it on a serving dish. Let the sauce cook down a bit and thicken it with beurre manié. Add a dash of cayenne and taste for seasoning. Pour the sauce over the lobster and serve.

LOBSTER NEWBURG, AMERICAN VERSION

1½ cups cooked lobster meat	1 cup heavy cream
4 tablespoons butter	3 egg yolks
¼ cup brandy	Salt, pepper

Cut the lobster meat in large pieces and sauté in butter for 5 minutes. Add the brandy and blaze. Mix the egg yolks and heavy cream together and heat in the upper part of a double boiler, stirring constantly until the mixture coats the spoon. Add the lobster and heat through, being careful not to let the mixture boil. Taste for seasoning. Serve in croustades or patty shells or on rice.

LOBSTER PHOCEENNE

Court bouillon (see index)	3 shallots
2-pound lobster	1 clove garlic
¼ cup olive oil	1 green pepper
Salt, pepper	¾ cup rice
Pinch of saffron	

Prepare a strong court bouillon and let it reduce half in volume. Strain. Cut the live lobster in half and remove the intestinal tract. Heat the olive oil in a deep pot and add the lobster, salt, pepper, shallots, garlic and green pepper. Toss the lobster in the oil to redden it, add the rice and saffron. Pour the court bouillon over all, cover tightly and bring to a boil. Reduce the heat and let it cook very slowly for about 20 minutes or until the rice is done. Serve the lobster on a bed of the rice.

STUFFED LOBSTER DROUANT

4 small lobsters	1 tablespoon dry mustard
Butter	Cayenne
2½ cups sauce béchamel (see index)	1 cup grated Switzerland Swiss cheese

Split the live lobsters and remove the intestinal tract. Butter them lightly and broil for 12 to 15 minutes, depending on their size. When cooked, remove the lobster meat from the shells and keep it hot.

Season the sauce béchamel with dry mustard and cayenne. Spread a thin layer of sauce in the empty lobster shells, add pieces of the lobster meat cut in thin slices and cover these with additional sauce. Sprinkle the top with grated cheese. Place in a 400° oven until heated through.

HOMARD THERMIDOR

This dish was first served at the famous Café de Paris in Paris. It was created by Monsieur Tony Girod and this is the original recipe.

1 lobster (about 2 pounds)	1 tablespoon chopped tar-
Salt, pepper	ragon or chervil and
⅔ cup olive oil	tarragon
⅔ cup white wine	1 cup sauce béchamel
⅔ cup bouillon (fish or meat	¾ cup heavy cream, mixed
stock)	with 2 egg yolks
1 tablespoon chopped shallot	1 teaspoon dry mustard
or green onion	Grated Parmesan cheese

Melted butter

Split the live lobster in half. Sprinkle with salt and pepper and brush with olive oil. Bake it in a 425° oven for approximately 18 minutes. Baste during the cooking with additional olive oil. When the lobster is cool enough to handle, remove the meat from the body and claws and dice it. Combine the wine, the broth and the herbs and cook until it is reduced to practically a glaze. Add this to the sauce béchamel and stir in the mixed cream and egg yolks. Allow this to heat without boiling. Add the mustard and taste for seasoning. When it is well thickened, add the lobster meat and heat through. Fill the lobster shells with this mixture, sprinkle with grated Parmesan cheese, brush with melted butter and brown in a 375° oven.

VARIATIONS

1. The American version of this recipe omits the mustard and tarragon and adds sautéed mushrooms and a little sherry wine.

2. Here is a quick version. Make a cream sauce and flavor it with sherry and plenty of mustard. Arrange frozen lobster meat in an ovenproof dish, add the sauce, sprinkle with grated cheese and brown in the oven.

HOMARD AUX AROMATES

4 lobsters (about 1½ pounds each)	4 tablespoons heavy cream
White wine court bouillon (see index. Add thyme, bay leaf, parsley, peppercorns and coriander.)	Beurre manié (see index)
	1 cup Hollandaise sauce (see index)
	Fresh tarragon

This dish is a favorite in France and there are a number of recipes for it. I give two that I regard as distinctive, each in its own way. This recipe will serve 4 people.

Poach the lobsters in the court bouillon. When they are cool enough to handle remove the meat from the bodies and claws. Reduce the court bouillon to 1½ cups of liquid, strain, and add the cream and beurre manié. Stir until thickened and add the Hollandaise sauce. Arrange the lobster shells on a serving dish, fill them with the lobster meat and cover with the sauce. Sprinkle generously with chopped tarragon.

VARIATION

Prepare 2 cups of sauce velouté (see index) using bouillon, white wine and cream in equal parts. Add chopped parsley, chervil, tarragon and fennel and stir in 2 egg yolks. Taste for seasoning. Arrange the lobster shells filled with lobster meat on a hot platter and cover with the sauce.

DEVILED LOBSTER

4 small lobsters	2 stalks celery
4 tablespoons butter	Salt, pepper
1 medium onion	Mustard
1 clove garlic	Cayenne
2 green peppers	2 cups bread crumbs
Butter	

Cook the lobsters in salted water. When cool enough to handle, split them and remove the meat. Dice it and mix it with the liver and lobster coral, if there is any.

Melt 4 tablespoons of butter in a skillet and sauté the finely chopped onion, garlic, green peppers and celery. When they are tender, season them to taste and combine them with half the bread crumbs and the lobster meat. Season highly with salt, pepper, mustard and cayenne and fill the lobsters shells with this mixture. Dot with butter and sprinkle with the rest of the crumbs. Bake in a 400° oven for 15 or 20 minutes or until nicely browned.

BAKED LOBSTER ITALIAN

1 lobster (about 2 pounds)	3 tablespoons butter
3 tablespoons olive oil	½ cup bread crumbs
1 clove garlic	Salt, pepper
Fines herbes (parsley, basil, oregano)	3 tablespoons butter
	Grated cheese

Split the lobster and remove the intestinal tract. Brush with olive oil. Sauté the garlic, minced, and the herbs for 3 minutes in 3 tablespoons of butter and mix with ½ cup of bread crumbs. Spread this paste over the lobster halves, salt and pepper to taste and dot with butter. Bake in a 400° oven for about 20 minutes. Sprinkle with grated Parmesan cheese and run under the broiler to brown.

SAUTEED LOBSTER WITH CURRY

¼ pound butter	1 pound cooked lobster (frozen is excellent)
½ cup shredded, blanched almonds	1 tablespoon chopped parsley
2 tablespoons grated onion or shallot	2 teaspoons curry powder
	½ cup heavy cream
Salt, pepper	

Melt the butter in a large skillet and add the almonds and onion (or shallot). Cook for 3 or 4 minutes. Add the lobster meat cut into scallops and toss lightly. Add the parsley and curry and blend in the cream. Let it just come to a boil and simmer for 3 minutes. Taste for seasoning and serve on fried toast rounds.

LOBSTER NORTH AFRICAN

To be authentic this dish should be made with langouste, but it can be prepared with any kind of lobster. This recipe will serve two people.

1 large lobster	1 medium onion
2 green peppers	6 tablespoons olive oil
3 tablespoons olive oil	1 small eggplant
1 cup tomato sauce	1 cup cooked rice
⅓ cup white wine	Cayenne
Salt, pepper	Oregano
¼ cup brandy or whiskey	

Cook the lobster in salt water for about 10 to 12 minutes, or until done. When cool enough to handle, remove the tail and cut it in half, cut the body in half and remove the claws. Take the meat from the claws.

Cut the green peppers julienne, and sauté them in 3 tablespoons of olive oil until they are soft. Then add the tomato sauce and wine and season with salt and pepper. Let it cook down for several minutes. Add the two sections of the tail and the meat from the claws and let it heat through. Remove from the fire but keep warm.

Peel and chop the onion and cook it in 6 tablespoons olive oil until soft. Peel and dice the eggplant and add it to the onion. Sauté until it is soft and slightly colored. Mix this with the rice and season well with salt, pepper, cayenne and oregano. Heap this on the two halves of the body of the lobster and top with the two halves of the lobster tail.

Add the brandy (or whiskey) to the tomato sauce, and cook it down for several minutes. Pour the sauce over the lobster halves and serve with additional rice.

SAUTEED LOBSTER WITH TOMATOES

4 tablespoons butter	Salt, pepper
4 tablespoons olive oil	Basil
1 cup chopped, seeded toma-	1 pound lobster meat
toes	

Heat the butter and olive oil and add the chopped tomatoes. Salt and pepper to taste and add a touch of basil. Simmer until the tomatoes form a paste. Add the lobster, cut into scallops, and cook until it is heated through. Serve on fried toast.

LOBSTER CARDINAL

1 lobster (2 to 3 pounds)	½ cup heavy cream
½ pound shrimp	2 egg yolks
Court bouillon	¼ cup brandy or whiskey
½ pound mushrooms	Salt, pepper
3 or 4 truffles (optional)	Grated Parmesan cheese
4 tablespoons butter	Melted butter
1 cup sauce béchamel	

Cook the lobster and the shrimp in court bouillon for about 10 to 12 minutes. When they are cool enough to handle, shell the shrimp and split the lobster in halves. Take the meat from the lobster tail and slice in even scallops. Remove the claws and take the meat from the body and claws and dice it. Dice the mushrooms and truffles, Sauté these with the diced lobster meat(set the meat from the lobster tail aside) in a little butter for a few minutes.

Grind or chop the shrimp very fine and mix with the béchamel, the cream, the egg yolks and the liquor. Stir over low heat until thickened but do not let it boil. Taste for seasoning. Mix a little of the sauce with the mushrooms and lobster meat and arrange this in the bottom of the lobster shells. Place the scallops of meat from the lobster tail on this bed of sauce, cover with more sauce, sprinkle with grated cheese and brush with melted butter. Run it under the broiler for a few minutes to brown.

LOBSTER SAUTE FINES HERBES

¼ pound butter
1 pound lobster meat
Salt, pepper

¼ cup mixed chopped
herbs (chives, parsley,
tarragon—or your own
choice)

¼ cup white wine

Melt the butter, add the lobster meat cut into scallops and sauté, tossing lightly, until browned. Season to taste, add the herbs and the wine. Turn the pieces of lobster so they are thoroughly covered with the herbs and wine. Serve on fried toast.

LOBSTER SAUTE MEXICAINE

3 sweet peppers, seeded and
finely chopped
2 tablespoons chopped onion
⅓ cup olive oil
3 tomatoes, peeled, seeded and
and chopped

½ cup white wine
2 teaspoons chili powder
Pinch of saffron
2 pimientos, finely cut
Salt, pepper
1 pound lobster meat

Sauté the peppers and the onion in the olive oil until soft. Add the tomatoes, the wine, the chili powder, saffron, and pimientos. Taste for seasoning. Cover and cook for 25 to 30 minutes over a low flame. Add the lobster meat and cook for another 10 to 12 minutes. Serve with rice or polenta.

LOBSTER SAUTE LOUISIANE

1 clove garlic
3 green onions
1 green pepper
6 tablespoons butter

½ cup tomato sauce
Salt, pepper
Cayenne
¼ cup heavy cream

1 cup cooked lobster meat

324

Chop the garlic and the onions and seed the pepper and cut it into julienne strips. Sauté them in butter for 5 minutes, add the tomato sauce and let it cook down a bit. Season to taste, stir in the cream and blend well. Add the lobster meat and heat it through. Serve on fried toast.

MOUSSE OF LOBSTER

1 pound lobster meat	2 cups heavy cream
2 egg whites	Butter
Ice	24 mushrooms caps
Salt, pepper	1 cup white wine
Paprika	Hollandaise sauce (see index)

Grind the lobster meat with the fine blade, putting it through the grinder twice. Or you may pound it in a mortar. Gradually work in the egg whites with a wooden spoon. Next, put the mixture through a puree machine or a fine sieve. Place a bowl over cracked ice, place the mixture in the bowl and, with a wooden spoon, work in salt, pepper and paprika to taste and the heavy cream.

Butter a ring mold or charlotte mold and decorate it with slices of truffle, if you wish. Fill the mold ¾ full with the lobster mixture. Place in a pan of hot water and cook, either over a low flame or in a moderate oven (350°), until set. This should take about 30 minutes. Unmold on a hot platter and decorate with mushrooms which have been poached briefly in the white wine. Serve with a Hollandaise sauce.

NOTE: Individual molds of the mousse may be made and served in the same way.

LOBSTER SOUFFLE

1 cup finely chopped lobster meat	½ cup cream
½ cup court bouillon	Salt, pepper
3 tablespoons butter	Cayenne
3 tablespoons flour	4 egg yolks
	6 egg whites

It is nice to prepare the lobster for this dish yourself. If you do, cook the live lobster in a court bouillon. When it is done, remove it from the bouillon and let the liquid cook down to ½ cup. Strain it and set it aside to use in the soufflé. After you have cleaned the lobster, be sure to chop the meat very fine, or put it through a food chopper, using the fine blade.

Melt the butter in a saucepan and add the flour. Cook until it is golden and thoroughly blended. Gradually stir in the bouillon and the cream, which you have mixed with the intestines of the lobster. Continue stirring until well thickened. Remove from the stove, season to taste and add the lobster meat. Gradually beat in the egg yolks, one at a time. Beat the egg whites until stiff and fold them into the lobster mixture. Pour the mixture into a well-buttered soufflé mold and bake at 375° for 30 to 35 minutes. Serve plain or with a Hollandaise sauce.

SOUFFLE OF LOBSTER PLAZA-ATHENEE

1 live lobster (2 to 2½ pounds)
Salt, pepper
Paprika
5 tablespoons butter
2 stalks celery, finely chopped
2 onions, finely chopped
2 carrots, finely chopped
2 ounces cognac
1 cup white wine
½ cup cream
3 egg yolks
½ cup sauce béchamel (see index)
5 egg whites

Split the lobster in half and remove the intestines, the liver and the coral. Season each half with salt, pepper and paprika. Melt 5 tablespoons of butter in a deep saucepan and add the finely chopped vegetables. Put the lobster halves in the pan and let them cook until the shells redden. Add the cognac and blaze. Pour the wine in the pan and let it all cook for 15 minutes. Remove the lobster and when cool enough to handle, take the meat from the body and claws and place it in a buttered casserole.

Add the cream and the lobster intestines, liver and coral to the broth in the saucepan. Heat through for a few minutes and then remove from the fire and force it through a fine sieve. If the sauce needs thickening, add egg yolks and cook gently but do not let it boil. Pour half of the sauce over the lobster meat.

Combine 3 beaten egg yolks with the sauce béchamel. Beat the 5 egg whites very stiff and fold them into the béchamel mixture. Pour this over the lobster and sauce in the casserole, place in a hot oven and let it cook 10 to 15 minutes or until it is puffy and delicately browned. Serve with the remaining sauce.

LOBSTER STEW NEW ENGLAND

6 tablespoons butter	2 egg yolks
2½ cups lobster meat	1 cup cream
1 pint lobster bouillon	Salt, pepper
1 quart milk	Paprika

To get 2½ cups of lobster meat for this dish you will probably need to prepare 2 lobsters. Cook them in a court bouillon (see index) and when they are done, remove the meat from the shells. Reduce the bouillon to 1 pint.

Melt the butter in a large saucepan, add the lobster meat and toss it for several minutes to brown it lightly. Add the bouillon and the milk, which has been scalded, and let it heat through. Beat the egg yolks with the cream, stir them in and continue stirring until the stew is very hot. Season to taste. Serve in bowls with a sprinkling of paprika.

Pilot crackers are the traditional accompaniment for this dish. Personally, I prefer plenty of good hot buttered toast.

LOBSTER PIZZA

Bread or brioche dough (see index)	1 pound lobster meat
Olive oil	Butter
Mozzarella cheese	Salt
	Grated Parmesan cheese

TOMATO SAUCE

¼ cup olive oil	1½ cups cooked tomatoes
3 cloves garlic	Basil
Salt, pepper	

To make the sauce, put ¼ cup of olive oil in a saucepan and add the garlic cloves finely chopped, the tomatoes and the seasonings. Let this cook down for 30 minutes and then force it through a fine sieve. It should be a thick, rich paste.

Oil a large flat pan and line it with bread or brioche dough rolled to about ½ inch thick. Brush the dough with olive oil and cover with slices of Mozzarella. Add a layer of the tomato sauce and then a layer of lobster meat. Dot with butter, sprinkle with salt and grated Parmesan cheese. Bake at 375° until the dough is done and the cheese melted.

Cold Lobster

Cold lobster is often served in the shell with a variety of different sauces. For hors d'oeuvre, a half lobster is an ample serving, but for a main course the usual portion is a whole lobster—unless it happens to be of tremendous size. Some of the very large langoustes popular on the Riviera will serve 3 to 4 people.

Serve cold lobster with any of the following sauces:

1. Mayonnaise
2. Rémoulade
3. Gribiche
4. Russian dressing
5. Vinaigrette

LOBSTER EN BELLEVUE, PARISIENNE

This is a classic French dish. You see it as often in France as you see cold decorated ham in America, and it is not really difficult if you are patient and clever with your hands. Lobster en Bellevue is an architectural triumph as well as a delicious morsel.

2 large lobsters	Lettuce
1½ quarts of aspic made from court bouillon (see index)	Bread
	Russian salad
	For decorating: truffles,
Mayonnaise	olives, black and
6 eggs	stuffed, parsley, chervil,
6 tomatoes	tarragon

Cook the lobsters in court bouillon. When they are cool enough to handle, carefully cut away the bottom part of each shell so that the back and tail remain in one perfect piece. Remove all the meat from the bodies of the lobsters and from the claws of one of them. Then gently loosen the meat in each tail and lift it out whole. Chill the lobster meat.

Prepare the aspic by clarifying the bouillon and adding gelatin, according to the recipe. Mix 1 cup of the aspic with 1 cup of mayonnaise and chill. Chill half of the plain aspic.

Cut the meat from the lobster tails into even scallops. Combine the rest of the meat with mayonnaise and season to taste. Hard-cook the eggs, and when cool cut them in half and trim them so they will stand. Peel the tomatoes, hollow them out and fill them with the lobster mixture. Cover the filled tomatoes and the eggs with the aspic and mayonnaise and dip each scallop of lobster meat in the same mixture, being sure it is thoroughly coated. Chill until firm.

Now you are ready for the decorating. If you use truffles, slice them. Then cut the sliced truffles and the black and stuffed olives into fancy shapes. (Pimientos can also be used.) Parsley, chervil and tarragon can be used to fashion tiny leaves. Chop the plain aspic very fine to use as garnish. Decorate each lobster scallop, each egg and tomato with these garnishes. But make some definite plan for your decoration so that it all forms a pattern. Place your decoration on each piece, then brush with a little of the unchilled jelly. Chill until it is firm and holds the decoration in place, then make a little border of some of the chopped aspic.

From a loaf of stale bread cut a cube about 4 or 5 inches square. Place this on a platter and cover with greens. Set the perfect lobster with the claws intact on the platter, resting the body on the bread cube. Stretch the tail across the bed of greens. If you have a decorative skewer, put one large perfect tomato or a small head of lettuce on the skewer and run it in between the lobster's eyes. Arrange the decorated scallops of lobster meat along the back of the lobster shell so that they overlap. Build them out fan-shaped at the bottom. Arrange the eggs and tomatoes around the shell and decorate the platter with additional chopped aspic.

Serve the dish with Russian salad and additional mayonnaise if you wish.

LOBSTER ASPIC

2 large lobsters	1 cup of mayonnaise
1 quart of aspic made from court bouillon (see index)	For decoration: olives, truffles, tarragon

RUSSIAN SALAD

1 cup potatoes, diced Mayonnaise mixed with aspic	½ cup each of finely cut green beans, carrots, peas

Cook the lobsters in court bouillon for 15 minutes. Remove and reduce the bouillon to 1 quart. Clarify and add gelatin for an aspic according to the recipe.

When the lobster is cool enough to handle, remove the tails and the claws. Cut the bodies in half and extract the meat. With a pair of sharp kitchen shears cut the shell of each tail so that the meat may be removed in one piece. Keep the claws whole for decoration. Slice the lobster meat from the tail into even scallops.

Pour the aspic into a mold (a ring mold, a decorative tail mold, or a flat mold—anything you choose) and place the mold in a large bowl filled with cracked ice. When the aspic has formed a thin film on the mold, gently pour off the rest of the jelly. Blend a little of this with mayonnaise and chill for several minutes.

On the aspic film in the mold make a decorative pattern with slices of truffle, stuffed olives, and black olives. You may cut these into fancy shapes if you wish and you may add slices of hard-cooked egg and pimiento. Arrange bits of tarragon in the decoration. Dip the scallops of lobster meat in the jellied mayonnaise and place them in the mold. If it is a ring mold overlap them in a circle; if it is a flat mold use a flat design. Pour the remaining jelly over all until the mold is full. Chill.

When ready to serve, place a bed of greens on a large platter and unmold the aspic on this. Place the Russian salad in the center of a ring mold or around the edge of a flat mold. Decorate with the lobster claws. Serve with additional mayonnaise.

To make the Russian salad: Cook the potatoes and vegetables until they are just tender. Combine them with mayonnaise that has been mixed with a little of the jelly. Taste for seasoning and chill.

Lobster Salads

TRADITIONAL LOBSTER SALAD

To my mind, this simple traditional salad is far better than many more complicated combinations.

Greens (lettuce or romaine)	Mayonnaise
2 cups diced lobster meat	Hard-cooked eggs
Capers	

Line a bowl with greens. Mix the lobster meat with mayonnaise and heap it in the bowl. Garnish with quartered hard-cooked eggs and capers.

VARIATION

Add 1 cup of diced celery.

SALADE PARISIENNE

2 cups mixed cooked vegetables	Mayonnaise
	Greens
2 cups lobster meat	10 scallops of lobster meat
Salt, pepper	Hard-cooked eggs
Onion juice	

Cut the vegetables (green beans, carrots, potatoes, tiny French peas) very fine and cook in salted water until they are just tender. Drain and cool. Mix them with the diced lobster meat, season to taste with salt, pepper and onion juice and bind with mayonnaise. Line a bowl with greens and arrange the salad on top. Decorate with the scallops of lobster meat and slices of hard-cooked egg.

VARIATION

This salad may be jellied. Make an aspic. Combine a little of it with mayonnaise. Line a mold with some of the aspic, fill with the salad, into which you have stirred the mayonnaise-aspic mixture. Cover with more aspic. Chill and serve with additional mayonnaise.

ENGLISH GARDEN PARTY SALAD

3 cups lobster meat
1 cup sliced cucumbers
1 cup pickled mushrooms caps
Mayonnaise
Greens
Asparagus tips

Dice the lobster meat coarsely. Peel and seed the cucumbers and cut in thin slices. Combine the lobster, the cucumber, and the mushroom caps with mayonnaise. Arrange a bed of greens on a platter and place the salad on top. Garnish with asparagus tips.

NOTE: If you cook your own lobster for this dish, you can use the claws as an added garnish.

LOBSTER SALAD REMOULADE

2 cups lobster meat
1 cup shredded celery root
Hard-cooked eggs
Rémoulade sauce
Greens

Combine diced lobster meat, shredded celery root and rémoulade. Arrange on a bed of greens and decorate with hard-cooked eggs.

COUPE D'AVOCADO A LA RITZ

½ cup lobster, diced
1 cup crabmeat
1 tablespoon tomato, peeled, seeded and chopped
½ teaspoon each of chopped tarragon, chervil, chives
½ teaspoon salt
3 tablespoons mayonnaise
½ teaspoon Worcestershire sauce
1 tablespoon chili sauce
1 avocado, halved and pitted

Greens

331

Combine all the ingredients except the avocado and greens. Arrange beds of greens on two plates. Place an avocado half on each plate and fill with the salad mixture. Garnish with additional mayonnaise.

Mussels

THE mussel is a rock-clinging mollusk with a rather soft, bluish-black shell that is slightly ribbed. It is one of the most abundant seafoods in America and one of the most neglected. In fact, so little attention has been paid to it that there is no accurate idea of the extent of the mussel beds around our shores. They are found in great profusion on both coasts, but on the Pacific Coast, where people have occasionally been poisoned by them, they are quarantined during the dangerous period and cannot be obtained.

It is interesting that in Europe mussels are so popular that the demand cannot be met from natural sources. For years they have been artificially propagated in enormous quantities.

The most common mussel dish known in this country is one served in nearly every French restaurant—moules marinière. It is often made incorrectly, but still people love it and order it over and over—dipping in with their fingers and lapping up the juice with great delight.

This is the most authentic recipe I know of for this really fine dish.

MUSSELS MARINIERE

(Mussels must be washed and the beard—the gathering of vegetation on the shell—must be removed.)

This recipe will serve 4 people.

2 quarts mussels	Pepper
1 large onion	1 cup white wine
2 or 3 sprigs of parsley	3 tablespoons butter
Pinch of thyme	Chopped parsley
3 or 4 tablespoons butter	Salt (if needed)

Wash and beard the mussels. Peel and chop the onion and place it in the bottom of a saucepan with parsley and thyme. Add the mussels, 3 or 4 tablespoons of butter and a good sprinkling of freshly ground black pepper. Pour over this the white wine, cover the saucepan, and let it steam over a low flame. Steam just until the mussels open. (If by chance any of them do not open, remove them at once and throw them away.)

When the mussels are open, you may remove the empty half of the shell or not, as you prefer. Arrange them in a large tureen or bowl. Add 3 tablespoons of butter and a handful of chopped parsley to the broth, taste for seasoning, (mussels, like clams, sometimes need no additional salt.) and pour it over the mussels. You'll need plenty of toasted French bread or toast with this dish to sop up the juice—and not a drop should be wasted.

VARIATIONS

1. Instead of the onion, use 3 cloves of garlic, finely chopped, and substitute olive oil for the butter.

2. If you like a thick sauce, add a little beurre manié (see index) and stir until smooth.

MUSSELS POULETTE

Prepare the mussels as for mussels marinière. Combine the broth with 1½ cups of heavy white sauce and stir until thoroughly blended and thickened. Add a few tablespoons of essence of mushrooms or mushroom broth and the juice of a lemon. Remove the empty half of the shell from the cooked mussels, and serve them with the sauce poured over them.

MUSSELS RAVIGOTE PASCAL

Steam the mussels as for mussels marinière. Remove the empty half of the shell and allow the mussels to chill. Add a spoon of sauce rémoulade (see index) to each mussel and serve as hors d'oeuvre. Six to 8 mussels will make a serving.

MUSSEL SALAD

Prepare the mussels as for mussels marinière. Take the mussels out of the shells and marinate them in a well-seasoned vinaigrette sauce (see index). Arrange them on a bed of shredded lettuce and mask with mayonnaise. Garnish with water cress, capers, and a good dash of paprika.

STUFFED MUSSELS

Prepare the mussels as for mussels marinière. Remove the mussels from the shells, but keep the half shells. Chop the mussel meat coarsely and combine with the following stuffing:

4 tablespoons chopped onion	4 tablespoons chopped
3 tablespoons chopped celery	parsley
1 tablespoon chopped green	1 cup toasted crumbs
pepper	1 teaspoon dry mustard
6 tablespoons butter	1 teaspoon salt
	Few grains cayenne

Sauté the onion, celery, and green pepper in the butter until just tender. Add the parsley, the toasted crumbs, and seasonings. Add the chopped mussels and enough of the broth from the mussels to make a moist mixture. Heap this into the half shells and dot with butter. Heat in a 450° oven until lightly browned.

CURRIED MUSSELS

Prepare 2 quarts of mussels as for mussels marinière. Remove the mussels from their shells. Prepare a sauce from the following:

5 tablespoons butter	1 cup mussel broth
2 tablespoons onion, chopped	½ cup heavy cream
1 clove garlic, chopped	1 tablespoon curry powder
4 tablespoons flour	1 teaspoon salt
Few grains of cayenne	

Melt the butter in a large skillet and sauté the onion and garlic until just soft. Add the flour, mix well, and let it cook gently for a minute or two. Gradually stir in the mussel broth, and continue stirring until the sauce is thickened. Add the cream slowly, add the seasonings and taste to be sure there is enough curry. Finally add the mussels and let them heat through. Serve with steamed rice, crisp fried onions and chutney.

STEAMED MUSSELS

Place 2 quarts of mussels with 1 cup of water in a saucepan. Cover and steam over a low flame until the mussels open. Taste the broth for salt. Serve the mussels with the broth and a little melted butter. This dish lacks the rich flavor of mussels steamed over white wine, but some people prefer this method.

MUSSELS CREOLE

Prepare 2 quarts of mussels as for mussels marinière. Remove the mussels from the shells. Prepare a sauce from the following:

1 medium onion, finely chopped	⅔ cup tomato puree
3 tablespoons butter	1 cup mussel broth
3 tablespoons olive oil	1 clove garlic, chopped
4 tablespoons chopped celery	¼ cup chopped parsley
4 tablespoons chopped green pepper	Pinch of thyme

Sauté the onion in the butter and olive oil. Add the celery, the pepper, the tomato puree and the broth and simmer for 30 minutes. Add more broth if the sauce gets too thick. Add the garlic, parsley and thyme, and taste for seasoning. Finally add the mussels. Serve with steamed rice or risotto.

BARBECUED MUSSELS

2 quarts mussels, steamed as for mussels marinière	1 clove garlic, finely chopped
4 tablespoons chili sauce	2 tablespoons whiskey
Few grains of cayenne	Salt (if needed)
	Beurre manié
Chopped parsley	

Steam the mussels as for mussels marinière. Remove the empty half shell. Strain the broth, put it over a brisk flame and reduce it to half its volume. Add the chili sauce, cayenne, garlic and whiskey. Taste for salt and thicken with a little beurre manié (see index). Pour this sauce over the mussels and sprinkle with chopped parsley. Serve with plenty of toasted French bread.

STUFFED MUSSELS PROVENCALE

Prepare 2 quarts of mussels as for mussels marinière. Remove the empty half shell. Blend together:

6 finely chopped shallots or green onions	1 teaspoon salt
	½ teaspoon pepper
2 cloves garlic, chopped	½ pound butter
½ cup chopped parsley	1 egg yolk
½ cup bread crumbs	

When all this is well blended, spoon it into the shells containing the mussels. Sprinkle with additional crumbs. Arrange in a baking pan with a little white wine in the bottom. Bake in a 400° oven until the sauce is melted and delicately browned.

MUSSELS IN CREAM

Wash and beard 2 quarts of mussels. Place them in a saucepan with a finely chopped onion, a branch of celery, and a sprig of parsley. Add 2 cups of water, cover the pan and steam until the mussels open. Remove the mussels from the shells and keep them warm.

Prepare 1½ cups of sauce béchamel (see index), using some of the mussel broth. Season well and add the mussels. Serve in patty shells, over rice, or on mounds of mashed potatoes. Sprinkle with paprika and chopped parsley.

MUSSEL FRITTERS

Prepare mussels as for mussels in cream. Heat fat or oil to 360° for deep-fat frying. Prepare beer batter (see index), dip each mussel into the batter, and fry in the hot fat for 3 to 5 minutes, or until nicely browned. Serve with tartar sauce (see index).

SPAGHETTI WITH MUSSEL SAUCE

See spaghetti with clam sauce.

Oysters

MANY gourmets, or so-called gourmets, tell you that to eat an oyster in any fashion except directly from the shell is to show ignorance of gastronomic tradition and the rules of good taste. This is nonsense. While there may be nothing quite so wonderful as a freshly opened oyster with just a squirt of lemon juice on it, still there are many delightful ways to eat these mollusks cooked.

The American oyster was a staple in the diet of our coast Indians, and the great piles of shells found in many areas along our shores are evidence of the magnitude of Indian appetites. And because the popularity of oysters has continued so strongly among those of us who have more recently taken oven this continent, most of the natural oyster beds are gone. We must rely now on cultivated beds. Over 90 million pounds of oysters are consumed in this country every year, and that is quite a few oysters.

Even so, we are actually sissies when it comes to eating oysters. Our grandfathers ate them by the gross, not the dozen. It was once commonplace for people to eat several dozen just as a first course. Today, in most European cities, a dozen oysters are considered a portion, rather than the half dozen usually served here.

There is great variety in types of oysters. Those from separate beds in the same area, such as Long Island, have decidedly different flavors, as you can readily find out for yourself by a comparative tasting of them. They contain different quantities of salt (Since some oysters need no additional salt in preparation, I have not included salt in many of the recipes that follow. I feel that the individual should season to suit his own particular taste.) or have different degrees of coppery flavor. Some are fat and plump, others are thin and very flat. The tiny Olympia oyster of the Pacific Coast has a most distinctive flavor, as have certain Eastern oysters that have been transplanted to the Pacific. The Chincoteagues of Chesapeake Bay have their unique qualities. Then there are the Japanese oysters that have been planted along the Western coastline. These are giants—so large no one would dare try to eat them on the half shell.

But no matter what sort of oyster you select or how you choose to prepare it, you are eating great gourmet fare.

OYSTERS ON THE HALF SHELL

By far the most common way to serve oysters is raw. Unfortunately, someone who was certainly no oyster lover started serving what is now known far and wide as "cocktail sauce" —usually nothing more than a fantastic mixture of tomato sauce, chili sauce, horseradish and other condiments. This is my pet abomination. A sauce of this kind entirely destroys the delicate flavor of the oyster. A freshly opened oyster, served on the half shell in a bed of ice, needs only a little squirt of lemon juice, and perhaps some freshly ground pepper. The only tolerable variation is the addition of a dab of caviar. Some gourmets will allow sauce mignonette—a combination of pepper, vinegar and a little shallot. Don't forget to drink the juice in the bottom of the shell—never waste it.

The usual portion is 6 oysters to a person. If they are medium-sized, serve 12. And you may figure that the average diner can eat 36 to 48 of the tiny Olympias. Always be sure that they are icy cold and serve them on ice so they will stay that way.

With all oyster dishes used as a first course, serve thin—paper-thin—slices of delicate rye or pumpernickel bread heavily buttered. A brisk dry white wine, such as a fine Chablis or a Pouilly Fuisse, is excellent with oysters. Some people prefer a light beer, and beer does do a wonderful job of complementing all seafoods and fish.

OYSTERS WITH COCKTAILS OR CHAMPAGNE

1. Several times in this country and many times in France I have been served oysters on the half shell with cocktails. Huge platters of them were passed and each guest helped himself.

2. Open-faced oyster sandwiches are another treat. Butter well some rounds of pumpernickel bread, spread with finely chopped onion, place a raw oyster on each and top it with a dab of caviar. Superb!

3. Butter some pumpernickel rounds, spread lightly with anchovy paste and top with a raw oyster. Delicious with cocktails.

4. Small oysters perfectly fried (see fried oysters) and served on fried toast rounds are wonderful hot tidbits with either cocktails or champagne. But they must be piping hot. You can spread the toast with anchovy paste before topping with the oyster if you wish.

5. Another unforgettable hot snack is creamed oysters in tiny patty shells. Make the shells yourself, or order them from your favorite bakeshop. Use a rich Hollandaise (see index) or a curry sauce (see index) for the oysters.

6. Any of the recipes for stuffed oysters may be served with cocktails if you pass small plates and forks so your guests can manage this food easily.

HUITRES FARCIES CASENAVE

6 shallots (or green onions), finely chopped
½ cup chopped parsley
¼ cup chopped chervil
3 ounces butter
12 oysters on the half shell
Salt, pepper

Mix the chopped herbs and shallots or onions with the butter, and top each oyster with a spoonful of the mixture. Salt and pepper to taste and bake on a bed of rock salt in a 475° oven for 4 or 5 minutes, or until the oysters are just heated through.

These may be run under the broiler instead, but be careful not to overcook them.

OYSTERS ROCKEFELLER

These are as many recipes for this dish as there are for bread. This may not be the original one, but it makes a delicious treat. In the old days it was necessary to pound the ingredients for the sauce in a mortar—a very tiring job—but with today's electric mixers, oysters Rockefeller is a simple treat to prepare.

¼ cup chopped shallot or green onion
¼ cup chopped celery
1 teaspoon chopped chervil
⅓ cup chopped fennel
⅓ cup chopped parsley
½ pound butter
2 cups water cress
⅓ cup bread crumbs
⅓ cup Pernod or anisette
Salt, pepper
Cayenne
2 dozen oysters on the half shell

Sauté the onion, celery and herbs in 3 tablespoons of butter for 3 minutes. Add the water cress and just let it wilt. Put this mixture with the rest of the butter, the bread crumbs and the Pernod or anisette in the electric blender. Season to taste with salt, pepper, and a few grains of cayenne. Blend for 1 minute. Put about 1 tablespoon of this on each oyster, place the oysters on beds of rock salt in individual containers and dampen the salt slightly. Bake at 450° to 475° for about 4 minutes, or until the butter is melted and the oysters heated through.

NOTE: Tin pie plates are excellent for baking this dish.

339

OYSTERS KIRKPATRICK

There are as many versions of this as there are of the famous Rockefeller recipe. This is my choice:

24 oysters on the half shell	3 tablespoons butter
½ cup finely chopped onion or shallot	⅔ cup tomato catsup
	Chopped parsley
1 tablespoon chopped green pepper	Bacon

Arrange oysters on the half shell on beds of rock salt. Sauté the onion and green pepper in the butter. Mix this with the catsup. Put a spoonful on each oyster, sprinkle with parsley and top with a partially cooked piece of bacon. Place in a 450° oven just long enough to brown the bacon and heat the oysters.

VARIATIONS

1. Sprinkle grated cheese over the top, dot with butter and top with the piece of bacon.

2. Simply spoon tomato catsup or chili sauce over the oysters and top with crumbs and the piece of bacon.

3. Cover the oysters with chopped green onion, tomato catsup, and top with pieces of partially cooked bacon. Bake in a 450° oven just long enough to brown the bacon and heat the oysters.

OYSTERS REMICK

36 oysters on the half shell	1 tablespoon prepared mustard
2 cups mayonnaise	½ teaspoon salt
4 tablespoons chili sauce	2 teaspoons lemon juice
¼ teaspoon paprika	2 tablespoons butter
Few grains cayenne	½ cup bread crumbs

Bacon

Place the oysters on beds of rock salt. Mix the mayonnaise and the seasonings and spoon it over the oysters. Sprinkle with buttered crumbs and top with pieces of partially cooked bacon. Bake in a 450° oven for 4 or 5 minutes, place under the broiler flame for 3 minutes—just until the edges curl.

OYSTERS AU GRATIN

Arrange oysters on the half shell on beds of rock salt. Add a dash of lemon juice to each oyster, cover with fine bread crumbs, a little melted butter and a sprinkling of cayenne. Bake in a 450° oven for a few minutes—just until the edges curl and the oysters are heated through. Sprinkle with chopped parsley just before you serve.

OYSTERS FLORENTINE

This is certainly a forerunner of the famous oysters Rockefeller, for it's a very old recipe—no one knows when it was introduced.

Poach oysters in their own liquor, with a little white wine added, just long enough for the edges to curl. Arrange oyster shells on a baking sheet and place a spoonful of chopped cooked spinach in each shell. Put an oyster on each spinach bed and top with sauce Mornay (see index). Sprinkle with a little grated cheese and run under the broiler flame for a minute or two to melt the cheese and brown slightly.

OYSTERS BRETON

Remove the oysters from their shells and arrange the shells in a baking dish or pans filled with rock salt. In each shell put a spoonful of chopped lobster meat which has been heated in butter and cream. On top of this place an oyster and cover with a heavy béchamel (see index) to which you have added more chopped lobster. Sprinkle with crumbs and brown under the broiler. Meanwhile sauté an equal number of oysters— dip them in egg and crumbs and brown quickly in butter. Just before serving top each oyster shell with a sautéed oyster and sprinkle with chopped parsley.

CURRIED OYSTERS

3 cups sauce béchamel
12 shrimp, finely chopped

1 tablespoon curry powder
24 oysters on the half shell
Toasted bread crumbs

Prepare the sauce béchamel and add the chopped shrimp and curry powder. Arrange the oysters on beds of rock salt and top each one with the curried shrimp sauce. Sprinkle with toasted crumbs and bake in a 475° oven for 4 or 5 minutes.

OYSTERS PAPRIKA

24 oysters on the half shell
3 medium onions, finely chopped
6 tablespoons butter
⅓ cup chopped mushrooms
1 cup sauce béchamel (see index)
1 tablespoon, or more, paprika
Toasted bread crumbs

Arrange the oysters on beds of rock salt. Sauté the onion in the butter until tender, but not browned. Add the mushrooms and blend well. Prepare the béchamel and add 1 tablespoon or more of paprika to color and flavor it. Combine with the onions and mushrooms. Spoon this over the oysters and sprinkle highly with crumbs and paprika. Bake in 475° oven for about 5 minutes or until the oysters are just cooked through.

CRUMBED OYSTERS

24 oysters on the half shell
1 cup toasted bread crumbs
8 tablespoons butter
Parsley
Chives

Arrange the oysters on beds of rock salt. Fry the bread crumbs in the butter until very crisp and brown. Top the oysters with the bread crumbs and sprinkle with chopped parsley and chives. Bake in 475° oven for about 5 minutes or until the oysters curl at the edges.

OYSTERS CASINO

Here again there are many versions of the recipe, so I include several. One thing on which everyone agrees is that oysters Casino always contain green pepper and bacon.

24 oysters on the half shell
½ cup butter
⅓ cup chopped shallots
¼ cup chopped parsley
¼ cup chopped green pepper
Lemon juice
Bacon, partially cooked

Arrange the oysters on beds of rock salt. Blend together the butter, the finely chopped shallots, parsley and green pepper. Spoon this over the oysters and add a dash of lemon juice to each one. Top with pieces of partially cooked bacon. Bake in a 450° oven until the bacon is brown and the oysters cooked through.

342

VARIATIONS

1. Try out ½ cup of finely chopped bacon. Add ⅓ cup of finely chopped onion, ⅓ cup of finely chopped green pepper, ¼ cup of finely chopped celery, 1 teaspoon of lemon juice, salt, pepper, Worcestershire sauce and a few drops of tabasco. Spoon this over the oysters which have been placed on beds of rock salt. Bake in a 350° oven for 10 minutes.

2. Sprinkle the oysters with finely chopped green pepper and onion and top each one with a piece of bacon. Bake in a 450° oven until the bacon is done and the oysters cooked through.

OYSTER LOAF

There is an old story that oyster loaves were always "guilty conscience" presents or peace offerings. To take home an oyster loaf in New Orleans and certain other places meant that you had been misbehaving and were trying to get back into good graces. I can remember homes in my youth where oyster loaves were so constantly served that surely bad deeds must have been the regular rule.

1 loaf of bread, unsliced　　　　　Butter
Fried or sautéed oysters

For this dish, try to find a really good loaf of bread—difficult these days, I know, but try. The round Italian loaves will do, or the regular loaf-pan loaves. Cut about a ⅔ inch slice off the top of the loaf. Scoop out the interior, leaving a wall about ½ inch thick all around. Toast the loaf in a slow oven until it is nicely browned and then brush it well with butter. Fill it with hot fried oysters and put the cover on. To serve, slice with a sharp knife.

These may be made in individual sizes as well. French rolls or, if you can find them, those rolls that are baked in miniature bread pans are ideal for this.

(NOTE: Any other type of seafood may be substituted for the oysters in this recipe.)

I hate to mention it, but the traditional condiment with any oyster loaf is tomato catsup or chili sauce.

OYSTER FRITTERS

Drain the oysters well and roll them in flour. Preheat fat or oil to 380°. Dip the oysters in beer batter (see index) and fry in the deep fat for about 2 minutes or until browned and crisp. Drain on absorbent paper and salt and pepper to taste. Serve with a tartar sauce (see index) or rémoulade (see index).

OYSTER CROUSTADES

Roll brioche dough ½ inch thick and cut it in small rounds. Place two oysters apiece on half of the rounds, sprinkle them with salt and pepper, add a dab of butter and some chopped parsley. Dampen the edges of the rounds. Cover each with another round of dough, press the edges together, and fry in deep fat, heated to 375°, until they have risen and browned. Turn once during the cooking. Serve with a tartar sauce or tomato sauce (see index). For brioche dough, see index.

VARIATION

Substitute rounds of roll or bread dough for the brioche.

OYSTER PAN ROAST

A pan roast is really oysters poached in butter—and they must have plenty of butter to be good. Personally, I think the tiny oysters of the Pacific Coast are far better for this dish than the larger ones.

1. Melt ½ cup of butter (¼ pound) in a skillet. Add 1 pint of drained oysters, salt, plenty of freshly ground pepper, a dash of cayenne and a good squirt of lemon or lime juice. When the oysters are plumped and puffy the pan roast is done. I like mine served on fried toast.

2. Proceed in the same way, adding 2 tablespoons of catsup and 1 tablespoon of Worcestershire sauce.

3. When the butter is melted, add ⅓ cup of chopped shallots or green onions and ¼ cup of chopped parsley. Add the drained oysters, a dash of red wine, and let it all boil up for 3 minutes.

4. Add 1 clove of crushed garlic, 3 tablespoons of tomato puree and 1 teaspoon of dry mustard to the butter. Then add the oysters and a dash of lemon juice.

5. Sauté ⅓ cup of chopped shallots or green onions and ⅓ cup of chopped green peppers in butter until tender. Add the drained oysters, salt and pepper. A dash of vermouth or white wine makes this extra good.

DEVILS ON HORSEBACK

Wrap oysters individually in thin rashers of bacon and broil under a hot flame until the bacon is crisp. Turn once while cooking. (For added dash, you may, before cooking, marinate the oysters in white wine flavored with garlic and black pepper.)

ANGELS ON HORSEBACK

Sprinkle oysters with fine chopped onion and parsley and wrap in paper-thin strips of smoked ham. Broil for 5 to 8 minutes, turning once. Serve on buttered toast with Hollandaise sauce (see index).

OYSTERS EN BROCHETTE I

For each brochette:

4 oysters	3 to 4 mushroom caps
Lemon juice	1 long strip of bacon
Salt, pepper	Butter

Parsley

Sprinkle the oysters with lemon juice, salt and pepper. At the end of the brochette place a mushroom cap. Next put the end of the bacon strip, then an oyster, then loop the bacon around the oyster onto the brochette again, add another mushroom, another oyster and continue until you have used four oysters. Brush with butter and broil over charcoal or under the broiler flame, turning several times. Sprinkle with chopped parsley and serve with lemon wedges.

OYSTERS EN BROCHETTE II

Alternate small cubes of beef tenderloin and oysters on a skewer. Brush well with butter and broil until the beef is delicately browned and the oysters cooked through. Salt and pepper to taste and brush with plenty of butter before serving.

OYSTERS EN BROCHETTE III

Alternate oysters, small tomatoes or small chunks of tomato, mushrooms and small cubes of cooked ham. Brush with butter and broil. Salt and pepper to taste and sprinkle with lemon juice.

CREAMED OYSTERS

1 pint sauce velouté	3 tablespoons sherry or Madeira
	1 pint oysters
	Patty shells or croustades

Make a sauce velouté, using some of the oyster liquor, and season well with salt and pepper. Add the wine. Add the drained oysters and cook them just long enough to curl the edges. Serve on croustades or in patty shells which have been heated through.

VARIATION

If your baker makes a good puff paste, order a vol au vent, or make it yourself. Fill it with oysters in the sauce velouté and serve it with a salad of beets, hard-cooked eggs and tender greens. Pass some crisp French bread and a cheese tray. This is an outstanding late evening supper. You can dramatize it by preparing the sauce in the chafing dish and filling the vol au vent at the table.

OYSTER PIE

This same creamed dish—the oysters in velouté—may be used for a pie. Fill a deep casserole or baking dish with the mixture and top it with a crust. Decorate the crust with designs, such as small leaves cut from the pastry. Bake for 15 or 20 minutes in a 425° oven.

If you make your pastry and roll it out ahead of time and chill it for several hours, it saves you trouble at the last minute and makes a better crust.

OYSTER SOUFFLE

1 cup heavy sauce béchamel	Salt, pepper
1 cup chopped oysters	Cayenne
1 tablespoon grated onion	4 egg yolks
	6 egg whites

Make the sauce béchamel with part of the oyster liquor. Add the chopped oysters, season with the grated onion and salt, pepper and cayenne to taste. Beat in the egg yolks. Beat the egg whites until stiff and fold half of them into the mixture, blending them in well. Then fold in the other half lightly. Pour it into a buttered soufflé dish and bake in a 375° oven for 40 or 50 minutes. Serve with a Hollandaise sauce.

OYSTER OMELET

Prepare omelets in your usual fashion. Fold in oysters in velouté sauce or fried oysters. Serve with shoestring potatoes and a delicate white wine.

OYSTER CHOWDER

4 tablespoons butter	Salt, pepper
3 tablespoons chopped onion	Sprig of thyme
¾ cup finely cut celery	1 cup fish broth or white
3 finely diced carrots	wine
2 cups diced potatoes	1 quart milk
	1 pint oysters
⅓ cup chopped parsley	

Melt the butter in a saucepan and add all the vegetables but the potatoes. Brown very quickly and salt and pepper to taste. Cover and let them cook for 5 to 8 minutes. Add the oyster liquor, the thyme, and the fish broth or white wine and bring to a boil. Add the potatoes, cover and simmer until the potatoes are tender. Add the milk and let it come just to the boiling point. Add the oysters and let them cook until the edges curl. Pour into bowls or a tureen and sprinkle liberally with chopped parsley.

OYSTER CLUB SANDWICH

This is a combination of fried oysters, bacon, tomato, lettuce and mayonnaise on toasted white or rye bread. A very good dish late at night or for luncheon.

SCALLOPED OYSTERS

This is a favorite old New England dish that has always had a place of honor at all functions—especially at holiday feasts —in that part of the country. It has never been popular with me but I can understand why many people like it.

347

Butter
1 cup freshly rolled cracker
    crumbs—Saltines, please
1 pint oysters
Salt, pepper
Nutmeg
¼ cup oyster liquor
4 tablespoons cream
½ cup buttered bread crumbs

Butter a baking dish and place a layer of cracker crumbs on the bottom. Place a layer of oysters over that and sprinkle with salt, pepper and a little nutmeg. Add 2 tablespoons of oyster liquor, 2 tablespoons of cream and dot well with butter. Add a layer of cracker and bread crumbs mixed, then another layer of oysters, seasonings and liquids. Dot with butter, cover with cracker crumbs and top with bread crumbs. Add a little more cream, sprinkle with salt, pepper and nutmeg and dot with butter. Bake at 425° for approximately 40 minutes.

OYSTER STEW I

4 tablespoons or more butter
½ pint milk
1 pint cream
1½ pints oysters and liquor
Salt, pepper
Cayenne

First of all heat the bowls. When they are hot, put a large piece of butter in each one and keep the bowls hot. Heat the milk, cream and oyster liquor to the boiling point. Salt and pepper to taste and add a dash of cayenne. Add the oysters and let it come to the boiling point again. Ladle into the hot bowls. You may add a dash of paprika, if you like. I prefer my stew with hot crunchy French bread, although crackers are the traditional accompaniment.

This recipe makes four generous or six medium-sized servings.

OYSTER STEW II

4 tablespoons butter
1½ pints oysters
1 quart milk or half cream and
    half milk
Salt, pepper
Paprika

Melt the butter, add the drained oysters and cook until the edges curl—about 3 minutes. Add the liquids, season to taste and bring just to the boiling point. Serve with a dash of paprika. This will serve six people.

OYSTER BISQUE

⅔ cup rice
1 pint oysters
1 small onion stuck with cloves
Bouquet garni (thyme, parsley, celery or fennel)

1 cup oyster liquor or oyster liquor and white wine mixed
1 pint cream
Salt, pepper

Paprika

Cook the rice in boiling salted water until very soft. Chop the oysters fine and do not lose any of the juice. Add the onion, the bouquet garni, the oyster liquor and cognac. Bring this to the boiling point and simmer for ten minutes. Remove the bouquet garni. Add the drained rice and put it all through a fine sieve. Add the cream. Taste for seasoning, return to the stove and bring to the boiling point. Serve with a dash of paprika on each bowlful.

VARIATIONS

1. If small oysters are available, poach several in white wine and oyster liquor, and float them in each serving.
2. Cook the oysters in 1 cup of tomatoes instead of in the oyster liquor.

FRIED OYSTERS

Among the most vivid gastronomical memories of my childhood are the visits we made to the home of friends who were in the oyster business. They had huge sacks of oysters sent to their beach home every week and when these arrived we knew we were in for many treats. The greatest treat of all would come after an early morning venture of clamming and crabbing followed by a dip in the surf. Then we would climb the sand dunes to the house with ravenous appetites, to be met by a wonderful aroma—a mixture of melting butter and coffee gently simmering. In the kitchen there would be a magnificent sight—dozens of freshly opened oysters dipped in beaten egg and rolled in crushed cracker crumbs. On the stove would be two huge iron skillets with a half inch of bubbling butter in each one, waiting to brown the delicate morsels as soon as we were seated at the table.

It was the man of the house who always cooked these oysters. He would never trust the women or the cook to do the job properly. Such perfection of cookery I have seldom encountered since, and the smell of those early morning oyster fries has stayed in my memory and enchanted me for years.

Here, so far as I can remember, is Mr. Hamblet's oyster recipe:

Butter	1 quart oysters (not too big)
3 eggs	
3 tablespoons heavy cream	Freshly rolled cracker crumbs (Saltines are best)

Salt, pepper

Melt plenty of butter in your skillet—it should be about ½ inch thick. (I usually use part oil so the butter will not burn.) Beat the eggs lightly and combine with the cream. Dip the oysters in the egg mixture, then in the crumbs and arrange on wax paper (far enough apart so they do not touch) and let them stand for a few minutes before cooking. They should be cooked just long enough to brown delicately and get a little crisp. Salt and pepper to taste and serve with wedges of lemon or with tartar sauce.

OLYMPIA OYSTER FRY

Olympia oysters are so tiny it is difficult to fry them separately. We used to have small individual pans for frying them. We would dip them in eggs and cracker crumbs and fry each portion in butter in its separate pan. We cooked them very quickly and turned them once with a large spatula. Then, with a quick twist of the wrist, we turned them out onto hot plates like pancakes.

OYSTER SAUTE

Oysters may be dipped in flour and sautéed in butter very quickly. You may season them with chopped herbs or a little white wine, or simply with salt and pepper. They are particularly good with tarragon and a little white wine, or with equal amounts of chives and parsley and a little white wine. They will cook in 3 or 4 minutes—be careful not to overcook them.

VARIATIONS

1. Sauté oysters in butter and serve on fried toast with a sauce made as follows: To the juices in the pan add 4 tablespoons of butter, 1 clove of garlic finely minced and 3 tablespoons of finely chopped parsley. Pour this over the oysters on the toast. Six or 7 oysters fixed in this manner will make a good serving for a first course at dinner or a main course at luncheon.

2. Sauté 24 oysters and arrange them on thin slices of frizzled ham. Garnish with sautéed mushroom caps and chopped parsley.

3. Sauté a chicken in butter with a little parsley and some white wine. Sauté 24 oysters in butter and combine with the chicken. This is an excellent combination of flavors.

4. Combine sautéed oysters with broiled fillets of any white-meated fish, such as sole. Grill the fillets or sauté them in butter and smother them with the oysters. Sprinkle with freshly ground black pepper and chopped parsley.

FRENCH-FRIED OYSTERS

Fat for frying (or oil)
2 eggs
3 tablespoons of cream
1 teaspoon salt
Flour
½ teaspoon pepper
Bread or cracker crumbs or corn meal
1 quart oysters

Heat fat for frying to 380°. Beat the eggs with the cream; add seasonings. Roll the crumbs very fine. Dip the oysters in flour, then in the egg mixture and then in the crumbs. Fry for about 2 minutes or until delicately browned. Drain on absorbent paper. Salt and pepper.

VARIATION

Add 1 tablespoon of curry powder to the egg mixture or to the crumbs.

HANGTOWN FRY

This mixture of eggs and oysters is made in several ways. Here are three popular methods.

1. Beat eggs with cream and seasonings, using 2 eggs for 4 large oysters. Sauté oysters in a skillet and pour the egg mixture over them. Continue cooking until the eggs are set. Turn out on a platter.

2. This is an Italian version, similar to a frittato. Fry the oysters until just delicately browned. Mix 2 eggs and 1 tablespoon of cream for each 4 oysters and combine with 3 tablespoons of grated Parmesan cheese. Pour over the oysters and place under the broiler until the eggs are set.

351

3. Fold fried oysters into scrambled eggs just before they are ready to serve.

Scallops

THE scallop is a mollusk that is so named because of its beautifully fluted and scalloped shell. There are two types found along most American shores. The tiny bay scallop is tenderer and more delicately flavored, and is so popular that the supply has been greatly depleted. Then there is the larger deep sea scallop which is more generally available.

In Europe, where they are called by the French term *Coquilles St. Jacques,* scallops are eaten whole. In this country, only the muscle that controls the shell movement is used—no one seems to know why—and the rest of the meat is used for bait or fertilizer. One pound will supply 3 average or 2 large servings.

SCALLOPS AS AN APPETIZER

Raw scallops are delicious, although few people eat them this way—possibly the idea has never been suggested to them. The bay scallops, tiny and tender, served like oysters with lemon, salt and pepper, have a delightful and unusual flavor.

BROILED SCALLOPS

Place the scallops on a flat tin—a baking sheet or pie tin. Dot them with butter and sprinkle lightly with salt and pepper. Place under the broiler, about 3 inches from the flame. They will take from 5 to 6 minutes to broil and become delicately browned. Serve with lemon juice.

SCALLOPS SAUTE FINES HERBES

Follow the same procedure as for scallops Provençale, omitting the garlic and adding 1 teaspoon of chopped tarragon and 1 teaspoon of chopped chives with the parsley.

SAUTEED SCALLOPS

1½ pounds scallops
Flour

6 tablespoons butter
Salt, pepper

¼ cup chopped parsley

Wash the scallops and pick out any bits of shell. Dry and dust lightly with flour. Melt the butter in a skillet, and add the scallops. Let them cook quickly and not too long or they will get tough and lose their delicious flavor. They should just heat through and brown lightly. Salt and pepper to taste, sprinkle with chopped parsley and serve with lemon wedges. Serves 4.

SCALLOPS SAUTE PROVENCALE

1½ pounds bay scallops
Flour
6 tablespoons olive oil

2 or 3 cloves garlic, finely
chopped
Salt, pepper

½ cup chopped parsley

Wash and dry the scallops and roll them in flour. Heat the olive oil, add the scallops and cook them very quickly, tossing them lightly in the hot oil. While they are cooking add the chopped garlic and mix it in well. Then salt and pepper to taste, and just before taking the pan from the stove, add the parsley and toss it around so that the scallops are nicely coated with it. Serve with lemon wedges. Scallops Provençale are often served in shells—a very attractive dish.

VARIATION

Peel, seed and chop 3 medium tomatoes. Sauté them in butter until soft and thick. Serve with the scallops.

SCALLOPS WITH CURRY I

2 medium onions
5 tablespoons butter
1½ pounds scallops
Flour

1 tablespoon curry powder
1 cup sauce béchamel
1 cup heavy cream

Chop the onions very fine and sauté lightly in butter until just transparent. Roll the scallops in flour and add them to the onions, tossing them gently until lightly browned. Add the curry and mix well. Add the béchamel and the cream and cook until the mixture is thick, smooth and well blended. Serve on a deep platter surrounded by mounds of rice. Chutney should accompany this.

SCALLOPS WITH CURRY II

3 tablespoons butter	Flour
3 tablespoons olive oil	1 teaspoon salt
1 finely chopped clove garlic	1 tablespoon curry
1 onion, finely chopped	⅓ cup dry vermouth
2 pounds scallops	Chopped parsley

Melt the butter in a skillet and add the olive oil. When it is hot add the garlic and onion and sauté for 3 minutes. Roll the scallops in flour and add them to the pan. Toss them around so that they brown quickly on all sides. Add salt, curry and vermouth and let it all blend well. Serve on fluffy rice and sprinkle liberally with chopped parsley.

SCALLOP STEW

See index for oyster stew.

FRIED SCALLOPS

2 pounds scallops	Fat or oil
Beer batter (see index)	Salt, pepper

Wash, drain and dry scallops on a dry cloth. Prepare the beer batter. Heat fat or oil for deep frying to 370°. Dip the scallops into the beer batter and drop by spoonfuls into the hot fat. Cook for 3 to 5 minutes or just long enough for them to brown nicely. Drain on absorbent paper. Salt and pepper to taste and serve with tartar sauce (see index).

SCALLOPS MORNAY

2 pounds scallops	Sauce Mornay (see index)
White wine to cover	Buttered crumbs
Bouquet garni (onion, parsley, thyme)	Grated Parmesan cheese

Poach the scallops in white wine with the bouquet garni for 3 to 5 minutes—until they are just cooked through. Drain them and use some of the white wine to prepare the sauce Mornay. Arrange the scallops in shells or small ramekins and cover with the sauce. Sprinkle with buttered crumbs and a little grated Parmesan cheese. Heat under the broiler for a few minutes to glaze the tops.

There is usually enough seasoning in the sauce; however, it is wise to taste for seasoning before you fill the ramekins.

VARIATIONS

1. Line individual casseroles with thin slices of frizzled smoked ham. Place scallops on top. With the aid of a pastry tube squeeze a ruffle of Duchess potatoes around the edge. Cover the scallops with sauce Mornay and sprinkle liberally with buttered crumbs. Bake in a 450° oven for 10 or 15 minutes to give a pleasant glaze to the sauce and brown the potatoes.

2. Poach the scallops in white wine. Prepare the sauce Mornay. Line a shallow oval baking dish with a border of Duchess potatoes piped through a pastry tube. Alternate scallops and mushroom caps which have been sautéed in butter for 6 minutes. Correct the seasoning and cover the scallops and mushrooms with the sauce Mornay. Sprinkle with crumbs and grated Parmesan and imported Swiss cheese mixed. Bake at 450° for 10 minutes or until nicely browned.

SCALLOPS DUXELLES

2 pounds scallops	6 tablespoons butter
2 cups white wine	3 tablespoons butter
Salt, pepper	4 tablespoons flour
1 onion, finely chopped	½ cup tomato puree
1 pound mushrooms, finely chopped	1 cup bouillon from the scallops

Buttered crumbs

Poach the scallops for 6 minutes in white wine to cover. Salt and pepper to taste. Drain and save the bouillon. Sauté the onion and half the mushrooms in 6 tablespoons of butter until they cook down thoroughly and are almost a paste. Add a little of the wine bouillon if necessary. Spread the bottom of shells or ramekins with this mixture.

Melt 3 tablespoons of butter in a small skillet and add the rest of the mushrooms. Cook for 3 minutes, add the flour and mix well. Add the tomato puree and bouillon and stir until the sauce is well blended and thickened. If it does not thicken enough add a little beurre manié (see index). Correct the seasoning. Cover the mushroom paste in the ramekins with scallops and top with the sauce. Sprinkle with crumbs and brown quickly in a very hot oven—500°—or under the broiler.

VARIATION

Use part scallops and part shrimp, mussels or clams. I like this dish made with one third scallops, one third shrimp, and one third oysters for a change. Poach the shrimp and scallops in white wine and add the oysters to the sauce at the last minute.

COQUILLES ST. JACQUES, MONTEIL

1½ pounds bay scallops	⅓ cup water
2 tablespoons butter	Juice of 1 lemon
6 shallots or green onions	½ teaspoon salt
Bouquet garni (parsley, onion, celery leaves, thyme, bay leaf)	¼ teaspoon pepper
	3 tablespoons butter
	2 or 3 tablespoons flour
1½ cups white wine	4 egg yolks
2 tablespoons butter	1 cup heavy cream
12 mushrooms	Grated Parmesan cheese

Bread crumbs

Wash the scallops and place in a saucepan with 2 tablespoons of butter, the chopped shallots and the bouquet garni. Barely cover with white wine and simmer for about 4 to 6 minutes until the scallops are done. Drain and save the cooking liquid. When the scallops are cool enough to handle, cut them into small pieces.

Melt 2 tablespoons of butter, chop the mushrooms fine and add them to the butter. Add the water, lemon juice, salt and pepper. Let this cook for about 5 or 6 minutes over a low flame. Drain the mushrooms and save the liquid.

Prepare a beurre manié with 3 tablespoons of butter and the flour. Add the combined cooking liquids from the scallops and mushrooms, and stir over a medium flame until thickened. Correct the seasoning. Add the scallops and let them heat in the sauce. Cool slightly. Combine the egg yolks and cream and stir into the mixture. Continue stirring over a low flame until it is well thickened, but take care that the mixture does not boil. Add the mushrooms. The sauce will be quite thick—stiff enough to be heaped into shells or individual casseroles. Sprinkle with bread crumbs and grated Parmesan cheese and glaze under the broiler.

VARIATION

You may use half scallops and half some other seafood.

SCALLOPS AND BACON EN BROCHETTE

Intertwine scallops and rashers of bacon on skewers. Put the bacon on first, then a scallop, then bacon, then a scallop, and so on. Brush the scallops well with butter, salt and pepper them, and broil until they are delicately browned and the bacon is cooked. Serve with lemon wedges.

Cold Cooked Scallops

SCALLOPS IN MAYONNAISE

2 pounds scallops	Lettuce
White wine	Potato salad
Bouquet garni (onion, pars-	Mayonnaise
ley, thyme)	Capers

Poach the scallops in white wine with the bouquet garni. Drain and let them cool. Arrange a bed of finely shredded lettuce. Cover it with a layer of sliced potato salad. Top with the scallops and mask with mayonnaise. Decorate with capers.

SCALLOP SALAD

Poach the scallops in white wine with the bouquet garni (see recipe above). Drain and let them cool. Pour over them a sauce vinaigrette and let them stand for 2 hours. Arrange lettuce and romaine in a bowl, add thinly sliced onion rings, quartered tomatoes and hard-cooked eggs. Put the scallops in the center. Decorate with capers and sliced cucumbers and serve with additional vinaigrette sauce (see index).

Shrimp

MORE shrimp, either fresh or canned, are sold in this country than any other type of shellfish. The fresh shrimp in our markets range in size from the great Mexican and Gulf shrimp, which comes 10 or 12 to the pound, to the tiny Alaskan or Icelandic shrimp, which average 40 to 45 to the pound. The large ones are ideal for spectacular dishes in which color and symmetrical arrangement are important. As for the tiny shrimp, I think they are much underrated in this country. They are remarkably good in salads and are excellent in some cooked dishes. A huge bowl of tiny shrimp, shelled, makes a perfect snack with cocktails.

You can now buy shrimp, quick-frozen, in nearly all parts of the country. They are obtainable both cooked and raw. In the raw state, they may be a greenish-gray color, pale pink or brown. People used to be warned that a raw shrimp that was pink had turned bad. But recently we have been getting a shrimp from the Gulf area that is naturally pale pink in its raw state. The brown shrimp come from Brazil.

Cooked shrimp are sold in shells, shelled, and sometimes both shelled and de-veined. In my opinion, shrimp that have been shelled and de-veined before cooking are more delicate in flavor and less apt to be gritty. Shelling is a simple job—just push the shell with your thumb and forefinger, and it comes off easily. You should leave the tails on for certain types of cookery, especially in preparing barbecued or grilled shrimp or scampi. While it is not necessary to de-vein shrimp, most people prefer to serve them that way. Use a sharp-pointed knife to cut along the curve in the body, removing the black vein. If you are making "butterfly" shrimp or scampi, by all means de-vein before cooking to enhance the appearance of the dish. Cut well through each shrimp so that the two halves nearly divide.

The unpardonable fault in preparing shrimp is overcooking. They should be cooked just long enough to give them color and firmness—about 3 to 5 minutes, certainly no longer. If you are adding shrimp to a sauce, don't cook them before adding them or they will be overcooked. If a recipe calls for bouillon from the shrimp, cook the shells and a couple of fish heads to get the required amount of broth. For shrimp to be served as hors d'oeuvre or in salads, poach them in a strong court bouillon.

Practically all shrimp sold in the markets have been decapitated, but in certain localities in the South and the West, you may find small sweet shrimp that are sold with their heads on. These are what the French call *bouquet* and are excellent served in shell as hors d'oeuvre—without sauce. The flavor is very delicate, and overwhelming them with sauces is unthinkable.

It is very difficult to tell you how many shrimp to buy per person. Sometimes I can eat a half pound as a first course at dinner, and for a main course I would want the same amount. So, if the appetites are very good, you might gauge about 1 pound of shrimp for two persons. If you are mixing the shrimp with a great deal of sauce, you may be able to make a pound stretch for four servings.

Shrimp as a First Course—Cold

In addition to the small shrimp, poached and served without sauce, there are almost endless ways in which shrimp may be used as appetizers. Large shrimp, cooked in court bouillon and cooled, may be served either shelled or unshelled. Arrange them on plates of greens and pass:

1. Sauce rémoulade
2. Sauce vinaigrette
3. Sauce mayonnaise
4. Sauce verte
5. Mustard sauce

You may use a cocktail sauce if you wish; personally I like to get as far away as possible from the bottled tomato sauce that is served so much as cocktail sauce. It smothers the flavor of the shrimp. So I give it a little dressing up. (see index for Cocktail Sauces.)

TOMATO SHRIMP APPETIZER I

For each person, peel, seed and hollow out a large ripe tomato. Into the bottom place a cold egg which has been poached in boiling salted water until the yolk has not quite set. Cover the egg with shrimp. Top with mayonnaise and garnish with finely chopped parsley, chives and tarragon.

TOMATO SHRIMP APPETIZER II

Hollow the tomato out as above, put in the egg and add the shrimp. Cover with a tomato aspic and chill until very firm. Prepare a mayonnaise chaudfroid with equal quantities of mayonnaise and aspic and cover each tomato with this sauce. Garnish with finely chopped egg, red pepper and parsley.

CUCUMBER SHRIMP APPETIZER

For each person make a cucumber boat. Cut a strip from one side of the cucumber and remove all the seeds, hollowing it out. Then cut a thin slice from the bottom so that the cucumber boat will stand steady on the plate. Salt and pepper the inside, and rub with olive oil and vinegar. Chill for 2 hours.

Fill the boats with well-seasoned shrimp that have been cooked in a court bouillon and chilled. Cover with a mayonnaise sauce, and garnish with slices of tomato, hard-cooked egg, and finely chopped fresh dill.

VARIATION

Season the cucumber boats well with chopped fresh dill and chives. Fill with the cooked shrimp, cover with dill-flavored sour cream, and garnish with chopped hard-cooked egg and capers.

SHRIMP ASPIC RING

2 quarts court bouillon (see index)
3 pounds large shrimp
3 envelopes gelatin
12 eggs
1 small onion, chopped
6 mushrooms
12 ripe olives, chopped
Mayonnaise
2 cucumbers
Romaine lettuce
2 or 3 knob celery (celery root)
Sauce rémoulade (see index)
Pimientos, olives, and other garnish

Prepare the court bouillon. Cook the shrimp 4 minutes and remove them from the bouillon to cool. Reduce the bouillon to 1 quart and strain. Dissolve the gelatin in ½ cup of cold water and combine with the bouillon. Cool, but do not let it set.

Hard-cook and peel the eggs. Cut 6 in half the long way, and 6 the round way, and remove the yolks. Crush the yolks with a little finely chopped onion, chopped mushrooms, and chopped ripe olives. Moisten with mayonnaise. Fill the egg halves with this paste piped through the large rosette end of a pastry tube. Chill.

Arrange the shelled shrimp in the bottom of a ring mold—making a solid ring of shrimp. Cover with a layer of the jelly and chill until firm. Score the skins of the cucumber by running the tines of a fork the long way, from tip to tip, in order to form scalloped edges on the cucumber slices. Then, slice them evenly. Arrange a layer of the cucumber slices in an overlapping ring on top of the shrimp and jelly. Add another layer of shrimp and cover with more aspic. Chill. Cover each stuffed egg with aspic and chill.

Arrange romaine on a large platter and unmold the ring on top. Fill the center with celery root that has been grated and mixed with sauce rémoulade. Decorate the stuffed eggs with pimientos and olives cut in slices or designs and arrange them around the edge of the platter. Serve with more rémoulade.

CUCUMBER ASPIC WITH SHRIMP

White wine court bouillon (see index)
2 pounds shrimp
1½ envelopes gelatin

2 or 3 cucumbers
Romaine
Green peppers
Russian salad (see index)

Prepare the court bouillon. Add shrimp shells and cook for ½ hour over a brisk flame to blend the flavors. Poach the shrimp for the last 4 minutes and remove from the bouillon to chill. Reduce the bouillon to 3 cups and strain through a linen napkin.

Dissolve the gelatin in ¼ cup of cold water. Combine it with the bouillon and season to taste with fresh tarragon or dill.

Peel the cucumbers and slice thinly. Arrange them in overlapping slices in the bottom of a ring mold. Add a little of the gelatin mixture and let it set. Pour the remaining gelatin over it and chill until firm. Arrange romaine on a round platter and unmold the ring on top. Fill the center with the cold poached shrimp. Decorate with strips of green pepper and surround with pepper cups filled with Russian salad (see index). Serve with sauce verte (see index).

INDIVIDUAL SHRIMP ASPICS

Court bouillon (see index)
2 pounds shrimp
2 envelopes gelatin
Fresh or dried tarragon

4 truffles
6 hard-cooked eggs
4 pounds asparagus
4 pimientos

Mayonnaise (see index)

361

Prepare the court bouillon. Peel and de-vein the shrimp and poach them for 4 minutes. Remove to cool. Reduce the bouillon to one half and strain through a linen cloth. Dissolve the gelatin in ½ cup of cold water. Combine with the bouillon and add a few leaves of fresh or dried tarragon. Taste for seasoning. Chill, but do not let it set.

Line individual molds with a large slice of truffle surrounded with slices of hard-cooked egg. Add a spoonful of the jelly mixture and let it set. Arrange the cooked shrimp in the molds in an even design. Place another slice of truffle in the center and cover with more jelly. Chill.

Clean the asparagus and cook in boiling salted water until just barely tender. Drain and cool. Arrange in a half sunburst of a large platter and garnish with strips of pimiento. Unmold the aspics and arrange them on the platter. Serve with mayonnaise.

SHRIMP BOATS

1½ pounds shrimp
    Court bouillon (see index)
2 cloves garlic
¼ cup olive oil

3 avocados
    Russian dressing (see index)

Shell and de-vein the shrimp. Prepare the court bouillon and poach the shrimp for 4 minutes. Cool.

Crush the garlic in a mortar or chop exceedingly fine and combine with the olive oil. Cut the avocados in half and remove the pits. Dress each one with a little of the oil and garlic mixture. Fill the centers with cold shrimp and serve with a Russian dressing.

PICKLED SHRIMP

These may be prepared with either shelled or unshelled shrimp and may be kept for quite a while in the refrigerator if you store them in covered fruit jars. They are exceedingly good with beer, with cocktails, and make a wonderful late evening snack with a bottle of chilled white wine. I like heavy rye or pumpernickel bread with them.

For 3 pounds of shrimp you will need 1 cup of wine vinegar (the white is better, but the red does add color), a cup of either olive oil or peanut oil, 2 cups of wine (white or red, depending upon the vinegar you use), a like amount of water, and a bouquet garni of 2 leeks or large green onions cut in pieces, 2 or 3 hot red peppers, a handful of parsley, some celery leaves, 6 to 8 whole peppercorns, 2 or 3 cloves, a sprig of fresh tarragon or a teaspoon of the dried, a sprig of thyme, a tablespoon of brown sugar, and a piece of stick cinnamon.

Cook this bouillon all together for about 15 minutes after it has started to simmer. Add the shrimp and cook 5 more minutes. Let the shrimp cool in the broth and store in jars until you wish to use them.

Scampi—Hot Shrimp Hors d'oeuvre

SCAMPI FRITTI

2 pounds shrimp	Flour
Butter	Salt, pepper
2 eggs	Paprika

Shell and de-vein the shrimp, leaving the tails on. Melt 5 tablespoons of butter in a skillet. Dip the shrimp in beaten egg, then in flour, and then in egg again. Fry in the butter until nicely browned. Season to taste and serve with a sauce rémoulade (see index) or a barbecue sauce (see index).

FRENCH-FRIED SHRIMP

2 pounds shrimp	Salt, pepper
1 teaspoon curry powder	Corn meal
1 teaspoon chili powder	3 eggs, beaten

Heat fat in your automatic fryer or deep fryer to 365°. Shell and de-vein the shrimp, leaving the tails on. Mix the seasonings with the corn meal. Beat the eggs. Dip the shrimp in the eggs and then roll in the corn meal. Fry a few at a time in the hot fat. Drain on absorbent paper. Serve with moutard mayonnaise (see index).

SHRIMP STRAWS PEKINESE

1 pound shrimp	2 egg whites
¼ pound fresh ginger	Slices of stale bread
1 large onion	Crumbs
Salt, pepper	Deep fat for frying

Shell and clean the shrimp and chop very fine. Peel and chop the ginger and onion very fine. Mix the shrimp and vegetables together, season to taste, and moisten with egg whites. Spread the mixture on stale bread cut into fingers. Dip in fine crumbs and fry in fat heated to 375° for 3 minutes. Drain on absorbent paper.

BUTTERFLY SHRIMP

2 pounds shrimp	Soft bread crumbs
2 eggs, beaten	Soy sauce
¾ cup milk	Mustard
Kumquat chutney	

Heat the fat in your French fryer to 360°. Shell and de-vein the shrimp, leaving the tails on. Split them almost in two and flatten them out. Beat the eggs with the milk. Dip the shrimp in the eggs and milk, then in the crumbs, and fry 2½ to 3 minutes, or until brown. Drain on absorbent paper. Serve with bowls of soy sauce, hot mustard, and kumquat chutney.

TEMPURA

2 pounds shrimp	1 cup sifted flour
2 eggs	1 tablespoon soy sauce
¾ cup beer	1 teaspoon mustard
1 tablespoon olive oil	Flour

Heat the fat in your French fryer to 365° or slightly over. Shell and de-vein the shrimp, leaving the tails intact. Separate the eggs, and beat the yolks with the beer, the oil, the flour and the seasonings and blend well. Beat the whites until stiff and fold them in. Dip the shrimp in flour and then into the egg batter. Lower them into the frying basket by spoonfuls. Cook 4 minutes. Drain on absorbent paper and serve with soy sauce and hot mustard. Thin slices of large white radish go well with this.

VARIATION

Wrap the shrimp in half slices of bacon.

SHRIMP FRITTERS

1 pound shrimp	½ teaspoon salt
3 cups chopped parsley	3 teaspoons baking powder
1 tablespoon fresh dill	2 eggs, well beaten
1 cup flour	½ cup milk
Dash of tabasco sauce	

Cook and clean the shrimp. Chop them and mix with chopped parsley and dill. Sift the dry ingredients, add the beaten eggs and the milk and mix until smooth. Combine with the shrimp and herbs and add a dash of tabasco sauce. Drop by spoonfuls into shortening heated to 380°. Fry until brown and crisp. Drain on absorbent paper. Serve as a first course. If you serve these as a cocktail snack, drop them from a small teaspoon into the fat.

BROILED BARBECUED SHRIMP

2 pounds shrimp	2 cloves garlic
1 cup olive oil	1 tablespoon tomato sauce
1 teaspoon salt	or chili sauce
3 tablespoons chopped parsley	1 teaspoon freshly ground
1 tablespoon basil	pepper

1 tablespoon wine vinegar

Shell and de-vein the shrimp, but leave the tails on. Make a sauce by mixing all the other ingredients together. Arrange the shrimp in a shallow pan—9 by 14 inches—and pour the sauce over them. Marinate for several hours. Broil for 5 to 8 minutes under a brisk flame. Arrange the shrimp on a serving dish or serve them in the broiling pan. You eat them by picking them up by the tail and dipping them into the hot sauce, so plates and plenty of paper napkins are needed with this dish.

BROILED SHRIMP ITALIAN

½ cup olive oil	1 cup tomato puree
2 pounds large shrimp	1 teaspoon salt
2 cloves garlic, chopped	1 teaspoon dry mustard
¼ pound Italian ham—	1 teaspoon oregano
prosciutto	1 teaspoon black pepper

½ cup red wine

Shell and clean the shrimp, leaving the tails intact. Heat the olive oil in a skillet and add the garlic. Sauté it gently without browning. Add the shredded ham and cook 2 minutes. Add the tomato puree, the seasonings and the red wine and blend well. Cool. Arrange the shrimp in a 9 by 14 inch pan and pour the sauce over them. Marinate for 2 hours. Broil in the sauce for about 7 to 9 minutes.

BROILED SHRIMP

2 pounds shrimp	1 tablespoon lemon juice
2 cloves garlic	3 tablespoons chopped
½ cup peanut oil	parsley
¼ cup soy sauce	¼ cup chili sauce

Shell and de-vein the shrimp, leaving the tails on. Press the garlic or chop it very fine and mix with the other ingredients. Marinate the shrimp in this mixture for 2 hours. Broil in the sauce for 7 or 8 minutes.

VARIATION

Leave the shells on the shrimp and let them soak in the marinade for 2 hours. Arrange them in a grill or on skewers and grill over or under coals or under a broiling unit. They should broil in about 5 minutes. Serve with plenty of napkins and plates, of course. Heat the marinade separately to be used as a dip, and let each person shell his own shrimp and dip them in the sauce.

WINE SCAMPI

2 pounds shrimp	1 clove garlic, minced
3 tablespoons butter	3 tablespoons white wine
	Salt, pepper

Shell and de-vein the shrimp. Melt the butter and add the garlic and wine. Place the shrimp on a flameproof dish and pour the garlic-wine butter over them. Salt and pepper to taste and broil for 5 minutes.

SHRIMP EN BROCHETTE

Any of the preceding recipes for broiling may be used for broiling *en brochette*. Remove the shrimp from the marinade and arrange them on the skewers. Brush them with oil or butter and broil for about 5 minutes. Heat the sauce separately and serve it as a dip.

SHRIMP AND MUSHROOMS EN BROCHETTE

Alternate large shrimp and mushrooms on a brochette. Salt and pepper and brush well with olive oil or butter. Broil about 5 minutes.

HELEN EVANS BROWN'S STUFFED
BROILED SHRIMP

Shell and clean the shrimp and cut them almost in half—as for butterfly shrimp. Poach them in court bouillon (see index). Place an anchovy fillet between the halves of each shrimp and press them together tightly. Wrap each shrimp in half a slice of bacon. Arrange 3 to 5 of these shrimp on a skewer and bake in a moderate oven or broil until the bacon is crisp. Serve as a first course with broiled tomato or with a cucumber salad.

Shrimp as a Main Course

SHRIMP IN CREAM

Shell and de-vein 2 pounds of shrimp and cook for 3 minutes in salted water. Prepare a shellfish velouté or béchamel (see index) and combine with the cooked shrimp. Heat until the fish is hot through and the flavors are blended. Serve with croustades, toast, patty shells, or vol au vent. Garnish with finely chopped hard-cooked egg.

SHRIMP WIGGLE

This dish, which used to be the delight of the chafing dish and the stand-by of the girls' dormitory, can be very delightful if correctly prepared.

Combine 1 large can of French peas (*petits pois*), which have been heated with 4 tablespoons of butter and 1 teaspoon of onion juice, with the recipe above for shrimps in cream. Use the liquid from the peas in preparing the velouté or béchamel.

SHRIMP SAUTE IN CREAM

2 pounds shrimp	Salt, pepper
Flour	1 tablespoon minced onion
3 tablespoons butter	1 tablespoon minced parsley
3 tablespoons olive oil	1 tablespoon minced tarragon

1½ cups heavy cream

Shell and de-vein the shrimp. Dredge them with flour. Melt the butter, add the oil, and sauté the shrimp until lightly browned and cooked through—about 3 or 4 minutes. Salt and pepper to taste. Add the seasonings and toss with the shrimp. Gradually pour in the cream, stirring carefully, and continue stirring until the sauce is thickened and thoroughly blended.

VARIATION

When the sauce is slightly thickened, pour the mixture into an ovenproof serving dish and sprinkle with 4 ounces of grated Switzerland Gruyère or good Cheddar cheese. Run under the broiler to melt the cheese and glaze the top.

SHRIMP NEWBURG

Follow directions for lobster Newburg.

SHRIMP A L'AMERICAINE

Follow directions for lobster à l'Américaine.

SHRIMP CREOLE

2 pounds shrimp	1 carrot
2 pounds tomatoes	⅓ cup olive oil
2 green peppers	Bouquet garni (thyme, parsley, fennel)
3 stalks celery	
3 cloves garlic	1 cup white wine
2 onions	½ cup tomato puree

Salt, pepper

Shell and clean the shrimp and keep the shells. Seed and chop the tomatoes and the green peppers. Cut the celery, garlic, onions, and carrot fine. Heat the olive oil in a large kettle and add the garlic and onion and brown lightly. Add the tomatoes, the shrimp shells, the peppers, celery, carrot, bouquet garni, and wine. Cover and simmer for 1 hour. Strain through a fine sieve with the aid of a wooden spoon, or put through a puree machine. Add the tomato puree and season to taste.

Return to the stove and bring to a boil. Add the shrimp and let them cook for 5 minutes in the sauce. Serve with rice prepared in your favorite fashion. This will serve 6 people.

NEW ORLEANS SHRIMP CREOLE

4 tablespoons butter	2 cups stewed or canned
2 onions, finely chopped	tomatoes
3 green peppers, finely chopped	1 teaspoon paprika
1 clove garlic, finely chopped	Salt, pepper
1½ pounds shrimp	

Melt the butter in a large skillet or Dutch oven. Add the onions, peppers and garlic and cook slowly until tender. Add the tomatoes and simmer for 30 minutes. Add the paprika, season to taste, add the shrimp, shelled and cleaned, and cook for 5 minutes. Serve with rice.

JAMBALAYA WITH SHRIMP

I have found that a great many of the recipes for jambalaya do not specify ham. Evidently almost any type of smoked meat was considered *jambon* in the old days.

4 tablespoons butter, lard, or	2 cups cooked or canned
bacon fat	tomatoes
2 tablespoons flour	Salt, pepper
3 onions, chopped	2 pounds shrimp
1 clove garlic, chopped	2 cups rice
¼ pound ham, cut in strips	
3 cups liquid (water, broth, or	
fish stock)	

Melt the fat in a large Dutch oven and blend in the flour. Add the onions, garlic and ham and cook just until the onion grows translucent. Add the tomatoes and cook them down for a few minutes. Salt and pepper to taste.

Shell and clean the shrimp. Wash the rice well and add with the shrimp to the sauce. Pour over it enough boiling water or stock to cover 1 inch above. Cover and simmer until the rice is cooked. It may be necessary to add more liquid as the rice cooks.

VARIATIONS

1. Some recipes omit the tomatoes and use more stock or liquid.

2. Some recipes include chili powder or gumbo file.

3. I prefer to add the shrimp during the last 5 minutes of cooking time when I make this dish. It is my opinion that the seafood is overcooked in the original recipe.

CHINESE SAUTEED SHRIMP WITH GINGER

½ cup peanut oil
1 piece ginger root
1 large onion
2 pounds shrimp

4 tablespoons soy sauce
2 tablespoons sugar
2 tablespoons sherry
½ cup water

Salt, pepper (if needed)

Heat the oil in a large skillet and brown the peeled and sliced ginger. Add the chopped onion and cook for a few minutes. Add the shelled and cleaned shrimp and fry about 4 minutes. Pour off most of the oil, add the soy sauce, sugar, wine, and a little water and cook until well blended. Taste for seasonings. Serve with rice.

FRIED RICE WITH SHRIMP

This Chinese recipe resembles jambalaya and is an interesting contrast. Which came first, no one knows.

⅓ cup peanut oil
½ cup diced celery
½ cup sliced water chestnuts
½ cup finely cut green onions
1 tablespoon chopped green pepper
3 tablespoons chopped Chinese parsley or curly parsley
3 cups cooked rice

½ cup finely shredded smoked or Chinese ham
Salt, pepper (or soy sauce and mustard)
1½ cups cooked shrimp
2 tablespoons butter
4 eggs
2 tablespoons water

Heat the oil in a large skillet and add all the vegetables. Sauté quickly for a few minutes. Add the rice and ham and mix well, adding more oil, if it is needed. Season to taste with salt and pepper, or soy sauce and mustard. Add the shrimp and simmer until heated through and well blended.

Melt the butter in a saucepan. Beat the eggs with 2 tablespoons of water and make a pancake of them. Cut the pancake into fine strips and top the rice-ham-shrimp dish with them.

SHRIMP AND CABBAGE SOUP

If you cannot get Chinese cabbage for this Chinese dish, buy a tender head of young cabbage.

2 cups shredded cabbage	Salt
½ cup shredded pork or ham	½ pound shelled shrimp
1 quart water	¼ cup sherry

Boil the cabbage and pork in the water for 15 minutes. Add salt to taste and the shrimp and simmer for 5 more minutes. Add sherry and serve.

PEKINESE FRIED NOODLES WITH SHRIMP
(HSIA JEN CHAO'MIEN)

This is not just an ordinary chow mein from the neighborhood chop suey house. It is an authentic old recipe from Peiping.

8 ounces fine Chinese noodles	½ cup soy sauce
4 tablespoons peanut oil	½ cup sherry
1 pound small shrimp	2 teaspoons sugar
1 ounce ginger root	6 tablespoons peanut oil

Cook the noodles in boiling salted water for 10 to 12 minutes. Drain and steam them over hot water for 3 minutes. Dry on a clean towel.

Heat 4 tablespoons of peanut oil in a large skillet and sauté the shelled and cleaned shrimp for 2 minutes. Add ¼ cup of soy sauce, ½ cup of sherry, and 1 teaspoon of sugar and cook for 1 minute more. Remove from the pan and keep warm.

Put 6 tablespoons of peanut oil in the pan and add the noodles. Stir them around and let them brown well. Add the remaining ingredients and the shrimp. Cook very briskly for 2 minutes.

SHRIMPS SWEET AND SOUR

2 pounds shrimp	⅔ cup pineapple cubes
Flour	1 large tomato, cut in
Beaten egg	eighths
Crumbs or corn meal	½ cup sugar
8 tablespoons olive or peanut	½ cup vinegar
oil	1 teaspoon dry mustard
3 green onions	¼ cup sherry
1 large green pepper	2 teaspoons soy sauce
1½ tablespoons cornstarch	

Shell and clean the shrimp. Dredge them in flour, dip in beaten egg, and roll in crumbs or corn meal. Sauté in the hot oil for about 4 or 5 minutes. Remove to a hot platter. Add the onions and green pepper cut in shreds, the pineapple cubes, and the tomato eighths. Mix the sugar and vinegar, add to the pan and bring it to a boil. Add the sherry and mustard mixed, and the soy sauce. Mix the cornstarch with a little water and stir it unto the sauce. Continue stirring until it is thickened and transparent. Pour the sauce over the shrimp and serve with rice.

SHRIMP DE JONGHE

No one seems to know where this dish originated, but it is very popular in the South and parts of the Middle West.

2 cloves garlic	Pinch each of nutmeg,
1 teaspoon each of chopped parsley, chopped chervil, chopped shallots, chopped tarragon	mace, freshly ground black pepper
	¼ pound butter
	⅔ cup bread crumbs
Salt	½ cup dry sherry

2 pounds shrimp

Crush the garlic with a fork and gradually work it and the other seasonings into the butter. Work in the crumbs and sherry.

Shell and clean the shrimp and cook in boiling salted water for 3 minutes. Butter 6 to 8 ramekins or individual baking dishes. Arrange layers of the shrimp and the herbed crumb mixture alternately in the ramekins. Top with buttered crumbs and bake in a 400° oven for 10 to 15 minutes.

PAIN DE CREVETTES—SHRIMP LOAF

1 pound shelled shrimp	½ cup heavy cream
1 teaspoon salt	1 whole egg
½ teaspoon freshly ground pepper	2 egg yolks
2 cups cold, thick sauce béchamel (see index)	Pinch of nutmeg

For this recipe you will need 1 pound of shelled raw shrimp, which should be about 1½ pounds of shrimp before shelling. Clean the shrimp, grind them twice, and pound them in a mortar or work them with a heavy wooden spoon. They must be thoroughly mashed and as smooth as possible. Add the salt, pepper, béchamel sauce, cream, egg, egg yolks, and nutmeg. Blend thoroughly and force through a fine sieve.

Pour the mixture into a buttered mold, place the mold in a pan of hot water, and bake at 350° for 25 to 30 minutes, or until the mixture is set. Unmold on a hot platter, decorate with whole cooked shrimp, and serve with a Hollandaise sauce or a shrimp sauce (see index).

This recipe will serve 6 people amply.

SHRIMP POLENTA

Polenta is an Italian and Southern French version of our old-fashioned corn-meal mush. It is actually a European adaptation of an original American dish with a Creole and perhaps a Mexican background.

2 pounds shrimp	1 cup yellow corn meal
2 slices salt pork	6 tomatoes
2 tablespoons butter	1½ teaspoons salt
1 onion	2 tablespoons chili powder
1 green pepper	⅔ cup grated cheese—
4 cups boiling water	Cheddar or Jack
	cheese

Shell and de-vein the shrimp. Try out the salt pork until crisp. Peel and chop the tomatoes and cook with 2 tablespoons of butter for 25 to 30 minutes. Peel and chop the onion. Seed and chop the green pepper.

Stir 1 cup of boiling water into the corn meal, and when it boils add the remaining 3 cups and salt to taste. Let it simmer for 10 minutes, stirring constantly to keep it smooth. Add the salt pork, onion, green pepper, tomatoes, and chili powder and cook over hot water for 20 minutes.

Butter an earthenware casserole well. Place a thin layer of the polenta in the bottom, then a layer of shrimp and a slight sprinkling of cheese. Repeat this pattern until all the ingredients are used, but be sure that the top layer in the casserole is polenta. Sprinkle with cheese and dot well with butter. Bake in a 350° oven for 20 to 25 minutes. Serve with a well-seasoned tomato sauce, spiked with additional chili.

SHRIMP CURRY

2 pounds shrimp	2 cloves garlic, finely
Court bouillon (see index)	chopped
1 onion, finely chopped	3 tablespoons butter
1 green pepper, finely chopped	1 tablespoon curry powder
	1 teaspoon cumin

Beurre manié (see index)

Shell and de-vein the shrimp and keep the shells to use in the bouillon. Prepare a court bouillon, add the shells and shrimp and cook for 5 minutes. Remove the shrimp and reduce the broth one half.

Sauté the onion, pepper, and garlic in the butter until just soft, but not browned. Add the curry powder and the cumin and blend well. If the curry powder is too bland, spike it with a little cayenne or Jamaica ginger.

Strain the bouillon and add it to the curry mixture. Taste for seasoning. If you wish a thickened sauce, add beurre manié. Add the shrimp and cook just long enough to heat through. Serve with rice pilaff, crisp fried onions, and chutney.

SHRIMP CURRY MANCHURIAN

2 pounds shrimp	½ cup tomato puree
2 pounds tomatoes	Salt
2 cloves garlic	2 tablespoons curry powder
2 onions	6 bananas
4 tablespoons olive oil	Butter
Brown sugar	

Shell and de-vein the shrimp. Peel, seed, and chop the tomatoes. Peel and chop the garlic and onions very fine. Sauté the onions and garlic in the olive oil until soft but not browned. Add the tomatoes and simmer for 1 hour. Add the tomato puree and salt to taste. Continue cooking for 20 minutes. Add the curry powder and strain through a fine sieve. Taste for seasoning. If the sauce is too thick, dilute it with a little broth or white wine.

Peel the bananas, place them in a baking dish, dot with butter, and sprinkle lightly with brown sugar. Bake in a 375° oven for 15 minutes, or until soft and delicately browned.

About 10 minutes before serving, add the shrimp to the sauce, bring it to the boiling point and simmer for 5 minutes. Serve with the baked bananas. Rice pilaff and crisp onion rings go with this, and grated coconut and chopped peanuts make wonderful additions.

QUICK SHRIMP CURRY

6 tablespoons butter	2 tablespoons chopped parsley
2 tablespoons finely chopped shallots or green onions	2 teaspoons curry powder
2 cups cooked shrimp	½ cup heavy cream
	Salt

Melt the butter in a skillet and cook the shallots until just transparent. Add the cooked shrimp and toss to brown lightly. Add the parsley, the curry powder and the cream. Salt to taste and simmer for 3 minutes. Serve on rice, in croustades, or in bouchées. Baked bananas and chutney go well with this dish.

NOTE: Serve this mixture in small bite-size bouchées at cocktail time. It is a delightful surprise.

SHRIMP AND MUSHROOM SAUTE POLONAISE

1 pound shrimp	¼ cup chopped parsley
1 pound mushrooms	¼ cup sherry or Madeira
6 to 8 shallots	Salt, pepper
4 tablespoons butter	Paprika
2 tablespoons olive oil	1 cup sour cream

Shell and de-vein the shrimp. Remove the stems from the mushrooms. Peel and chop the shallots.

Melt the butter, add the oil and sauté the shallots for 2 minutes. Add the mushrooms and sauté gently for 10 minutes, tossing them frequently. Add the parsley and wine. Let it come to the boiling point and add the shrimp. Cook for 4 to 5 minutes, or until the shrimp turn pink. Season to taste with salt, pepper, and paprika. Stir in the sour cream and heat thoroughly but do not boil. Serve with a rice pilaff or with kasha.

VARIATION

Omit the mushrooms and add more shrimp.

SHRIMP AND ASPARAGUS MORNAY

2 pounds shrimp	24 large asparagus tips, or
Court bouillon	36 medium ones
1½ cups sauce béchamel	2 egg yolks
(made with fish stock)	½ cup grated Switzerland
Salt	Gruyère cheese
Few grains cayenne	3 tablespoons heavy cream

Shell and clean the shrimp. Cook in a court bouillon (see index) for 3 to 5 minutes. Remove to a hot dish. Reduce the bouillon to 1 cup and strain. Prepare a sauce béchamel (see index) using the fish broth and a little milk. You will need about 1½ cups of sauce. Season to taste with salt and cayenne.

Cook the asparagus tips and arrange them on the bottom of a large oval baking dish. Top with the shrimp. Combine the sauce with the egg yolks and the cheese and heat until the cheese is melted. *Do not let it boil.* Add the cream and pour over the shrimp, but leave the tip ends of the asparagus uncovered. Top with additional grated cheese, run under the broiler to brown, and serve at once.

VARIATION

This may be prepared with broccoli instead of asparagus.

SHRIMP FLORENTINE

1 pound shrimp	4 egg yolks, slightly beaten
1 package frozen chopped spinach	Salt, pepper
	Pinch of nutmeg
2 tablespoons butter	2 teaspoons chopped parsley
2 tablespoons flour	2 teaspoons minced onion
2 cups milk	¼ cup grated Parmesan cheese

Shell and clean the shrimp and cook in boiling salted water for 3 to 5 minutes. Cook spinach according to the directions on the package. Melt the butter in a saucepan. Stir in the flour and make a smooth paste. Gradually add the milk and continue stirring until the sauce thickens. Add the egg yolks and heat the mixture through, but do not let it boil. Season to taste, and add the nutmeg, parsley and onion. Butter 4 individual casseroles and place a layer of spinach in the bottom of each one. Add a layer of shrimp and pour the sauce over the top. Sprinkle with grated Parmesan cheese. Bake in a 400° oven for about 10 minutes, or brown under the broiler flame.

SHRIMP AND CORN SAUTE

This is a delicious dish to make in the summer when fresh corn is in season.

1 finely chopped green pepper	1½ cups cooked shelled shrimp
4 to 6 tablespoons butter	½ cup heavy cream
1½ cups corn kernels	Salt, pepper

Paprika

Sauté the green pepper in the butter. Add the corn and let it heat through. Add the shrimp and the cream and mix thoroughly. Cover the pan and let it simmer for 3 or 4 minutes. Season to taste with salt, freshly ground black pepper, and paprika.

FRENCH-FRIED SHRIMP LOAF

1 pound loaf of unsliced bread (Italian, French, or regular)
¼ pound butter
1 clove garlic
French-fried shrimp (see index)

Curry or Hollandaise sauce or Russian or Louis dressing with greens, olives, pickles

Cut the top off the loaf of bread and scoop out the center, leaving a wall about ½ inch thick. Brush well with butter mixed with chopped or pressed garlic. Toast in a slow oven until nicely browned and crisp, but not hard.

Fry the shrimp and stuff the loaf with them, using a little additional melted butter if needed.

This dish may be served hot with a curry or Hollandaise sauce (see index) or cold on a bed of greens with an olive and pickle garnish, and Russian or Louis dressing (see index).

Shrimp Salads

SHRIMP SALAD I

Shell and clean 2 pounds of shrimp. Cook in a court bouillon (see index) for 5 minutes. Remove and chill. Combine with a well-seasoned mayonnaise and arrange in a bowl lined with greens. Garnish with sliced hard-cooked eggs and onion rings.

VARIATION

Add walnut halves.

SHRIMP SALAD II

Combine cooked, chilled shrimp with greens in a salad bowl and toss with a sauce vinaigrette (see index) well-flavored with dry mustard.

377

Make beds of shredded lettuce or other greens on salad

1. Shrimp may be added to any tossed salad.

2. Combine shrimps with anchovy fillets and toss with greens. Dress with an olive oil dressing heavily laced with garlic.

SHRIMP AND ORANGE SALAD

Combine cooked, chilled shrimp with orange sections and onion rings and toss with a sauce vinaigrette (see index). Serve on romaine or endive.

OLD-FASHIONED SHRIMP SALAD

I remember from childhood the shrimp salad that was always served at our family's favorite resort hotel. Its sauce was, I realize now, a true old-fashioned boiled dressing.

Combine 2 cups of broken pieces of cooked, chilled shrimp with 2 cups of finely chopped cabbage. Dress with a boiled dressing and add a little sour cream. Let it stand for 1 hour.

SHRIMP LOUIS

plates. Top with cooked, chilled shrimp. Dress with a Louis dressing (see index), and decorate with tomato wedges and quartered hard-cooked eggs.

I think that the smaller shrimp are much better for this dish than the larger varieties.

SHRIMP SALAD EDWARDIAN

Marinate 2 cups of cooked shrimp in a vinaigrette sauce (see index) heavily flavored with dill. Let it stand for 2 hours. Drain, and combine with 1 cup of finely cut celery, 2 tablespoons of grated onion and enough mayonnaise to bind the salad. Serve with asparagus tips and quartered hard-cooked eggs.

TERRESTRIAL ANIMALS
PREPARED LIKE FISH

Frogs' Legs

THERE are plenty of wild frogs in this country for people who enjoy the sport of catching and skinning them. Fortunately for most of us, frogs are also grown commercially in the Middle West and in Florida, Louisiana and California. Besides our native product, we receive some frogs' legs shipped frozen from Japan.

Frogs' legs come in many sizes—for my taste the small ones are by far the best. They are delicately flavored, tender, and cook very quickly. About 6 pairs of the small sort are a good portion.

Frogs' legs are better if soaked in milk for an hour or more before cooking.

FROGS' LEGS SAUTE

Sautéeing is by far the most common way of preparing frogs' legs. There are a number of variations, but the general procedure is the same. It's a good idea to use half butter and half olive oil. The oil prevents burning and adds a great deal of flavor to the frogs' legs.

Use one or two good-sized spatulas to turn the legs. They are very tender and are apt to stick to the pan. Cook them quickly—they need only about 5 minutes. Flavor them at the last, just before serving.

For a plain sauté, soak frogs' legs in milk for an hour or more. Dry them on a towel, then roll in flour and sauté very quickly in butter and olive oil mixed, turning them so that they become delicately browned on all sides. Salt and pepper to taste and serve with lemon wedges.

FROGS' LEGS SAUTE FINES HERBES

Soak the frogs' legs in milk. Dry on a clean towel and roll in flour. Chop parsley, chives and tarragon very fine and add

381

to toasted buttered bread crumbs. (For four people use 1 cup of crumbs and 2 tablespoons each of the herbs.)

Melt butter and olive oil in a skillet. Saute the legs very quickly and when they are nicely browned, add the herbed crumbs. Mix these well with the frogs' legs, salt and pepper to taste, and serve with lemon wedges.

FROGS' LEGS SAUTE PROVENCALE

Soak the frogs' legs in milk, dry and roll them in flour. Sauté them very quickly in olive oil (omitting the butter). When nicely browned, add chopped garlic and parsley and blend well. (Use about 1 clove of garlic for each portion. Plenty of parsley, of course.) Salt and pepper to taste.

FROGS' LEGS SAUTE NICOISE

Follow the recipe for sauté Provençale (see above). For each person, peel, seed and chop one tomato. Cook the tomatoes down in butter until they are a paste. Add a spoonful or so of this paste to each serving of frogs' legs.

FROGS' LEGS SAUTE ITALIENNE

Soak the frogs' legs in milk, dry them, and roll them in flour. Sauté in olive oil. Just before they are done, add mushrooms and onion, very finely chopped, to the pan. Salt and pepper to taste and serve sprinkled with chopped parsley.

DEVILED FROGS' LEGS

Soak the frogs' legs in milk and dry them. Roll them in flour, dip them in beaten egg, and roll in crumbs. Sauté in butter and olive oil. When nicely browned remove from the pan. Add salt, pepper, lemon juice, dry mustard, Worcestershire sauce and a dash of brandy or whiskey to the pan. Swirl it around and mix well. Pour this sauce over the frogs' legs.

FROGS' LEGS POULETTE

Poach frogs' legs for about 5 minutes in just enough white

wine to cover them. Serve with a sauce poulette (see index), using some of the white wine broth as a base.

WILLIAM PALMER'S FROGS' LEGS VINAIGRETTE

For this dish you really must have the small frogs' legs. Use about 3 pairs per serving as a first course at dinner or as a main luncheon course.

Poach the legs in a light court bouillon (see index) for about 5 minutes. Or poach them in a mixture of half white wine and half water. Season to taste with salt and pepper. Chill.

Serve on romaine or lettuce leaves and top with the following very highly seasoned sauce vinaigrette:

For 4 servings:

1 cup olive oil	½ teaspoon dry mustard
¼ cup wine vinegar, or half vinegar and half lemon juice	¼ teaspoon oregano
	1 tablespoon chopped shallot or green onion
½ teaspoon salt	1 tomato, peeled, seeded and finely chopped
½ teaspoon freshly ground pepper	1 tablespoon capers
3 tablespoons chopped parsley	

Mix all together thoroughly. You may add anything you choose to this sauce—chopped pickle, hard-cooked egg, chopped olives. Spoon the sauce over the frogs' legs.

SOUTHERN-FRIED FROGS' LEGS

Soak the frogs' legs in milk. Roll them in flour, dip in the milk again, and roll in dry bread crumbs or cracker crumbs. Melt 6 tablespoons of butter and 5 tablespoons of oil in a large skillet. Sauté the frogs' legs quickly in the hot fat and when nicely browned, remove them to a hot platter. Pour off all but 4 tablespoons of the fat. Combine this with 4 tablespoons of flour and mix it well, being sure to scrape up all the bits of brown from the pan. Add 1½ cups of light cream and stir until thickened. Season to taste with salt and pepper and pour over the frogs' legs or serve separately.

VARIATION

Add 3 tablespoons of sherry or Madeira to the sauce just before pouring over the frogs' legs.

383

FRIED FROGS' LEGS I

Soak frogs' legs in milk for 30 minutes. Roll in flour, dip in beaten egg and milk, and roll in crumbs. Heat deep fat for frying to 370°. Fry the legs for 2 minutes or until brown. Remove to absorbent paper and sprinkle with salt and pepper. Serve with lemon or with tartar sauce (see index).

FRIED FROGS' LEGS II

Soak frogs' legs in milk for 30 minutes. Dip them in beer batter (see index). Fry in deep fat heated to 375° for 3 or 4 minutes or until brown and crisp. Drain on absorbent paper and serve with a sauce rémoulade (see index) or a tartar sauce (see index).

NOTE: It is my opinion that frying frogs' legs robs them of their delicate flavor and their delightful juiciness. I much prefer one of the methods for sautéing, frogs' legs poulette, or Wililam Palmer's recipe with the vinaigrette sauce.

Snails

SNAILS can be terrestial, fresh-water, or marine. The terrestial variety, which is the most commonly eaten, is admittedly not a shellfish, but a land-loving vegetarian. It is included in this book because it is similar in many ways to the sea snail, or periwinkle, and because all snails, whether native to land or water, may be cooked by the same recipes.

Some people are revolted even by the thought of eating snails. Usually such people have never tasted them. Addiction to snails is growing. Lately I have been pleasantly surprised at the number of my friends and acquaintances who tell me that they have become snail enthusiasts.

Most snails eaten in this country come canned, accompanied by a bag of polished shells so that they may be served in the approved way. Moroccan and Tunisian snails are available fresh in the markets, along with a smaller quantity of periwinkles.

French cook books give startling directions for cooking snails, and some of the French dishes take days or even weeks to achieve. Complicated procedure is not necessary for preparing and cooking the fresh snails found in American markets. Soak them in warm water just long enough to break the membrane that covers the shell. Any snails that do not emerge should be discarded. The remaining snails should be brought to a boil in salted water or court bouillon. They can then be used in several fashions.

SNAILS BOURGUIGNONNE WITH CANNED SNAILS

1 cup creamed butter
½ cup minced parsley

3 or 4 garlic cloves, minced
Salt to taste

Cream the above ingredients together to make a beurre d'escargots (snail butter). Rinse the snails with ½ cup of white wine. Butter the inside of each shell lightly. Insert a snail and cover the entrance of the shell with the snail butter. Arrange on snail platters or on a large baking sheet, and let them stand for several hours before you cook them, if you have the time. About 10 minutes before serving, place the snails in a 450° oven and let them heat through thoroughly. Serve with plenty of good crisp French bread and white wine.

VARIATION

Prepare the snails as above and add ½ cup of white wine to the pan in which you cook them.

SNAILS LASSERE

48 mushroom caps (medium
    size, about 1 inch across)
6 tablespoons butter

Snail butter (see above)
⅔ cup walnuts
48 snails

Fried toasts

Sauté the mushroom caps in butter until just slightly tender. Prepare the snail butter. Chop the walnut meats coarsely. Arrange the mushrooms, cup side up, on a baking sheet. Place a snail in each mushroom cup, cover with a little snail butter, and sprinkle with chopped nuts. Cook in a 400° oven for about 10 minutes, or until thoroughly heated through. Serve on fried toasts.

SNAILS BOURGUIGNONNE WITH FRESH SNAILS

Soak the snails until they come out of their shells and put

them in salted water or court bouillon. After you have brought this to a boil, remove them from their shells, and rinse them with a little cold water or white wine. Wash the shells, and then follow the preceding recipe for canned snails.

FRESH SNAILS POULETTE

Snails	2 cloves garlic
White wine and water mixed	6 tablespoons butter
1 large onion stuck with	2 tablespoons butter
2 cloves	3 tablespoons flour
1 bay leaf	½ cup heavy cream
Pinch of thyme	3 egg yolks
3 medium onions	1 tablespoon lemon juice

¼ cup chopped parsley

Prepare the fresh snails as for snails Bourguignonne with fresh snails (see index). After you have removed them from the boiling salted water, transfer them to a mixture of half white wine and half water. Add the onion stuck with cloves, the bay leaf, and the thyme. Bring to a boil and simmer for 35 to 40 minutes. Sauté the onions and garlic, finely chopped, in 6 tablespoons of butter until they are soft but not browned. When the snails are tender, remove them from the bouillon, and keep them hot in their shells in a hot serving dish.

Remove the large onion and the bay leaf from the bouillon and taste for seasoning. Add the sautéed onions, bring to a boil, and simmer for 15 minutes. Make beurre manié by kneading 2 tablespoons of butter with 3 tablespoons of flour. Mix the heavy cream with the egg yolks, and add the beurre manié and the cream-egg mixture to the broth. Stir until well blended and thickened, but do not let it boil. Add lemon juice and chopped parsley and pour over the snails. Serve with plenty of hot French bread.

Turtle, Tortoise and Terrapin

TURTLES come in many different sorts, sizes and colors, and once the word *turtle* covered all of them. Now some people restrict the term just to the sea turtles. A *tortoise* is a turtle that prefers the land, and a *terrapin* is a variety of turtle that inhabits rivers and coastal swamps along the Eastern seaboard and Gulf.

386

Green turtle is the most famous of sea turtles and the turtle soup that comes from it is extraordinary. If you have never tasted thick, gelatinous turtle soup, freshly made, then you have a great treat awaiting you. The canned green turtle soup is also excellent. Look for brands with turtle fat or meat in the jar or tin; add a little Madeira or sherry to the soup, heat, and serve with a thin slice of lemon and finely chopped parsley.

Commercial fishing for green turtle is centered around Key West, and turtle steak is much fancied in the South. I have eaten it when it resembled the finest veal. Also delicious is turtle liver, which, ideally, should be sautéed in butter with shallots and parsley. Neither steaks nor liver reach the markets very often, so there is not much use longing for them.

Diamondback terrapin has always had enthusiasts in the Eastern part of the country. It was expensive even around the turn of the century—about $120 a dozen. Now it is very scarce, and red-bellied turtle is marketed in Eastern cities as a substitute. Snapper turtle, which is found all through the East in lakes, rivers and canals, is very popular in some areas, especially eastern Pennsylvania.

In the South, people like a tortoise known as a "gopher," found in high sandy areas and pine woods. Other Southern varieties include the "Suwannee chicken," caught in salty coastal waters or clear streams; the "cooter" of country ponds and marshes; the Florida peninsular turtle; the spotted pond turtle; and the box turtle of the Gulf area.

In the Mississippi Valley, "sawbuck" is eaten as a substitute for terrapin. And there are still other local varieties, such as the Pacific pond turtle and Blanding's turtle of the Great Lakes region. All have local popularity, but they are rarely obtainable commercially.

I have said that turtle steak is rare. Here is a recipe just in case you come across some or can arrange to have some sent to you by air:

TURTLE STEAK FLORIDIAN

Have 1½ pounds of turtle cut paper-thin. Pound the steaks with the edge of a plate. Dip them in flour. Melt 6 tablespoons of butter in a skillet that has a cover, and brown the pieces of turtle very quickly. Salt and pepper them to taste and add 1 tablespoon of paprika. Pour over them ½ cup of white wine, cover, and simmer for 1 hour. Remove the pieces of turtle to a hot platter. Add 1 cup of sour cream to the pan and stir well until it is heated through and blended. Pour the sauce over the turtle steaks and sprinkle with paprika and chopped parsley.

TERRAPIN MARYLAND

Terrapin is a food that people either like tremendously or dislike violently. If you can stand the rather unique odor, you may enjoy it. To me, terrapin is offensive.

For this recipe, 1 terrapin will serve 3 people.

Bring a kettle of water to a rolling boil and toss the terrapin in alive. Let it boil for 5 minutes. Remove it from the water and rub it with a coarse towel—preferably a Turkish towel—to take the skin off the feet and head. Cook it in boiling salted water until the feet fall off and the shell is cracked. Remove it from the water and place it on its back.

When it is cool enough to handle, draw the nails from the feet. Cut under the shell and remove the meat. Be careful in removing the gall bladder, the sandbags, and the large intestines. These are to be discarded. Cut the meat into 1 to 2 inch strips. Cut up the liver and the small intestines and add them to the meat. Add the eggs, if there are any. Add ¾ cup of the broth and simmer for 25 minutes. Add 4 tablespoons of butter, salt and pepper to taste, and a dash of cayenne.

Combine a little of the broth with 2 slightly beaten egg yolks and stir it in carefully. Add ¼ cup of Madeira or sherry to the mixture just before serving.

VARIATION

Terrapin, Philadelphia Style. Cut the meat very fine, add the broth and simmer for 25 minutes. Make 1 cup of velouté (page 24) with some of the broth and cream. Add this to the terrapin. Beat 2 egg yolks with ½ cup of cream, and stir this into the mixture slowly. Do not let it boil. Add sherry or Madeira just before serving. You may add 1 cup of sautéed mushrooms if you wish.

SOUTHERN TERRAPIN STEW

Boil and pick 3 terrapin according to the directions given

above. Strain and clarify the stock and add a little concentrated turtle broth to it.

Rub the yolks of 6 hard-cooked eggs through a sieve and combine them with 3 tablespoons of flour and ½ pound of butter to form a paste. Season with ¼ teaspoon of freshly grated nutmeg, 2 tablespoons of grated onion, 1 tablespoon of Worcestershire sauce, the grated rind of 1 orange, and the juice of 1 lemon. Heat 3 cups of the turtle broth until boiling, stir in the seasoned paste, reduce the heat and continue stirring until well blended. Add 1 cup of Madeira and 1 pint of heavy cream and continue stirring until the mixture is thickened and smooth. Be careful not to burn or curdle it. Add the heated terrapin eggs, the meat, and the chopped whites of the 6 hard-cooked eggs. Heat thoroughly and taste for seasoning. Serve with hot buttered toast.

TURTLE FINS

The flippers or fins of the sea turtle are excellent eating. They must be simmered in boiling water until tender and then skinned. After this initial preparation they can be prepared in various ways:

1. Dip the fins in seasoned flour, brown them in butter or oil. When they are nicely browned, add a little white wine and a pinch each of tarragon and fennel. Simmer until tender.

2. Dip in seasoned flour, brown in butter or oil. When brown add white wine and sauce à l'Américaine (see index). Simmer until tender.

3. Brown the turtle fins as above, add white wine and simmer until nearly done. At the last add a little sauce Mornay (see index), sprinkle with grated cheese and run under the broiler flame to brown.

SNAPPER TURTLE SOUP

Cut off the head of a 10-pound snapper turtle and let it bleed. Wash it thoroughly, scrubbing it with a stiff brush. Run a sharp knife around each shell, pull out the legs, pull the shells open and extract the meat.

To the shell, skin and bones of the turtle, add several veal knuckles cracked into pieces. Place this mixture in a large oven-proof pan with 1 cup of butter, 2 or 3 chopped onions, several stalks of celery, chopped, several chopped carrots, a pinch of thyme, 1 bay leaf, 4 cloves, and salt and pepper to taste. Roast in a hot oven until brown. Stir in 1 cup of flour and cook for 30 minutes longer.

Place this mixture in a large kettle, add 3 quarts of beef broth and 2 cups of canned tomatoes, strained. Simmer for 2 hours. Strain the broth. Cut the turtle meat into small pieces and add these to the strained broth. Add 1 cup of sherry and simmer for 10 minutes or until the turtle's meat is tender. Taste for seasoning. Serve garnished with chopped hard-cooked egg and lemon slices.

MINORCA GOPHER STEW

Marjorie Kinnan Rawlings in her book *Cross Creek Cookery* (Charles Scribner's Sons) has a mouth-watering section on turtles and gophers. Here is her recipe for gopher stew:

"Wash the decapitated gopher. Cut the shell away from the meat. Scald the feet until the skin and claws can be removed. Discard entrails. Cut meat in two-inch pieces. Simmer until thoroughly tender in two cups water to every cup of meat, adding one half teaspoon salt and a dash of pepper to every cup of meat.

"In a deep kettle or Dutch oven, heat fat, preferably olive oil, allowing one quarter cup of fat to every cup of meat. Brown in fat one large chopped onion to every cup of meat, one small can of tomatoes and one green pepper, finely cut. Simmer gently while gopher is cooking. More tomatoes may be added if mixture cooks down too much. When gopher is tender, turn the sauce into the gopher pot. There should be enough liquid to make plenty of gravy. Thicken by mashing the yolks of hard-boiled eggs, two eggs to every cup of meat, and stirring into the stew. Add more salt and pepper to taste. Stir in three tablespoons dry sherry to every cup of meat. Serve at once, preferably directly from pot.

"Thin corn sticks make a good bread to serve with the stew, and spring onions, ripe olives and a green salad usually accompany it."

TURTLE EGGS

Turtle eggs are a rare delicacy and hard to get, but if you

ever happen to come on some, here is what Marjorie Kinnan Rawlings has to say about them:

"They are boiled in heavily salted water for twenty minutes. The white never solidifies, but the hard-boiled yolk is rich, rather grainy, with a fine and distinct flavor. They are eaten 'out of hand,' from the shell, breaking off the top of the shell, dotting the egg with salt and pepper and butter, and popping the contents of the shell directly into the mouth. A dozen turtle eggs, with plain bread and butter and a glass of ale, make all I ask of a light luncheon or supper."

INDEX

397

399

403